EMISSIONS TRADING SCHEMES

Over the last four decades emissions trading has enjoyed a high profile in environmental law scholarship and in environmental law and policy. Much of the discussion is promotional, preferring emissions trading above other regulatory strategies without, however, engaging with legal complexities embedded in conceptualising, scrutinising and managing emissions trading regimes. The combined effect of these debates is to create a perception that emissions trading is a straightforward regulatory strategy, imposable across various jurisdictions and environmental settings. This book shows that this view is problematic for at least two reasons. First, emissions trading responds to distinct environmental and non-environmental goals, including creating profit-centres, substituting bureaucratic control of resources and ensuring regulatory compliance. This is important, as the particular purpose entrusted to a given emissions trading regime has, as its corollary, a particular governance structure, according to which the regime may be constructed and managed, and which trusts the emissions market, the state and rights in emissions allowances with distinct roles. Second, the governance structures of emissions trading regimes are culture-specific, which is a significant reminder of the importance of law in understanding not only how emissions trading schemes function but also what meaning is given to them as regulatory strategies. This is shown by deconstructing emissions trading discourses: that is, by enquiring into the assumptions about emissions trading, as featuring in emissions trading scholarship and in debates involving law and policymakers and the judiciary at the EU level. Ultimately, this book makes a strong argument for reconfiguring the common understanding of emissions trading schemes as regulatory strategies, and sets out a framework for analysis to sustain that reconfiguration.

Emissions Trading Schemes

Markets, States and Law

Sanja Bogojević

·HART·
PUBLISHING
OXFORD AND PORTLAND, OREGON
2013

Published in the United Kingdom by Hart Publishing Ltd
16C Worcester Place, Oxford, OX1 2JW
Telephone: +44 (0)1865 517530
Fax: +44 (0)1865 510710
E-mail: mail@hartpub.co.uk
Website: http://www.hartpub.co.uk

Published in North America (US and Canada) by
Hart Publishing
c/o International Specialized Book Services
920 NE 58th Avenue, Suite 300
Portland, OR 97213-3786
USA
Tel: +1 503 287 3093 or toll-free: (1) 800 944 6190
Fax: +1 503 280 8832
E-mail: orders@isbs.com
Website: http://www.isbs.com

British Library Cataloguing in Publication Data
Data Available

ISBN: 978-1-84946-405-5

Typeset by Hope Services, Abingdon
Printed and bound in Great Britain by
TJ International Ltd, Padstow

PREFACE

This book is ambitious. It challenges what is understood to be the common understanding of emissions trading as a straightforward regulatory tool and proposes a revised framework of analysis for emissions trading regimes in law. It does this by taking a unique exploration of discourses surrounding emissions trading on the part of scholars,[1] and by setting out three models – the *Economic Efficiency*, the *Private Property Rights*, and the *Command-and-Control* models – it demonstrates that emissions trading is a nuanced regulatory concept, which refers to distinct governance regimes and whose definition is contextual and culture-specific.

I recognise that not all scholars commit to the oversimplified and uniform vision of emissions trading that this book addresses. The significance of this study lies in the fact that it digs deep into the emissions trading scholarship, unpacks legal complexities embedded in these discussions and explains *why* oversimplifications relating to emissions trading regimes, nonetheless, exist. As such, this book makes an important contribution to environmental law scholarship. However, it is not only written for lawyers but also for a non-legal audience – albeit for slightly different reasons. To the non-legal community, this book presents a valuable reminder as to why it is crucial to consider law in thinking about emissions trading schemes. It shows that the way in which emissions trading is conceptualised as a regulatory strategy has important implications on how the trading scheme is constructed and how it operates. In other words, it evidences the legal complexities of emissions trading. To legal scholars, this book sets out a revised methodology in analysing the use of markets in law and shows why environmental law scholars need to reconsider their approach and role in debates on environmental markets. In this context, it highlights legal themes and questions relating to emissions trading that need to be pursued.

This book was initially written as a DPhil thesis, which I completed in November 2011 at the University of Oxford. Except from certain editorial facelifts and updates on the case law, this book is for the most part the same as my doctoral thesis – despite the fact that significant legal developments have occurred to the global climate change regime,[2] the EU Emissions Trading Scheme,[3] and individual

---

[1] As well as the European Commission and the EU Courts in relation to the EU Emissions Trading Scheme.

[2] See in particular United Nations Framework Convention on Climate Change (UNFCCC) Decision of 11 December 2011 on Establishing an Ad Hoc Working Group on the Durban Platform for Enhanced Action, 1/CP.17.

[3] The EU Emissions Trading Scheme, which is used as a case study in this book, has been revised. See Directive 2009/29 of the European Parliament and of the European Council amending the Directive 2003/87 so as to improve and extend the greenhouse gas emission allowance trading scheme of the Community, [2009] OJ L140/63.

emissions trading schemes elsewhere[4] in the year that followed my submission and indeed whilst I was writing my doctorate. There are two key reasons as to why I have declined to commit to a full revision of my original thesis.

First, this book is a series of 'snapshots'[5] of emissions trading discourses, as opposed to a comprehensive analysis of a particular emissions trading regime. Together, these snapshots illustrate both past and present understandings of emissions trading as a regulatory mechanism. The significance of such a portrayal is not to tell the full story concerning emissions trading but rather to show the pluralistic understandings of these trading regimes as a regulatory concept, and bring to light legal complexities involved in conceptualising and applying emissions markets in law. With the help of the snapshots I thus reorient and reframe the debate on emissions trading and highlight the need to engage in emissions trading discourses from a legal perspective.

Second, this book is only the first step in a much broader project on the use of markets as a control mechanism in environmental law. This first step has been to paint a kaleidoscopic legal prism through which to view emissions trading as a regulatory concept. More precisely, the *Economic Efficiency*, the *Private Property Rights*, and the *Command-and-Control* models demonstrate that emissions trading responds to a variety of environmental and non-environmental objectives, each objective creating a distinct governance regime in which different roles are ascribed to the state, the market and rights in emissions allowances. Neither the models nor this book considers all the necessary themes that are relevant to emissions trading. However, this study is significant in demonstrating that markets, states, and law exist in a symbiosis and that emissions trading regimes raise important questions regarding co-production.

Finally, it is important to note that this book does not tell you how emissions trading schemes ought to be constructed nor how the reader should think about emissions trading.[6] Rather, this is a book that informs the reader about the type of legal issues that are central to properly appreciate the concept of emissions trading, and commits the author to further intellectual challenges.

11 February 2013

---

[4] Norway, Switzerland, Japan, Australia (and specifically New South Wales), Canada, Russia and various states in the US (primarily California) have shown interest in, and in certain cases already developed links with the EU Emissions Trading Scheme.

[5] The use of 'snapshots' takes inspiration from E Fisher, *Risk Regulation and Administrative Constitutionalism* (Hart Publishing, Oxford, 2010).

[6] This approach is inspired by E Fisher, B Lange and E Scotford, *Environmental Law: Text, Cases and Materials* (Oxford University Press, Oxford, 2013).

ACKNOWLEDGEMENTS

Writing this book required long periods of solitary work but it is a book I could not have written on my own. I am indebted to the following people and institutions for their help in completing this manuscript.

To start where it all started, I am thankful to Maria Lee, who first brought the concept of emissions trading to my attention, as I studied for her course 'EU Environmental Law and Policy' whilst an undergraduate at King's College London. Maria was the first to encourage me to study further in this field, and her support has not faltered since. For that I remain deeply grateful. Before starting this project at Oxford University, three people deserve thanks for encouraging me to do so: Tariq Baloch, who correctly predicted that Corpus Christi College would be the right environment in which to develop my research, Sionaidh Douglas-Scott and Ludwig Krämer, who supported this project even before it had taken any written form.

I would like to thank Corpus Christi College for providing a friendly and stimulating setting, in which I carried out the bulk of my writing. This study was also deeply influenced by research I conducted whilst on research trips to the Max Planck Institute for Research on Collective Goods in Bonn, the New York University School of Law, and the Humboldt University School of Law. All three institutions provided outstanding research opportunities and, in particular, I wish to thank Katrina Wyman, Richard Stewart, Richard Revesz, Richard Epstein, Vanessa Casado Pérez, Christoph Engel, Stefan Magen and Christoph Paulus for their hospitality and the time they took to deliberate and engage with several issues raised in this book. Thanks are also due to the Law Faculty at Lund University, where the final edits for this book were carried out. I especially thank Xavier Groussot for his encouragement, enthusiasm and wit.

Much of this study has been presented at a variety of conferences and seminars in the US, Australia, China and across Europe. Additionally, earlier versions of chapters two and five have been published as journal articles and as a book chapter. During these reviewing processes and presentations, Chris Hilson, Kim Rubenstein, Brad Jessup, Paul Craig, Bettina Lange and Lisa Vanhala provided particularly valuable comments, for which I am grateful. I am also thankful to Joanne Scott and Stephen Weatherill, who examined this work as a DPhil thesis and supported its broader application. The entire team at Hart Publishing is also owed much thanks.

In writing this book, my greatest source of inspiration was Elizabeth (Liz) Fisher, who supervised the doctoral thesis that this manuscript is based upon. From the outset, Liz armoured me with the necessary confidence to carry the research through to the final stage, teaching me that scholarship demands utmost frankness. Without Liz's endless patience, heartfelt encouragement and unrelenting support, this book could not have been brought to fruition. I also thank Eloise Scotford for being a generous and supportive colleague and a wonderful friend throughout the writing process. Eloise's doctorate (DPhil thesis, Oxford 2010) provided another important source of inspiration, especially in conceptualising my framework of analysis. Ulrika Carlsson deserves special thanks for editing the first draft of this manuscript and being a friend I have always been able to rely on. I am thankful to Sandra Šćepanović for her deep sense of collegiality, as well as to Silvia Pronk, Henrik Isackson, Anja Lindahl, Elisabeth Lange-Stas, Jenny Brenke, Sara Mikrut, Emma German, Sarah Stephanou, Amia Srinivasan, Linnéa Ottervik-Clearfield, Ester Herlin-Karnell, Harro van Asselt, and Benjamin Spagnolo for being, at all times, only a phone call away with good advice.

My final thanks are to my family, who provided strong support during the writing of this book. I am thankful to my grandparents, Stanka and Milutin, and Radmila and Milojko (who sadly died before I finished) for cheering me on from the sidelines. I thank Slađan and Slađana for being always encouraging of my work. Thanks are also due to the newest family members, Simon and Andrej, for comic relief. My profoundest thanks go to my parents, Zorica and Dragiša, for providing a loving and nurturing home, and for their efforts, which include leaving their home country, to provide for a better future for their children. Ову књигу посвећујем вама.

CONTENTS

TABLE OF CASES

Chronological

United Kingdom

TABLE OF LEGISLATION

Decisions

Directives

United States of America

TABLE OF CONVENTIONS, TREATIES ETC

1

From Uniformity to Legal Particularities of Governance Regimes: Revising the Framework of Analysis for Emissions Trading Schemes in Law

I. Introduction

This is a study of environmental law scholarship and the way in which scholars[1] understand emissions trading as a regulatory concept. The aim that underpins this book is undeniably bold – I seek to challenge a certain vision and methodology applied in analysing emissions trading schemes that I take to be prevalent in environmental law scholarship. I intend to discard the generically uniform prism through which emissions trading tends to be projected and subsequently understood as a straightforward instrument that is based on common design features and thus imposable in public law from jurisdiction to jurisdiction to the same effect. In its place, I will set out a more pluralistic view of emissions trading, responding to diverse environmental and non-environmental problems – including creating profit-centres, establishing a governance regime aimed at substituting state control of common resources, and ensuring regulatory compliance – and as such, capable of establishing distinct governance regimes, each regime embedded in its own legal cultural and historical contingencies.

Analysing emissions trading schemes in their respective legal setting poses a methodological challenge that is central to this book. The challenge lies in accommodating emissions trading discourses that are intrinsically cross-jurisdictional, vastly interdisciplinary (albeit with overarching influences from economics), and continuously evolving in accordance with, or in differentiation to, the political climate, within a legal framework that rejects generalisations and mere technical portrayals of emissions trading schemes. The way in which this book responds to this challenge is by developing a methodology that 'zooms out' of emissions trading debates, and with an overview of these discourses, explores the type of environmental governance regimes that are furthered when emissions trading schemes are promoted. The current investigation shows that the understanding of emissions

---

[1] As well as law- and policymakers and the judiciary, see chs 4 and 5 respectively.

trading is mediated by three distinct and competing visions of how these trading schemes function or ought to function. As part of the analysis, I develop three models – the *Economic Efficiency*, the *Private Property Rights* and the *Command-and-Control* models – in which these portrayals are distinctly projected. According to the *Economic Efficiency Model*, emissions trading schemes function as a means of securing economic benefits, the *Private Property Rights Model* promotes emissions trading schemes as a substitution for central governance of common resources, and the *Command-and-Control Model* views emissions trading schemes as a neo-regulatory mechanism. These three visions, in turn, have as corollaries three different governance structures according to which a trading scheme may be constructed and managed, each structure conferring a different legal status upon the rights created in emissions allowances, whilst subscribing to competing visions of what role the state plays, or ought to play, in the construction and management of the emissions market.

The significance of this methodology and the models is to establish a new framework of analysis for emissions trading schemes in law that enhances the idea of emissions trading as distinct governance regimes, thereby rejecting any generalisations that suggest that emissions trading schemes are simple regulatory tools that may be used across jurisdictional borders with equal simplicity and to the same effect. The models show that each governance regime created by emissions trading schemes is deeply grounded in the roles that are ascribed to the state and the market in environmental regulation. Although the emissions trading discourse tends to be dichotomous in this regard,[2] the models highlight that the view of the state and the market are co-produced; that is, they exist in a symbiosis and the idea regarding the function of the one, directly affects the idea regarding the function of the other. At the heart of emissions trading debates, therefore, stands the legal dilemma of how and to whom to allocate regulatory power[3] to decide on the construction and management of emissions trading.

It is important to note that the models form a theoretical framework of analysis that, as such, is incapable of determining what legal structures a particular emissions trading regime ought to take. With the intention of exploring the applicability of the models in law, and to show that the governance regimes underpinning emissions trading schemes can only be understood in the context of legal specificities, I examine the EU Emissions Trading Scheme (EU ETS) against the backdrop of the legal order of the European Union (EU). More specifically, this exploration surveys the EU ETS by focusing first on how law – and policymakers[4]

---

[2] See ch 6.

[3] Much regulatory theory deals with the meaning of 'regulatory power', covering questions, such as, who can exercise regulatory power, from whom is it transferred, and on what grounds and who can challenge it. See B Morgan and K Yeung, *An Introduction to Law and Regulation: Texts and Materials* (Cambridge University Press, Cambridge, 2007) chs 1, 3, 5 and 6. For the purpose of this book, I use a very simple definition: namely, the capability to organise, manage and construct emissions trading regimes.

[4] Here referring to the European Commission.

at the EU level, and second the Court of Justice of the European Union (CJEU)[5] – reason and give meaning to emissions trading. This close analysis of policy-based and judicial discourses surrounding the EU ETS reveals a strong mismatch in the understanding of the rationale and functionality of the EU emissions trading regime as envisioned by the European Commission (Commission), the EU Courts and the litigants. Mapping the *Economic Efficiency*, the *Private Property Rights* and the *Command-and-Control* models onto the EU ETS judicial discourse helps to categorise and flesh out these discrepancies and show that competing visions of the construction, role and impact of the EU ETS exist and give rise to an ever-increasing case law. In effect, pointing to the multiple visions that exist in a single jurisdiction regarding an emissions trading scheme challenges the scholarly assumption that furthers emissions trading as a straightforward tool that can be applied across different legal settings with generic outcome. In its place, the case analysis unveils complex multi-level governance structures created by the emissions trading scheme in the EU jurisdiction.

The aim of this book is to undertake a positivist analysis of environmental law scholarship and explore the EU ETS with the intention of showing that emissions trading as a regulatory concept reflects different governance structures, which are dependent on their specific cultural context for meaning and implication. From the viewpoint of other established areas of law, this exercise is not novel; ultimately any control system is certain to create a particular governance structure that relies on its legal specification for content and impact. In environmental law, nonetheless, and especially with regard to emissions trading schemes, this approach is significant because environmental law scholarship has yet to develop a methodology that accommodates thorough legal analysis for emissions markets. The current nature and framing of environmental law scholarship instead induce discussions that overlook the impact of legal culture and encourage simplistic and generic portrayals of this particular regulatory mechanism.[6] Understanding *why* environmental law scholarship is shaped in this manner involves reflecting critically and broadly on the nature, promise and deficiencies of this particular strand of scholarship. As such, this book makes an important contribution to environmental law more broadly, outside the domain of emissions trading debates.

This chapter provides a two-step introduction to this book. First, it briefly highlights the high profile of the use of emissions trading in environmental law and policy and environmental law scholarship, pointing to the common assumptions of the virtues of this regulatory control mechanism. This overview aims to orient the discussion on emissions trading but also to highlight the pressing need to revise the existing analytical framework through which these emissions trading schemes are viewed. In effect, it paints the general picture of the problem that this

---

[5] Formerly the European Court of Justice (ECJ) and the Court of First Instance (CFI). Since the Lisbon Treaty, the CJEU compromises the Court of Justice, the General Court and specialised courts, as listed in Art 19 TEU. 'TEU' refers to Consolidated Versions of the Treaty on European Union (TEU), [2008] OJ C115/13.

[6] See ch 6.

book addresses. Second, it outlines the particular methodology applied in this study, and explains how its application paves the way for a robust and mature framework of analysis for emissions trading schemes in law. Before starting, however, it is useful to introduce emissions trading with which this book is concerned.

Describing emissions trading in general terms is conceptually difficult, as each portrayal adheres to one particular governance structure that I intend to explore in chapter two. Thus merely as a brief introduction, one way of presenting emissions trading is to state that it is a scheme under which the government imposes a limit on the total quantity of emissions, issues allowances adding up to that total, and then allows emitters to buy and sell surplus allowances among each other.[7] The idea is that this control system creates a clear incentive to reduce emissions and sell allowances at a profit. This formulation, however, is open-textured and on this basis different from, for instance, a rights-based view of emissions markets that sees the creation of a tradeable property right in emissions allowance as pivotal in the establishment of an emissions market. Dales explains this particular analysis:[8]

> Because *transferable (or full) property rights* always command an explicit price, the establishment of such Rights *makes it easy to establish a market* in them. In turn, the buying and selling of the Rights in an open market and the consequent establishment of an explicit price for the right to discharge a ton of waste into water (or air) system results in a theoretically efficient allocation of 'anti-pollution effort' as between different dischargers. (Emphasis added).

Thus, in the view of Dales, transferable property rights in emissions (and water) rights are central in the construction of environmental markets, as it is through these that trading schemes in emissions allowances can be created in a straightforward manner. This view is again different from, for instance, a state-focused description of emissions trading where these trading schemes are defined as:[9]

> [A] 'command and control *plus*' instrument, with often even stronger [than traditional direct regulation] government intervention and control, in particular in relation to monitoring of emissions, and high non-compliance sanctions.

The obvious distinction between this explanation, compared with the previous two, is the focus on the state rather than on market forces in managing the emissions trading scheme. This suggests that the core structure and function of emissions trading will differ depending on through which prism this regulatory strategy is viewed. Listing these descriptions is not to suggest that these portrayals are preferred, or in any way representative of particular formal explanations of emissions trading. Indeed these illustrations are set out in different jurisdictions,

---

[7] R Stewart, 'Models for Environmental Regulation: Central Planning Versus Market-Based Approaches' (1992) 19 *Boston College Environmental Affairs Law Review* 547, 553.

[8] J Dales, *Pollution, Property and Prices: An Essay in Policy-Making and Economics* (University of Toronto Press, Toronto, 1970) 107.

[9] J Lefevere, 'Greenhouse Gas Emission Allowance Trading in the EU: A Background' (2003) *Yearbook of European Environmental Law* 149, 154.

periods and contexts and as such unsurprisingly diverse.[10] The fact that they, nonetheless, frame the conceptualisation of emissions trading differently, shows, as chapter two discusses, that in debating emissions trading, distinct governance regimes for pollution control are ascribed to.

II. Emissions Trading Schemes and their High Profile in Environmental Law

Emission trading is not a novel regulatory strategy. The general principles underlying emissions trading are based on scholarly proposals put forward in the late 1960s as part of theories concerning the optimal solution to the allocation of resources to various commons.[11] Coase, belonging to this category of scholars, and known as the 'grandfather of pollution trading',[12] revolutionised the way in which pollution control is viewed by arguing that pollution is simply a factor of production, and that by turning it into well-defined, transferable legal rights, the market, as opposed to the government, can play a crucial role in the way in which pollution is regulated.[13] This scholarly contribution, coupled with several other by now classic articles,[14] comprise the foundation for theorising about market-based mechanisms, including emissions trading schemes in environmental law, and have subsequently helped inspire legislative action.[15]

In the five decades that followed the publication of Coase's paper, the high profile of emissions trading schemes in environmental law and policy, as well as in environmental law scholarship, has thrived to the extent that it is impossible to debate regulatory choice for air pollution control without considering emissions

---

[10] Implications of the cross-jurisdictional nature of emissions trading scholarship are discussed in ch 6.

[11] G Brown, 'Renewable Natural Resource Management and Use Without Markets' (2000) 38 *Journal of Economic Literature* 875. The notion of 'commons' and how emissions trading is understood to regulate common resources is discussed in ch 2.

[12] L Lohmann, 'Carbon Trading: A Critical Conversation on Climate Change, Privatisation and Power' (2006) 48 *Development Dialogue* 4, 55.

[13] R Coase, 'The Problem of Social Cost' (1960) 3 *Journal of Law and Economics* 1. Coase's theory regarding the allocation of social cost of externalities, or pollution is discussed in ch 2.

[14] These include G Hardin, 'The Tragedy of the Commons' (1968) 162 *Science* 1243, J Dales, 'Land, Water, and Ownership' (1968) 1 *Canadian Journal of Economics* 791, H Demsetz, 'Toward a Theory of Property Rights' (1967) 57 *American Economic Review* 347, T Crocker, 'The Structuring of Atmospheric Pollution Control System' in H Wolozin (ed), *The Economics of Air Pollution* (WW Norton & Co, New York City, 1966) 61, W Montgomery, 'Markets in Licenses and Efficient Pollution Control Programs' (1972) 5 *Journal of Economic Theory* 395.

[15] In the1970s – almost two decades after Coase first published his article – the so-called 'off-set policy', an early form of emissions trading, was introduced in the US. Under these schemes, polluters were encouraged to voluntarily reduce their emissions levels below their legal requirements on the basis that the Environmental Protection Agency would verify any excess reductions as emissions reduction credits, see T Tietenberg, *Emissions Trading: Principles and Practice* (2nd edn, Resources for the Future, Washington DC, 2006) 6–7.

trading regimes.[16] Although a strong sentiment exists in environmental law for the need to apply a mix of regulatory mechanisms to environmental problems,[17] emissions trading schemes, falling within the broader scope of market-based mechanisms,[18] are widely considered 'superior'[19] to other direct regulatory options, and their application is furthered as an obvious choice '*unless* one can show they are somehow deficient' (emphasis added).[20] From this angle, emissions trading is seen as 'the holy grail of environmental policymaking',[21] and its use in environmental law and policy 'close to politically correct'[22] – a point that is illustrated throughout this book.

The profile of emissions trading schemes in environmental law has particularly

[16] Academic journals, collections of essays, environmental law textbooks, as well as scholarship on regulation more generally, examine and discuss emissions trading, see, eg R Baldwin, M Cave and M Lodge, *Understanding Regulation: Theory, Strategy, and Practice* (2nd edn, Oxford University Press, Oxford 2012) ch 10, N Gunningham, P Grabosky and D Sinclair, *Smart Regulation: Designing Environmental Policy* (Clarendon Press, Oxford, 1998) 424, R Macrory, *Regulation, Enforcement and Governance in Environmental Law* (Hart Publishing, Oxford, 2010) 11, J Holder and M Lee, *Environmental Protection, Law and Policy* (2nd edn, Cambridge University Press, Cambridge, 2007) 428, Morgan and Yeung, *An Introduction to Law and Regulation* (n 3) 85, A Ogus, *Regulation: Legal Form and Economic Theory* (Clarendon Press, Oxford, 1994) 249, J Wiener, 'Global Environmental Regulation: Instrument Choice in the Legal Context' (1999) 108 *Yale Law Journal* 677, 709, S Bell and D McGillivray, *Environmental Law* (7th edn, Oxford University Press, Oxford, 2008) 509, C Olsen Lundh, 'Koldioxidhandeln Inom EU ETS – Stärkt och Expanderad?' (2008) 2 *Europarättslig Tidskrift* 350.

[17] See B Rittberger and J Richardson, 'Old Wine in New Bottles? The Commission and the Use of Environmental Policy Instruments' (2003) 81 *Public Administration* 575, N Gunningham and D Sinclair, 'Regulatory Pluralism: Designing Policy Mixes for Environmental Protection' (1999) 21 *Law and Policy* 49, E Donald, 'Environmental Markets and Beyond: Three Modest Proposals for the Future of Environmental Law' (2001) 29 *Capital University Law* 245, 246, L Krämer, 'Some Reflections on the EU Mix of Instruments on Climate Change' in M Peeters and K Deketelaere (eds), *EU Climate Change Policy: The Challenge of New Regulatory Initiatives* (Edward Elgar, Cheltenham, 2006) 279. The idea of using a mix of regulatory instruments is also supported by the IPPC Directive, Council Directive 2008/1/EC of 15 January 2008 concerning integrated pollution prevention and control [2003] OJ L 24/8 and the Kyoto Protocol to the United Nations Framework Convention on Climate Change, opened for signature 11 December 1997, 37 ILM 22 (entered into force 16 February 2005).

[18] Market-based mechanisms are defined to fall into two general categories: regimes founded on effluent taxes and tradable pollution permit regimes, see J Nash, 'Too Much Market? Conflict between Tradable Pollution Allowances and the "Polluter Pays" Principle' (2000) 24 *Harvard Environmental Law Review* 465, 482.

[19] As explained by L Heinzerling, 'Selling Pollution, Forcing Democracy' (1995) 14 *Stanford Environmental Law Journal* 300, 302. Economists in particular tend to compare market-based mechanisms to 'conduct rules', which specify behaviour or technology, and on this basis proclaim control mechanisms, such as emissions trading, superior. J Wiener and B Richman, 'Mechanism Choice' in D Farber and A O'Connell (eds), *Research Handbook on Public Choice and Public Law* (Edward Elgar, Cheltenham, 2010) 363, 370, J Freeman and C Kolstad, 'Prescriptive Environmental Regulations versus Market-Based Incentives' in J Freeman and C Kolstad (eds), *Moving to Markets in Environmental Regulation: Lessons After Twenty Years of Experience* (Oxford University Press, Oxford, 2006) 3, 4.

[20] Freeman and Kolstad, 'Prescriptive Environmental Regulations versus Market-Based Incentives' ibid 5.

[21] L Raymond, 'The Emerging Revolution in Emissions Trading Policy' in B Rabe (ed), *Greenhouse Governance: Addressing Climate Change in America* (The Brookings Institute, Washington DC, 2010) 101, 105.

[22] R Stavins, 'Market-Based Environmental Policies: What Can We Learn from US Experience (and Related Research)?' in J Freeman and C Kolstad (eds), *Moving to Markets in Environmental Regulation: Lessons from Twenty Years of Experience* (Oxford University Press, Oxford, 2007) 19, 19. Note that here emissions trading is part of a broader debate on market-based environmental policies.

flourished in recent decades due to the inclusion of emissions trading in international environmental law and as part of the Kyoto Protocol (Protocol), in which emissions trading scheme is suggested as a strategy that may be applied to meet quantified emission limitations and thereby comply with international emissions targets.[23] The earlier success of the so-called 'acid rain program' in the US,[24] which used emissions trading schemes to reduce sulphur dioxide, played a crucial role in the decision to place emissions trading at the centre of the international attempt to fight climate change[25] and make this regulatory option 'fashionable'[26] as a control mechanism across various jurisdictions.[27] In EU environmental law, emissions trading is a 'key trend'[28] and the EU ETS,[29] which will be scrutinised in this book, is described as one of the 'cornerstones'[30] of environmental protection policy of the Union. Environmental lawyers and policymakers alike promote this particular regulatory option as one of the leading regulatory strategies for addressing the proliferation of threats imposed by greenhouse gases and climate change,[31] or even 'for nearly every pollution problem'.[32]

The application of trading schemes to air pollution has received most of the media and scholarly attention; market-based mechanisms, however, are applied, or urged to be applied to a wide spectrum of environmental problems beyond air

[23] Kyoto Protocol, Art 17. For a brief overview of the Protocol and the outlook on its aftermath see J Aldy and R Stavins, 'Climate Policy Architecture for the Post-Kyoto World' (2008) 50 *Environment* 7.

[24] For an overview see H Waxman, 'An Overview of the Clean Air Act Amendments of 1990' (1991) 21 *Environmental Law* 1721, R Martella, 'Market-based Regulation under the Clean Air Act' (2010) 4 *Carbon and Climate Law Review* 139. For an overview by EPA employers directly involved with the acid rain programme, see S Napolitano and others, 'The US Acid Rain Program: Key Insights from the Design, Operation, and Assessment of a Cap-and-Trade Program' (2007) 20 *The Electricity Journal* 47.

[25] D Driesen, 'Economic Instruments for Sustainable Development' in B Richardson and S Wood (eds), *Environmental Law for Sustainability* (Hart Publishing, Oxford, 2006) 277, 298.

[26] D Helm and D Pearce, 'Economic Policy Towards the Environment: An Overview' in D Helm (ed), *Economic Policy Toward the Environment* (Blackwell Publishers, Oxford, 1991) 1, 15.

[27] Trading schemes have been set up across various states in the US, see C Cinnamon, 'Climate Change Policies an Ocean Apart: United States and European Union Climate Change Policies Compared' (2006) 14 *Penn State Environmental Law Review* 435. Also, Norway, Switzerland, Japan, Australia (and specifically New South Wales), Canada, Russia have showed interest in, and in certain cases, started developing linking opportunities with the EU ETS, see N Anger, 'Emissions Trading Beyond Europe: Linking Schemes in a Post-Kyoto World' (2008) 30 *Energy Economics* 2028.

[28] Emissions trading, together with 'out-sourcing' of responsibility, is thought of as the key regulatory mechanism in EU environmental law to achieve emissions reductions on the behalf of the Union, J Scott, 'The Multi-Level Governance of Climate Change' in P Craig and G de Burca (eds), *The Evolution of EU Law* (2nd edn, Oxford University Press, Oxford 2011) 805, 806.

[29] Council Directive 2003/87 establishing a scheme for greenhouse gas emission allowance trading within the Community and amending Directive 96/61, [2003] OJ L275/32 ('Directive'), which is amended by Directive 2009/29 of the European Parliament and of the European Council amending the Directive 2003/87 so as to improve and extend the greenhouse gas emission allowance trading scheme of the Community, [2009] OJ L140/63 ('revised Directive').

[30] Case C-127/07 *Arcelor Atlantique and Lorraine and Others v Commission* [2008] OJ C44/8, Opinion of AG Maduro, para 2.

[31] C Carlarne, *Climate Change Law and Policy: EU and US Approaches* (Oxford University Press, Oxford, 2010) 177.

[32] Raymond, 'The Emerging Revolution in Emissions Trading Policy' (n 21) 107. See also Dales, *Pollution, Property and Prices* (n 8) 100.

pollution, or 'whenever they can reliably achieve environmental objectives'.[33] For instance, these are employed to help curb overfishing,[34] conserve biodiversity,[35] resolve land use problems,[36] and manage water allocation.[37] Market-based mechanisms of this kind are understood to be 'the hottest growth industry in environmental law',[38] whose application in law has developed into a 'virtual orthodoxy'.[39] In short, and as predicted by Dales, the use of markets in environmental law has become the strategy 'no policy-maker can afford to do without'.[40]

This is not to say that the enthusiasm towards the use of emissions trading schemes as a regulatory strategy has been consistent or, remained unchallenged.[41] Indeed, in the aftermath of the financial and credit crises, the application of markets is faced with somewhat dampened zest and a new level of scepticism.[42] Moreover, in the EU, the interest in emissions trading has been adversely affected[43] by incidents concerning cyber attacks on emission permits registers,[44] VAT

---

[33] D Schoenbrod, R Stewart and K Wyman, *Breaking the Logjam: Environmental Protection that Will Work* (Yale University Press, New Haven, 2010) 36.

[34] See K Wyman, 'The Property Rights Challenge in Marine Fisheries' (2008) 50 *Arizona Law Review* 511, A Rieser, 'Prescription for the Commons: Environmental Scholarship and the Fishing Quotas Debate' (1999) 23 *Harvard Environmental Law Review* 395. The Commission has also recently proposed to reform the common fisheries policy by creating a market in fisheries quotas, see Commission of the European Communities, Proposal for a Regulation on the Common Fisheries Policy, COM(2011) 425 final.

[35] M Drechsler and F Hartig, 'Conserving Biodiversity with Tradable Permits under Changing Conservation Costs and Habitat Restoration Time Lags' (2011) 70 *Ecological Economics* 533.

[36] eg New York City employed a trading scheme approach to the preservation of landmark buildings, see Driesen, 'Economic Instruments for Sustainable Development' (n 25) 288 and further J Costonis, 'The Chicago Plan: Incentive Zoning and the Preservation of Urban Landmarks' (1972) 85 *Harvard Law Review* 574, 576.

[37] L Godden, 'Governing Common Resources: Environmental Markets and Property in Water' in A McHarg and others (eds), *Property and the Law in Energy and Natural Resources* (Oxford University Press, Oxford, 2010), M Bond and D Farrier, 'Transferable Water Allocations-Property Rights or Shimmering Mirage' (1996) 13 *Environmental and Planning Law Journal* 213.

[38] In particular when compared to traditional direct regulation, see E Orts, 'Reflexive Environmental Law' (1995) 89 *Northwestern University Law Review* 1227, 1241.

[39] Freeman and Kolstad, 'Prescriptive Environmental Regulations' (n 19) 4.

[40] Dales, *Pollution, Property and Prices* (n 8) 100.

[41] For criticism of the use of market-based mechanisms as regulatory control systems see, eg D Satz, *Why Some Things Should Not Be For Sale* (Oxford University Press, Oxford, 2010), R Goodin, 'Selling Environmental Indulgences' (1994) 47 *Kyklos* 573. The way in which this type of scholarship is framed, and the consequences thereof, is discussed in ch 6.

[42] For an overview of possible parallels between the financial and debit crisis and carbon markets, see M Chan, 'Lessons Learned from the Financial Crisis: Designing Carbon Markets for Environmental Effectiveness and Financial Stability' (2009) 2 *Climate and Carbon Law Review* 152, L Lohmann, 'Regulatory Challenges for Financial and Carbon Markets' (2009) 2 *Climate and Carbon Law Review* 161, Baldwin, Cave and Lodge, 'Understanding Regulation' (n 16) 209. Also Hedegaard recognises the adverse impact of the financial and debt crises on the EU ETS, see EU's Climate Action Commissioner Connie Hedegaard, 'First Annual Report on the EU ETS to Focus on Timing Auctions' (Brussels, 19 April 2012) europa.eu/rapid/pressReleasesAction.do?reference=MEMO/12/264, accessed 10 September 2012.

[43] Following the closure of the EU ETS due to cyber attacks on the registry system, traders labelled this particular emissions scheme a 'Mickey Mouse carbon market'. As cited in T Macalister, 'Traders Condemn EU's "Mickey Mouse" Carbon Market After Botched Trading Statement', *The Guardian*, London, 21 January 2011.

[44] EUROPA, 'Announcement of Transitional Measure: EU ETS Registry System' (19 January 2011) ec.europa.eu/clima/news/articles/news_20110119011_en.htm, accessed 11 September 2012, T Macalister,

fraud,[45] and the crash in carbon prices following the over-allocation of emissions permits.[46] Despite these drawbacks, scholars have generally remained loyal to supporting the application of markets in environmental law, arguing, for instance, that emissions trading 'works far better'[47] than any other regulatory alternative. Equally, policy- and lawmakers in the EU have extended the time frame in which emissions trading can be used,[48] and at the international level it has been decided to maintain and build upon the existing flexible mechanism, including emissions trading, which was established under the Kyoto Protocol.[49] Also, the US State of California has been inspired by the EU ETS to launch its own trading scheme,[50] while Australia and the EU have agreed to create a two-way link between emissions trading in Australia and the EU ETS, allowing the relevant business to use carbon units from either trading scheme for compliance. Such collaboration is seen to 'reaffirm that carbon markets are the prime vehicle for tackling climate change and the most efficient means of achieving emissions reductions'.[51] Thus, notwithstanding the experienced problems, the steadfast support for emissions trading clearly indicates that this regulatory option is significant and retains a strong position in environmental law, which further confirms that it certainly is worthy of a thorough legal examination.

The high profile of emissions trading schemes in environmental law and policy at international, regional and national level invites wide-ranging academic scrutiny of

---

'European Carbon Market Reopens but Traders Stay Away', *The Guardian,* London, 4 February 2011, T Macallister, 'European Union Faces Legal Action Over Fraudulent Carbon Emissions Trading', *The Guardian,* London, 20 February 2011.

[45] EUROPOL, 'Further Investigations into VAT Fraud Linked to the Carbon Emissions Trading Scheme' (28 December 2010) mobile.europol.europa.eu/content/press/further-investigations-vat-fraud-linked-carbon-emissions-trading-system-641, accessed 11 September 2012, A Seager, 'European Taxpayers Lose 5bn in Carbon Trading Fraud', *The Guardian,* London, 14 December 2009.

[46] For an overview see D Ellerman and P Joskow, *The European Union's Emissions Trading System in Perspective* (Pew Center on Global Climate Change, Washington, 2008).

[47] R Epstein, 'Carbon Dioxide: Our Newest Pollutant' (2010) 43 *Suffolk University Law Review* 797, 825. See also D Schoenbrod, R Stewart and K Wyman, *Breaking the Logjam* (n 33), R Lazarus, *The Making of Environmental Law* (Chicago University Press, Chicago, 2004) 232–33, R Repetto, *America's Climate Problem: The Way Forward* (Earthscan, London, 2011). Note that emissions trading schemes tend to be supported within a broader framework of market-based instruments.

[48] The revised Directive (n 29) shows the Union's ambition to continue to use emissions trading also after the Kyoto Protocol's first commitment period has passed.

[49] United Nations Framework Convention on Climate Change (UNFCCC) Decision of 11 December 2011 on Establishing of an Ad Hoc Working Group on the Durban Platform for Enhanced Action, 1/CP.17, Section E, Art 78.

[50] See California Environmental Protection Agency, Air Resource Board, arb.ca.gov/cc/capandtrade/capandtrade, accessed 11 October 2012, S Manea, 'Defining Emissions Entitlements in the Constitution of the EU Emissions Trading System' (2012) 1 *Transnational Environmental Law* 303, 307.

[51] This according to the Australian Minister for Climate Change and Energy Efficiency, Greg Combet MP, see EUROPA, 'Australia and European Commission agree on pathway towards fully linking Emissions Trading systems' (Joint Press Release) (Brussels, 28 August 2012) europa.eu/rapid/pressReleasesAction.do?reference=IP/12/916&format=HTML&aged=0&language=EN&guiLanguage=en, accessed 15 September 2012. Similarly, Connie Hedegaard, EU's Climate Action Commissioner, envisions linking between the EU ETS and carbon trading in California. F Carus, 'EU Plans to Link Emissions Trading Scheme with California: Connie Hedegaard in Discussions on how to join the World's Largest and Second Largest Carbon Markets', *The Guardian,* London, 7 April 2011.

these regulatory measures in different contexts. The Kyoto Protocol, which establishes the legal skeleton for international emissions trading, does not prescribe any global emissions trading model on which trading schemes worldwide are to be based;[52] rather, Parties to the Protocol are encouraged to create their own respective trading schemes.[53] Yet debates on this topic assume that the understanding of emissions trading as a regulatory concept is uniformly understood and that emissions trading schemes are devised, or need to be devised according to a generic technique that includes establishing so-called common 'design features'.[54] As such, emissions trading is reduced to a mere tool that may be used across different jurisdictions, or to regional and national levels.[55] Indeed, emissions trading is often defined as being part of a 'regulator's toolbox',[56] implying that as long as this regulatory mechanism is *picked* before other available regulatory 'tools', it is able to fix the designated problem independently of the legal contexts to which it is applied.[57] Following this view, emissions trading schemes may be defined as legal constructions that are 'propagated in identical sterile laboratories'[58] to which legal particularities are irrelevant.[59] The problem with this particular approach toward emissions trading schemes is the assumption that a successful emissions trading story, for instance the US acid rain programme, may be replicated with equal success across jurisdictions.[60] As a conse-

---

[52] United Nations Framework Convention on Climate Change (UNFCCC) Decision of 30 November 2005 on Modalities, Rules and Guidelines for Emissions Trading under Art 17 of the Kyoto Protocol, 11/CMP.1 sets out general and non-legal guidelines suggesting to Parties to the Protocol how to fulfil Art 17 of the Kyoto Protocol and thereby determine the modalities, rules and guidelines on emissions trading. The extent to which the Protocol is a top-down regime is discussed in D Bodansky, 'A Tale of Two Architectures: The Once and Future UN Climate Change Regime' (2011) 43 *Arizona State Law Journal* 697.

[53] 'The Conference of the Parties shall define the relevant principles, modalities, rules and guidelines, in particular for verification, reporting and accountability for emissions trading'. Kyoto Protocol, Art 17. Distinctions between emissions trading as set out in international environmental law and the EU ETS are explained in more detail in ch 3.

[54] See, eg Tietenberg, *Emissions Trading* (n 15) 17, D Mavrakis and P Konidari, 'Classification of Emissions Trading Scheme Design Characteristics' (2003) 13 *European Environment* 48, 52.

[55] The type of scholarship and its framing of emissions trading as a regulatory mechanism is discussed in ch 6.

[56] Phrase used by Wiener and Richman, 'Mechanism Choice' (n 19) 363, 365. A similar view is portrayed in Schroeder, see C Schroeder, 'Public Choice and Environmental Policy' in D Farber and A O'Connell (eds), *Research Handbook on Public Choice and Public Law* (Edward Elgar, Cheltenham, 2010) 450, 474.

[57] Discourses about the 'regulatory toolbox' has the ability to undermine the complexity of law, see E Fisher, 'Unpacking the Toolbox: Or why the Public/Private Divide is Important in EC Environmental Law' in M Freedland and J-B Auby (eds), *The Public Law/Private Law Divide: Une Entente Assez Cordiale? la Distinction du Droit Public et du Droit Privé: Regards Français et Britanniques* (Hart Publishing, Oxford, 2006) 215.

[58] Description borrowed from L Zedner, 'Comparative Research in Criminal Justice' in L Noaks, M Maguire and M Levi (eds), *Contemporary Issues in Criminology* (University of Wales Press, Cardiff, 1995) 8, 14.

[59] This point is unpacked in ch 6. For an analysis of the ways in which international law frameworks, and in particular the Kyoto Protocol, overlook 'locality' see C Fogel, 'The Local, the Global, and the Kyoto Protocol' in S Jasanoff and M Martello (eds), *Earthly Politics: Local and Global in Environmental Governance* (MIT Press, Cambridge, Mass, 2004) 103.

[60] M Hanemann, 'Cap-and-Trade: A Sufficient or Necessary Condition for Emission Reduction?' (2010) 26 *Oxford Review of Economic Policy* 225, 227, J Johnston, 'Problems of Equity and Efficiency in

quence, legal complexities particular to a certain trading scheme are overlooked and law is mistakenly framed as uniform strategy applicable at all times and in all public law settings.[61]

The implication of assuming that trading schemes are uniform legal constructions applicable with equal effect across jurisdictional borders, is to presuppose that these are *straightforward* regulatory measures. In one of the landmark pieces on emissions trading, Ackerman and Stewart indentify four administrative tasks in setting up an emissions trading, ranking cap-setting on the top of the list followed by establishing an auction system for emissions allowances, a title registry, and a penalty system before concluding 'that's that'.[62] This description is part of a broader argument that suggests that emissions trading is *easier* to establish than traditional direct regulation,[63] and that a generic step-by-step design model exists for creating emissions trading schemes.[64] As a consequence, emissions markets tend to be perceived as 'intuitively simple'[65] processes. It is important to note that the understanding of emissions trading as a straightforward regulatory control system builds on a particular vision of the state. As described by Stewart in a more recent publication, the state is thought to play a 'simplified role'[66] in emissions trading. The idea is that once the emissions market is introduced, the market, as opposed to the state, will deliver the assigned regulatory objectives. This alleged division between the market and the state is analysed in detail in chapter six; here the point that I wish to make is that the assumed simple and generic legal architecture of emissions trading is used to further emissions trading as an easy regulatory tool.

the Design of International Greenhouse Gas Cap-and-Trade Schemes' (2009) 33 *Harvard Environmental Law Review* 405, 429–30, S Sorrell and J Skea, 'Introduction' in S Sorrell and J Skea (eds), *Pollution For Sale: Emissions Trading and Joint Implementation* (Edward Elgar Publishing, Cheltenham, 1999) 1, 23, L Heinzerling, 'The Environment' in M Tushnet and P Cane (eds), *The Oxford Handbook of Legal Studies* (Oxford University Press, Oxford, 2003) 701, 712–13. Note that Heinzerling's argument in this regard is directed at how environmental law scholars further this regulatory strategy across environmental settings, as opposed to jurisdictions.

　[61] This argument was first set out in S Bogojević, 'Global Gazing: Viewing Markets Through the Lens of Emissions Trading Discourses' in B Jessup and K Rubenstein (eds), *Environmental Discourses in Public and International Law* (Cambridge University Press, Cambridge, 2012) 331.

　[62] B Ackerman and R Stewart, 'Reforming Environmental Law' (1985) 37 *Stanford Law Review* 1333, 1347. More recent scholarly contributions apply an equally systematic and straightforward description of the way in which emissions trading schemes are constructed. Nash and Revesz, for instance, categorises the construction into three steps: 1) setting the acceptable level of pollution; 2) allocate the allowances; 3) allow trading, J Nash and R Revesz, 'Markets and Geography: Designing Marketable Permit Schemes to Control Local and Regional Pollutants' (2001) 28 *Ecological Law Quarterly* 569, 575–76. Bell and McGillivray also categorise the construction of emissions trading into six stages, including establishing general policies on the environment, setting standards, applying these, enforcing permissions, providing information and monitoring, see S Bell and D McGillivray (n 16) 224.

　[63] As explained in D Driesen, 'Capping Carbon' (2010) 1 *Environmental Law* 1, 11.

　[64] Driesen, ibid, explains how the notion of 'cap-and-trade' in particular suggests simplicity in creating and managing emissions markets.

　[65] J Skjærseth and J Wettestad, *EU Emissions Trading: Initiation, Decision-Making and Implementation* (Ashgate Publishing, Burlington, 2008) 154.

　[66] R Stewart, 'Instrument Choice' in D Bodansky, J Brunnée and E Hey (eds), *The Handbook of International Environmental Law* (Oxford University Press, Oxford, 2007) 145, 156.

To summarise the discussion above it is useful to point to the key common assumptions concerning emissions trading that this book addresses. As explained, this regulatory option enjoys a high profile in environmental law and policy, and environmental law scholarship, which inflicts high hopes on the abilities of emissions trading to 'implement any anti-pollution policy that you or I can dream up'.[67] In other words, emissions trading tends to be seen as the obvious regulatory choice in discussing attempts to control pollution. This enthusiasm in using and promoting emissions trading as a regulatory option, however, is not limited to pollution problems only but is furthered across different environmental contexts and jurisdictions. In effect, trading schemes are thought of as equally imposable in most, if not all, public law settings. These visions are tied to a broader picture of emissions trading as a regulatory mechanism that is simple to construct and operate, and in which law plays only a minor part.[68] It is these assumptions that this book challenges about emissions trading that are described next.

III. The Importance of Methodology

The methodology of this book is based, in part on a positivist analysis of environmental law scholarship, and in part on an exploration of the EU ETS and the way in which the Commission and the EU Courts understand and give reason to this regulatory strategy in an EU context. The scope and reasons for this particular method, employed to establish a revised framework of analysis for emissions trading schemes in law, are outlined next.

A. Positivist Analysis of Environmental Law Scholarship

The positivist analysis of environmental law scholarship is set out in this book in three stages. First, in chapter two, environmental law scholarship is examined by focusing on emissions trading discourses. With the aim of unpacking the multifaceted governance structures that emissions trading schemes may take, an enquiry is made into assumptions about emissions trading schemes; that is, 'how' emissions trading schemes are understood as regulatory options. These findings are categorised in three models – the *Economic Efficiency*, the *Private Property Rights* and *Command-and-Control* models – that help project the wide range of hopes and objectives that scholars assign to emissions trading as a regulatory mechanism and governance regime. In the second stage of this positivist analysis, chapter six examines the scholarly motivation for, and methodological limitations involved in, analysing emissions trading schemes in environmental law scholarship to date. The

---

[67] Dales, *Pollution, Property and Prices* (n 8) 100.
[68] Scholarship that portrays law in this way is discussed in ch 6.

aim is to unwrap the reasons 'why' environmental law scholars have failed to develop a more robust methodology to the study of emissions markets through which claims about emissions trading schemes can be challenged from a legal perspective. Finally, in chapter seven, I explain how the analysis applied in this book is a revised framework of analysis for emissions trading schemes in law that is able to meet these challenges.

This positive analysis of emissions trading debates and environmental law scholarship more broadly is adopted for two reasons. First, an in-depth analysis of various scholarly conceptualisations of emissions trading helps to flesh out discrepancies regarding the role, construction and management of trading schemes that may be noticed in practice.[69] Taking a step back and examining the relevant emissions trading *discourse*, rather than particular trading schemes, provides the opportunity to examine emissions trading schemes as a regulatory idea. Although scholarly contributions since the 1960s have influenced the way in which emissions trading is understood in environmental law,[70] no study to date has examined the precise picture of emissions trading that these further, nor contrasted it with other existing understandings of the role of emissions trading. Instead, it is assumed that the way in which Coase, for instance, illustrates a regulatory system in which rights to pollution are traded, is effectively one picture of a trading scheme, applicable to different contexts, disciplines and time.[71] The positivist analysis of emissions trading in this book challenges this assumption and sets out models that present a more nuanced picture of emissions trading as a regulatory strategy. This book thus fills an important gap in the existing emissions trading scholarship.

Second, a positivist analysis of environmental law scholarship invites consideration of the development of environmental law methodologies, which to date are still in their infancy.[72] In order to create a coherent and rigid framework for environmental law scholarship, and to develop environmental law expertise,[73] it is crucial to bring to light the type of challenges that environmental law scholars face in applying law to a particular area of research. By better appreciating these obstacles, scholars can be better equipped, from a methodological viewpoint, to overcome them, which indeed is the aim of this book, as well as the specific topic of chapter six.

---

[69] The operation of these discrepancies in practice is examined in chs 4 and 5.

[70] The emissions trading scholarship is examined in ch 6.

[71] Heinzerling observes that lawyers tend to accept, as oppose to challenge, claims set out in disciplines other than their own at face value. Heinzerling, 'The Environment' (n 60) 723.

[72] E Fisher and others, 'Maturity and Methodology: Starting a Debate about Environmental Law Scholarship' (2009) 21 *Journal of Environmental Law* 213.

[73] E Fisher, 'The Rise of Transnational Environmental Law and the Expertise of Environmental Lawyers' (2012) 1 *Transnational Environmental Law* 43.

B. The EU Emissions Trading Scheme as a Case Study

In the second stage of this book, the focus is on the crucial role that legal culture plays in understanding emissions trading schemes. Here, the EU ETS is used as a case study. First, chapter three examines the unique legal environment in which the EU ETS operates, which acts as an introduction to chapters four and five where the EU ETS case study is set out. More precisely, the EU emissions trading regime is scrutinised by analysing the Commission's and the EU Courts' narrative relating to this regulatory strategy. The aim therewith is to highlight the different ways in which policy- and lawmakers, as well as the judiciary give meaning to emissions trading in the context of the EU legal order. In terms of how this case study is carried out, it is concerned with mapping the *Economic Efficiency,* the *Private Property Rights,* and the *Command-and-Control* models, when applicable, to EU ETS-related discourses as issued by the Commission and the EU Courts. The reason for this exercise is to show the applicability of the models in law, and more importantly, to demonstrate that any meaningful examination of emissions trading must be tied to the legal culture in which the specific trading scheme operates.

The EU ETS is picked to be the heart of this case study for two reasons. First, it is the largest multi-country and multi-sector greenhouse gas emission trading scheme anywhere in the world[74] and on this basis alone deserves attention from environmental legal scholars. Second, and more importantly, the EU ETS tends to be projected as a scheme that can be applied elsewhere. More precisely, it is based on a regulatory idea that has travelled from the US to the Kyoto Protocol, and following this path, been introduced top-down to the EU legal order, where, as a key EU climate change law, EU policy- and lawmakers tend to project the EU ETS as applicable worldwide.[75] As such, the EU ETS constitutes an ideal case study in which to show the uniqueness of each trading scheme and refute any suggestions of its direct transferability.

The reason why, in chapter four, I examine the discourse of the Commission, as opposed to any other institution or actor, is because beyond the Commission's usual obligation of initiating policy in the EU,[76] the Commission played an 'extraordinarily strong role'[77] in the process of creating emissions trading in Europe, as well as in establishing EU's position in climate change negotiations at

---

[74] See European Communities, *EU Emissions Trading: An Open Scheme Promoting Global Innovation to Combat Climate Change* (European Commission, Brussels 2005).

[75] As explained in chs 3 and 6 respectively.

[76] According to Art 17(1) TEU, 'The Commission shall promote the general interest of the Union and take appropriate initiatives to that end'. Literature on the Commission's policy-initiating powers is vast, see, eg S Douglas-Scott, *Constitutional Law of the European Union* (Pearson Education, Harlow, 2002) 54, D Chalmers and others, *European Union Law: Text and Materials* (Cambridge University Press, Cambridge, 2006) 93, P Craig and G de Burca, *EU Law: Text, Cases and Materials* (4th edn, Oxford University Press, Oxford, 2008) 43 and ch 4.

[77] J Wettestad, 'The Making of the 2003 EU Emissions Trading Directive: An Ultra-Quick Process due to Entrepreneurial Proficiency?' (2005) 5 *Global Environmental Politics* 1, 2.

Kyoto, where the idea of implementing emissions trading in the EU legal context first emerged.[78] The EU ETS is ultimately the 'Commission's baby',[79] and as such, the Commission is positioned as an obvious part in the EU ETS case study.

The second part of the EU ETS case study is focused on the EU Courts' understanding of emissions trading as regulatory concept. The relevance of the courtroom to this book is two-fold. First, the EU emissions trading scheme has been fiercely litigated,[80] and as such, studying the EU ETS case law is an obvious part of any legal examination of this regulatory strategy. Importantly, emissions trading discourse tends to predict that the use of emissions trading regimes will significantly reduce litigation,[81] which is an assumption that fits the concept of emissions trading schemes as straightforward regulatory tools. The case study employed in this book challenges that assumption.

Second, only a study of case law before the EU Courts allows for a close enough legal examination of emissions trading schemes to reveal their legal rationale and construction as understood in the EU legal context.[82] As so-called 'interpretative communities',[83] the EU Courts judicially constructs the European legal order by defining constitutional limits and interpreting divisions of competencies between the Member States and the Union.[84] In other words, the judiciary determines the question as to whom the regulatory power to construct and manage the emissions trading regime is to be allocated. More generally, the CJEU constructs the relationship between states and markets, in particular because its judgments determine not only the constitutional limits to state intervention in the market but also the level of government at which regulation is legitimate.[85] As a result, case law

---

[78] The Commission is reported to have acted as a 16th Member State in this regard. Y Slingenberg, 'The International Climate Policy Developments of the 1990s: The UNFCCC, the Kytoto Protocol, the Marrakech Accords and the EU Ratification Decision' in J Delbeke (ed), *EU Energy Law: The EU Greenhouse Gas Emissions Trading Scheme* (Claeys & Casteels, Leuven, 2006) 15, 23.

[79] J Wettestad, 'European Climate Policy: Toward Centralized Governance?' (2009) 26 *Review of Policy Research* 311, 313.

[80] See ch 5.

[81] R Stewart, 'Economic Incentives for Environmental Protection: Opportunities and Obstacles' in R Revesz, P Sands and R Stewart (eds), *Environmental Law, the Economy and Sustainable Development: The United States, the European Union and the International Community* (Cambridge University Press, Cambridge, 2000) 171, 202, D Ellerman, 'Are Cap-and-Trade Programs More Environmentally Effective than Conventional Regulation?' in J Freeman and C Kolstad (eds), *Moving to Markets in Environmental Regulation: Lessons From Twenty Years of Experience* (Oxford University Press, Oxford, 2007) 48–63.

[82] E Scotford, *The Role of Environmental Principles in the Decisions of the European Union Courts and New South Wales Land and Environment Court* (DPhil thesis, University of Oxford, 2010) 25, as well as E Scotford, *Environmental Principles and the Evolution of Environmental Law* (Hart Publishing, Oxford, forthcoming).

[83] R Cotterrell, 'Is there a Logic of Legal Transplants?' in D Nelken and J Feest (eds), *Adapting Legal Cultures* (Hart Publishing, Oxford, 2001) 71, 79, P Legrand, 'What "Legal Transplants"?' in D Nelken and J Feest (eds), *Adapting Legal Cultures* (Hart Publishing, Oxford, 2001) 55, 57–59.

[84] A Sweet Stone, *The Judicial Construction of Europe* (Oxford University Press, Oxford, 2004) 9, G Conway, 'Introduction and Overview – Interpretation and the European Court of Justice' in G Conway (ed), *The Limits of Legal Reasoning and the European Court of Justice* (Cambridge University Press, Cambridge, 2012) 1.

[85] M Egan, *Constructing a European Market* (Oxford University Press, Oxford, 2001) 107. Maduro sets out a similar claim regarding the Courts role in interpreting the free movement provisions,

analysis is an ideal part of a study of the interpretation of a specific regulatory mechanism in a particular legal setting.

C. Limitations in Revising the Framework of Analysis for Emissions Trading Schemes in Law

At the outset of this book I stated that it is ambitious. There are, nonetheless, significant caveats to this study. First, it is a positive rather than a normative analysis of emissions trading schemes in environmental law and policy, and environmental law scholarship. As such, this book refrains from engaging in prescriptive accounts of the role, design, or impact that emissions trading schemes have or ought to have in environmental law, or in the EU legal order. The reason for employing this particular methodology relates back to the aim of this book: my intention is not to provide definite answers as to whether regulation via emissions trading schemes ought to be applauded, or how such trading scheme ought to be constructed. Rather, the objective is to establish a framework, which may be used to critically assess emissions markets as part of environmental law, and in that way contribute to a richer understanding of regulatory responses to the initiative to use emissions trading schemes as a control system.

This also means that I do not reject the use of emissions trading schemes in law, nor do I discard scholarly contributions that favour the application of emissions trading schemes. As explained by Heinzerling, enthusiasm for the use of market-based mechanisms more broadly has 'spiralled into irrational exuberance'[86] but rather than rejecting scholarship that manifests this enthusiasm, my aim is to examine *why* emissions trading schemes are regarded with such zest and *how* this reflects on methodologies used to portray this particular regulatory measure in law. In this regard, I critique the current environmental law scholarship on the basis of its failure to challenge portrayals of emissions trading as a straightforward regulatory mechanism. I recognise that there are scholars who take a more sophisticated view of emissions trading and who do not merely consider that emissions trading is a tool, imposable everywhere.[87] This book helps to explain why methodologies through which to address these claims are, nonetheless, still immature and by revising the framework of analysis for emissions trading schemes in law, it suggests ways in which this trend may be reversed.

M Maduro, *We the Court: The European Court of Justice and the European Economic Constitution – A Critical Reading of Article 30 of the EC Treaty* (Hart Publishing, Oxford, 2002).

[86] Heinzerling, 'The Environment' (n 60) 713.

[87] See, eg N Graham, 'The Mythology of Environmental Markets' in D Grinlinton (ed), *Property Rights and Sustainability* (Martinus Nijhoff Publishers, Leiden, 2011) 149, D Ellerman and others, *Markets for Clean Air: The US Acid Rain Program* (Cambridge University Press, New York City, 2000) 321–22, Baldwin, Cave and Lodge, 'Understanding Regulation' (n 16) 197, and several publications in the recently established journal on transnational environmental law; J Peel, L Godden and R Keenan, 'Climate Change Law in an Era of Multi-Level Governance' (2012) 1 *Transnational Environmental Law* 245, 256, T Etty and others, 'Transnational Dimensions of Climate Governance' (2012) 1 *Transnational Environmental Law* 235, 235, C Carlarne and D Farber, 'Law Beyond Borders: Transnational Responses to Global Environmental Issues' (2012) 1 *Transnational Environmental Law* 13, 19.

Moreover, although the EU ETS forms the basis of the case study in this book, it is not used as a prototype of the legal construction and rationale of emissions trading schemes in law, or markets more generally. In brief, environmental markets are different from other 'general' markets for the simple reason that they trade public goods that are privately produced.[88] Additionally, the EU ETS is distinct from other environmental markets on the basis of its specific scale and goal,[89] and because it was implemented in the EU legal order top-down following political deliberation and specific international obligations under the Kyoto Protocol.[90] As such, the EU ETS stands in contrast to, for instance, voluntary markets, such as the Chicago carbon market, which are created without direct interference by the state.[91] What this means, and what this book explains, is that environmental markets, and emissions trading regimes more specifically, must be understood in their specific legal contexts. Thus, in examining the EU emissions trading regime, this is done from an EU law point of view. The account of the EU ETS, however, is far from complete; it is portrayed only through snapshots of how the Commission and the judiciary view this particular environmental market. In other words, this study provides only glimpses of the competing and, at times, contradictory understandings of emissions trading, as a regulatory concept, in the EU. These glimpses, nonetheless, suffice to illustrate the various nuances of emissions trading regimes that are capable of existing in a single jurisdiction.

Additionally, even though the case analysis in this book is concerned with the regulatory framework of the EU ETS, this study, and in particular chapters two and six, relies heavily on US-based literature concerning emissions trading. The reason is the extensive expertise that US-based academics hold in this subject; research concerning environmental regulation instruments is far advanced in the US whilst in the EU it is only slowly emerging.[92] Considering that all theory-based discussions regarding emissions trading schemes stem from the US, and that in the process of constructing and implementing the EU ETS, EU officials directly relied on expertise from US academics and policymakers,[93] it is impossible to study this topic without also examining the relevant US-based debates. Obviously

---

[88] G Chichilnisky and G Heal, 'Introduction' in G Chichilnisky and G Heal (eds), *Environmental Markets: Equity and Efficiency* (Colombia University Press, New York City, 2000) 1, 3.

[89] J Delbeke, 'Putting the Emerging Global Carbon Market on Solid Footing' (Speech for the opening of ICAP Global Cabron Market Forum, 19–20 May 2008) www.icapcarbonaction.com/index.php?option=com_content&view=article&id=18&Itemid=17&lang=ja, accessed 11 September 2012.

[90] As explained in Skjaerseth and Wettestad, *EU Emissions Trading* (n 65).

[91] Although Vis argues that lessons that may be learned from voluntary and mandatory schemes are reinforcing and consistent. P Vis, 'Basic Design Options for Emissions Trading' in J Delbeke (ed), *EU Energy Law: The EU Greenhouse Gas Emissions Trading Scheme* (Claeys & Casteels, Leuven, 2006) 39, 54. For an overview of voluntary markets see R Sandor, 'Creating New Markets: The Chicago Climate Exchange' in I Kaul and P Conceicao (eds), *The New Public Finance: Responding to Global Challenges* (Oxford University Press, Oxford, 2006).

[92] Stewart, 'Instrument Choice' (n 66) 148.

[93] D Ellerman, F Convery and C de Perthuis, *Pricing Carbon: The European Union Emissions Trading Scheme* (Cambridge University Press, Cambridge, 2010) 3, Skjaerseth and Wettestad, *EU Emissions Trading* (n 65) 154, F Convery, 'Reflections – The Emerging Literature on Emissions Trading in Europe' (2009) 2 *Review of Environmental Economics and Policy* 121, 127.

this poses certain challenges since this approach means that the EU ETS is tested against portrayals of emissions trading that are written in a US context. This, in fact, is one of the methodological problems that face environmental lawyers researching this topic and which this book seeks to address.

Finally, in this study, the term 'governance' enjoys much limelight; in particular in describing that emission trading schemes, as a regulatory concept, refer to different 'governance' regimes. To speak of governance, however, is ambiguous, especially since the concept is 'catch-all',[94] which may comprise any strategy for controlling or, exercising authority in a specific space.[95] Here, this term has a narrow meaning and refers to the relationship between markets, the state and law as established within specific emissions trading regimes, and as understood in emissions trading scholarship, and by the law- and policymaker and the judiciary in the EU context.

---

[94] N Rose, *Powers of Freedom: Reframing Political Thought* (Cambridge University Press, Cambridge, 1999) 15.
[95] Fisher and others (n 72) 235, G de Burca and J Scott, 'Introduction' in G de Burca and J Scott (eds), *Law and New Governance in the EU and the US* (Hart Publishing, Oxford, 2006) 1, 2.

2

Deconstructing Emissions Trading Discourses

I. Introduction

As noted in the previous chapter, emissions trading is commonly understood to be a regulatory system that, at its core, controls pollution, or broadly speaking, the exploitation of commons[1] in air.[2] Unpacking emissions trading discourses and going beyond this initial characterisation shows that a complex picture of emissions trading exists and in debating this regulatory regime, scholars present different views as to what the underlying principle of emissions trading schemes is or ought to be. More precisely, an enquiry into the assumptions in the emissions trading literature about the specific nature of the problem of exploitation, and how emissions trading is supposed to solve it – a 'deconstruction' of emissions trading discourses – demonstrates that competing visions of emissions trading exist, each depending on a different 'interpretative map'.[3] In this chapter, these different perceptions of emissions trading are set out in three models: the

---

[1] The notion of a 'commons' is contentious. For instance, Nonini defines these as a 'global idea' of an ensemble of resources, D Nonini, 'The Global Idea of "the Commons"' in D Nonini (ed), *The Global Idea of 'the Commons'* (Berghahn Books, New York, 2007) 1, 1–3 and Ostrom, famously, refers to these as 'common pool resources', E Ostrom, *Governing the Commons: The Evolution of Institutions for Collective Action* (Cambridge University Press, Cambridge, 1990). Commons have also been defined as 'open access' systems, see K Anttonen, M Mehling and K Upston-Hooper, 'Breathing Life into the Carbon Market Legal Frameworks of Emissions Trading in Europe' (2007) 16 *European Environmental Law Review* 96, 97. Note that 'open access' systems and 'commons' are arguably distinguishable on the basis that the former notion defines a system open to *all* with no entry or exit restrictions, while the latter refers to a group *within* a certain system – eg a farm family – to which no exclusionary rights within that set group are applied, see H Dagan and M Heller, 'The Liberal Commons' (2001) 110 *Yale Law Journal* 549, 552.

[2] T Tientenberg, 'The Tradable Permits Approach to Protecting the Commons: What Have We Learned ?' in E Ostrom and others (eds), *The Drama of the Commons* (National Resource Council, Washington DC, 2003) 197, L Raymond, 'The Emerging Revolution in Emissions Trading Policy' in B Rabe (ed), *Greenhouse Governance: Addressing Climate Change in America* (The Brookings Institute, Washington DC, 2010) 101, 102, R Hahn and G Hester, 'Marketable Permits: Lessons for Theory and Practice' (1989) 16 *Ecological Law Quarterly* 361, 361, R Stewart and J Wiener, 'The Comprehensive Approach to Global Climate Policy: Issues of Design and Practicality' (1992) 9 *Arizona Journal of International and Comparative Law* 83, 83.

[3] A term used by Freeden to describe that the way in which we understand things will depend on merits that correspond to our values and beliefs that we impose on the case. M Freeden, *Ideology: A Very Short Introduction* (Oxford University Press, New York, 2003) 8.

Economic Efficiency, the *Private Property Rights*, and the *Command-and-Control* models. In the *Economic Efficiency Model*, exploitation of the commons is understood as an externality. The role of emissions trading is to help internalise these by putting a price tag on emissions and making emission reductions a lucrative business. Thus conceived, the role of emissions trading is that of a 'profit center'.[4] In the *Private Property Rights Model* emissions trading forms part of a certain world-view in which government control of the commons has given rise to ever-deteriorating environmental quality and emissions trading is projected as a system in which citizens, via private property rights, are able to defend and manage commons independently of governmental programmes. Finally, according to the *Command-and-Control Model*, the exploitation of clean air occurs due to ineffective direct pollution control regimes. Emissions trading is envisioned as an innovative regulatory strategy that 're-regulates'[5] environmental law by making it administratively flexible though without dislodging the state and its regulatory control of the commons.

Besides offering an overview of the nature and content of key debates in emissions trading literature – literature that is fundamentally complex due to its cross-jurisdictional, interdisciplinary, and dynamic character[6] – there are three other key reasons why these models are significant. The first is that the models demonstrate that emissions trading can be viewed through diverse lenses, each lens setting out a different framework through which to construct and understand the functionality and objective of emissions trading schemes. The fact that various conceptualisations of emissions trading in emissions trading discourses exist is significant because these determine the expectations that are imposed on emissions trading as a regulatory idea, which, in turn has an impact on the way in the legislation upon which emissions trading schemes are based is constructed and interpreted. The models thus show that emissions trading discourses imagine *distinct* regulatory regimes in discussing emissions trading. As this chapter highlights, each regime is mediated by different visions of how the market, the state, and the legal status of emissions allowances operate, or ought to operate.

The second reason why the models are important is that they discard the oversimplified view of emissions trading schemes as a straightforward and uniform regulatory strategy, as highlighted in chapter one, by pointing to three distinct images of emissions trading. These are projected in the emissions trading literature, and show that emissions trading responds to different environmental and non-environmental problems, each image setting out a distinct regulatory regime

---

[4] Description borrowed from R Stewart, 'Economic Incentives for Environmental Protection: Opportunities and Obstacles' in R Revesz, P Sands and R Stewart (eds), *Environmental Law, the Economy and Sustainable Development: The United States, the European Union and the International Community* (Cambridge University Press, Cambridge, 2000) 171, 186.

[5] Term borrowed from G Majone, 'Introduction' in G Majone (ed), *Deregulation or Re-Regulation? Regulatory Reform in Europe and the United States* (Pinter Publishers, London, 1990) 1. Note that here 're-regulation' is understood to allow for administrative flexibility, as explained in section III(C).

[6] Emissions trading literature that forms the basis of this study is examined in ch 6.

that underpins emissions trading schemes. In other words, or more bluntly, the models demonstrate that emissions trading is a far more nuanced and sophisticated regulatory concept than what is to date assumed in environmental law and policy, and in environmental law scholarship.

Third, the models shed light on core legal dilemmas in promoting emissions trading schemes, which are concerned with questions of 'how' and 'to whom' to allocate regulatory power under such schemes. There is no consensus between the models in answering these questions; according to the *Economic Efficiency Model* emissions trading is understood to function according to free market mechanisms; in the *Private Property Rights Model* regulatory power is entrusted to the citizens, or private property holders, who decide on their own terms the control systems of common resources; and in the *Command-and-Control Model* regulatory power is vested in the central government. What the models thus show is that emissions trading responds to a broad definition of control, imposed either by the state, the market or the private property holders, and generates important legal questions concerning the relationship between these. It is important to note that the models do not provide any answers as to how regulatory power in emissions trading is in practice allocated. This would require attending rather to legal culture and examining an emissions trading scheme in legal isolation. Such research is carried out in the next three chapters, using the EU ETS as a case study and examining this particular trading scheme in the context of the EU legal order.

This chapter is structured as follows. In section II, I define the role and significance of the *Economic Efficiency, Private Property Rights,* and *Command-and-Control* models, as well as the meaning of 'discourses' and the act of 'deconstructing' emissions trading literature in light of the aims of this chapter. It is crucial to understand these definitions accurately and in the context of this book, as the validity of the methodology applied in this chapter depends on it. In section III, I deconstruct emissions trading discourses by setting out the three above-mentioned models, each model categorising a particular way in which emissions trading is understood as a regulatory concept in the emissions trading literature. Subsequently, these models are examined separately. In section IV the models are compared and evaluated, and in the following part, section V, their application to practice is considered. In this context emissions trading as a regulatory concept is compared to a parallel example of regulating a commons: parking on public roads. The aim of this comparison is to highlight that emissions trading – just like another example of commons regulation – is capable of creating multiple regulatory regimes depending on the underlying world-view. In the last part of this chapter, section VI, the findings of the chapter are recapitulated.

Three points should be made before starting. First, this chapter does not prescribe ways in which emissions trading ought to be viewed or constructed. Rather it demonstrates, using the models, that competing visions exist in the emissions trading literature of how emissions trading systems function or ought to function – without deciding which of the models, if any, ought to be preferred. Second, the models employed in this chapter project *theoretical* understandings – as opposed to descriptions of a particular regulatory reality – of the way in which emissions trading discourses view emissions trading schemes as a regulatory concept. In order to investigate the applicability of the models in practice, these have to be read in the legal context of a particular trading scheme and jurisdiction, which is the task set out in the next chapter. Third, the list of emissions trading literature, explored in this chapter, and upon which the models are based, is not exhaustive. What is referred to as 'emissions trading literature' is in fact a 50-year scholarly debate on the regulation of common resources, which is categorised and scrutinised in chapter six. Obviously it would be impossible, within the limited scope of this book, to dig into all pockets of this rich and extensive discourse and so what is offered is only a glimpse thereof. This brief glance, nonetheless, suffices to highlight the divergent portrayals of emissions trading schemes that exist in emissions trading debates, each portrayal corresponding to a distinct emissions trading governance regime.

II. Defining Basic Concepts

This chapter deconstructs emissions trading discourses and appreciating its significance requires understanding the purpose of employing models as a methodological tool. Considering that the terms 'model', 'deconstruction' and 'discourses' admit of different interpretations in different contexts, it is particularly important to specify how these notions are understood in this book.

A. Deconstructing *Discourses*

The *Economic Efficiency*, the *Private Property Rights* and the *Command-and-Control* models, which are based on emissions trading discourses, constitute the core of the analysis in this chapter. Defining the notion of a 'discourse' first, it is worth noting that this concept has different meanings in different scholarly areas[7] and the bourgeoning literature on discourse theory and discourse analysis shows

---

[7] The notion of 'discourse' tends to be associated with works by Foucault, who examined in particular social discourses and the relationship between power and discourse, see, eg M Foucault, *Discipline and Punish: The Birth of the Prison* (Penguin Books, Harmondsworth, 1991), M Foucault, *The History of Sexuality* (Penguin Books, Harmondsworth, 1981), M Foucault, *The Order of Things: An Archeology of the Human Science* (Routledge, London, 2002). This chapter does not apply Foucault's theories to the study of emissions trading schemes but Foucault's work has been applied to environmental studies, see É Darier (ed), *Discourses of the Environment* (Blackwell Publishers, Oxford, 1999).

that there are also many distinct methods of studying it.[8] According to Dryzek, a discourse is by definition a collection of[9]

> shared concepts, categories, and ideas that enable actors to understand situations. Thus, any particular discourse will entail and include judgments, assumptions, capabilities, dispositions, and intentions, establishing the foundations for analysis, debates, agreements, and disagreements. Those who subscribe to a discourse will then be able to put together pieces of information into coherent accounts organized around storylines that can be shared in ways that are meaningful to fellow subscribers.

This definition brings to light two important ideas regarding discourses; first, they are projections of a particular world-view, and second, each discourse creates an analytical platform for a set of beliefs. Congruent to this explanation, a discourse may be viewed as a shared way of apprehending the exterior,[10] and an ensemble of ideas, concepts, and categories to which disparate views, values, and interests may be attached,[11] and which become the medium through which actors try to impose their view of reality on others.[12] Importantly, a discourse is able to project 'one version of the world in the face of competing versions',[13] and as such, it is based on a particular narrative, which suggests unity and a common thought within a particular group or debate that is part of a broader and often more complex discussion.[14] In the context of legal scholarship, a discourse may be understood as a particular framework through which the legal environment and the regulatory mechanisms applied thereto are interpreted.[15] Together these accounts suggest

[8] For an overview of the many different ways in which discourse, and in particular discourse analysis, is applied, see M Hajer, *The Politics of Environmental Discourse: Ecological Modernization and the Policy Process* (Clarendon Press, Oxford, 1995) 43, J Torfing, 'Discourse Theory: Achievements, Arguments, and Challenges' in D Howarth and J Torfing (eds), *Discourse Theory in European Politics: Identity, Policy and Governance* (Palgrave Macmillan, Hampshire, 2005) 1, 5, A Bryman, *Social Research Methods* (3rd edn, Oxford University Press, Oxford, 2008) 501. Possible applications of discourse theory in an EU context are discussed in D Howarth and J Torfing (eds), *Discourse Theory in European Politics: Identity, Policy and Governance* (Palgrave Macmillan, Hampshire, 2005). What this literature shows is that discourse analysis is a study itself.
[9] J Dryzek, 'Paradigms and Discourses' in D Bodansky, J Brunnée and E Hey (eds), *The Oxford Handbook of International Environmental Law* (Oxford University Press, Oxford, 2007) 44, 46.
[10] J Dryzek, *The Politics of the Earth: Environmental Discourses* (2nd edn, Oxford University Press, Oxford, 2005) 9.
[11] M Hajer, 'Coalitions, Practices, and Meaning in Environmental Politics: From Acid Rain to BSE' in D Howarth and J Torfing (eds), *Discourse Theory in European Politics: Identity, Policy and Governance* (Palgrave Macmillan, Hampshire, 2005) 297, 300.
[12] M Hajer, 'Discourse Coalition and the Institutionalisation of Practice: The Case of Acid Rain in Britain' in F Fischer and J Forester (eds), *The Argumentative Turn in Policy and Planning* (UCL Press, London, 1993) 43, 47.
[13] R Gill, 'Discourse Analysis' in M Bauer and G Gaskell (eds), *Qualitative Research with Text, Image and Sound: A Practical Handbook* (Sage, London, 2000) 172, 176.
[14] Hajer, 'Discourse Coalition' (n 12) 46.
[15] For a collection of essays that portrays different kinds of environmental discourses and their implications on international law, public law, and environmental law, see B Jessup and K Rubenstein (eds), *Using Environmental Discourses to Traverse Public and International Environmental Laws* (Cambridge University Press, Cambridge, 2012), and with regard to the focus of this book, see S Bogojević, 'Global Gazing: Viewing Markets Through the Lens of Emissions Trading Discourses' in B Jessup and K Rubenstein (eds), *Environmental Discourses in Public and International Law* (Cambridge University Press, Cambridge, 2012) 331.

that each discourse paints a picture and encompasses a particular attitude or position against which experiences and facts may be tested or analysed.

Using Dryzek's term of 'storylines' to describe discourses may appear abstract,
especially since this analogy falls short of explaining the impact that discourses
may have on the particular topics they orbit. In this regard, it is crucial to flag the
importance of language.[16] Obviously discourses depend on the existence and use
of language for a story to be told but a discursive 'storyline' is not a mere anecdote
or just a matter of words; rather it is part of reality.[17] This argument rests on the
idea that language is constructive and that the way in which environmental problems are interpreted, explained, discussed and analysed has consequences.[18] A
particular use of language constructs a particular view of social reality,[19] and even
if we do not subscribe to the view in question, we cannot avoid being influenced
by it. Hajer furthers a similar argument, claiming that the collective understanding of language has moved away from viewing words and expressions as merely
descriptive to appreciating these as a *medium*; that is, 'a system of signification
through which actors not simply describe but *create* the world'.[20] This definition
of discourses infers, in the context of this chapter, that the *Economic Efficiency*, the
Private Property Rights and the *Command-and-Control* models are based on particular narratives concerning the role of emissions trading schemes as a regulatory
concept, which, albeit mere positive descriptions, have real implications for how
emissions trading is understood to function. In other words, the models construct
regulatory realities. The role of discourses in this chapter is further explained by
defining 'deconstruction' and 'models' in the same context.

B. *Deconstructing* Discourses

The notion of 'deconstruction' also allows for different interpretations in different contexts, although it tends to be associated with the act of analysing philosophical and literary works with the aim of examining assumptions implicit in

[16] M Wetherell, 'Themes in Discourse Research: The Case of Diana' in M Wetherell, S Taylor and
S Yates (eds), *Discourse Theory and Practice: A Reader* (Sage, London, 2001) 14, 16. The importance of
language in discourse analysis lies at the heart of debates in contemporary social science, epistemology
and 20th century philosophy, see, eg L Wittgenstein, *Philosophical Investigations* (4th edn, Wiley-
Blackwell, West Sussex, 2009), J Austin, 'A Plea For Excuses' (1956) 57 *Aristotelian Society* 57.

[17] Hajer, 'Discourse Coalition' (n 12) 44. Dryzek explains that language and power – as examined by
Foucault (n 7) – is central in analysing discourses, and that social actions are always associated with
language that establish their meaning, see Dryzek, *Paradigms and Discourses* (n 9). See also S Jasanoff,
'The Idiom of Co-Production' in S Jasanoff (ed), *States of Knowledge: The Co-Production of Science and
Social Order* (Routledge, London, 2004) 1, in which the idea of co-production between state-making
and knowledge-making (inter-relationships between society and technology) is analogous to the use
of language to portray a particular version of reality.

[18] Dryzek, *Politics of the Earth* (n 10) 10.

[19] Bryman, *Social Research Methods* (n 8) 501.

[20] Hajer, *Discourse Coalition* (n 12) 44. Gill, 'Discourse Analysis' (n 13) 172 sets out a similar argument.

different forms of expression.[21] Deconstruction, following this description, is similarly carried out in this chapter only that philosophical and literary texts are exchanged with emissions trading discourses, and deconstruction passed by enquiring into the assumptions set out in emissions trading debates about the objectives of emissions trading schemes.

Upon this scrutiny, patterns surface that reflect different ways in which the rationale of emissions trading are understood in the scholarly debate. These patterns show that the portrayal of the problems that emissions trading schemes are supposed to remedy, is inescapably linked to the way in which emissions trading, as a regulatory strategy, is conceived.[22] In other words, the view of the problem is symptomatic of the suggestions as to how to ameliorate or solve it.[23] With the aim of highlighting these links, the three models – the *Economic Efficiency*, the *Private Property Rights*, and the *Command-and-Control* models – are set out, each model illustrating a different understanding of why the overexploitation of the commons has occurred ('portraying the problem'),[24] and how emissions trading does or ought to remedy it ('understanding the solution').

The aim of this exercise is to flesh out differences, as well as to acknowledge overlaps, in the way emissions trading schemes are understood in the literature. Deconstruction therefore means exploring emissions trading discourses, and the way in which emissions trading schemes, as regulatory concepts, are narrated but without rejecting or criticising these descriptions. Ultimately, the intention is to shed light on diverse conceptualisations of emissions trading and show how these set out distinct governance regimes for emissions trading schemes.

It is important to understand *how* different discourses have been distinguished and mapped out in the models, even before I set out and use the models in this chapter. Differences in understanding emissions trading as a regulatory concept in the emissions trading literature are manifested rhetorically, through various catch phrases, and vocabularies of motive, as well as metaphors and analogies employed in discussing this pollution control system.[25] To a certain extent the models overlap but their distinction is clear in the language used in defining and explaining emissions trading schemes. In the *Economic Efficiency Model* the focus is on the cost-effectiveness of the emissions market. Advocates of this model come

---

[21] See J Derrida, *Writing and Differences* (Chicago University Press, Chicago, 1978), J Derrida, *Of Grammatology* (Johns Hopkins University Press, Baltimore, 1974).

[22] Similarly Jasanoff (n 17) argues that the ways in which we understand the world is inseparably linked to the ways in which we seek to organise and control it.

[23] Bodansky, for instance, argues that the way in which problems are defined is linked to our values, see D Bodansky, *The Art and Craft of International Environmental Law* (Harvard University Press, Cambridge, Massachusetts, 2010) 55, 59. 'Framing' is particularly important in this context, see S Jasanoff, 'Heaven and Earth' in S Jasanoff and M Martello (eds), *Earthly Politics: Local and Global in Environmental Governance* (MIT Press, Cambridge, Mass, 2004) 31, 49.

[24] As explained in section I of this chapter, the literature seems to agree upon that the exploitation of commons is the problem that emissions trading schemes should remedy. However, scholars take different views as to *why* the exploitation has occurred in the first place.

[25] R Kemp, 'Why Not In My Backyard? A Radical Interpretation of Public Opposition to the Deep Disposal of Radioactive Waste in the United Kingdom' (1990) 22 *Environment and Planning* 1239.

mainly from economics, and the debates therefore revolve around ideas of 'internalising externalities', creating 'incentives', 'bargaining systems' and 'profit-centres' that produce 'cost-efficient' results in managing the commons in air. This model reflects views that underpin international climate negotiations, and global trade agreements.

In the *Private Property Rights Model*, on the other hand, the focal point is the market as a 'free' forum in which citizens of a community, rather than the state, are able to decide over and control common resources. Key phrases embedded in these discourses include 'liberty', 'bureaucratic coercion', 'privatisation', and 'private property rights'. In distinction from the other two models, visions of central government in the *Private Property Rights Model* are shared with certain classic public choice theorists – in particular the view that the sole aim of government officials is to be re-elected to office, even if that comes at the cost of protecting a common good, such as clean air.[26] This places the *Private Property Rights Model* in opposition to any common or top-down approaches to public and international law.

In the *Command-and-Control Model*, the discussion shifts to regulatory reform and the manner in which emissions trading can ensure smoother environmental law implementation and compliance with regulatory obligations. Key words in this model are 're-regulation', 'regulatory and administrative flexibility', 'permits' and 'authorisation'. The *Command-and-Control Model*, in contrast to the two previous models, has a strong public law tradition, in which implementing administratively flexible regulation is the focal point of discussion.

It may appear to the reader that deconstructing emissions trading discourses by focusing on vocabulary employed in these debates is a rather frivolous affair, or at least, an activity without any serious implications. What this study, however, aims to show is that dominant legal and non-legal vocabulary associated with emissions trading schemes project a particular vision of emissions trading schemes, which has an important impact on how these are constructed and promoted. Fleshing out the diverse understandings of emissions trading as a regulatory mechanism is where the significance of the models – as described next – lies.

C. Significance of the Models

The *Economic Efficiency*, the *Private Property Rights*, and the *Command-and-Control* models that this chapter is based upon, show that the understanding of

---

[26] Literature on public choice is vast, classic public choice scholarship includes A Downs, *An Economic Theory of Democracy* (Harper, New York, 1957), J Buchanan and G Tullock, *The Calculus of Consent: Logical Foundations of Constitutional Democracy* (University of Michigan Press, Ann Arbor, 1965), K Arrow, *Social Choice and Individual Values* (Yale University Press, New Haven, 1963). For a recent overview, see J Mashaw, 'Public Law and Public Choice: Critique and Rapprochment' in D Farber and A O'Connell (eds), *Research Handbook on Public Choice and Public Law* (Edward Elgar, Cheltenham, 2010) 19, D Farber and A O'Connell, 'A Brief Trajectory of Public Choice and Public Law' in D Farber and A O'Connell (eds), *Research Handbook on Public Choice and Public Law* (Edward Elgar, Cheltenham, 2010) 1.

emissions trading in emissions trading discourses is mediated by three distinct and competing visions of how these trading schemes function or ought to function. The models thus highlight three distinct governance regimes, upon which emissions trading schemes may be based, each suggesting a different role for the market, the state, and rights in emissions allowances in such a scheme.

The models are significant for three reasons. First, they show that emissions trading schemes can be part of different paradigms, each setting out a different mould according to which these trading schemes may be constructed. Determining the nature of a particular trading scheme may only be done in legal isolation of such a scheme, and the models demonstrate that the role of the market, the state, and the legal rights envisioned for emissions allowances are crucial indicators of the type of regulatory structure that a particular emissions trading scheme may seek to establish. In fact, deciding where to allocate regulatory power under an emissions trading regime – to the market, the rights holders, or the central government – is the key consideration in creating such a governance structure. Second, therefore, the models highlight that the allocation of regulatory power is the core dilemma in emissions trading debates. Third, the models make obvious that emissions trading cannot be generalised or described as a straightforward regulatory strategy; rather these trading schemes must be viewed through a kaleidoscope of hopes and objectives that, in effect, construct the way emissions trading schemes are created and interpreted. In this context, my aim is not to describe *why* these different perceptions have arisen, but rather to show that these exist and point to their implications.

There exist important limitations to the role of models as described. To start with, the models contain elements both of what the emissions trading discourses argue in relation to emissions trading, and of that which I understand these discourses to state regarding emissions trading. As these models are my own, they can impossibly overcome the oversimplification of this kind of categorisation. In this regard, it is crucial to note the scope and the use of models in this chapter. First, the models are neither prescriptive nor normative and therefore *do not* create a strict pattern of how emissions trading must be understood. The models are instead created so as to establish a forum for reflection and debate in environmental law scholarship about the way in which scholars understand and portray emissions trading as a regulatory strategy and then examine the implications thereof in law.

Second, the models are limited in scope; they are based on my own selection of emissions trading literature and further narrowed by focusing on discourses that promote emissions trading as a regulatory strategy.[27] The reasons for these limita-

---

[27] Environmental ethics literature, for instance, is omitted from this analysis. For a brief overview of the critique of emissions trading based on ethics, see M Sagoff, 'Controlling Global Climate: The Debate over Pollution Trading' in V Gehring and W Galston (eds), *Philosophical Dimensions of Public Policy* (Transaction Publishers, New Brunswick, 2002) 311, R Goodin, 'Selling Environmental Indulgences' (1994) 47 *Kyklos* 573. Also much writing on climate change and emissions trading is based on ethical concerns looking at distributive justice in particular, see, eg H Sue, 'Climate' in D Jamieson (ed), *A Companion to Environmental Philosophy* (Blackwell Publishing, Oxford, 2001) 449,

tions are twofold: first, it is practically impossible to include all emissions trading literature in a book limited in scope. The second reason relates back to chapter one, in which I illustrated how emissions trading schemes have thrived in environmental law and policy, and in environmental law scholarship, one key regulatory appeal in this regard being their presumed straightforwardness.[28] Unpacking these debates and analysing reasons why emissions trading is promoted shows that there are competing images and establishes thereby that these are neither uniform nor straightforward.

Third, the models do not to reflect *a* particular regulatory reality, and as such, they do not project the functionality or construction of a specific emissions trading in practice. There are two reasons why this is the case. First, many influential scholarly contributions that constitute cornerstones of the emissions trading literature do not analyse emissions trading schemes per se. For instance, Coase,[29] who, as explained in the previous chapter, is considered to be the 'grandfather of pollution trading',[30] discusses optimal solutions to the allocation of resources in various commons without, however, exploring or creating a specific regulatory agenda for emissions trading schemes. Yet his work forms an intrinsic part of emissions trading discourses. Similarly, Hardin,[31] whose scholarship is at the heart of any regulatory debate concerning the control of the commons, envisions a number of different regulatory solutions, including privatisation, subsidies, taxes, and direct regulation, which may be applied to common resources.[32] In fact, neither Coase nor Hardin – two central figures in theory-based emissions trading scholarship – analyse emissions trading schemes. On this basis the models are mere *theoretical* frameworks. Second, any examination of the functionality or construction of emissions trading in practice must be carried out against the backdrop of the legal culture in which the emissions trading scheme in question operates. That is why in chapters four and five, the applicability of the *Economic Efficiency*, the *Private Property Rights*, and the *Command-and-Control* models to narratives relating to the EU ETS will be examined in the context of the EU's legal milieu.

Fourth, my intention is not to try to convince the reader that the categorisation of the emissions trading literature presented in this chapter is the only possible or correct type of modelling. Rather, my argument is that although we may disagree about the exact distinctions as to how emissions trading schemes are understood in emissions trading literature and set out in the models, it is nonetheless obvious

---

M Paterson, 'International Justice and Global Warming' in B Holden (ed), *The Ethical Dimensions of Global Change* (Macmillan, London, 1996) 181, G Michael, 'Seeking Fair Weather: Ethics and the International Debate on Climate Change' (1995) 71 *International Affairs* 463.

[28] How this straightforwardness is portrayed and why it is assumed is discussed in ch 6.

[29] R Coase, 'The Problem of Social Cost' (1960) 3 *Journal of Law and Economics* 1.

[30] L Lohmann, 'Carbon Trading: A Critical Conversation on Climate Change, Privatisation and Power' (2006) 48 *Development Dialogue* 4, 55.

[31] G Hardin, 'The Tragedy of the Commons' (1968) 162 *Science* 1243.

[32] ibid 1254.

that different conceptualisations about these trading schemes exist. The importance of understanding these conceptual differences relates back to earlier discussions in this chapter about the significance of language and may be further explained by allusion to Mashaw's comment on Picasso's portrait of Gertrude Stein.[33]

Commenting on his portrait of Gertrude Stein, Pablo Picasso is reported to have said:

'Everybody thinks she is not at all like her picture, but never mind, in the end she will manage to look just like it.'

Picasso's statement may have been a product of his famous ego, but it contains an important insight. We are often the captives of our pictures of the world, and in the end, if the world does not look just like them, their influence on our perceptions is nevertheless profound.

Mashaw explains that although many would disagree with the way in which Picasso painted Stein, his portrait still *influences* our perceptions. He summerises: 'Our vision of what *is* guides our approach to what *ought* to be'.[34] This point is crucial, as it explicates the weight and vigour of pictures – both painted and written. Similarly, the models may be seen as distinct canvasses, each exhibiting a different view of emissions trading as a regulatory strategy. Although these pictures may not reflect existing trading schemes or the way in which, if given the choice, we personally might depict them, the fact remains that the way in which they are portrayed in the models frames certain perceptions of emissions trading. The legal implications are manifested in the prescription of distinct roles to the market and the state, as well as to the legal status of emissions allowances in emissions trading. As such, the models highlight various governance regimes according to which emissions trading schemes are based.

In sum, the models in this chapter encompass different understandings as to why the exploitation of commons has occurred and how emissions trading ought to remedy it. Although these models are simple archetypes based on emissions trading literature, they frame the way in which the role of the market, the state, and the legal status of emissions allowances are understood with regard to emissions trading schemes. In this sense, the models highlight important themes concerning regulatory strategies applied to commons in air. The hope is by better understanding emissions trading models, there is better hope of creating systems mindful of regulatory disparity, local legal culture and diverse public law traditions.

---

[33] J Mashaw, *Greed, Chaos, and Governance: Using Public Choice to Improve Public Law* (Yale University Press, New Haven, 1997) 1.

[34] ibid. These notes draw inspiration from a similar analysis set out in E Fisher, B Lange and E Scotford, *Environmental Law: Text, Cases and Materials* (Oxford University Press, Oxford, 2013) ch 1.

III. The Three Models

Below, the *Economic Efficiency, Private Property,* and *Command-and-Control* models are set out and examined separately. This analysis is carried out by first listing the problem that emissions trading is understood to remedy ('portraying the problem') and thereafter the role that is envisioned for emissions trading schemes in remedying these ('understanding the solution'). The following sub-sections contain the bare analysis of the emissions trading discourse in this regard, leaving the exercise of evaluating the models to section IV.

A. Economic Efficiency Model[35]

In the *Economic Efficiency Model,* emissions trading is understood to solve the problem of externalities. The belief is that externalities (such as air pollution) are created due to a lack of incentives to protect the commons. Emissions trading is identified as being able to circumvent this exploitation by turning externalities into transferable rights that are cost-efficiently allocated, via the market, to their highest bidder (thus internalising them). This idea is inspired by Coase's theory about removing externalities by creating a bargaining system, in which externalities are turned into property rights and thereafter traded.[36] In order to incentivise this kind of internalisation, the core consideration in constructing emissions trading is ensuring that the trading scheme functions cost-efficiently.[37] From this perspective, emissions trading is defined as a profit-centre,[38] which does not reduce emissions in itself but which makes it profitable to do so.

[35] Literature that falls under this model forms part of theory-based scholarly discussions concerning emissions trading and stems mainly from economics. Examples thereof include Coase, 'Problem of Social Cost' (n 29), H Demsetz, 'Toward a Theory of Property Rights' (1967) 57 *American Economic Review* 347, W Montgomery, 'Markets in Licenses and Efficient Pollution Control Programs' (1972) 5 *Journal of Economic Theory* 395, J Dales, *Pollution, Property and Prices: An Essay in Policy-Making and Economics* (University of Toronto Press, Toronto, 1970). From a legal perspective see B Ackerman and R Stewart, 'Reforming Environmental Law' (1985) 37 *Stanford Law Review* 1333. For an overview of theory-based debates on emissions trading see W Baumol and W Oates, *The Theory of Environmental Policy* (2nd edn, Cambridge University Press, Cambridge, 1988) 177 and A Myrick Freeman III, 'Economics' in D Jamieson (ed), *A Companion to Environmental Philosophy* (Blackwell Publishing, Oxford, 2001) 277, 287.

[36] Coase, ibid. It is crucial to note that although this model is inspired by certain theories advocated by Coase, it is not a truly Coaseian model. As explained in section II(C) above, theory-based literature, including studies by scholars such as Coase, form part of emissions trading discourses although it does not discuss emissions trading per se. Thus, even if this model is heavily influenced by Coase, it is a mere application and not a mirror image of Coase's theories.

[37] Note that 'efficiency' may be defined in various ways; a measure may be deemed inefficient if it costs more than the benefit it reaps, or if it is more costly than alternative ways of reaching the same objective. J Holder and M Lee, *Environmental Protection, Law and Policy* (2nd edn, Cambridge University Press, Cambridge, 2007) 421. In this chapter the latter definition applies.

[38] Stewart, 'Economic Incentives for Environmental Protection' (n 4) or, as explained by Raymond, 'Emerging Revolution in Emissions Trading Policy' (n 2) 102, emissions trading offers 'bang for the buck'.

1. Portraying the Problem

In the *Economic Efficiency Model*, externalities are flagged as the problem that emissions trading has as its regulatory rationale to remedy. In short, externalities are costs that are not reflected in free market prices.[39] A firm that discharges its waste into a river rather than purifying it is a typical example of an externality. By treating the river as a free resource, or a commons, the cost of polluting the river is imposed neither on the consumer who purchases the firm's product, nor on the polluter, but on society as a whole.[40] Costs of pollution, however, are not only externalised by private entities and in isolated markets but also by jurisdictions and sovereign.[41] Bodansky explains:[42]

> For example, one country emits sulphur dioxide that causes acid rain to fall on its neighbour downwind or it discharges pollution into a river, causing damage to lower riparians. To the extent that a country is able to 'externalize' the costs of polluting, it has no economic incentive to stop.

Following from this description, externalities arise because there is a lack of incentive to internalise them. This theory is further elucidated by allusion to Hardin's description of the 'Tragedy of the Commons'.

Hardin describes the idea behind this 'tragedy' by analogy to the management of agricultural land, or more specifically to herdsmen with access to a 'pasture open to all'.[43] Without imposing any entrance or exit restrictions on the use of the pasture, every rational herdsman will seek to add additional grazing animals to the pasture with the aim of capitalising on the benefit he gains by having his cattle grazing for free. This might not in itself lead to utility problems. However, since all rational herdsmen will follow this path of reasoning and each add an extra animal to the common pasture, overgrazing will quickly become a problem. 'Therein is the tragedy'.[44] The underlying problem that Hardin describes is that there is no system in the commons that incentivise the herdsmen to internalise the costs imposed on the remaining herdsmen when extra animals on the pasture are added. In a 'reversed'[45] way, the tragedy of the commons appears also in the problem of pollution; rather than extracting from natural resources, air pollution puts something into a system and in that sense it creates externalities in the form

---

[39] B Harrison, C Smith and B Davies, *Introductory Economics* (Macmillan Press, London, 1992) 40.

[40] ibid.

[41] Fisher, Lange and Scotford, *Environmental Law* (n 34) ch 5.

[42] D Bodansky, J Brunnée and E Hey, 'International Environmental Law: Mapping the Field' in D Bodansky, J Brunnée and E Hey (eds), *The Oxford Handbook of International Environmental Law* (Oxford University Press, Oxford, 2007) 1, 9.

[43] Hardin, 'Tragedy of the Commons' (n 31) 1244. Note that Hardin re-frames his argument in later studies in which he claims that rather than regulating the commons, via, eg privatisation, human behaviour directly ought to be controlled. G Hardin, 'The Tragedy of the Unmanaged Commons: Population and the Disguise of Providence' in R Andelson (ed), *Commons Without Tragedy* (Shepheard-Walwyn Publishers, London, 1991) 162.

[44] Hardin, 'Tragedy of the Commons' (n 31) 1244.

[45] ibid 1245.

of purification costs or opportunities lost to subsequent or concurrent users.[46] The calculation of utility remain the same; the rational man finds that his share of the cost of the waste he discharges into the commons less than the cost of purifying the waste before releasing it.[47] The problem of externalities is understood to be particularly acute as human population increases and economic activities advance and become more complex.[48] As a result, certain externalities, such as greenhouse gases, are allowed to increase to levels that cause climate change, which is a threat in particular to vulnerable communities.[49] Subsequently, the effects of externalities become extensive, making the need for the application of a regulatory strategy for the commons pressing.

What the discussion above shows is that in the *Economic Efficiency Model* emissions trading is understood to be a regulatory strategy that seeks to solve the problem of externalities in the commons. Externalities are said to arise due to lack of incentives to internalise them.

2. *Understanding the Solution*

The legal solution proposed by the *Economic Efficiency Model* to the above problem is heavily influenced by academics such as Coase who argue that externalities can be resolved by creating a bargaining system in which these are traded.[50] In this regard, externalities are seen as being left to the market to deal with on its own.[51] Central to this model is the belief that the problem with externalities is of a 'reciprocal nature'.[52] This means that by prohibiting activities which give rise to externalities (for example, forbidding the herdsmen in Hardin's example from accessing the grazing area), all herdsmen in that specific commons – and not only the herdsmen whose activities give rise to externalities – will be negatively affected.[53] Instead of banning externalities outright (for example via regulation), rights – either to cause harm or to be free from harm – are assigned to one party. In this way, the possibility of bargaining for the entitlement is created. The theory is that, subject to transaction costs, the party who values (in economic terms) the entitlement the most will obtain it.[54] In the context of air pollution, the cost of an entitlement to emit gases is the cost of opportunity lost to breathe unpolluted air, and

[46] Harrison, Smith and Davies, *Introductory Economics* (n 39).

[47] Hardin, 'Tragedy of the Commons' (n 31) 1245.

[48] eg Hardin defines the problem of pollution to correlate with increased levels of population, see ibid 1245.

[49] See J Shaw and R Stroup, 'Global Warming and Ozone Depletion' in W Block (ed), *Economics and the Environment: A Reconciliation* (The Frasier Institute, Vancouver, 1990) 159, S Farrall, T Ahmed and D French (eds), *Criminological and Legal Consequences of Climate Change* (Hart Publishing, Oxford, 2012), J McAdam (ed), *Climate Change and Displacement* (Hart Publishing, Oxford, 2012), G White, *Climate Change and Migration: Security and Borders in a Warming World* (Oxford University Press, Oxford, 2011).

[50] Coase, 'Problem of Social Cost' (n 29).

[51] Bodansky, *International Environmental Law* (n 23) 49.

[52] Coase, 'Problem of Social Cost' (n 29) 2.

[53] ibid 2–3, 27.

[54] J Wiener, 'Global Environmental Regulation: Instrument Choice in the Legal Context' (1999) 108 *Yale Law Journal* 677, 709.

only if the entitlement is valued more than clean air, will air pollution occur.[55] This means that the allocation of rights to unpolluted air or rights to emit pollution is not based on environmental considerations but is, rather, substituted by economic calculations. As a result, the acceptable limit of air pollution is, according to this model, defined not by the regulator but by the market.

Indeed, according to the *Economic Efficiency Model*, the market plays a central role in emissions trading because it is understood to provide the most cost-effective allocation of externalities. Its cost-effectiveness lies in the low cost of private transactions, which is contrasted with the traditionally high costs of administrative regulation.[56] As a consequence, questions such as what interest should prevail or what payment is paid for the right to externalities should not be defined by the regulator but are decided instead by market mechanisms.[57] In effect, price and allocation of externalities in this model are seen to depend on the shrewdness of the various bargainers in emissions markets.[58] This theory is, however, based on the premise that there are no transaction costs.[59] In real life, transaction costs exist, and when these are high, the *Economic Efficiency Model* explains that government intervention in the emissions market may be required.[60] To be more specific, if the government provides solutions for internalising externalities at a lower cost than can the market, the role of the government should be to limit the costs of trading by regulatory intervention.[61] Therefore, when a regulatory strategy is applied to the commons, it should be constructed so as to provide the most cost-effective solutions instead of assuming that either the government or the market work 'costlessly'.[62] From this viewpoint, emissions trading is seen as a pragmatic economic process of allocation of externalities rather than as a doctrinal laissez-faire theory.[63]

---

[55] Coase, 'Problem of Social Cost' (n 29) 44.

[56] The cost-effectiveness of emissions trading, compared to direct regulation, is widely discussed in emissions trading literature, see, eg Ackerman and Stewart (n 35) 1362, T Tietenberg, *Emissions Trading, An Exercise in Reforming Pollution Policy* (Resources for the Future, Johns Hopkins University Press, Washington DC, 1985) 16, J Nash, 'Too Much Market? Conflict between Tradable Pollution Allowances and the "Polluter Pays" Principle' (2000) 24 *Harvard Environmental Law Review* 465, 481, R Stavins, 'Policy Instruments for Climate Change: How Can National Governments Address a Global Problem?' (1997) *University of Chicago Legal Forum* 293, 297–98, J Wiener, 'Global Environmental Regulation: Instrument Choice in the Legal Context' (1999) 108 *Yale Law Journal* 677, 682, 766–67.

[57] Note that Pigou, as a contrast, argues that the government ought to internalise externalities, and according to Pigou, via taxation. A Pigou, *Wealth and Welfare* (Macmillan, London, 1912). Coase's study differs from Pigou's theory in the sense that Coase sees the market – due to its allocative efficiency – as opposed to the state, to internalise externalities.

[58] Coase, 'Problem of Social Cost' (n 29) 5.

[59] ibid 17.

[60] The greater the number of parties involved, the higher the bargaining costs and the greater the potential for strategic behaviour and free-riding. This is why externalities, such as pollution, are difficult to manage and may require state intervention, see Bodansky *International Environmental Law* (n 23) 49–50.

[61] H Demsetz, 'The Cost of Transacting' (1968) 82 *The Quarterly Journal of Economics* 33, 34, Coase, 'Problem of Social Cost' (n 29) 18.

[62] R Posner, 'Nobel Laureate: Ronald Coase and Methodology' (1993) 7 *Journal of Economic Perspectives* 195, 202.

[63] ibid.

According to the *Economic Efficiency Model* it is imperative to ensure that the object of trade, in this context emissions allowances, is well-defined as legal rights. Here it is suggested that in theory the exact legal status of these rights is immaterial as long as the rights are clear and thus do not create an obstacle to trade. The belief is that, subject to transaction costs, these will always be allocated to their highest bidder.[64] However, because transaction costs exist, the legal definition of emission allowances has a direct impact on the economic activity in the market, as it may affect investment.[65] With the single aim of providing security for investment in emissions trading schemes, emissions allowances in the *Economic Efficiency Model* are often defined in property rights terms.[66] This shows that the key consideration in constructing emission trading schemes according to this model is to ensure that investments in the market are secured and the cost-effectiveness of the market safeguarded.

In sum, according to the *Economic Efficiency Model* emissions trading follows the rationale of a profit-centre that ensures allocative efficiency of externalities, and in this context, air pollutants. The market plays a crucial role in this regard as it is seen as internalising costs of pollution at the optimal price level, whilst the state intervenes in this market only when it is cost-beneficial to do so.

B. Private Property Rights Model[67]

In the *Private Property Rights Model* the problem which emissions trading should solve is government control of the commons. State officials are understood to over-exploit the commons for their own benefit. By pleasing the industry and creating jobs, they secure their own re-election.[68] The formulation of the problem, which emissions trading in this model is seen to remedy, reflects a certain outlook on government control. Creating private property rights that are tradable in an emissions market is understood as a substitute for government control of common resources

---

[64] Coase, 'Problem of Social Cost' (n 29) 19.

[65] ibid.

[66] See, eg G Chichilnisky and G Heal, 'Markets for Tradable Carbon Dioxide Emission Quotas: Principles and Practice' in G Chichilnisky and G Heal (eds), *Environmental Markets: Equity and Efficiency* (Colombia University Press, New York, 2001) 13, 17, R Hahn and G Hester, 'Where Did All the Markets Go? An Analysis of EPA's Emissions Trading Program' (1989) 6 *Yale Journal on Regulation* 109, 140, and as explained in G Xu, 'The Role of Property Law in Economic Growth' in M Faure and J Smits (eds), *Does Law Matter? On Law and Economic Growth* (Intersentia, Cambridge, 2011) 331, 333.

[67] Literature that falls under this model includes scholarly contributions by free market environmentalists, such as Anderson and Leal, as well as public choice inspired literature that identifies the government as the core of environmental protection problems, see, eg T Anderson and D Leal, *Free Market Environmentalism* (Westview Press, Oxford, 1993), E Brubaker, *Property Rights in the Defence of Nature* (Earthscan, London, 1958) and G Heal, 'Markets and Sustainability' in R Revesz, P Sands and R Stewart (eds), *Environmental Law, the Economy and Sustainable Development: The United States, the European Union and the International Community* (Cambridge University Press, Cambridge, 2000) 410.

[68] R Stroup and S Goodman, 'Property Rights, Environmental Resources, and the Future' (1992) 15 *Harvard Journal of Law and Public Policy* 427, 430.

altogether. Here, privatisation of the commons is a symbol of liberty. By transferring these private property rights to citizens, government control is diminished, and property owners are left to manage the commons on their own terms via the 'free' market (or in other words, 'free' from regulatory intervention).[69]

1. Portraying the Problem

According to the *Private Property Rights Model* government control of common resources is the key problem to the exploitation of the commons. State officials are described as squandering property rights in the commons for their personal benefit.[70] The reason is that a strong economy and a high level of employment guarantee popularity in elections, and so, the government has a selfish interest in pleasing industries that can secure national prosperity, rather than reducing pollution.[71] It is described that in case after case, 'government regulations have made it easier – and cheaper – for industries to pollute'.[72] In effect, both the *Economic Efficiency Model* and the *Private Property Rights Model* are based on the belief that incentives matter. The distinction lies in the fact that the *Economic Efficiency Model* identifies the *lack* of incentives, as opposed to acting according to the *wrong* incentives (which is the idea envisioned in the *Private Property Rights Model*), as the key problem that emissions trading addresses.

Examples used to illustrate in what manner governments place jobs and revenue from industries before nature preservation are predominantly conservation cases in North America.[73] For instance, governments are described as having licensed and bankrolled polluters, who have 'turned forests into wastelands, emptied oceans of fish, and dammed rivers that were once magnificent'.[74] For the personal benefit of state officials, governments allegedly pressured property owners via, for example, taxation, subsidies or expropriation to allow industries to be set up ahead of securing pollution control or nature preservation.[75] Also, costly court proceedings, difficulties of court challenges, and complex causal chain justifications between pollution and harm are identified as administrative burdens leaving people powerless to protest against activities that cause, for example, high levels of air pollution.[76]

---

[69] This signifies a regulatory shift from the government to the individual. Brubaker (n 67) 174.

[70] ibid 160–62, T Anderson and D Leal, 'Free Market Versus Political Environmentalism' (1992) 15 *Harvard Journal of Law and Public Policy* 297, 301. This idea is similar to those present in public choice literature, see n 26.

[71] Brubaker, *Property Rights in the Defence of Nature* (n 67) 105.

[72] ibid.

[73] The argument is that previous cases of environmental destruction bring to light what may happen to the remaining environment if governments are allowed to continue to control it, Heal, 'Markets and Sustainability' (n 67) 411.

[74] Brubaker, *Property Rights in the Defence of Nature* (n 67) 19–20.

[75] ibid 161.

[76] Block argues that instead of encouraging respect of property rights, governments all too often override them and that 'this lies at the bottom of many of our pollution-related problems'. W Block, 'Environmental Problems, Private Property Rights Solutions' in W Block (ed), *Economics and the Environment: A Reconciliation* (The Frasier Institute, Vancouver, 1990) 281, 282, ibid 113, 130.

Because politicians and bureaucrats are seen as being rewarded for responding to political pressure groups, this model projects a strong disbelief in the ability and will of the political system to ever guarantee the environment's protection. Environmental legislations, therefore, are understood as manifestations of favours to special interest groups, even if these are destined to prevent pollution and more generally to safeguard the environment.[77] As such, the *Private Property Rights Model* sees the central government as an example of institutional failure, both with regard to its interventions (by the introduction of certain laws) and omissions (by non-interference in favour of industries) in managing common resources.[78] The emphasis in this model is subsequently on governmental manipulation of the commons, which is understood to have created victims of pollution for the personal benefit of bureaucrats.

What the above discussion shows is that the *Private Property Model* portrays government control as the main reason for the exploitation of the commons. Government ownership and control of natural resources are considered to undermine sound management of natural resources and since no private property rights exist in commons resources, state control over such resources is retained and the commons are accordingly continuously abused.

2. *Understanding the Solution*

According to the *Private Property Rights Model*, the role of emissions trading is to replace government control of the commons by establishing tradable private property rights in common resources. The market, the state, and emissions allowances in these emissions trading schemes are not defined as mere components of a cost-effective allocation process (as in the *Economic Efficiency Model*) but as the cornerstones of a free society.

Creating tradable private property rights in the commons is considered essential in the *Private Property Rights Model*. Here, privatisation of common resources is thought to equal liberty: via private property rights, property holders are empowered to use and manage the commons on their *own* terms.[79] This means that the regulatory power which bureaucracies are thought to have misused in managing the commons is shifted to individuals and communities.[80] Individual preference is central, then; it is believed that through the aggregated expression of individual values in the market, resource shortage is avoided and environmental

---

[77] T Anderson and D Leal, 'Rethinking the Way We Think' in J Dryzek and D Schlosberg (eds), *Debating the Earth: The Environmental Politics Reader* (Oxford University Press, Oxford, 2005) 117, 211, Anderson and Leal, *Free Market Environmentalism* (n 67) ch 6.

[78] ibid.

[79] Brubaker, *Property Rights in the Defence of Nature* (n 67) 161–62. Note that creating private property rights to the atmosphere, although promoted, is recognised as being more technologically challenging than creating property rights to land. Anderson and Leal, 'Free Market Versus Political Environmentalism' (n 70) 309–10.

[80] Brubaker, *Property Rights in the Defence of Nature* (n 67) 174.

protection achieved.[81] Property holders are believed to avoid bad management decisions simply because their wealth in the property will depend on it.[82] Also, the idea that ownership secures material independence, which in turn facilitates political and even moral independence, saturates this model.[83] In effect, the underlying argument is that 'the further a decision maker is removed from this discipline – as he is when there is political control – the less likely it is that good resource stewardship will result'.[84] This approach does not seek to guarantee an overarching environmental standard or goal in a community, rather it advocates for these standards to be set by the will of the individuals or, more narrowly, private property holders.

Although the *Private Property Rights Model* and the *Economic Efficiency Model* are similar in the sense that both advocate for the creation of property rights in emissions allowances, the meaning of property rights here is very different from the understanding of property rights in the previous model. In the *Private Property Rights Model*, privatisation is thought to bestow upon property holders an 'unmatched power'[85] to protect the commons and to use property as a weapon to 'their own defence'.[86] Property rights empower citizens both to manage and protect the commons from any further overexploitation independently of governmental programmes. This stands as a contrast to the *Economic Efficiency Model*, which defines emission allowances in property right terms merely as a way of offering security for investments.[87]

Also the relationship between the market and the state in emissions trading is understood in a particular way in the *Private Property Rights Model*. The role of the market is vital as it is thought to ensure autonomy for the individual. Only the free market, it is argued, can provide individual liberty, 'and without that human freedom, environmental quality will be of little consequence'.[88] According to this view, allowing citizens to trade in emissions allowances leads to a rise in environmental quality while expanding individual liberty.[89] Freedom in this context consists of the breadth of possibilities that the market offers every citizen for finding exchanges of private property rights on the best terms possible for that particular person.[90]

[81] W Sunderlin, *Ideology, Social Theory, and the Environment* (Rowman and Littlefield Publishers, Lanham, 2003) 88.

[82] Anderson and Leal, 'Rethinking the Way We Think' (n 77) 208.

[83] This idea dates back to works, such as J Mill, *On Liberty; and Other Essays* (Oxford University Press, Oxford, 1991) and J-J Rousseau, *The Social Contract and Discourses* (Dent, London, 1913). For an analysis of the interrelationship between property rights, liberty and natural resources, see R Barnes, *Property Rights and Natural Resources* (Hart Publishing, Oxford, 2009) 37.

[84] Anderson and Leal, *Free Market Environmentalism* (n 67) 3.

[85] A Scott, 'Foreword' in E Brubaker (ed), *Property Rights in the Defence of Nature* (Earthscan, London, 1995) 16.

[86] ibid 8.

[87] See n 66.

[88] Anderson and Leal, 'Free Market Versus Political Environmentalism' (n 70) 310.

[89] According to free market environmentalism proponents, including Anderson and Leal, private property rights and a free market from regulatory interventions are two essential components for wise custodianship of the environment, see Sunderlin, *Ideology, Social Theory, and the Environment* (n 81) 88.

[90] A Alchian, *Pricing Society* (The Institute of Economic Affairs, Leicester, 1967) 8.

The element of freedom that is understood to exist in markets is contrasted with coercive bureaucratic pollution control. For instance, regulators are described as having failed the citizens and squandered common resources,[91] and since the aim of emissions trading is to hinder the exploitation caused by this bureaucratic mismanagement, any direct government control of the commons under the emissions trading regime is rejected.[92] As such, this model overlaps with certain politics of Reagan – or today's Tea Party[93] – who identified the government, not as the solution, but as the problem.[94] The market, on the other hand, is portrayed as 'the only non-arbitrary solution',[95] and a substitute for non-functioning government control of the commons. Emissions trading schemes are seen as being able to manage the commons independently of governmental programmes.[96] Still, the *Private Property Rights Model* recognises the need for policy-makers to establish the basic parameters of a market,[97] which in the context of emissions trading includes the legislator defining private property rights and the judiciary enforcing these.[98]

Clearly there are overlaps between this and the previous model; the way in which governmental exploitation is discussed in this model shows strong resemblance to Hardin's example of herdsmen who exploit the commons for their personal use. Also, Coase's theory about creating a market in which rights to a commons, such as air, are traded is another idea that the two models share. It is therefore worth recapping the differences. In the *Economic Efficiency Model* the focus is directed at the creation of a cost-effective trading scheme that helps to incentivise internalisation of pollution costs. Questions about whether the market is 'free' or heavily regulated, or whether the role of the state in emissions trading is laissez-faire or profoundly interventionist, are irrelevant as long as the emissions trading scheme constructed produces cost-effective results.[99] The *Private Property Rights Model*, on the other hand, is not equally flexible in this regard.

---

[91] Brubaker, *Property Rights in the Defence of Nature* (n 67) 162.

[92] In other words, the belief is that due to excessive government control and interference in the management of commons, environmental problems arise, see Sunderlin, *Ideology, Social Theory, and the Environment* (n 81) 87.

[93] In this context, I understand the Tea Party to be based on a sceptical attitude toward 'the expansion of government rolling forth from Washington, DC' as described in J O'Hara, *A New American Tea Party: The Counterrevolution Against Bailouts, Handouts, Reckless Spending and More Taxes* (John Wiley & Sons, Hoboken, New Jersey, 2010) 4.

[94] In his first inaugural address, Reagan stated that 'government is not the solution to our problems, government is the problem', as cited in C Schroeder, 'Public Choice and Environmental Policy' in D Farber and A O'Connell (eds), *Research Handbook on Public Choice and Public Law* (Edward Elgar, Cheltenham, 2010) 450, 452.

[95] Block, 'Environmental Problems, Private Property Rights Solutions' (n 76) 302.

[96] Brubaker, *Property Rights in the Defence of Nature* (n 67) 161–62.

[97] Dryzek explains that the majority of the scholarship that argues that the role of the government is to simply leave the market be, still recognise the role of the policymakers in first creating the market, see Dryzek, *Politics of the Earth* (n 10) 121.

[98] Anderson and Leal, *Free Market Environmentalism* (n 67) 3.

[99] Although there is a presumption in the *Economic Efficiency Model* that the emissions market is most cost-effective when government interventions are strictly limited, see n 60.

Here, the debates revolve around the problems of bureaucratic mismanagement. Emissions trading is understood as an empowering mechanism by which citizens, via the creation of private property rights in common resources, are able to prevent state officials from continuing to exploit the commons for their own profit. Private property rights in commons resources are therefore not mere components of a cost-effective market transaction – as in the *Economic Efficiency Model* – but a symbol of a free and just society.[100] Additionally, the role of central governance in emissions trading cannot be compromised but is limited to the legislator defining rights in these trading systems and the judiciary enforcing them. The role of the market, therefore, is to ensure liberty, not only as underpinning a cost-effective and autonomous market – as in the *Economic Efficiency Model* – but more as a way of assisting citizens in establishing a system in which they can manage the commons on their own terms and conditions, according to their own values and independently of state control and bureaucratic meddling.[101]

In sum, in the *Private Property Rights Model* emissions trading is envisioned as turning common resources into tradable private property rights, thereby replacing state control of the commons and allowing property holders to manage and protect common resources on their own terms.

C. Command-and-Control Model[102]

According to the *Command-and-Control Model* the reason why the exploitation of the atmosphere occurs is traced to direct regulation, or commonly named command-and-control. The role of emissions trading is portrayed as that of re-regulating classic command-and-control by turning outdated legislation into flexible and administratively effective regulation that caps and reduces diffuse pollutants. Re-regulating in this regard does not mean stripping the regulator of regulatory powers to manage the emissions market, or necessarily creating a profit-centre, as suggested in the previous models. Rather, it refers to the idea of creating a more suitable version of direct regulation, a so-called "'command and

---

[100] In this context, 'free society' means that citizens are free to access common resources, possess and control these on their own terms and independently from coercive state interference and state pollution programmes. Brubaker, *Property Rights in the Defence of Nature* (n 67) 161–62.

[101] The argument that emissions trading schemes may reinforce democracy by fostering and allowing for democratic debates about environmental values relates to this point about direct representation in emissions trading, see B Ackerman and R Stewart, 'Reforming Environmental Law: The Democratic Case for Market Incentives' (1988) 13 *Colombia Journal of Environmental Law* 171, Sunstein makes an analogous claim. C Sunstein, 'Panel II: Public Versus Private Environment Regulation' (1994) 21 *Ecological Law Quarterly* 455, 459.

[102] Literature that falls under this model is mainly contemporary and often EU-based, projecting emissions trading as an administrative tool. See, eg M Faure and M Peeters (eds), *Climate Change and European Emissions Trading: Lessons for Theory and Practice* (Edward Elgar, Cheltenham, 2008), A Sinden, 'The Tragedy of the Commons and the Myth of a Private Property Solution' (2007) 78 *University of Colorado Law Review* 533, B Thompson, 'Markets for Nature' (2000) 25 *William and Mary Environmental Law and Policy* 261, D Driesen, 'Is Emissions Trading an Economic Incentive Program?: Replacing the Command and Control/Economic Incentive Dichotomy' (1998) 55 *Washington and Lee Law Review* 289.

control *plus*" instrument'[103] that builds flexibility, so as to reduce the levels of certain air pollutants, into existing command-and-control regulatory regimes.

1. Portraying the Problem

In the *Command-and-Control Model* exploitation of the atmosphere is explained to occur due to the failings of direct regulation to respond to and control mobile and diffuse pollutants. The traditional licensing and command-and-control mechanisms that usually are applied to pollution control are thought to place too impossible administrative demands on central government to gather information, set standards, monitor and then enforce these in cases of highly complex and novel environmental problems, such as climate change.[104] The concern is that fixed environmental standards or licenses are quickly outpaced and outdated both by more effective technology and increasingly complicated environmental problems.[105] Moreover, direct regulation is understood to offer no incentive to implement new technology or go beyond the set pollution standards,[106] and so, the *Command-and-Control Model* identifies a regulatory stalemate in applying command-and-control to certain new pollutants. The problem that emissions trading is seen to address is to regulate these high-risk, invisible and multiple pollution sources that direct regulation is viewed inapt to successfully manage.[107]

It is important to note that this model considers command-and-control techniques effective when applied to stationary and point sources of pollution. In contrast to the *Private Property Right Model*, which uses examples of conservation cases in North America to show the failings of government control of commons, the *Command-and-Control Model* refers to examples of traditional environmental protection to show that the application of bureaucratic management over the past few decades has helped decrease visible pollution.[108] This means that the *Command-and-Control Model* calls for re-regulation of command-and-control to specific types of pollution that are problematic rather than seeking to overhaul the entire governance regime of regulating the environment.

---

[103] Description borrowed from J Lefevere, 'Greenhouse Gas Emission Allowance Trading in the EU: A Background' (2003) *Yearbook of European Environmental Law* 149, 154.

[104] Extensive literature exists on this point, and starting in the 1980s, an entire wave of scholarship criticised the use of direct regulation to deal with new environmental law problems, such as diffuse air pollution, see, eg J Scott, *Environmental Law* (Longman, London, 1998) ch 2, C Hilson, *Regulating Pollution. A UK and EC Perspective* (Hart Publishing, Oxford, 2000) ch 6, R Baldwin, M Cave and M Lodge, *Understanding Regulation: Theory, Strategy, and Practice* (2nd edn, Oxford University Press, Oxford, 2012) ch 10.

[105] JB Ruhl, 'Thinking of Environmental Law as a Complex Adaptive System: How to Clean Up the Environment by Making a Mess of Environmental Law' (1997) 34 *Houston Law Review* 933, 984, Ackerman and Stewart, 'Reforming Environmental Law' (n 35).

[106] R Stewart, 'Regulation, Innovation, and Administrative Law: A Conceptual Framework' (1981) 69 *California Law Review* 1256.

[107] M Lee, *EU Environmental Law: Challenges, Change and Decision-Making* (Hart Publishing, Oxford, 2005) 187.

[108] Hilson (n 104) 127.

Ultimately all emissions trading discourses promote a particular version of emissions trading against the backdrop of the failings of direct regulation, and so it is inevitable that criticism of traditional environmental regulation appears in all three models. In the *Economic Efficiency Model* the criticism focuses on the fact that externalities persist whilst in the *Private Property Rights Model* the extensive government control is the main objection to direct regulation. It is in these academic debates that the term 'command-and-control' has emerged as a way of describing governmental control as a form of 'draconian bureaucracy',[109] coercing firms and consumers into something that is ineffective and which is described to bring to mind 'Soviet style interference in private life'[110] that allegedly are 'at odds with the worldwide recognition of the failures of state socialism'.[111] What the two first models thus do is to label any type of government interference 'command-and-control', even when, as explained in the *Economic Efficiency Model*, such interference is cost-effective.

In the *Command-and-Control Model*, on the other hand, the problem that emissions trading addresses is framed neither as an externality issue nor as a rejection of government control of common resources; rather, the only disputed 'commanded and controlled' parts of state interference concern primarily regulatory mechanisms that demand fix implementation exercises.[112] This means that the *Command-and-Control Model* is not based on a particular objectionable view of central government, as is the *Private Property Rights Model*. As such, central government control of common resources is not discarded nor is emissions trading understood to work in lieu of, or as opposed to, central management of the commons.[113] The *Command-and-Control Model* is nonetheless similar to the *Economic Efficiency Model* in that it too portrays certain direct regulations as cost-ineffective.[114] The difference between the two is nonetheless that at the heart of the *Command-and-Control Model* lies the aim to establish a regulatory strategy that successfully complies with regulatory obligations and reduces pollution levels rather than creating a profit-centre per se.

---

[109] M Jacobs, *The Green Economy: Environment, Sustainable Development, and the Politics of the Future* (Pluto Press, London, 1991) 151.

[110] See Lee, *EU Environmental Law* (n 107) 183, Dryzek, *Politics of the Earth* (n 10) 135.

[111] R Stewart, 'Introduction' in R Revesz, P Sands and R Stewart (eds), *Environmental Law, the Economy and Sustainable Development: The United States, the European Union and the International Community* (Cambridge University Press, Cambridge, 2000) 1, 19.

[112] Such requirements range from the setting of maximum level of pollution release (eg target standards) to specifying methods of how to achieve this (eg specific standards). Lee, *EU Environmental Law* (n 107) 183.

[113] See Driesen, 'Replacing Command and Control / Economic Incentive Dichotomy' (n 102) 310, Lefevere (n 103) 152, L Krämer, 'Some Reflections on the EU Mix of Instruments on Climate Change' in M Peeters and K Deketelaere (eds), *EU Climate Change Policy: The Challenge of New Regulatory Initiatives* (Edward Elgar, Cheltenham, 2006) 279. Sinden, 'Tragedy of the Commons' (n 102) 538 states that the fact that property rights in common resources and markets are generated as an alternative to government regulation of environmental problems – and as encompassed here in the *Private Property Rights Model* – 'is in fact nothing more than a mirage'.

[114] See n 56.

What the discussion above shows is that in the *Command-and-Control Model*, traditional regulation is portrayed as ineffective in dealing with air pollution control. The motivation behind emissions trading is to establish a revised regulatory framework, which deals with specific types of air pollutants in a flexible and administratively effective manner.

2. Understanding the Solution

As explained, in the *Command-and-Control Model* emissions trading is presented as re-regulation of classic command-and-control applied to certain air pollutants. The notion of 're-regulation' elucidates that such a trading scheme is not a matter of challenging regulatory powers of central government but rather reforming the existing legal framework to address new regulatory challenges.[115] The key regulatory adaption that emissions trading is thought to achieve is the creation of a less 'imposing'[116] regulatory tool where polluters are allowed considerable flexibility in complying with pollution targets. Rather than imposing definitions as to 'how', 'where', and 'when' compliance must be achieved – which direct regulation is understood to do – and in that sense command a particular behaviour or technology that industries must follow and apply, emissions trading is seen to delegate the question of which route to take to compliance.[117] More precisely, allowing polluters to trade rights in emissions allowances and so decide on their own whether to reduce emissions and sell their surplus, stay within the regulatory equilibrium, or increase emissions and buy additional emissions rights, flexibility that emissions trading schemes are hailed for, is achieved.[118] This administrative flexibility is thought not only to unburden the central government from micro-level management of a myriad of pollutants, their sources and technologies to apply to reduce these but also lead to innovation and in particular incentivise firms to invest in clean technologies so as to be able to sell any potential surplus in emissions allowances.[119] As such, from the viewpoint of the *Command-and-Control Model*, emissions trading is able to cure the

---

[115] In more general literature on regulation, re-regulation has been defined as 'fine tuning' of markets without 'going back' to direct regulation, see M Ghertman, 'The Puzzle of Regulation, Deregulation and Reregulation' in C Ménard and M Ghertman (eds), *Regulation, Deregulation, Reregulation: Institutional Perspectives* (Edward Elgar, Cheltenham, 2009) 351, 367. According to Majone (n 5) 3, re-regulation is a form of regulatory reform, which fits the description of re-regulation as encompassed in the *Command-and-Control Model*. Re-regulation in this context thus does not signify the abolishment of regulation but rather achieving regulatory objectives by a new form of (less administrative burdensome) rules.

[116] B Rittberger and J Richardson, 'Old Wine in New Bottles? The Commission and the Use of Environmental Policy Instruments' (2003) 81 *Public Administration* 575, 575.

[117] Literature that advocates for emissions trading schemes due to their flexibility is vast and the following are mere examples, see J Wiener and B Richman, 'Mechanism Choice' in D Farber and A O'Connell (eds), *Research Handbook on Public Choice and Public Law* (Edward Elgar, Cheltenham, 2010) 363, 370, D Dudek, R Stewart and J Wiener, 'Environmental Policy for Eastern Europe: Technology-Based Versus Market-Based Approaches' (1992) 17 *Colombia Journal of Environmental Law* 1, 3, R Stewart, 'A New Generation of Environmental Regulation?' (2001) 29 *Capital University Law Review* 21.

[118] Stewart, 'Regulation, Innovation, and Administrative Law' (n 106).

[119] ibid.

failings of classic command-and-control by decentralising compliance methods from the central government and offering innovation incentives to industries by creating tradable rights in emissions allowances.

The *Command-and-Control Model* is similar to the *Economic Efficiency Model* in that both stress the importance of flexibility and effectiveness in managing commons in air. Moreover, both rely on incentives that markets offer to change the behaviour of the regulated. There is nonetheless an important difference in the role of the state as envisioned by these two models, as well as by the *Private Property Rights Model*. In the *Economic Efficiency Model* the role of the central government is determined according to its *impact* on the functioning of the market and the cost-effectiveness of market transactions, while in the *Private Property Rights Model*, the role of central governance is limited to the legislator defining private property rights and the legislator enforcing these. In the *Command-and-Control Model*, however, the regulator's role is not compromised. The regulatory is vested with the discretion to determine, for instance, the quantity of emissions, the form of allocation, the recognition of entitlements and the enforcement of sanctions.[120] These are important regulatory powers, even with the regulated having the right to decide where and how to emit and whether to reduce, buy or sell emission allowances.[121] Subsequently, in the *Command-and-Control Model* emissions trading is seen to function around obligations that the government creates, just like any other command-and-control type of regulation,[122] and on this basis it is explained that emissions trading 'cannot be equated with "market forces"'.[123] As such, emissions trading is presented as regulation albeit of 'a different *form* from command-and-control'.[124] Moreover, this model recognises emissions trading schemes also as part of a global emissions trading scheme, in which nation states – rather than private property holders – are the primary actors both for agreeing to such trading schemes and implementing them in their legal orders.[125] The image and role prescribed to the central government in emissions trading is, in fact, what distinguishes the *Command-and-Control Model* from the *Economic Efficiency* and the *Private Property Rights* models.

[120] M Peeters, 'Enforcement of the EU Greenhouse Gas Emissions Trading Scheme' in M Peeters and K Deketelaere (eds), *EU Climate Change Policy: The Challenge of New Regulatory Initiatives* (Edward Elgar, Cheltenham, 2006) 169.
[121] Driesen elucidates this point with reference to property rights and how the thought of 'ownership' with regard to emissions allowances is a misguided description, D Driesen, 'What's Property Got To Do With It?: A Review Essay of "Pollution and Property: Comparing Ownership Institutions for Environmental Protection" by Daniel Cole' (2003) 30 *Ecology Law Quarterly* 1003, 1012–15.
[122] B Morgan and K Yeung, *An Introduction to Law and Regulation: Texts and Materials* (Cambridge University Press, Cambridge, 2007) 315, Sinden, 'Tragedy of the Commons' (n 102) 538, Driesen, 'Replacing Command and Control/Economic Incentive Dichotomy' (n 102) 338.
[123] Hilson, *Regulating Pollution* (n 104) 103.
[124] ibid. Similar point raised in Jacobs, *Green Economy* (n 109) 151.
[125] Morgan and Yeung, *Law and Regulation* (n 122) 316, M Peeters, 'Towards a European System of Tradable Pollution Permits?' (1993) 2 *Tilburg Foreign Law Review* 117, G Pring, 'A Decade of Emissions Trading in the USA: Experience and Observations for the EU' in M Peeters and K Deketelaere (eds), *EU Climate Change Policy: The Challenge of New Regulatory Initiatives* (Edward Elgar, Cheltenham, 2006) 188.

Moreover, in comparison to the *Economic Efficiency* and *Private Property Rights* models, the *Command-and-Control Model* is far more critical of the role that markets are able to play, or ought to play in emissions trading. In the two previous models, the market is depicted as 'free', meaning that no room is envisaged for governmental intervention in relation to emissions trading – unless it is cost-effective, as explained in the *Economic Efficiency Model*. In the *Command-and-Control Model*, markets are not understood to exist in this kind of legal vacuum but in the constant presence of the regulator.[126] There is no so-called invisible hand of the market but rather the state is there to regulate it. The task of the regulator is defined as ensuring fair competition via government intervention in the emissions market – a view contrary to the *Private Property Rights Model*. Unregulated markets are described as giving rise to dominant market players, who have the possibility of raising costs for rivals or blocking the entry of new competitors by means of predation, pre-emption, exclusion, and collusion – unless the regulator intervenes.[127] Emissions trading is viewed as a regulation strategy in which the government artificially shapes competition so as to prevent this.[128] Moreover, the regulator – not the market – is envisioned to limit and target the quantity of emission allowances so as to create scarcity and ensure that the market functions.[129] Therefore, the market is not understood as 'free' in the *Command-and-Control Model* but at best as 'partial and incomplete'[130]; as a mere device through which regulatory obligations can be carried out.

With regard to the legal status of emissions allowances, these are inconsistently defined in the *Command-and-Control Model* including, for instance, 'environmental obligations', 'licences', 'pollution rights' or 'permits'.[131] As such, it is not always clear as to what is traded,[132] suggesting that here emissions allowances are seen as 'hybrid rights'.[133] Although these definitions arguably fall

---

[126] Driesen, 'Replacing Command and Control / Economic Incentive Dichotomy' (n 102) 338.

[127] ibid.

[128] E Rehbinder, 'Market-Based Incentives for Environmental Protection' in R Revesz, P Sands and R Stewart (eds), *Environmental Law, the Economy and the Sustainable Development* (Cambridge University Press, Cambridge 2000) 245, 249.

[129] Lefevere, 'Greenhouse Gas Emissions Allowance Trading' (n 103) 151.

[130] Morgan and Yeung, *Law and Regulation* (n 122) 316.

[131] Lefevere, 'Greenhouse Gas Emissions Allowance Trading' (n 103) 151, for instance, sees emissions allowances as a 'right to emit a particular quantity of [in this context] greenhouse gases'. Driesen, 'What's Property Got To Do With It?' (n 121) 1013, similarly, names these 'environmental obligations'. For a list of the variety of rights that emissions rights may take see G Libecap, 'Property Rights Allocation of Common Pool Rescources' in C Ménard and M Ghertman (eds), *Regulation, Deregulation, Reregulation: Institutional Perspectives* (Edward Elgar, Cheltenham, 2009) 27, 40.

[132] J Button, 'Carbon: Commodity or Currency? The Case for an International Carbon Market Based on the Currency Model' (2008) 32 *Harvard Environmental Law Review* 571, L Rajamani, 'The Increasing Current and Relevance of Rights-Based Perspectives in the International Negotiations on Climate Change' (2010) 22 *Journal of Environmental Law* 391.

[133] Note that 'hybrid' in this context describes a range of non-property based emission allowances and is therefore not employed in the same way as in C Rose, 'Expanding the Choice for the Global Commons: Comparing Newfangled Tradable Allowance Schemes to Old-Fashioned Common Property Regimes' (1999) 10 *Duke Environmental Law and Policy Forum* 45.

under a broad legal spectrum, privatisation of emission allowances is not envisaged in this model – a direct contrast to the *Private Property Rights Model*. This is because private property rights would diminish government's control over the commons and this disagrees with how the *Command-and-Control Model* envisions the role of the regulator. In other words, emission allowances are legally defined so as to facilitate emissions trading without removing the regulator's control over it.

In sum, the *Command-and-Control Model* presents emissions trading as a regulatory response to the failings of classic command-and-control pollution control systems. The re-regulation is manifested in the creation of emissions trading schemes that allows flexible implementation of regulatory obligations through a trade system of surplus in emission allowances. This regulatory framework is, nonetheless, understood to operate against the backdrop of government control and at the direction of the regulator. As such, the *Command-and-Control Model* furthers emissions trading schemes due to their regulatory flexibility but without compromising the role of the central government in constructing and managing this regulatory strategy.

IV. Evaluating and Comparing the Models

The analysis of the *Economic Efficiency*, the *Private Property Rights* and the *Command-and-Control* models above highlights emissions trading as a shared paradigm, meaning that the scholarship on emissions trading is informed by a wide variety of intellectual disciplines and thoughts. Accordingly competing visions regarding the role that these trading schemes play or ought to play in managing the commons in air, as understood by the academic community, exist. The models demonstrate that underpinning the overarching theme in emissions trading discourses of managing the exploitation of the commons, lie nuanced discussions regarding distinct environmental and non-environmental problems to which emissions trading is thought to respond. These relate to establishing a profit-centre (the *Economic Efficiency Model*), a governance system that replaces central control of common resources (the *Private Property Rights Model*), and a regulatory system that complies with regulatory goals effectively (the *Command-and-Control Model*). Each narrative in the three models envisions the governance regime of emissions trading differently, as manifested in the dissimilar roles that the market, the state, and the legal status of emissions allowances are understood to play in these trading schemes. Table 1 below illustrates these findings as encompassed by the models.

Table 1: The models compared

	Economic Efficiency Model	Private Property Rights Model	Command-and-Control Model
PORTRAYING THE PROBLEM			
Problem	Externalities	Government control of the commons	Ineffective cross-boundary pollution regulation
Reason for the Problem	Lack of incentive to internalise externalities	Lack of private property rights in the commons	Lack of administratively flexible and effective regulatory strategies
UNDERSTANDING THE SOLUTION			
Role of the Market	Enable the creation of 'profit- centres'	Safeguard personal liberty (that is, ensuring transfer of private property rights on the terms of property holders)	Regulatory device
Role of the State	Regulatory intervention if cost-effective	The legislator defines private property rights and the judiciary enforces these	Creates and manages the emissions trading scheme
Legal Nature of Emissions Allowance	Secured financial right	Private property right	Hybrid right

This table highlights very different forms of emissions trading schemes and it is useful to summarise these findings before evaluation. In the *Economic Efficiency Model*, emissions trading is understood as trying to solve the problem of externalities. In this model, the key aim is to create a cost-effective emissions trading scheme that induces internalisation of externalities. The role of the market and the state depend therefore on whether it is cost-effective to have a heavily regulated or a 'free' market. Equally, emissions allowances are defined in property rights terms with the aim of providing financial security for investors. Thus the role of emissions trading is to act as a profit-centre, so as to secure participation in the emissions market, and in this sense, induce the internalisation of externalities.

In the *Private Property Rights Model*, emissions trading is understood to remedy poor government control of the commons. State officials are described as having squandered these for their personal benefit, and are thus found unsuitable for controlling common resources. By privatising the commons, emissions trading is seen as empowering citizens to manage common resources on their own terms, and more importantly, independently of governmental programmes. Hence the role of central authority in emissions trading is limited to the legislator defining private tradable property rights and to the judiciary enforcing these. The market thus plays a crucial role in ensuring liberty by assisting citizens in establishing a system in which they can trade rights to common resource and in this way manage these on their own conditions. Ultimately, emissions trading is considered a substitute for government control of the commons.

In the *Command-and-Control Model*, emissions trading addresses the problem of ineffective direct pollution regulation. In contrast to the two previous models, the *Command-and-Control Model* portrays the emissions market as a device, rather than the central component of emissions trading, through which regulatory obligation is created. The market is therefore not 'free' but heavily regulated. Since emissions trading is not understood as stripping the regulator of its control of the commons – as envisaged in the *Private Property Rights Model* – emission allowances are not defined in property rights terms but are rather seen as falling within a wide range of administrative permits, or hybrid rights. From this perspective, the role of emissions trading is to re-regulate and establish a flexible and administratively effective air pollution strategy.

Having bared the emissions trading discourses in the described manner, none of the models may seem particularly appealing. For instance, the *Private Property Rights Model* sits uncomfortably with any current international agreement that uses emissions trading schemes as a top-down means to combat a common problem, such as climate change. Although the *Economic Efficiency Model* and the *Command-and-Control Model* seem less politically radical in comparison (depending on one's own political views), they too are dogged in specific agendas, such as the creation of economic opportunities and re-regulation respectively. It may be argued that the models are not appealing because they constitute three extremes of the emissions trading literature. In light of this argument, the following points need to be raised.

It is not demanded from the reader to show alliance to any model as listed in this chapter. Ultimately these models are limited in scope as they are based on only a small part of the extensive scholarly landscape that is the emissions trading literature.[134] Moreover, there is the constant risk of bias in the selection and categorisation of literature. To start with, environmental problems are 'interconnected and multidimensional; they are, in a word, complex'.[135] This gives rise to equally complex debates that are extremely hard to conceptualise and categorise

---

[134] eg literature that rejects the use of emissions markets to environmental problems have, to a large extent, been excluded from this analysis, see J Mintz, 'Economic Reform of Environmental Protection: A Brief Commentary on a Recent Debate' (1991) 15 *Harvard Environmental Law Review* 149. Also, scholarly contributions that offer regulatory solutions, beyond the use of markets, to help limit and halt the exploitation of the commons, have similarly been omitted from this study, see B Yandle and A Morriss, 'The Technologies of Property Rights: Choice Among Alternative Solutions to Tragedies of the Commons' (2001) 28 *Ecology Law Quarterly* 123, 168, M Heller, *The Gridlock Economy: How Too Much Ownership Wrecks Markets, Stops Innovation, and Costs Lives* (Basic Books, New York City, 2008), E Ostrom, *Governing the Commons: The Evolution of Institutions for Collective Action* (Cambridge University Press, Cambridge, 1990).

[135] Dryzek, *Politics of the Earth* (n 10) 8.

in distinct models. Because cataloguing broad-ranging discourses on a topic, such as emissions trading, is hard, the risk of oversimplification is high – especially in this chapter, as these models are based on no previous system of categorising emissions trading scholarship. A way of avoiding this would have been to resort to existing theoretical grouping of regulation instead of defining models according to my own analysis of the set literature. For example, the *Private Property Rights Model* reflects ideas shared with public choice theorists.[136] In broad terms, public choice theorists critically analyse the way in which governments make decisions,[137] arguing that politicians set out policies with the single aim of being re-elected.[138] In the *Private Property Rights Model* governments are similarly portrayed as squandering the commons for the benefit of industries, which guarantee jobs and therefore also votes. Indeed, environmental discourses and public choice arguably 'grew up together'[139] and so strong similarities between the two are bound to exist. As another alternative, emissions trading debates could have been mapped onto environmental discourses as defined by Dryzek.[140] In particular 'economic rationalism', which is defined as relying on the 'free market' and the idea of private property holders being able to trade in natural resource rights, overlaps greatly with the *Private Property Rights Model* – especially with regard to its non-negotiable rejection of central management of environmental protection.[141] The reason why the *Economic Efficiency*, the *Private Property Rights* and the *Command-and-Control* models have not been mapped on already existing scholarly patterns is that emissions trading literature demands separate attention. Although similarities between the *Private Property Rights Model* and public choice and economic rationalism in environmental discourses are apparent, these particular theories of regulation are only two amongst a range of different influences on emissions trading discourses. Stating that these discourses are mere mirror images of different regulatory theories would not only undervalue the specific nature and complexity of emissions trading literature but also the significance of the models.

Moreover, although the models should not be read as the only possible categorisation of the emissions trading literature, they still perform one type of categorisation. This particular categorisation is useful in highlighting a chronological development of emissions trading debates, which may serve as a valuable outline of emissions trading discourses more generally. For instance, the *Economic Efficiency Model* projects theory-based emissions trading debates that stem from economics

[136] Drew notes that much emissions trading literature in fact relies on public choice theory, particularly in highlighting the risks of regulatory failure, see A Drew, 'Two Directives, Two Politics – Prospects for the EU ETS' (Law Society Economy Working Papers 11/2010, LSE Law 2010) www.lse.ac.uk/collections/law/wps/WPS2010-11_Drew.pdf, accessed 11 September 2012.
[137] P Samuelson and W Nordhaus, *Economics* (McGraw-Hills Book Co, London, 2005) 745.
[138] See n 26.
[139] See Schroeder (n 94) 451.
[140] These are administrative rationalism, democratic pragmatism and economic rationalism. Dryzek, *Politics of the Earth* (n 10) 121–28.
[141] ibid 121.

and that gained support in legal academia in the 1980s.[142] The view of emissions trading here is that it creates an economic opportunity and allows the emissions market to regulate pollution with limited input from the state. Following the most recent debt and financial crises, enthusiasm for this model and unregulated markets may seem to have faltered.[143] Arguably, the *Command-and-Control Model*, which places regulation – albeit of a different form to direct regulation – at the forefront in creating and managing emissions market, is instead gaining more widespread support.[144] Ideas and visions of emissions trading as portrayed in the *Private Property Rights Model*, on the other hand, were prominent in the US in the 1970s and again in the 1990s but have been less forceful in the EU and multilateral contexts.[145] Reasons for this (as discussed in chapter three) is that EU law has not developed a sense of 'property' due to constitutional questions about competence,[146] and that the *Private Property Rights Model* rejects the idea of top-down imposed control that the EU and multilateral contexts build upon. Viewing the models as chronological indicators and showing that certain views encompassed in a particular model are more favourable at different times and in different legal contexts, as well as responding to various political climates, reinforces the idea that emissions trading schemes are not static but complex regulatory strategies that feed off current affairs and respond to particular regulatory agendas. Although the models fail to answer *why* certain depictions of emissions trading schemes are more appealing than others, they help to show that these fluctuations exist.

The significance of setting out models based on emissions trading literature is to illustrate that emissions trading schemes are nuanced and complex regulatory concepts that do not allow for generalisation. Indeed, and as explained in chapter one, emissions trading tends to be linked with the ascendancy of market-oriented thinking, tied to capitalism and seen as a natural process of privatisation more generally.[147] These ideas are rooted in the *Private Property Rights Model*, and in

---

[142] The scholarly piece by Ackerman and Stewart, 'Reforming Environmental Law' (n 35) first introduced emissions trading schemes to environmental law scholarship.

[143] Even Alan Greenspan – 'the highest priest of laissez-faire economics' – has admitted that he may have gone too far in believing that markets could be self-regulating, as cited by Stiglitz. J Stiglitz, 'Government Failure vs Market Failure: Principles of Regulation' in E Balleisen and D Moss (eds), *Government and Markets: Toward a New Theory of Regulation* (Cambridge University Press, Cambridge, 2010) 1.

[144] This seems at least to be the case in examining the EU ETS and the Commission's emissions trading-related discourse, as illustrated in ch 4.

[145] This correlates with the fact that public choice discourse more generally is less popular in the EU and at the global level, see J Dunoff, 'Levels of Environmental Governance' in D Bodansky, J Brunnée and E Hey (eds), *The Oxford Handbook of International Environmental Law* (Oxford University Press, Oxford, 2007) 85, 98, Dryzek, *Politics of the Earth* (n 10) 121–28.

[146] Art 345 TFEU shows the very sensitivity of the notion of property at EU level, stating that 'The Treaties shall in no way prejudice the rules in the Member States governing the system of property ownership'. 'TFEU' refers to the Consolidated Versions of the Treaty on the Functioning of the European Union (TFEU), [2008] OJ C115/49.

[147] eg the use of markets in fisheries took off in New Zealand at the same time as privatisation, see K Wyman, 'Why Regulators Turn to Tradeable Permits: A Canadian Case Study' (2002) 52 *University of Toronto Law Journal* 419. See also Lee, *EU Environmental Law* (n 112) 186, D Satz, *Why Some Things Should Not Be For Sale* (Oxford University Press, Oxford, 2010) 3.

part, also in the *Economic Efficiency Model*. However, re-regulatory focus in the *Command-and-Control Model* shows that ensuring cost-effectiveness and responding to market failures is not the sole reason for regulating the commons. These regulatory rationales subsequently result in emissions trading schemes taking different legal forms, which means that the picture of the emissions trading scheme as a regulatory concept is fragmented and complex. In other words, the models help to demote the assumption that emissions trading schemes are straightforward regulations that are applicable with the same objective and effect across different jurisdictions. The models also importantly highlight that emissions trading regimes differ in relation to the role of the state, the market and the legal status of emissions allowances. As such, the models set out a framework through which to further investigate emissions trading schemes.

V. Applicability of the Models

The reader should now be familiar with the argument that emissions allowance discourses refer to different roles and objectives for emissions trading schemes in promoting this regulatory strategy to control commons in air. The implications of this finding have as yet not been crystallised and it is to these that I now turn.

Emissions trading schemes are broadly understood as dealing with the management of the commons. One idea that is shared in these debates, and which the *Economic Efficiency,* the *Private Property Rights* and the *Command-and-Control* models highlight, is that confronting resource users with the need to obtain, or purchase rights to utilise the commons – in the context of this chapter, emitting emissions into the atmosphere – leads to the husbandry of resources for the purpose of securing economic opportunities (the *Economic Efficiency Model*), liberty (the *Private Property Rights Model*), or regulatory compliance (the *Command-and-Control Model*). Although these objectives are divergent and no consensus exists as to *how* to achieve them, all three models imagine some form of governance authority that imposes restraints on the use of the commons recourses. According to the *Economic Efficiency Model* the regulatory authority lies within the market, as it is according to market forces that property rights in emissions allowances are allocated; in the *Private Property Rights Model* private property holders are vested with regulatory authority in deciding, on their own terms, whether to sell, keep, squander or safeguard their property; and in the *Command-and-Control Model* the regulatory power is entrusted to the central government. An implication of the models is the emphasis that emissions trading discourses orbit the legal dilemma of 'how' and 'to whom' to allocate regulatory power. Considering that each model imagines a different regulatory authority to govern emissions trading, it follows that each model refers to a distinct governance structure for these trading schemes.

An implication of this kind may not seem novel. New sources of regulatory power are obviously created when rules, such as emissions trading, are applied to a resource that used to belong to all. Questions that then arise, include how to create rules governing the commons,[148] who legislates or ought to legislate,[149] whom are, or whom ought scarce resources be allocated to and how.[150] Indeed, the questions about how environmental decisions are made and who makes them; that is, questions of environmental governance, lie 'at the heart of environmental law and policy'.[151] Yet the models highlight a different and important point that breaks away from the existing methodology in emissions trading discourse and environmental law scholarship in two specific ways.

First, the models show that the roles that scholars ascribe to the market, the state and emission allowances under emissions trading exist in a symbiosis; in other words, they are co-produced.[152] This means that a particular picture of the state – irrespective of its negative or positive understanding of the state's capabilities when entrusted with regulatory powers – directly affects the roles suggested for the market and emissions allowances under emissions trading schemes. For environmental lawyers working in this area, this means examining the three entities as part of a broader mosaic that constitutes emissions trading. By assuming that the state's entrusted role – whether according to the *Economic Efficiency*, the *Private Property Rights*, or the *Command-and-Control* model – defines the trading regime, this three-legged approach to studying emissions trading schemes breaks away from any suggestion that trading schemes are straightforward or operating outside of the spheres of law.

The models also show that determining the allocation of regulatory power within an emissions trading scheme is central to understanding how the governance structure underpinning such a scheme is imagined. Governance-related discussions in environmental law scholarship are expansive, in particular considering the multi-level governance structures of numerous environmental laws.[153] As such, questions concerning the allocation of regulatory power within a wider global environment governance system[154] and the fit of emissions trading within

---

[148] N Fligstein, *The Architecture of Markets: An Economic Sociology of Twenty-First Century Capitalist Societies* (Princeton University Press, Princeton, 2001) 4, R Revesz, *NYU Casebook: Environmental Law and Policy* (Foundation Press, New York City, 2008) 1–20.

[149] This is particularly clear in the EU context, as the competence to legislate on environmental matters is shared between the Member States and the Union. For an overview, see, eg J Jans and H Vedder, *European Environmental Law – After Lisbon* (4th edn, Europa Law Publishing, Groningen, 2011) chs 1–3.

[150] R Malloy, *Law in a Market Context: An Introduction to Market Concepts in Legal Reasoning* (Cambridge University Press, Cambridge, 2004) 22, D Schoenbrod, R Stewart and K Wyman, *Breaking the Logjam: Environmental Protection that Will Work* (Yale University Press, New Haven, 2010) 28.

[151] Dunoff, 'Levels of Environmental Governance' (n 145) 86.

[152] Terminology borrowed from Jasanoff, 'Idiom of Co-Production' (n 17).

[153] See, eg P Birnie, A Boyle and C Redgwell, *International Law and the Environment* (3rd edn, Oxford University Press, Oxford, 2009), Fisher, Lange and Scotford (n 34) ch 5.

[154] See Dunoff, 'Levels of Environmental Governance' (n 145), R Revesz, 'Federalism and Environmental Regulation: An Overview' in R Revesz, P Sands and R Stewart (eds), *Environmental Law, the Economy and Sustainable Development: The United States, the European Union and the International Community* (Cambridge University Press, Cambridge, 2000) 37, M Betsill, 'Global

this multi-level governance frame,[155] are well-known important and unresolved issues. The models, however, stress a different point. They show that emissions trading as a single regulatory *concept* envisions and allows different governance regimes to be established. In other words, the models demonstrate that emissions trading schemes correspond to nuanced and complex regulatory strategies that cannot be generalised.

To make this point clear, it is useful to set the discussion about emissions trading in a broader regulatory debate. In doing so, I will briefly outline and draw comparisons between emissions trading and an altogether different regulatory scenario; Epstein's study of the allocation of parking rights on public roads in Chicago.[156] These have in common their general objective: managing the commons. More importantly, however, Epstein points to the same conclusions as I have with the help of the models; namely that regulating the commons allows for different governance regimes to be established, each depending on a particular world-view. Epstein's analysis of parking on public roads is a study that[157]

> looks at bottom-up regimes for parking which are based on possession of particular spaces for limited periods of time, and top-down systems of allocation, such as metered parking and parking permits, which are based on such factors as place of residence or disability.

In this study, Epstein is particularly concerned with the allocative effectiveness of the different regimes available to control public road parking, establishing that bottom-up systems do better in this regard. The argument is that bottom-up systems tend to reduce the dead time associated with parking spaces and maximise the use of parking spots by providing access to these only for the specific time needed.[158] The reason why maximising the use of common land is thought advantageous depends on a specific economic rationale; guaranteeing a high flux of cars being able to park, Epstein suggests, would enable any commercial stores nearby public roads to profit from the high number of potential customers that can subsequently access the stores:[159]

> There is a powerful correlation between the amount of business traffic and the turnover rate of parking. Merchants will sell a lot more merchandise if 1,000 cars park on their street for 2 hours each than if 250 cars park there for the full business day.

This shows that the lens that Epstein applies in furthering a particular governance regime for parking on public roads is based on a particular economic rationale. He

Climate Change Policy: Making Progress or Spinning the Wheels?' in R Axelrod, D Downie and N Vig (eds), *The Global Environment: Institutions, Law, and Policy* (CQ Press, Washington DC, 2005) 103.

[155] See J Scott, 'The Multi-Level Governance of Climate Change' in P Craig and G de Burca (eds), *The Evolution of EU Law* (2nd edn, Oxford University Press, Oxford, 2011) 804.

[156] R Epstein, 'The Allocation of the Commons: Parking on Public Roads' (2002) 31 *Journal of Legal Studies* 515.

[157] ibid.

[158] ibid.

[159] ibid 534.

explains that business owners could ratio these spaces on their own and thereby help increase the volume of business through price charges, one such example being auctioning rights to parking spaces, which would also bring revenue.[160]

Epstein, however, concludes that this type of auctioning seldom realises, and the reasons he offers set out a second lens through which parking on public roads may be viewed. More precisely, he argues that the political process does not allow auction in this context on the basis that it would create an exclusionary market in which citizens, who cannot afford higher prices, would be excluded from accessing parking on public roads. It is this view, Epstein clarifies, which is the reason why parking spaces that would cost 8–10 US dollars per hour on the 'free' market, are capped to cost well below the market price to one US dollar.[161] This type of market intervention may seem objectionable on the grounds of cost-effectiveness.[162] However, the point is that governance regimes applied to commons do not always have as their prime aim to stimulate and steer the economy to profit but can also target guaranteeing access as a general right.

Epstein's study may seem an altogether different regulatory scenario from emissions trading but it overlaps with the *Economic Efficiency*, the *Private Property Rights* and the *Command-and-Control* models. For instance, regulating parking on public roads via a system of metered parking to which parking rights are auctioned resembles the *Economic Efficiency Model:* both regulatory regimes focus on allocative efficiency that yields most economic opportunities, including the profit centre that revenue from auctioning would harvest and the optimal number of customers being able to access the relevant merchants. Alternatively, by assigning a stronger role to the state in this regulatory system and instead of auctioning, capping metered parking prices below market prices so as to guarantee a wider overall access to common land, it seems clear that what Epstein discusses is a *Command-and-Control Model* type of approach to regulating commons. Here, the key consideration is no longer merely to create economic opportunities but to establish a regulatory regime within the public sphere that is flexible enough to allow high numbered utility of the roads. This system is therefore not left to the 'free market' to allocate rights to common resource but rather the state regulates market preferences to the use of parking spaces. Although not mentioned in the latter example from Epstein's study, the *Private Property Rights Model* would, in terms of regulating public roads, correspond to a case of substituting the metered parking for parking allocation via occupation or place of residence, which Epstein defines as a top-down approach.[163] This means that the property rights holder, based on his/her property right, is entitled to parking at all times – independently of the cost-effectiveness or fairness of such a regulation.

[160] ibid.
[161] ibid.
[162] For an overview of what 'free' parking costs the society at large see T Cowen, 'Free Parking Comes at a Price', *New York Times*, New York, 14 August 2010.
[163] Epstein, 'Parking on Public Roads' (n 156).

Beyond mapping the models onto Epstein's study and shedding light at certain parallels between the two, this exercise shows that it is possible to envision multiple regimes for the use of common space. Epstein concludes that bottom-up systems 'do better in an economics sense'[164] but economic sensibility, as he shows, is not always the rationale of a particular regulatory system.[165] Second, and more importantly, the fact that multiple ways exist to regulate common resources is true not only because different regulatory *methods* are available but also because each regulatory mechanism is applied according to a particular world-view and regulatory agenda. In Epstein's examples, parking on public roads could be regulated to stimulate business or ensure fair and equal access to common land, as well as to potentially protecting property holders by offering rights based on residence. Ultimately, the way in which the regulatory regime applied to these commons is structured will depend on the role that is given to the market, the state, and rights in land, which are similar to the central points found in emissions trading literature, clearly indicating that regulating the commons is never a straightforward affair.

Ultimately what the discussion above demonstrates is that in debating emissions trading, diverse regulatory strategies are referred to, in which the roles of the market, the state, and the legal status of emissions allowances are understood differently. Upon closer scrutiny of the models, it appears that the way in which emissions trading is conceptualised has direct implications for the way in which allocation of regulatory power under such a scheme is constructed, each creating a different regulatory model – both in the case of regulating commons in air and parking rights on public roads.

VI. Conclusion

At the outset of my book I explained that it follows a bold aim that is to re-configure the way in which scholars discuss and portray emissions trading schemes as a regulatory strategy. In this chapter I have provided three distinct lenses through which to view emissions trading schemes. From the perspective of the *Economic Efficiency Model* emissions trading is a profit centre in which the market is envisioned as free, and the role of the state limited. In the *Private Property Rights Model* private property rights holders stand at centre stage of emissions trading with vested regulatory powers to manage common resources on their own terms. In the *Command-and-Control Model* emissions trading is understood as an administratively flexible regulatory mechanism, in which, nonetheless, the state is entrusted with all regulatory

---

[164] ibid 515.
[165] Similarly, albeit from a moral philosopher's point of view, Bromme, argues that in regulating climate change a calculation of value is not enough to determine whether a policy ought to be chosen or not but rather justice needs to be reconsidered. J Broome, *Counting the Cost of Global Warming* (White Horse Press, Isle of Harris, 1992) 19.

powers. The implication of this finding is that emissions trading, as a regulatory concept, encompasses distinct regulatory structures, each regulatory regime suggesting a different role for the state, the market and the legal nature of emissions allowances. The models thus show that although emissions trading is broadly understood to respond to the exploitation of the commons, it is a regulatory concept that allows for distinct regulatory regimes to be established, each addressing different environmental and non-environmental problems.

The models, however are theoretical frameworks meaning that they do not map how emissions trading schemes in practice functions. In order to understand how the role of the market, the state, and the legal status of emissions allowances are defined in a particular emissions trading scheme, the legal context in which the set trading scheme operates must be taken into consideration. The next chapter explains the importance of legal culture in more detail, before, in chapters four and five, I investigate the applicability of the *Economic Efficiency*, the *Private Property Rights* and the *Command-and-Control* models in law.

3

The EU Emissions Trading Scheme and the Importance of Legal Culture

I. Introduction

In the previous chapter my focus was on how scholars understand emissions trading as a regulatory concept and illustrating these diverging conceptions by establishing the *Economic Efficiency,* the *Private Property Rights,* and the *Command-and-Control* models. In chapters four and five respectively, these models are mapped onto EU ETS-related discourses[1] so as to test the models' utility and relevance in law and provide a close examination of the EU emissions trading regime. Preliminary to such an analysis, this chapter emphasises a different, albeit highly correlated point, which is that any discussion about the EU emissions trading regime, including the dilemma of which role to entrust to the market, the state, and emissions allowances, are fundamentally an expression and part of EU legal culture.

To show the importance of legal culture, this chapter examines the unique legal environment in which the EU ETS operates. In particular, the intention is to demonstrate how in the EU legal order, environmental protection and environmental law are historically tied to a particular idea of market creation as integration. This, in addition to the distinctive role of the EU Courts and the regulatory character of the EU, has contributed to the creation of a single competitive market that is based on a particular integration-based market objective. On the basis of this close nexus between markets, the judiciary, and environmental law in the EU, I argue that it is impossible to discuss the EU ETS – irrespective of whether this particular market is thought of as 'free', a symbol of liberty, or a regulatory device – without paying attention to its legal context, and the specific market discourse pertinent to European integration. The purpose of this study is twofold.

First, showing that laws are embedded in and filtered by a particular legal and institutional setting – here, the EU legal order – the aim is to reject any suggestions that emissions trading is a basic design structure equally imposable in different jurisdictions. This point is particularly important to make in the context of emissions trading and the EU ETS mainly because the Directive, upon which the

---

[1] As voiced by the Commission (ch 4) and the CJEU (ch 5).

EU ETS is based,[2] appears simple and is believed to be able to 'travel'[3] and become a 'role model'[4] for other trading schemes beyond the EU jurisdiction. This is indeed a common assumption regarding successful trading schemes; as explained in chapter one, the sulphur dioxide emissions trading scheme in the US is similarly presumed to be able to be replicated with equal success.[5] By emphasising the significance of legal culture, this chapter thus discards such assumptions.

Second, highlighting the importance of legal culture has a methodological significance in this study. More precisely, engaging in a debate on legal culture aims to demonstrate that the common legal questions that emissions trading discourses orbit, and that the previous chapter sets out – that is, the roles entrusted to the market, the state, and emissions allowances in emissions trading – can only be answered against the background of legal specificities. As such, this chapter lays out the justification for a close contextual analysis of the EU emissions trading regime, which is carried out in chapters four and five, and gives reasons why it is insufficient to study the EU ETS through an examination only of the plain text of the Directive upon which it is based.

Ultimately, my concern in this chapter is to establish the validity of legal culture as a lens through which to view and understand the governance structure of emissions trading schemes. I do so by first introducing the reader, in section II, to the EU ETS, which is the emissions trading scheme that I use as a case study in this book. In particular, I highlight the basic structure of the EU ETS Directive and show how the simple form of this legal text sits comfortably with the idea that the EU emissions trading regime is transferable across jurisdictions. Moreover, and equally to explain the idea of transferability of emissions trading schemes, I describe how the emissions trading, as a regulatory strategy applied to air pollution, first entered the EU legal order from international environmental law and under the influence of the highly successful US sulphur dioxide trading scheme. In the same section, I elucidate the use of 'legal culture' in this book, and highlight its significance in understanding the pitfalls of assuming emissions trading to be a generic regulatory strategy. In section III I sketch some of the key feature of the EU legal culture, and highlight how market creation and market maintenance, the extensive interpretative role of the EU Courts, and environmental law overlap and co-exist in the EU legal order. The aim therewith is to illustrate – albeit roughly – the complex legal landscape in which the EU ETS exists. More importantly, the purpose is to demonstrate that markets in the EU legal order are not

---

[2] Council Directive 2003/87 establishing a scheme for greenhouse gas emission allowance trading within the Community and amending Directive 96/61, [2003] OJ L275/32 (Directive), Directive 2009/29 of the European Parliament and of the European Council amending the Directive 2003/87 so as to improve and extend the greenhouse gas emission allowance trading scheme of the Community, [2009] OJ L140/63 (Revised Directive). The latter Directive applies from 2013 onwards.

[3] The potential 'travels' of laws are further defined and explained in section II.

[4] A Runge Metzger, 'The Potential Role of the EU ETS for the Development of Long-Term International Climate Policies' in J Delbeke (ed), *EU Energy Law: The EU Greenhouse Gas Emissions Trading Scheme* (Claeys & Casteels, Leuven, 2006) 253, 273.

[5] See in particular L Heinzerling, 'The Environment' in M Tushnet and P Cane (eds), *The Oxford Handbook of Legal Studies* (Oxford University Press, Oxford, 2003) 701, 712–13.

generic design structures, as is often believed in emissions trading discourses[6] but rather constructed by the judiciary and part of a particular rationale of market integration. Finally, in section IV these findings are evaluated and in section V the conclusion of this chapter is set out.

Before starting I need to enter a number of caveats. First, this chapter is not intended to provide a full exposé of the meaning of EU legal culture; nor is the aim to explain the complete process of constructing a European market through judicial progressiveness and market-rulemaking. My objective is rather to simply highlight a few examples of how markets, the judiciary and environmental law and policy in the EU context are interconnected, and therewith sketch the complex market-discourse in the EU legal order that the EU ETS is inevitably part of. Second and subsequently, any questions that address whether EU legal culture is 'converging' or 'diverging',[7] or examining EU legal culture bottom-up with focus on various legal cultures of the Member States[8] fall outside the scope of this chapter, as does any discussion of culture as understood in Title XIII TFEU.[9] Third, in introducing the legal framework of the EU ETS, I focus on the initial Directive, despite its amendments.[10] This is because to understand how the EU ETS is thought to be replicable beyond the EU jurisdiction it is necessary to consider the premises on which emissions trading was first set out in the EU legal order. These, as will be explained, are clearly projected in the initial Directive.

---

[6] This point is discussed in ch 6.

[7] Defining legal culture in the EU tends to be layered with political difficulties concerning the determination of the real borders of Europe and whether political, historical and religious ties constitute essential ingredients for a common culture, see F Wieacker, 'Foundations of European Legal Culture' (1990) 38 *American Journal of Comparative Law* 1. In fact, debates on EU legal culture apt to focus on the legal culture of the Member States separately, or in blocks of, eg 'civil' and 'common' law traditions, using these analyses so as to establish whether legal cultures within the EU legal framework are converging or diverging, see, eg J Gibson and G Caldeira, 'The Legal Cultures of Europe' (1996) 30 *Law and Society Review* 55, P Legrand, 'Against a European Civil Code' (1997) 60 *MLR* 44.

[8] One way of understanding EU legal culture is by defining it as a bottom-up convergence of various European legal cultures, which together create a coherent and dynamic picture of the EU legal culture, or rather, it is this exercise that determines whether a common EU legal culture exists or could exist, see C Lyons, 'Perspectives on Convergence Within European Integration' in P Beaumont, C Lyons and N Walker (eds), *Convergence and Divergence in European Public Law* (Hart Publishing, Oxford, 2001) 79, 96.

[9] Art 167 TFEU is the specific Article on culture and includes, eg the need for the Union to 'take cultural aspects into account' when legislating under the Treaty. For an overview of the development of this provision, see R Craufurd Smith, 'The Evolution of Cultural Policy in the European Union' in P Craig and G de Burca (eds), *The Evolution of EU Law* (Oxford University Press, Oxford, 2011) 869.

[10] Ch 4 lists some of the key amendments. See also S Bogojević, 'The EU ETS Directive Revised: Yet Another Stepping Stone' (2009) 11 *Environmental Law Review* 279, S Bogojević, 'Legalising Environmental Leadership: A Comment on the CJEU's Ruling in C-366/10 on the Inclusion of Aviation in the EU Emissions Trading Scheme' (2012) 24 *Journal of Environmental Law* 345.

II. EU Emissions Trading Scheme

The EU emissions trading scheme constitutes an important environmental law in the EU legal context. It is identified as the 'flagship measure',[11] the 'eight-hundred-pound gorilla'[12] and the 'parade horse'[13] of EU climate change policy, as well as one of the 'cornerstones of Community environmental protection policy'[14] – descriptions that clearly highlight its significance. The EU ETS was codified in the EU legal order on 13 October 2003, as the Parliament and the Council adopted Directive 2003/87 establishing a scheme for greenhouse gas emission allowances trading within the Union to start operating on the first day of 2005. In the words of the Directive, its aim is to contribute to fulfilling the commitments of the Union and its Member States under the Kyoto Protocol 'more effectively, through an efficient European market in greenhouse gas emission allowances, with the least possible diminution of economic development and employment',[15] and to promote reductions of greenhouse gas emissions 'in a cost-effective and econom-ically efficient manner'.[16] The way in which the Directive organises this trading system, and how law- and policymakers, as well as the CJEU interpret these meas-ures is discussed in detail in the next two chapters. Here, and as an introduction to the EU ETS, two correlated points regarding the Directive are specifically high-lighted: its basic structure and its origin. It is against these two points that the relevance of legal culture to this study will be raised.

A. EU Emissions Trading Scheme: A Basic Structure

In general terms, the Directive prescribes the system of emissions trading to func-tion by demanding each of the relevant installations to obtain a permit in order to emit pre-determined levels of pollution, which, if there is a surplus, is tradable.[17] The idea is that if an installation does better than its target, it can sell its surplus allowances, and if it does worse, it has to buy additional allowances on the emissions market.[18] The rationale is to allow sources with high abatement costs to invest in

---

[11] S Dimas, EU Environment Commissioner, 'Improving Environmental Quality through Carbon Trading' (Speech at the Carbon Expo Conference, Köln 2 May 2007) europa.cu/rapid/pressReleases Action.do?reference=SPEECH/07/265, accessed 19 September 2012.

[12] N Singh Ghaleigh, '"Six Honest Serving-Men": Climate Change Litigation as Legal Mobilization and the Utility of Typologies' (2010) 1 *Climate Law* 31, 48.

[13] K Deketelaere and M Peeters, 'Key Challenges of EU Climate Change Policy: Competence, Measures and Compliance' in M Peeters and K Deketelaere (eds), *EU Climate Change Policy: The Challenge of New Regulatory Initiatives* (Edward Elgar, Cheltenham, 2006) 3, 8.

[14] Case T-263/07 *Estonia v Commission* [2009] ECR II-03395, para 57.

[15] Directive (n 2), Preamble 5.

[16] Art 1, ibid.

[17] Art 5, ibid. Note that it is the allowance limit specified in the permit rather than the permit itself that is tradable.

[18] J Lefevere, 'Greenhouse Gas Emission Allowance Trading in the EU: A Background' (2003) *Yearbook of European Environmental Law* 149, 151.

industries with lower abatement costs by buying allowances freed up by these, thereby reducing the costs of compliance.[19] This market, it is important to note, covers only certain private sectors, including the power and the heavy industry sector across the Union,[20] and certain emissions thereof,[21] meaning that it is limited in scope.[22] To date, nonetheless, it is the largest carbon market in the world, worth a total value of US $126 billion in 2008 and enjoying an impressive growth since.[23]

One of the key features of the EU ETS initial legal architecture is its decentralised trading regime: the private sector is entrusted with monitoring and reporting emissions,[24] and the Member States are vested with the regulatory discretion of deciding on the total national level of greenhouse gases that may be emitted,[25] granting emissions permits,[26] determining the allocation mechanism of emission permits to the industry,[27] verifying emissions levels,[28] and imposing penalties for non-compliance.[29] Considering that the EU ETS is based on a Directive, this legal feature is not surprising. According to the Treaty, such a legal measure should only establish a regulatory framework, leaving the method and content of implementation to the Member States.[30] Equally, Prechal explains that Directives are often used in creating or facilitating the functioning of markets on the basis that any market measures inevitably cut into the administration and economic structures of the Member States, and rather than seeking to harmonise national practices in this regard, Directives regulate but without affecting any national decision-making processes.[31] What is remarkable with the legal construction of this Directive, however, is that beyond its decentralised quality, it is in part

---

[19] ibid.

[20] Annex I lists categories of activities, which, if an installation emits, signifies the application of the Directive (n 2).

[21] The Directive (n 2) covers the following six greenhouse gases: carbon dioxide, methane, nitrous oxide, hydrofluorocarbons, perfluorocarbons, sulphur hexafluoride, see Annex II.

[22] Art 30, however, allows the Directive (n 2) to expand in scope to also include other sectors and gases. Indeed, the EU ETS has been extended to also cover emissions from aviation, see Bogojević, 'Legalising Environmental Leadership' (n 10).

[23] R Baldwin, M Cave and M Lodge, *Understanding Regulation: Theory, Strategy, and Practice* (2nd edn, Oxford University Press, Oxford 2012) 196, J Scott, 'The Multi-Level Governance of Climate Change' in P Craig and G de Burca (eds), *The Evolution of EU Law* (2nd edn, Oxford University Press, Oxford 2011) 805, 808.

[24] Directive (n 2), Art 6.

[25] Art 9, ibid.

[26] Art 6, ibid.

[27] Art 10, ibid. Note that 95% of the allowances are allocated free of charge, and from 2008 90%.

[28] Art 15, ibid.

[29] Art 16, ibid.

[30] According to Art 288 TFEU 'A directive shall be binding as to the result to be achieved, upon each Member State to which it is addressed, but shall leave to the national authorities the choice of form and methods'.

[31] S Prechal, *Directives in EC Law* (Oxford University Press, Oxford, 2005) 4–5. In comparison to environmental laws in the US, Carlarne explains that EU environmental law tends to be less detailed, focusing on establishing overarching goals, dependent on the Member States for implementation. Decentralisation of this kind is thus an inherent feature of EU environmental law. C Carlarne, *Climate Change Law and Policy: EU and US Approaches* (Oxford University Press, Oxford, 2010) 250–51.

'void'[32] in its stipulations, meaning that it omits to set out important legal definitions, including the legal status of emissions allowances.[33] One of the underpinning reasons for this is that the Directive is set out to establish a simple governance system. Indeed, throughout the legislative process that led to the implementation of the Directive, the Commission endeavoured the Directive to 'remain as simple as it can be'[34] as a way of rallying support for this particular regulatory strategy.[35] This has resulted in a Directive that *claims* simplicity by leaving out complex rules on trading and *appears* simple because it is, as a consequence of the previous, a very short legal document[36] that is open-textured.[37] The effect of this 'lite'[38] regulation is that the EU ETS seems a straightforward pollution control system that involves no loser, and most importantly, that can act as a legal model for emissions trading across jurisdictions.

Indeed emissions trading is commonly understood to be a legal instrument that allows cross-fertilisation, and often the EU ETS is used as an example thereof.[39] Prior to the implementation of the Directive, emissions trading was foreign to EU environmental law and seen as 'an alien'[40] regulatory mechanism. With the exception of domestic trading schemes in certain Member States – including Denmark, the Netherlands, and the United Kingdom[41] – and isolated scholarly debates on the topic,[42] the Union lacked knowledge and experience related to

---

[32] Description borrowed from C Bourbon-Seclet, 'Legal Aspects of Climate Change in Europe: Is the European Emission Trading Scheme Greater than the Sum of the Parts? Part 1' (2008) 23 *Journal of International Banking Law and Regulation* 252, 261.

[33] This is contrasted with commodities, such as oil and gas, with which emissions allowances have been compared. S Manea, 'Defining Emissions Entitlements in the Constitution of the EU Emissions Trading System' (2012) 1 *Transnational Environmental Law* 303, 304.

[34] Commission of the European Communities, 'Proposal for a Directive of the European and of the Council establishing a scheme for greenhouse gas emission allowance trading within the Community and amending Council Directive 96/61/EC', COM(2001) 581 final, 5 and Commission of the European Communities, 'Green Paper on Greenhouse Gas Emissions Trading Within the European Union', COM(2000) 87 final, 12.

[35] The Commission pushed for the Directive to remain simple also on a request from the industry, ibid. Note that the EU ETS emerged on the law- and policymaking table following the 'ill-fated' attempt to introduce carbon tax, see Commission of the European Communities, 'Commission Proposal for a Council Directive Introducing a Tax on Carbon Dioxide Emissions and Energy', COM(92) 226 final, Scott, 'The Multi-Level Governance of Climate Change' (n 23) 808.

[36] It consists of 33 Articles and 5 Annexes.

[37] eg in the EU ETS case law, it is stipulated that 'Directive 2003/87 is not a legal act that has been greatly elaborated'. See Case C-504/09 *Commission v Poland* [2012] ECR II-000, para 31.

[38] Term borrowed from Baldwin, who describes such measures to deliberately leaving out complexity and detail so as to favour the dominant powers regulated. R Baldwin, 'Regulation Lite: The Rise of Emissions Trading' (2008) 2 *Regulation and Governance* 193.

[39] See, eg J Wiener, 'Better Regulation in Europe' (2006) 59 *Current Legal Problems* 447.

[40] H van Asselt, 'Emissions Trading: The Enthustiatic Adoption of an "Alien" Instrument?' in A Jordan and others (eds), *Climate Change Policy in the European Union* (Cambridge University Press, Cambridge, 2010) 125.

[41] For an overview, see M Rodi, 'Legal Aspects of the European Emissions Trading Scheme' in B Hansjürgen (ed), *Emissions Trading for Climate Policy: US and European Perspectives* (Cambridge University Press, Cambridge, 2005) 177, 177.

[42] M Peeters, 'Towards a European System of Tradable Pollution Permits?' (1993) 2 *Tilburg Foreign Law Review* 117.

emissions trading schemes.[43] As such, adopting the Directive was thought to add a 'new dimension'[44] to EU environmental law, in particular due to the fact that it was imposed top-down, or through international environmental law, as part of a collective effort to deal with threats of climate change.

The problem of climate change was first addressed at the UN Framework Convention on Climate Change (UNFCCC),[45] which was followed by the Kyoto Protocol[46] that is designed, inter alia, to utilise a series of so-called 'flexible mechanism'[47] to help limit and reduce the level of a set of greenhouse gas emissions.[48] Signatories to the Protocol pledged to reduce set greenhouse gases by a certain percentage during the first commitment period from 2008–12,[49] and whilst each party to the Protocol is responsible for drawing up its own policies to meet these targets, the Protocol flags emissions trading as one of the flexible mechanisms able to help achieve the reduction obligations. The importance of the Protocol is the introduction of emissions trading to international environmental law[50] and to the

---

[43] Commission of the European Communities, 'Communication from the Commission on Preparing for Implementation of the Kyoto Protocol', COM(1999) 230, 14–15.

[44] See M Peeters, 'Emissions Trading as a New Dimension to European Environmental Law: The Political Agreement of the European Council on Greenhouse Gas Allowance Trading' (2003) 12 *European Environmental Law Review* 82.

[45] United Nations Framework Convention on Climate Change (UNFCCC) opened for signature 9 May 1992, 31 ILM 849 (entered into force 21 March 1994).

[46] Kyoto Protocol to the United Nations Framework Convention on Climate Change, opened for signature 11 December 1997, 37 ILM 22 (entered into force 16 February 2005).

[47] Flexible mechanisms encompass international emission trading (IET) and project-based mechanisms that allow for emissions reductions for projects in developing countries through Joint Implementation (JI) and Clean Development Mechanism (CDM). For an overview of the two latter mechanisms, see respectively C Streck, 'Joint Implementation: History, Requirements, and Challenges' in D Freestone and C Streck (eds), *Legal Aspects of Carbon Trading: Kyoto, Copenhagen, and Beyond* (Oxford University Press, Oxford, 2005) 107, and E Meijer and J Werksman, 'Keeping it Clean - Safeguarding the Environmental Integrity of the Clean Development Mechanism' in D Freestone and C Streck (eds), *Legal Aspects of Carbon Trading: Kyoto, Copenhagen, and Beyond* (Oxford University Press, Oxford, 2005) 191.

[48] D Freestone, 'The UN Framework Convention of Climate Change, the Kyoto Protocol, and the Kyoto Mechanisms' in D Freestone and C Streck (eds), *Legal Aspects of Implementing the Kyoto Protocol Mechanisms* (Oxford University Press, Oxford, 2005) 3, 3. Gases that fall under the scope of the Protocol are carbon dioxide, methane, nitrous oxide, hydrofluorocarbons, perfluorocarbons, and sulphur hexafluoride. Literature concerning more broadly the significance and implications following lengthy international negotiations before and after the Protocol is vast. For an overview see D Freestone and C Streck (eds), *Legal Aspects of Carbon Trading: Kyoto, Copenhagen, and Beyond* (Oxford University Press, Oxford, 2009) and M Grubb, C Vrolijk and D Brack, *The Kyoto Protocol: A Guide and Assessment* (The Royal Institute of International Affairs, London, 1999).

[49] The Union and its Member States committed themselves to reduce their emissions of these gases by 8% during the period 2008–12 in comparison with their levels in 1990, see Decision 1600/2002/EC of 10 September 2002 laying down the Sixth Community Environment Action Programme [2002] OJ L 242/6, Art 5.

[50] A Runge Metzger, 'The Potential Role of the EU ETS for the Development of Long-Term International Climate Policies' in J Delbeke (ed), *EU Energy Law: The EU Greenhouse Gas Emissions Trading Scheme* (Claeys & Casteels, Leuven, 2006) 253, 254. Another major significance of the Protocol is obviously the fact that the Parties to the Protocol committed to reducing their emissions of greenhouse gases, see R de Witt Wijnen, 'Emissions Trading under Article 17 of the Kyoto Protocol' in D Freestone and C Streck (eds), *Legal Aspects of Implementing the Kyoto Protocol Mechanisms: Making Kyoto Work* (Oxford University Press, Oxford, 2005) 403, 407.

EU, which, as a signatory of the Protocol, initiated a discussion regarding the use of emissions trading in Europe as a response to the Protocol.[51] Quickly thereafter, the Directive was adopted.[52]

Although the EU bound itself at Kyoto to tackling climate change problems as addressed at the international level, it did *not have to* implement an emissions trading scheme to respect its regulatory commitments.[53] In this regard, the success of the US acid rain emissions trading programme played a crucial role in making this regulatory strategy popular[54] – both at the international level by including it as a compliance method in the Protocol,[55] and in influencing the EU to adopt it as a key climate change law.[56] What is often understood to derive from US trading experience in sulphur dioxide is that emissions trading is a regulatory strategy that can be equally successfully applied elsewhere[57] – that it indeed can travel both vertically and horizontally to international and national legal regimes respectively.[58] Similarly, the EU ETS – now the biggest and first supranational trading scheme[59] – is predicted to become the 'blueprint',[60] 'cornerstone',[61] and 'role model'[62] for other schemes and the emerging global emissions trading regime.[63]

[51] See Commission of the European Communities, 'Communication from the Commission on Climate Change – Towards an EU Post-Kyoto Strategy, COM(1998) 353.

[52] The Directive was adopted within three years of its official initiation, see J Wettestad, 'The Making of the 2003 EU Emissions Trading Directive: An Ultra-Quick Process due to Entrepreneurial Proficiency?' (2005) 5 *Global Environmental Politics* 1.

[53] Art 17 of the Kyoto Protocol (n 46) states that emissions trading is only a regulatory option for compliance. This point is also discussed in J Skjærseth and J Wettestad, *EU Emissions Trading: Initiation, Decision-Making and Implementation* (Ashgate Publishing, Burlington, 2008) 35.

[54] There has been much debate amongst political scientists as to why the Directive was finally adopted, which fall outside the scope of this chapter. For such an overview, see ibid.

[55] J Wiener, 'Something Borrowed for Something Blue: Legal Transplants and the Evolution of Global Environmental Law' (2001) 27 *Ecological Law Quarterly* 1295, 1312.

[56] J Delbeke, 'The Emissions Trading Scheme (ETS): The Cornerstone of the EU's Implementation of the Kyoto Protocol' in J Delbeke (ed), *EU Energy Law: The EU Greenhouse Gas Emissions Trading Scheme* (Claeys & Casteels, Leuven, 2006) 1, 7–8.

[57] J Johnston, 'Problems of Equity and Efficiency in the Design of International Greenhouse Gas Cap-and-Trade Schemes' (2009) 33 *Harvard Environmental Law Review* 405, 429–30.

[58] Wiener, 'Something Borrowed for Something Blue' (n 55).

[59] van Asselt, 'Enthusiastic Adoption of an "Alien" Instrument?' (n 40).

[60] Delbeke, 'The Cornerstone of the EU's Implementation' (n 56) 13. Similarly, Aldy and Stavins examine the architecture of the EU ETS in hope of advancing it to an eventual global climate regime, see J Aldy and R Stavins, 'Introduction: International Policy Architecture for Global Climate Change' in A Joseph and S Robert (eds), *Architectures for Agreement: Addressing Global Climate Change in the Post-Kyoto World* (Cambridge University Press, Cambridge, 2007) 1.

[61] C Egenhofer and others, *The EU Emissions Trading Scheme: Taking Stock and Looking Forward* (Mistra, Brussels, 2006) 1.

[62] Runge Metzger, 'The Potential Role of the EU ETS' (n 50) 273.

[63] J Peel, L Godden and R Keenan, 'Climate Change Law in an Era of Multi-Level Governance' (2012) 1 *Transnational Environmental Law* 245, 254.

What the above shows is that the EU ETS is clearly 'on the move':[64] it entered the EU legal order – to which it is not native[65] – following the encouraged promulgation of emissions trading regimes by the Protocol and the US emissions trading experience. These type of travels, or 'legal transfers'[66] are not uncommon:[67] following the growth of markets, the proliferation of means of communication, and the stronger role of mass media – each of which encourages and facilitates jurisdictions to come together – the migration of regulatory ideas are becoming increasingly frequent.[68] The danger, however, with assuming that particular legal mechanisms can travel across borders is to underestimate the impact of legal culture in which the set law operates. In the case of the EU ETS, two types of caution must be raised against the assumption: one relates to the concrete procedural differences between the EU ETS and the international emissions trading scheme, as set out under the Protocol, and the second to legal culture as defined below.

1. *Kyoto Protocol and the EU Emissions Trading Scheme*

As explained, emissions trading was introduced in the EU legal order through international environmental law and from this viewpoint it tends to be argued that emissions trading in the EU would not exist 'were it not for the Protocol'.[69] The crucial point to make here is that despite this strong relationship between the EU ETS and international environmental law – including both the Protocol and the Protocol's successor[70] – the EU ETS stands as an independent climate change

---

[64] 'On the move' as defined by Nelken who describes the travels of regulatory ideas as legal transfers from one legal entity to another. D Nelken, 'Comparatists and Transferability' in D Nelken (ed), *Beyond Law in Context: Developing a Sociological Understanding of Law* (Ashgate, Surrey, 2009) 255, 255.

[65] Harro, 'Enthusiastic Adoption of an "Alien" Instrument?' (n 40) 125. The Commission has also remarked on the fact that this regulatory strategy is new to the EU legal order, Commission of the European Communities, 'Communication from the Commission on Preparing for Implementation of the Kyoto Protocol', COM(1999) 230, 14.

[66] Nelken, 'Comparatists and Transferability' (n 64).

[67] Similarly, EU regulation on chemicals is an example of laws 'migrating' from the EU to the US legal order, see J Scott, 'From Brussels with Love: The Transatlantic Travels of European Law and the Chemistry of Regulatory Attraction' (2009) 57 *American Journal of Comparative Law* 897. The 'better regulation' agenda in the EU is equally thought of as 'borrowed' from the US see, Wiener, 'Better Regulation in Europe' (n 39).

[68] Nelken, 'Comparatists and Transferability' (n 64). Laws are understood to travel from dominant countries in particular sectors to the rest of the world, see D Levi-Faur, 'The Global Diffusion of Regulatory Capitalism' (2005) 598 *ANNALS of the American Academy of Political and Social Science* 12, 24–25. In this regard, Friedman describes how Japan and Turkey 'swallowed whole codes of law from Europe' L Friedman, 'Some Comments on Cotterrell and Legal Transplants' in D Nelken and J Feest (eds), *Adapting Legal Cultures* (Hart Publishing, Oxford, 2001) 93, 93. Van Hoecke and Warrington systemise the study of legal cultures by dividing these into different legal families, see M van Hoecke and M Warrington, 'Legal Cultures, Legal Paradigms and Legal Doctrine: Towards a New Model for Comparative Law' (1998) 47 *ICLQ 495*, 498.

[69] As explained in D Ellerman and P Joskow, *The European Union's Emissions Trading System in Perspective* (Pew Center on Global Climate Change, Arlington VA, 2008) 1.

[70] See United Nations Framework Convention on Climate Change (UNFCCC) Decision of 11 December 2011 on Establishing of an Ad Hoc Working Group on the Durban Platform for Enhanced Action, 1/CP.17.

regime that is embedded in legal culture and a constituent of a rich legal system that is the EU jurisdiction. Over and above legal culture, four procedural differences between the emissions trading in the EU and the international climate change regime highlight the *sui generis* of the EU ETS in this regard.

First, the Protocol regulates trading only between its signatories at state level and not at the level of installations, as is the case under the EU ETS.[71] This means that the Protocol is negotiated between governments imposing reduction targets on a country's total emissions, whereas the EU ETS is a scheme at industry level, regulating emissions of specific installations.[72] Second, the commitments to reduce emissions by the EU are shared amongst its Member States according to the so-called Burden Sharing Agreement. This means that the EU ETS is based on emissions limits that are specific to the EU legal order – despite its origins in the Protocol and the overall emissions limits that the Protocol imposes.[73] Third, the two trading systems follow different timelines: the EU ETS was enacted before the Protocol became legally binding in international and EU law, and it was clear that the EU ETS would be put in operation – even if the Protocol had not taken effect.[74] The first period of trading under the EU ETS therefore fell entirely outside of the scope of the Protocol. Fourth, the EU ETS is based on a legal framework that continues after 2012, which is, beyond the initial time frame of the Protocol.[75]

Moreover, the fact that the EU emissions market is established as a legal response to international environmental law has no bearing on the construction and management of the EU ETS. This is not only because of the impact and

---

[71] Y Slingenberg, 'The International Climate Policy Developments of the 1990s: The UNFCCC, the Kytoto Protocol, the Marrakech Accords and the EU Ratification Decision' in J Delbeke (ed), *EU Energy Law: The EU Greenhouse Gas Emissions Trading Scheme* (Claeys & Casteels, Leuven, 2006) 15, 19.

[72] R Dornau, 'The Emissions Trading Scheme of the European Union' in D Freestone and C Streck (eds), *Legal Aspects of Implementing the Kyoto Protocol Mechanisms: Making Kyoto Work* (Oxford University Press, Oxford, 2005) 417, 421.

[73] In other words, this means that any changes to the burden sharing agreement would not have any effect on international law, see Y Slingenberg, 'Community Action in the Fight Against Climate Change' in M Onida (ed), *Europe and the Environment: Legal Essays in Honour of Ludwig Krämer* (Europa Law Publishing, Groningen, 2004) 211, 218. The distribution of the internal emissions reduction commitments are set with regard to national conditions, including current greenhouse gas emissions, opportunity to reduce them, and the level of economic development, see Council Decision 2002/358 of 25 April 2002 concerning the approval, on the behalf of the European Community, of the Kyoto Protocol to the United Nations Framework Convention on Climate Change and the joint fulfilment of commitments thereunder, [2002] OJ L130. Based on these considerations, different Member States may emit to different extents – for quantification of the respective emission levels of the Member States, see Commission Decision of 14 December 2006 determining the respective emissions levels allocated to the Community and each of its Member States under the Kyoto Protocol pursuant to Council Decision 2002/358/EC, [2006] OJ L358/87.

[74] Ellerman and Joskow, *The European Union's Emissions Trading System in Perspective* (n 69).

[75] The revised EU ETS Directive applies from 2013 onwards, see Revised Directive (n 2). Although the international community has agreed to an afterlife of the Protocol (see n 70), such an amending Protocol will only be adopted by 2015 and come into effect from 2020. For an analysis of how emissions trading will play out at the EU ETS and the international level in the meantime, see M von Unger, D Conway and J Hoogzaad, *Carbon Offsetting in Europe Post 2012: Kyoto Protocol, EU ETS, and Effort Sharing* (Climate Focus, Frankfurt am Main, 2012).

importance of legal culture discussed in the following section, but also due to the Protocol establishing simply a 'skeleton market'.[76] In other words, the Protocol contains few details of the trading scheme, or rather, the bare minimum,[77] leaving the 'relevant principles, modalities, rules and guidelines, in particular for verification, reporting and accountability'[78] to be determined at subsequent Conferences of the Parties.[79] As a consequence, different trading schemes may arise following the Protocol,[80] in particular because – and as the models show more generally in the previous chapter – Parties involved in the Protocol may have different concepts of emissions trading.[81]

What these four procedural differences show is that although international environmental law has been essential to the introduction and later implementation of emissions trading to the EU regulatory scene, the EU ETS stands as an EU-specific legal construction, independent of the global climate change law framework. The impact and importance of legal culture in this regard are considered next.

2. What has Legal Culture Got to Do with it?

Over and above the procedural difference between emissions trading at international and at EU level, emissions trading regimes depend on their specific legal culture for meaning. This is because each rule or legal framework has a particular meaning tied to a particular place and time,[82] and each legal concept and line of legal argument operates in pre-determined traditional contexts that spring from different cultural traditions – or, according to a so-called *mentalité*.[83] As such, a rule or

---

[76] D MacKenzie, *Material Markets: How Economic Agents are Constructed* (Oxford University Press, Oxford, 2009) 153.

[77] Grubb, Vrolijk and Brack, *The Kyoto Protocol* (n 48) 129.

[78] Kyoto Protocol, Art 17.

[79] Following the Protocol, five conferences finally lead to a political agreement in Bonn that were translated into legal documents at Marrakech. United Nations Framework Convention on Climate Change Report of the Conference of the Parties on its Seventh Session, FCCC/CP/2001/13/Add.1, 21 January 2002. For an overview of these conferences see Slingenberg, 'Climate Change Developments' (n 71) 214–15.

[80] Grubb, Vrolijk and Brack, *The Kyoto Protocol* (n 48) 207–08, identifies three possible trading schemes under this global regime: at one extreme, governments might simply transfer title deeds for part of their assigned amount to corporations and authorise these to corporations to trade internationally. Another option is for the government to define emission permits and to allow corporations to obtain these against assigned amounts specifically designated for international exchanges. A third option is to allow national companies to trade amongst themselves in a legal framework created by the central government, the latter also assuming responsibility for the trade under the Protocol.

[81] de Witt Wijnen, 'Emissions Trading under Article 17' (n 50) 415.

[82] P Legrand, 'What "Legal Transplants"?' in D Nelken and J Feest (eds), *Adapting Legal Cultures* (Hart Publishing, Oxford, 2001) 55, 57–58.

[83] Ibid 65. Similar points are raised in various strands of EU law studies, see, eg C Joerges, 'The Europeanization of Private Law as a Rationalization Process and as a Contest of Disciplines – an Analysis of the Directive on Unfair Terms in Consumer Contracts' (1995) 3 *European Environmental Law Review* 175, 183, N Questiaux, 'Implementing EC Law in France: The Role of the French Conseil d'Etat' in P Craig and C Harlow (eds), *Lawmaking in the European Union* (Kluwer International London, 1998) 479.

regime cannot be examined only as a black-letter text; rather it must be scrutinised through a culture-specific lens, taking into consideration its legal culture.[84]

'Legal culture', however, is a ubiquitous concept.[85] It reflects a fusion of social, political, and economic forces that impact a law's development, significance and process of implementation, as well as expressing the institutional and historical traditions through the legal language in a particular jurisdiction.[86] An appreciation of legal culture therefore agrees that the study of a legal concept and the examination of a law that is thought to have 'travelled' – as is the case in this chapter – will mirror these influences. Although there is a rich literature on this topic that suggests various methods and framework of how to study laws in comparison or laws that appear to be 'on the move', there is no overriding, uniform or straightforward guidance as to how to examine a law's particularities.[87] One analytical framework[88] proposes that legal culture is the study of finding the 'right fit'[89] between a law, which is travelling and the hosting legal body to which it travels. From this viewpoint, legal transfers are seen as legal 'transplants'[90] that must be 'domesticated' to fit into their new context,[91] or the transfer would run the risk of being 'rejected'[92] and the transplant proven a failure.[93] This illustration aims to show that no transplant, not even a legal one, is simple and that in order to have a chance at succeeding in applying foreign legal elements to a domestic legal system,

[84] Legrand, 'What "Legal Transplants"' (n 82) 65.

[85] Gibson and Caldeira, 'Legal Cultures of Europe' (n 7). See also, R Cotterrell, 'The Concept of Legal Culture' in D Nelken (ed), *Comparing Legal Cultures* (Darthmouth Publishing, Aldershot, 1997) 13, 14.

[86] E Scotford, *The Role of Environmental Principles in the Decisions of the European Union Courts and New South Wales Land and Environment Court* (DPhil thesis, University of Oxford, 2010) ch 1.

[87] eg legal culture may be treated as an aggregating concept that captures everything that is part of law in a particular field, or it may be viewed as an explanatory tool that helps to explain particular attitudes to laws that are culture-specific, see J Webber, 'Culture, Legal Culture, and Legal Reasoning: A Comment on Nelken' (2004) 29 *Australian Journal of Legal Philosophy* 27, 27–28.

[88] A related, albeit different, use of legal culture is to demonstrate that legal transplants are in fact never possible, or that law can never successfully be borrowed or transferred between legal systems. The argument is that when a law is translated from one legal system to another, instead of experiencing integration or, rejection, the imported law instead triggers a set of new and unexpected events and thereby creates a new law with a new meaning. These so-called 'legal irritants' are understood to be resistant to domestication, and thus unable to transform 'from something alien into something familiar'. These are instead understood to unleash 'an evolutionary dynamic' that results in a significant change both to the meaning of the rule and the context to which it is applied. This approach employs legal culture to show that legal culture is an undeniable and non-transferable part of a law's life and to highlight each law's uniqueness, see G Teubner, 'Legal Irritants: Good Faith in British Law or How Unifying Law Ends Up in New Divergences' (1998) 61 *MLR* 11, 12.

[89] Nelken, 'Comparatists and Transferability' (n 64).

[90] A Harding, 'Comparative Law and Legal Transplantation in South East Asia' in D Nelken and J Feest (eds), *Adapting Legal Cultures* (Hart Publishing, Oxford, 2001) 199.

[91] D Nelken, 'Towards a Sociology of Legal Adaption' in D Nelken and J Feest (eds), *Adapting Legal Cultures* (Hart Publishing, Oxford, 2001) 7, 13. Here, knowledge is required about the law and its 'web of meaning'. D Nelken, 'Using the Concept of Legal Culture' (2004) 29 *Australian Journal of Legal Philosophy* 1, 10.

[92] Nelken, 'Sociology of Legal Adaption', ibid.

[93] L Zedner, 'Comparative Research in Criminal Justice' in L Noaks, M Maguire and M Levi (eds), *Contemporary Issues in Criminology* (University of Wales Press, Cardiff, 1995) 11–12.

such as emissions trading to the EU, knowledge of both the implementing law and the hosting legal system is required. Such a study may be carried out by focusing on legal culture as a series of 'internal' factors – including judicial decisions, written law, scholarly comments, architecture of legal institutions – and/or 'external' elements – comprising social behaviour, attitudes to judicial decisions and informal organisation of behaviour within a community.[94]

The reference to legal culture in this chapter is not intended to turn into a socio-legal study; that is, the external elements concerning the EU emissions trading regime will not be examined. It is also worth noting that the concept of 'legal culture' is not employed for comparative purposes, as I only examine the EU ETS. Rather, I use the term so as to demonstrate that the legal features of the EU emissions trading regime are highly contingent on the legal system in which it operates, and that the legal architecture of this trading scheme – albeit appearing to be simple – is tied to complex questions concerning power-allocation that are specific to the EU. In fact, this is the reason why the *Economic Efficiency*, the *Private Property Rights*, and the *Command-and-Control* models are mapped onto EU ETS discourses, and the roles of the emissions market, the central government (here referring to the balancing of competence between the Member States and the Commission), and the legal status of emissions allowances, as envisioned by law- and policymakers and the EU Courts, are scrutinised in a close contextual legal analysis in chapters four and five respectively. This book thus adopts an 'internal' meaning of legal culture and engages in an analysis of emissions trading beyond the crude legal text of the Directive, examining in particular the institutional and jurisdictional forces that shape the EU emissions trading regime.

Before I start with a scrutiny of how the Commission and the EU Courts understand the EU ETS, it is useful to first sketch the general market discourse in the EU. This is so as to show that in these debates, the work of the judiciary is strongly tied to market construction and maintenance, and environmental protection. This rough outline aims to show that markets in the EU legal context are constructed according to a particular legal rationale, which is difficult, if at all possible, to duplicate elsewhere. This thus justifies a close examination of EU ETS, and highlights the importance of legal culture in understanding law.

III. EU Legal Culture: Intersections between Markets, the Judiciary and Law

EU legal culture is part of a vibrant evolution: the Union was created as a *sui generis* polity in 1958 and has since passed different legal processes of Treaty amendments

---

[94] See L Friedman, 'The Concept of Legal Culture: A Reply' in D Nelken (ed), *Comparing Legal Cultures* (Darthmouth Publishing, Aldershot, 1997) 33, Scotford, *Environmental Principles* (n 86).

and revisions, dramatic programmes of deregulation and re-regulation,[95] aimed at creating a particular economic and political 'ever closer union'.[96] These developments have occurred in different phases[97] and the Treaty Articles, secondary Union legislation, the EU Courts, and the institutions have all been important in realising this progress of creating an integrated Europe.[98] Such integration has evolved around markets and market-creation,[99] mainly because market liberation is seen as the main promoter of consolidating 'co-operation and integration that would make pan-European armed conflict inconceivable'[100] – a goal that is traditionally at the heart of the EU. Indeed, a market shared by Member States, in which free movement of goods and factors of production are safeguarded, was identified by the founders of the Treaty as key to generating economic growth, wealth,[101] and ultimately securing political unity across Europe.[102] As such, the use of markets in this context has a double-edged quality: it husbands economic activities and furthers European integration that is the centrepiece of EU legal culture.

Here it is important to highlight that it is impossible to generalise about markets,[103] including markets in a single jurisdiction, or in the EU, simply because they hold different meanings depending on the type of law employed and the law's purpose. For instance, within the scope of competition law, a particular market and market definitions are carried out so as to assess whether a firm or

[95] E Fisher, *Risk, Regulation and Administrative Constitutionalism* (Hart Publishing, Oxford, 2010) 168.

[96] Art 1 TEU states that the Lisbon Treaty 'marks a new stage in the process of creating an ever closer union among the peoples of Europe'. See also D Dinan, *Ever Closer Union: An Introduction to European Integration* (3rd edn, Palgrave Macmillan, Hampshire, 2005).

[97] Warleigh defines these developments to have occurred 'gradually and elliptically'. See A Warleigh, 'Purposeful Opportunists? EU Institutions and the Struggle over European Citizenship' in R Bellamy and A Warleigh (eds), *Citizenship and Governance in the EU* (London, Continuum, 2001) 19, 34. For an overview of the development of European integration and EU competences, see, eg P Craig and G de Burca (eds), *The Evolution of EU Law* (2nd edn, Oxford University Press, Oxford 2011), and in light of the key case law, see M Maduro and L Azoulai (eds), *The Past and Future of EU Law: The Classics of EU Law Revisited on the 50th Anniversary of the Rome Treaty* (Hart Publishing, Oxford, 2010).

[98] P Craig, 'The Evolution of the Single Market: Unpacking the Premises' in C Barnard and J Scott (eds), *The Law of the Single European Market* (Hart Publishing, Oxford, 2002) 1, 40.

[99] Illustrating the essence of the single European market to EU's governance and vice versa, Joerges explains the argument of EU functioning as a 'market without a State' as much as it could be 'States without market'. C Joerges, 'What is Left of the European Economic Constitution? A Melancholic Euology' (2005) 30 *EL Rev* 461, 475.

[100] C Barnard, *The Substantive Law of the EU: The Four Freedoms* (3rd edn, Oxford University Press, Oxford, 2010) 29.

[101] T Burns, 'Better Lawmaking? An Evaluation of Lawmaking in the European Community' in P Craig and C Harlow (eds), *Lawmaking in the European Union* (Kluwer Law International, London 1998) 435, 440.

[102] As epitomised by the former President of the European Commission, Jacques Delors, who is understood to have exclaimed: 'We're not here just to make a single market – that doesn't interest me – but to make a political union'. As cited in G Rachman, 'Greece Threatens More than the Euro', *Financial Times*, London February 23 2010.

[103] M Callon, 'An Essay on Framing and Overflowing: Economic Externalities Revisited by Sociology' in M Callon (ed), *The Laws of the Markets* (Blackwell Publishers, Oxford, 1998) 244, D MacKenzie, *Material Markets: How Economic Agents are Constructed* (Oxford University Press, Oxford, 2009) 182.

firms possess market power and whether to apply competition law.[104] Competition law merits,[105] however, are different to how a market is defined in applying, for example, the integration principle in the EU legal environment.[106] Discussions about the scope of the single European market further complicate matters. As illustrated by Armstrong, the single European market can be seen 'to have the qualities of Russian dolls'[107] in the sense that increasingly narrow or, increasingly broad definitions can be applied to define it. In the strictest sense, this market refers to the Treaty definition of establishing an internal market,[108] which connects to the Commission's 'White Paper on Completing the Internal Market' and the objectives stipulated therein, such as abolishing barriers to trade, harmonising and approximating legislation with the aim of facilitating firms work across borders.[109] Yet, even in adopting this allegedly narrow definition, the internal market cannot be precisely defined simply because the Commission's targeted goals in finalising the internal market are ongoing rather than an 'historical artefact'.[110]

Clearly, market discourses in the EU legal order are dynamic and complex. The idea behind this chapter is not to try to capture the entire essence of these discourses nor to depict the complete picture of the part that markets play in establishing an EU legal culture. Rather the objective here is to show, through snapshots, that the emission market in the EU operates in a broader market-based legal framework, in which the judiciary plays a progressive role in constructing a high level of environmental protection and integration, and in which market discourse are underpinned by particular regulatory agendas aimed at creating

---

[104] By pinning down the product and geographical area of a certain market, it is thereafter possible to determine the competitive constraints upon undertakings in that particular market and apply competition policies thereto. At EU level see Commission of the European Communities, Notice from the Commission on the Definition of the Relevant Market for the Purposes of Community Competition Law, [1997] OJ C372/5, and at UK level, see Office of Fair Trade, Competition Act 1998 Market Definition, March 1999, OFT 403. See R Whish and D Bailey, *Competition Law* (Oxford University Press, Oxford, 2012) 27.

[105] Note that markets also within competition law may be differently defined depending on the competition problem at hand, see ibid.

[106] Certain integration principles under the TFEU, such as the environmental integration principle in Art 11 TFEU have general application and as such must be integrated into the definition and integration of the Union's policies and activities, stretching beyond market definitions relevant to competition provisions. For an overview of various integration principles under the Lisbon Treaty see H Vedder, 'Treaty of Lisbon and European Environmental Law and Policy' (2010) 22 *Journal of Environmental Law* 285, 289.

[107] K Armstrong, 'Governance and the Single Market' in P Craig and G de Burca (eds), *The Evolution of EU law* (Oxford University Press, Oxford, 1999) 745, 747.

[108] Art 26(2) TFEU states that the 'internal market shall compromise an area without internal frontiers in which the free movement of goods, persons, services and capital is ensured in accordance with the provisions of the Treaties'.

[109] Commission of the European Communities, 'White Paper on Completing the Internal Market', COM(85) 310 final.

[110] Barnard (n 100) 12. See also, L Gormley, 'The Internal Market: History and Evolution' in N Shuibhne (ed), *Regulating the Internal Market* (Edward Elgar Publishing, Cheltenham, 2006) 14. Over the years and following the White Paper, ibid, the Commission has set out various ambitious goals to finalise the internal market project, for an overview see S Weatherill, *Cases and Materials on EU Law* (8th edn, Oxford University Press, Oxford, 2007) 238–42.

competitive and integrated markets. Although mere snapshots, it is in the light of these that the legal role of the emissions market in the EU can be made sense of and the relevance of a close examination of this market system appreciated.

A. *Markets*, the Judiciary and Environmental Law

The Union enjoys extensive market-making powers that tend to be exercised directly or indirectly to state measures.[111] Provisions on the control of fiscal barriers[112] and the free movement provisions[113] are clear examples of Treaty stipulations that may be applied to ensure market harmonisation by limiting domestic regulatory measures.[114] The process of creating the single European market thus realises economic freedoms but establishes that it is not *just* a market. Rather, what is described by Weiler as 'a highly politicized choice of ethos, ideology and political culture'[115] is crafted, which follows an economic rationale,[116] whilst seeking to protect high social and environmental standards. This can be seen in Article 3(3) TEU, which provides that the Union shall establish an internal market that is 'a highly competitive social market economy, aiming at full employment and social progress, and a high level of protection and improvement of the quality of the environment'. Moreover, Article 114(3) TFEU, which vests regulatory power with the Union to approximate laws on the grounds of the functioning of the internal market, obliges the Commission to consider a high level of environmental and consumer protection in its legislative proposals. What this shows is that the internal market follows deep social structures that stretch far beyond laissez-faire policies of a market.[117]

This idea of establishing a market with a particular regulatory goal, including that of environmental protection, dates back to the First Environmental Action Programme, which admitted that

a harmonious development of economic activities and a continuous and balanced expansion cannot now be imagined in the absence of an effective campaign to combat

[111] S Weatherill and P Beaumont, *EU Law* (3rd edn, Penguin Publishing, London, 1999) 1000.
[112] See Arts 30 and 110 TFEU.
[113] Arts 34 and 35 TFEU control quantitative physical and technical barriers and Arts 45, 49, and 56 TFEU control obstacles to the free movement of persons and services.
[114] See E Szyszczak, 'State Intervention and the Internal Market' in T Tridimas and P Nebbia (eds), *European Union Law for the Twenty-First Century: Rethinking the New Legal Order* (Hart Publishing, Oxford, 2004) 217, N Boeger, 'Minimum Harmonisation, Free Movement and Proportionality' in P Syrpis (ed), *The Judiciary, the Legislature and the EU Internal Market* (Cambridge University Press, Cambridge, 2012) 62, and Case C-142/05 *Åklagaren v Percy Mickelsson and Joakim Roos* [2009] ECR 1-4273 that is a clear example of the legitimate restriction on use according to the CJEU.
[115] J Weiler, 'The Transformation of Europe' (1991) 100 *Yale Law Journal* 2403, 2477.
[116] For an overview of various attempts by the Commission to measure the economic gains from the internal market and in this sense highlight areas where further regulatory action is needed, see P Craig and G de Burca, *EU Law: Text, Cases and Materials* (5th edn, Oxford University Press, Oxford, 2011) 605–09.
[117] See B de Witte, 'Non-market Values in Internal Market Legislation' in N Shuibhne (ed), *Regulating the Internal Market* (Edward Elgar Publishing, Cheltenham, 2006) 61.

pollution and nuisance or of an improvement in the quality of life and the protection of the environment.[118]

At the time when this action programme was issued, EU environmental law lacked a distinct legal base in the Treaties,[119] which, in light of EU constitutional law, would mean that the EU could not stipulate any measures in this particular field.[120] A rising number of legislative acts that enhanced environmental protection were, nonetheless, adopted during this period, based on the so-called 'gap filler clause'.[121] That is, Article 308 EC[122] and Article 95 EC,[123] which allow harmonisation of national laws on the basis of furthering the establishment of the internal market, and create residual general powers for the Union to safeguard the functioning of the internal market respectively, were employed to safeguard and uphold environmental standards.[124] The Drinking Water Directive[125] is but one example based on an internal market provision.[126] This legal measure supposed to regulate disparity in national provisions on the quality of water that may create differences in conditions of competition, and thereby 'affect the operation of the common market'.[127] Although different environmental standards are known to be able to create trade barriers,[128] environmental considerations 'undoubtedly played a part'[129] in establishing this type of legislative measure.

These snapshots show two things. First, market discourses in the EU are clearly embedded in a kaleidoscope of aims, including the creation of prosperity, social security and environmental protection. This demonstrates that the market men-

---

[118] Declaration of the Council of the European Communities and of the representatives of the Governments of the Member States meeting in the Council of 22 November 1973 on the programme of action of the European Communities on the environment, [1973] OJ C112/1.

[119] The Single European Act [1987] OJ L169/1 (SEA) introduced Arts 130r–t, which provide the first explicit codified legal base for environmental measures.

[120] Art 5(2) TEU states that 'the Union shall act only within the limits of the competences conferred upon it by the Member States in the Treaties to attain the objectives set out therein. Competence not conferred upon the Union in the Treaties remain with the Member States'. Plentiful cases exist on this topic, see, eg Case C-178/03 *Commission v European Parliament and Council* [2006] ECR I-107 .

[121] I von Homeyer, 'The Evolution of EU Environmental Governance' in J Scott (ed), *Environmental Protection: European Law and Governance* (Oxford University Press, New York City, 2009) 1, 2.

[122] Currently Art 352 TFEU. Note that this amendment does not refer to the internal market.

[123] Currently Art 114 TFEU.

[124] J Usher, 'The Gradual Widening of European Community Policy on the Basis of Articles 100 and 235 of the EEC Treaty' in J Schwarze and H Schermers (eds), *Structure and Dimension of European Community Policy* (Nomos, Baden Baden, 1988) 25, C Knill and D Liefferink, 'The Establishment of EU Environmental Policy' in A Jordan and C Adelle (eds), *Environmental Policy in the EU: Actors, Institutions and Processes* (Routledge, Abingdon, 2013) 13, A Haagsma, 'The European Community's Environmental Policy: A Case-Study in Federalism' (1989) 12 *Fordham International Law Journal* 311.

[125] Directive 80/778/EEC of 15 July 1980 relating to the quality of water intended for human consumption as amended by Directive 81/858/EEC and 91/692/EEC, [1980] OJ L229.

[126] Indeed, in the period leading up to the Single European Act (n 119), some 200 environmentally-related measures were adopted, see R Schütze, *From Dual to Cooperative Federalism: The Changing Structure of European Law* (Oxford University Press, Oxford, 2009) 271.

[127] J Holder and M Lee, *Environmental Protection, Law and Policy* (2nd edn, Cambridge University Press, Cambridge, 2007) 159.

[128] J Scott, *Environmental Law* (Longman, London, 1998) 12–15, Schütze (n 126) 265–79.

[129] J Jans and H Vedder, *European Environmental Law - After Lisbon* (4th edn, Europa Law Publishing, Groningen, 2011) 3.

tality at an EU level is neither neutral nor purely profit-oriented. Second, the maintenance of the internal market and the process of market-creation in the EU are historically used for 'economic spillovers', or more exactly, to expand the EU's regulatory competence to environmental matters. Discussing EU environmental law, as explained in more detail below, is thus inevitably tied to a broader market discourse particular to the EU.

B. Markets, *the Judiciary* and Environmental Law

In order to understand the relationship between the complex market-rationale and environmental law in the EU context, it is necessary to examine, albeit briefly, the role of the EU Courts.[130] According to Article 19 TEU, the CJEU 'shall ensure that in the interpretation and application of the Treaties the law is observed'. This means that the judiciary possesses the capacity to define the constitutional framework according to which all other organs of governance in the EU, including the Member States, the EU's legislative institutions and the courts interact.[131] Relying on this Treaty provision, the CJEU has continuously supported European integration – both by ruling in favour of the creation and maintenance of a market geared toward integration[132] and by constructing EU environmental law.[133] The goals of the single market, however, give rise to a number of conflicting tensions in establishing EU environmental policies,[134] which are clearly exemplified in the *ADBHU* case.[135] This preliminary ruling concerned the Directive on the disposal of waste oils, which placed an obligation on the Member States to set up a system for the safe disposal of waste spills. Such a system was based on zones, within which specifically licensed companies had to carry out the collection and disposal of oil, giving rise to incompatibility concerns with the free movement provisions.[136] Ruling on this clash between environmental and free movement priorities, the CJEU held that environmental protection is 'one of the Community's essential objectives'[137] that, as such, justifies certain limitations to the activities in the common market that do not 'go beyond the inevitable restrictions which are justified

---

[130] The role of the CJEU is further explored in ch 5.
[131] A Stone Sweet, 'The European Court of Justice' in P Craig and G de Burca (eds), *The Evolution of EU Law* (Oxford University Press, Oxford, 2011) 121, 131.
[132] See, eg M Maduro, *We the Court: The European Court of Justice and the European Economic Constitution – A Critical Reading of Article 30 of the EC Treaty* (Hart Publishing, Oxford, 2002), K Alter (ed), *The European Court's Political Power: Selected Essays* (Oxford University Press, Oxford, 2009).
[133] R Cichowski, 'Integrating the Environment: The European Court and the Construction of Supranational Policy' (1998) 5 *Journal of European Public Policy* 387.
[134] D Vogel, 'Environmental Policy in the European Community' in S Kamieniecki (ed), *Environmental Politics in the International Arena: Movements, Parties, Organizations, and Policy* (State University of New York Press, Albany, 1993) 181.
[135] Case 240/83 *Procureur de la République v Association de Défense Des Brûleurs D'huiles Usagées (ADBHU)* [1985] ECR 531.
[136] A Haagsma, 'The European Community's Environmental Policy: A Case-Study in Federalism' (1989) 12 *Fordham International Law Journal* 311, 323–26.
[137] *ADBHU* (n 135) para 13.

by the pursuit of the objective of environmental protection'.[138] This is the first time that the Court recognises the importance of safeguarding the environment,[139] and what is more remarkable is the timing – this judgment was delivered before the codification of environmental competences in the Treaties. This shows not only the sharp intersection between market and environment norms but also, and more importantly, the progressiveness of the Court in developing environmental values and expanding on EU environmental competences. To appreciate the evolution of EU environmental law is thus to consider the significant role of the Court in interpreting free movement provisions in favour of undeclared environmental goals.[140]

Over the course of various Treaty amendments, the Union has developed competences to legislate on environmental matters.[141] In the present constitutional arrangement, Title XX provides the legal basis for environmental policy.[142] Despite these developments, environmental and market-specific competences overlap in EU regulatory measures, subsequently giving rise to litigation before the EU Courts. One reason why this is the case is the dilemma that policy- and lawmakers face in choosing the right legal base for measures that, for instance, may have an impact on the internal market but target an environment-oriented objective.[143] Considering that the Union may only act upon its conferred powers, this is a significant choice to make, which, if wrong, leads to the invalidation of the measure.[144] This is a seemingly straightforward rule but the Treaty, and the extent to which it allows the Member States vis-à-vis the Union to enjoy regulative discretion, can be difficult to define.[145] This unclear cut between competences in regulating the internal market and trade on the one hand, and safeguarding the environment on the other, is clearly manifested in the CJEU's Opinion on the conclusion of the Cartagena Protocol.[146] Here the Court examined whether the conclusion of an international

---

[138] ibid, para 15.

[139] Jans and Vedder, *European Environmental Law* (n 129) 6.

[140] As clearly illustrated by Haagsma (n 124) 315, the word 'environment' was not even mentioned in any of the first Treaties of today's Union.

[141] See n 119, P Sands, 'European Community Environmental Law: The Evolution of a Regional Regime of International Environmental Protection' (1991) 100 *Yale Law Journal* 2511.

[142] Currently these are encompassed in Arts 114(3), 191–93 TFEU.

[143] J Jans, H Sevenster and J Janssen, 'Environmental Spill-Overs Into General Community Law' (2008) 31 *Fordham International Law Journal* 1360, 1362. Indeed, in the run-up to the Commission's proposal for the EU emissions trading scheme, the Commission considered whether Art 95 EC, which has as its goal to establish the EU's internal market, is more suited as a legal base for the EU ETS Directive than the environmental competence codified in Art 175 EC. The fact that it could not be shown that emissions trading schemes were causing distortion to the internal market made the internal market competence inapplicable, see D Meadows, 'The Emissions Allowance Trading Directive 2003/87/EC Explained' in J Delbeke (ed), *EU Energy Law: The EU Greenhouse Gas Emissions Trading Scheme* (Claeys & Casteels, Leuven, 2006) 63, 64.

[144] According to Art 5 TEU the limits of Union competences are governed by the principle of conferral. The use of Union competences is governed by the principles of subsidiarity and proportionality.

[145] S Douglas-Scott, *Constitutional Law of the European Union* (Pearson Education, Harlow, 2002) 213, Craig and de Burca, *EU Law* (n 116) ch 3, R Schütze, *European Constitutional Law* (Cambridge University Press, Cambridge, 2012) ch 5.

[146] Opinion 2/00 of the Court of 6 December 2001 concerning the Cartagena Protocol [2001] ECR I-09713.

agreement, which aimed to control the transboundary movement and management of living modified organisms, should be classified a trade measure and thus based on Articles 133 and 300 EC,[147] or as an environmental agreement within the ambit of Article 175 EC.[148] The fact that the Court engaged in a lengthy examination of the context, aim and content of the set Protocol to show that it should be classified as an environmental, as opposed to a trade measure, demonstrates the interwoven nature of environmental law and market regulation in the EU legal order, and the difficult role of the Court in distinguishing these.

Moreover, the EU Courts frequently engage in balancing between environmental and economic objectives in the application of free movement provisions. Cases such as *Bluhme*[149] and *Preussen Elektra*[150] are now classic examples of instances where the Court found measures with environmental objectives to fall within the scope of Article 34 TFEU but justified these on the grounds of protecting and preserving the bee population, and promoting renewable energy respectively. Similarly, restrictions to trade – both distinctly[151] and indistinctly applicable measures[152] – have been justified, the Court concluding that the 'protection of the environment is one of the Community's essential objectives'.[153] These are mere examples of the vast case law on environmental and trade related disputes[154] but they help to show that the EU Courts play a vital role in supporting a particular market mentality that includes considering broad social and environmental values in deciding the legitimacy of market rules.

What the discussion above shows is that the CJEU plays a significant part in the development of both the internal market and environment protection in the EU jurisdiction, and that EU environmental law is inherently tied to a particular market mentality specific to the EU. More precisely, the EU Courts have legitimised market measures aimed at protecting the environment when the EU lacked strict competence for such regulatory activities, and pushed for environmental protection in balancing trade and free movement objectives against environmental objectives. Ultimately, to appreciate EU environmental law, attention must be paid to the progressive role of the EU Courts and their construction of the internal market and environmental protection.

---

[147] The Commission argues that the conclusion of the Protocol falls within commercial activities and ought thus be based on former Arts 133 and 300 EC (Arts 284 and 218 TFEU), which would give the Commission the exclusive competence to implement the agreement.

[148] Art 192 TFEU.

[149] Case C-67/97 *Bluhme* [1998] ECR I-8033. Case dealing with a legislation prohibiting the keeping of certain kinds of bees on the Danish island of Laesö.

[150] Case C-379/98 *Preussen Elektra* [2001] ECR I-2099. Case concerning German legislation that obliged suppliers of electricity to purchase electricity from renewable energy sources at minimum price.

[151] Case 302/86 *Commission v Denmark (Danish Bottles)* [1988] ECR 4607. Case concerning a Danish system that requires manufactures and importers to market beer and soft drinks only in reusable containers that have to be approved by the National Agency for the Protection of the Environment.

[152] Case C-2/90 *Commission v Belgium* [1992] ECR I-14431.

[153] *Danish Bottles* (n 151).

[154] For an overview see L Krämer, *Casebook on EU Environmental Law* (Hart Publishing, Oxford, 2002) 33.

C. Markets, the Judiciary and *Environmental Law*

The EU is 'regulatory in nature',[155] meaning that it constructs the internal market through regulation and regulatory interpretation. Indeed, setting out the foundation of the internal market was a 'gigantic regulatory project'[156] that includes the adoption of more than 300 Directives and Regulations only in the first five years, aimed at creating a market without frontiers. This particular tier of governance can be described to follow a catchy motto of 'freer markets, more rules'.[157] Here it is important to note that the *type* of rules that are enacted in the EU are of importance, also in adopting environmental laws. Environmental legislation has typically been 'command-and-control'; that is, direct regulation that determines the technique and methodology required for compliance.[158] This particular regulatory mechanism is accredited to accommodate market transactions by imposing stable and clear obligations.[159] As such, EU environmental regulation has not only aimed at enhancing environmental protection but also safeguarding and furthering the functionality of the internal market. Indeed, EU environmental law has traditionally addressed only the most direct forms of market failures, such as pollution from one Member State to another primarily because of the likely distorting effects of national environmental laws on the European market.[160]

By the end of the 1980s, the use of command-and-control type of regulation started attracting criticism. More precisely, considerations regarding the inability of this regulatory method to address complex and varied environmental problems were raised,[161] and its effects on the internal market questioned. Command-and-control was described as 'obscure, complex and inaccessible',[162] and as such, harming 'the competitiveness of European business, damaging the employment prospects of European citizens and inhibiting economic growth'.[163] The two key regulatory movements that emerged to address this regulatory inertia are the

---

[155] Description borrowed from S Weatherill, 'The Challenge of Better Regulation' in S Weatherill (ed), *Better Regulation* (Hart Publishing, Oxford, 2007) 1, 3. A similar description exists in G Majone, 'The Rise of Statutory Regulation in Europe' in G Majone (ed), *Regulating Europe* (Routledge, Abingdon, 1996) 47, 55.

[156] R van Gestel and H-W Micklitz, 'Revitalizing Doctrinal Legal Research in Europe: What About Methodology?' in U Neergaard, R Nielsen and L Roseberry (eds), *European Legal Method – Paradoxes and Revitalisation* (DJOP Publishing, Copenhagen, 2011) 25, 42.

[157] S Vogel, *Freer Markets, More Rules: Regulatory Reform in Advanced Industrial Countries* (Cornell University Press, Ithaca, 1996). Vogel explains that the reason why rules are necessary is because governments cannot simply allow competition; they have to *create* it. S Vogel, 'Why Freer Markets Need More Rules' in M Landy, M Levin and M Shapiro (eds), *Creating Competitive Markets: The Politics of Regulatory Reform* (Brookings Institution Press, Washington DC, 2007) 25, 34.

[158] As defined in M Lee, *EU Environmental Law: Challenges, Change and Decision-Making* (Hart Publishing, Oxford, 2005) 183.

[159] D Chalmers, 'Inhabitants in the Field of EC Environmental Law' in P Craig and G de Burca (eds), *The Evolution of EU Law* (1st edn, Oxford University Press, Oxford, 1999) 653, 659.

[160] Holder and Lee, *Environmental Protection* (n 118) 162, ibid 660.

[161] Majone (n 155) 54–56, ibid 164.

[162] Burns, 'Better Lawmaking' (n 101) 435.

[163] Citing the Molitor Group as stated in ibid.

Better Regulation agenda[164] (succeeded by the Smart Regulation agenda)[165] and ecological modernisation. Both regulatory programmes seek to establish a strong interrelationship between competitive markets and environmental protection, thereby highlighting the close nexus between market maintenance and environmental law in the EU legal order.

More precisely, creating *better* regulation became a clear priority following the Lisbon Agenda in which regulation was identified as pivotal in making the EU 'the most competitive and dynamic knowledge-based economy in the world'.[166] The Better Regulation agenda subsequently set out to simplify legislation, reduce administrative burdens, and thereby increase economic competitiveness,[167] which is why it is aligned with the growth and job priorities of the Lisbon Agenda.[168] Regulatory objectives forming part of the Better Regulation agenda cover a wide range of initiatives,[169] including securing high levels of both social and environmental protection, effective implementation of laws, and easy access to regulation,[170] which is further linked to good governance.[171] Indeed, Better Regulation narratives are fluid and dynamic,[172] and suggest both strict regulatory standards, as well as deregulation to achieve the prescribed goals.[173] Relevant to the discussion about environmental laws is the focus of both the Better and Smart Regulation agendas on the idea that better and smarter regulation can enhance competition.[174] The idea is to create 'win-win' situations that will allow companies to behave responsibly and maximise profits at the same time.[175] The focus on creating 'win-win' solutions

[164] Commission of the European Communities, 'Communication from the Commission on Better Regulation for Growth and Jobs in the European Union', COM(2005) 97 final.

[165] Commission of the European Communities, 'Communication from the Commission on Smart Regulation in the European Union', COM(2010) 543 final. In regulatory scholarship 'smart regulation' is furthered as a regulatory design in which a mix of institutions and regulations work together for a common regulatory goal, see N Gunningham, P Grabosky and D Sinclair, *Smart Regulation: Designing Environmental Policy* (Clarendon Press, Oxford, 1998). Note that the better regulation agenda does not always lead to smart regulation as understood by Gunningham, Grabosky and Sinclair, although there is consistency between the two agendas. R Baldwin, 'Is Better Regulation Smarter Regulation?' (2005) *Public Law* 485, 502.

[166] Presidency Conclusions (EU) Lisbon European Council (23 and 24 March 2000) www.europarl.europa.eu/summits/lis1_en.htm, accessed 27 September 2012.

[167] Communication, 'Better Regulation' (n 164).

[168] C Radaelli, 'Whither Better Regulation for the Lisbon Agenda?' (2007) 14 *Journal of European Public Policy* 190, 204.

[169] Baldwin argues that the better regulation agenda is not so much a single idea as a collection of ideas that have come together to form an initiative. R Baldwin, 'Better Regulation: The Search and the Struggle' in R Baldwin, M Cave and M Lodge (eds), *The Oxford Handbook of Regulation* (Oxford University Press, Oxford, 2010) 258, 275.

[170] These were set out in the Manderlkern Report as the basis for better regulation in the EU. Manderlkern Group on Better Regulation (2001) ec.europa.eu/governance/better_regulation/documents/mandelkern_report.pdf, accessed 27 September 2012.

[171] Commission of the European Communities, 'Commission White Paper on European Governance', COM(2001) 428, 5.

[172] Radaelli, 'Better Regulation' (n 168) 200.

[173] ibid 197.

[174] Communication, 'Smart Regulation' (n 165) 12, Communication, 'Better Regulation' (n 164).

[175] R Haythornthwaite, 'Better Regulation in Europe' in S Weatherill (ed), *Better Regulation* (Hart Publishing, Oxford, 2007) 19, Baldwin (n 165) 507.

shows that ecological modernisation concepts have 'put an imprint' on the Union's portrayal of regulatory reform.[176] The idea is that more efficiency at the level of regulation is able to secure competitiveness and employment, as well as evade any environmental crises.[177] This movement aims to unite the forces that drive technical change and economic development to improve the quality of the environment.[178] Dimas summarises this goal by stating that Europe 'needs to invest more in innovative ways to protect the environment while boosting the EU's competitiveness'.[179] This idea, clearly influenced by the thought of ecological modernisation, has been steered toward the use of more flexible environmental regulation, and in the EU context the use of a mix of Regulations and deregulation.[180] What it signifies is the overlap between market progressiveness and environmental protection and that the two are interwoven in debates on regulation and regulatory reform in the EU.

These regulatory discussions, however, are part of an agenda that is not unique to the EU,[181] as indeed most governments are faced with demands for regulatory improvement.[182] As such, most public and private actors across Europe are devout 'in the pilgrimage toward the holy shrine of 'Better Regulation''.[183] There are nonetheless two key reasons, as identified by Weatherill,[184] why these regulatory reform programmes in the EU are different from anywhere else and ultimately, why any EU-rule is inevitably intertwined in the EU legal culture. The first reason is that any assessment and reform of EU legislation is directly linked to the EU's institutional framework.[185] This includes taking into consideration the Commission's 'policy entrepreneurship'[186] or, right of policy initiation, as well as the position of the Council and the Parliament to co-decide most matters that fall under the scope of the Treaty according to the ordinary legislative procedure.[187] The question of how

---

[176] M Andersen and I Massa, 'Ecological Modernization: Origin, Dilemmas and Future Directions' (2000) 2 *Environmental and Planning Law Journal* 337, 339.

[177] I Massa and M Andersen, 'Special Issue Introduction: Ecological Modernization' (2000) 2 *Journal of Environmental Policy and Planning* 265, 265.

[178] Holder and Lee, *Environmental Protection* (n 127) 164.

[179] As cited in European Commission, 'Member States need to Embrace Reform More Decisively to Create More Growth and Jobs' (Brussels, 27 January 2005) europa.eu/rapid/pressReleasesAction.do?reference=IP/05/100&format=HTML&aged=1&language=EN&guiLanguage=en, accessed 27 September 2012.

[180] Holder and Lee, *Environmental Protection* (n 127) 165.

[181] Wiener, 'Better Regulation' (n 39) argues that the better regulation agenda in the EU has been borrowed from the US.

[182] It is an agenda furthered also by international bodies, including the Organisation for Economic and Co-operation development (OECD), see R Baldwin, M Cave and M Lodge, 'Regulation – The Field and the Developing Agenda' in R Baldwin, M Cave and M Lodge (eds), *The Oxford Handbook of Regulation* (Oxford University Press, Oxford, 2010) 3, 8.

[183] S Weatherill, 'The Challenge of Better Regulation' in S Weatherill (ed), *Better Regulation* (Hart Publishing, Oxford, 2007) 1, 4.

[184] ibid.

[185] ibid 2.

[186] G Majone, 'The European Commission as Regulator' in G Majone (ed), *Regulating Europe* (Routledge, Abingdon, 1996) 61.

[187] Weatherill, 'Challenge of Better Regulation' (n 183) 2. Art 294 TFEU sets out the ordinary legislative procedure.

the EU regulates *better* is inevitably linked to this particular process of policy-deliberation. Examining the various methods of legislative processes thus helps to explain why an environmental measure, such as an EU-wide carbon energy tax[188] that requires unanimity in the decision-making process,[189] is less likely to be implemented and considered better regulation compared to, for instance, an emission trading regime that is based on the ordinary legislative procedure. Moreover, the subsidiarity principle forms an intrinsic part of this examination. This principle encapsulates a core constitutional rule that says that policy areas that do not fall within its exclusive competence, the Union shall legislate only when there is a real need and where it is clear that the objective cannot be reached effectively by national measures.[190] In the context of environmental law, this is particularly pertinent considering that the Union shares competence with the Member States to legislate on environmental matters.[191] This means that environmental measures under Articles 191–93 TFEU must be adopted according to the subsidiarity principle and Article 5(3) TEU.[192] Due to the political profile of the subsidiarity principle, each environmental law measure that is tested for improvement, faces an assessment on whether the Union can, but also whether it should, legislate.[193] According to Lenaerts, emissions markets are preferred to traditional direct regulation in controlling pollution *because* of their conformity to the subsidiarity principle. More precisely, he understands emissions trading regimes to leave it to the market to determine ways in which the tolerated level of pollution will be allocated among the several pollution sources, meaning that the government then only has to set the tolerated level of pollution, organise a system of tradable emission permits, and ensure that emissions do not exceed the amount authorised by the permits that every polluter holds. Lenaerts explains that this indeed is 'an expression of "subsidiarity"'.[194]

Second, creating *better* regulation is inherently value-based and as such tied to its legal context for proper assessment.[195] For instance, smart regulation, which

---

[188] Commission of the European Communities, 'Commission Proposal for a Council Directive Introducing a Tax on Carbon Dioxide Emissions and Energy', COM(92) 226 final.

[189] Art 192(2)(a) TFEU.

[190] See Art 5(2) TEU, ibid and E Olivi, 'The EU Better Regulation Agenda' in S Weatherill (ed), *Better Regulation* (Hart Publishing, Oxford, 2007) 191, 191.

[191] Art 4(e) TFEU.

[192] Art 5(3) TEU says that under 'the principle of subsidiarity, in areas which do not fall within its exclusive competence, the Union shall act only if and insofar as the objectives of the proposed action cannot be sufficiently achieved by the Member State, either at central level or at regional and local level, but can rather, by reason of the scale of effects of the proposed action, be better achieved at Union level'.

[193] Holder and Lee, *Environmental Protection* (n 127) 152. The subsidiarity debate is contentious, see, eg G Davies, 'Subsidiarity: The Wrong Idea, in the Wrong Place, at the Wrong Time' (2006) 43 *CML Rev* 63, A Biondi, 'Subsidiarity in the Courtroom' in A Biondi, P Eeckhout and S Ripley (eds), *EU Law After Lisbon* (Oxford University Press, Oxford, 2012) 211, X Groussot and S Bogojević, 'Subsidiarity as a Procedural Safeguard of Federalism' in L Azoulai (ed), *The European Union as a Federal Order of Competences* (Oxford University Press, Oxford, forthcoming).

[194] K Lenaerts, 'The Principle of Subsidiarity and the Environment in the European Union: Keeping the Balance of Federalism' (1993) 17 *Fordham International Law Journal* 846, 893.

[195] Weatherill, 'Challenge of Better Regulation' (n 183) 4.

builds on the foundation of better regulation, identifies regulation as playing a key role in curing market failure:[196]

> They [markets] exist to serve a purpose which is to deliver sustainable prosperity for all, and they will not always do this on their own. Regulation has a positive and necessary role to play.

Here the Commission raises the importance of regulation in ensuring a well-functioning market but this goal leaves the question how to balance protection from market failures on the one hand, and commercial freedom on the other unanswered.[197] Indeed this is the dilemma of better regulation: under its umbrella stand a wide range of goals including endeavoring to facilitate growth and job creation and regulation that will be 'of benefit to all economic actors in the least burdensome and most cost-effective way possible',[198] as well as 'high levels of both social and environment protection'.[199] Understanding how these interests can be combined is an assignment, which, as this section has attempted to show, is EU-specific.

What the above illustrate is that debates on regulation are central to the Union: it constructs the internal market via regulation and it is through the use and interpretation of these regulations and the relevant competences that the internal market has progressed to secure high standards of environment protection in the EU. At the same time, environmental law tends to be constructed and reformed so as to help enhance this market and its competitiveness, indicating a clear symbiosis between the two. The significance of this is that environmental law discourses in the EU are inherently tied to the internal market, and more precisely the EU legal order.

IV. All Together Now: International Climate Change Law, the Internal Market, EU Courts, EU Environmental Law and the EU ETS

The discussions above point to at least two key reasons why legal culture matters in examining emissions trading schemes. One refers to legal culture scholarship more broadly and the idea therein that each law is inherently tied for understanding to its specific legal environment. The second reason relates to emissions trading schemes more specifically, and the tendency to regard these as imposable

---

[196] Commission of the European Communities, 'Communication from the Commission on Smart Regulation in the European Union', COM(2010) 543 final 2.

[197] Weatherill, 'Challenge of Better Regulation' (n 183) 4.

[198] Commission to the European Communities, 'Commission Working Paper on Better Regulation and the Thematic Strategies for the Environment', COM(2005) 446 final, 2.

[199] Communication, 'Better Regulation' (n 164).

across various public law regimes. This is clearly seen in the context of the EU ETS, which, as a regulatory idea stems from the US and was imposed top-down following the EU's commitment to fight climate change as set out in the Protocol. Moreover, the EU ETS is believed to establish a straightforward model for emission trading that is predicted to build on and create a global emissions trading scheme. The argument here is that these legal 'travels' must be set in their legal context, and any assumed direct borrowing of legal regimes rejected – both on the basis of procedural differences between the EU ETS and the international climate change treaties, and legal culture.

By setting out snapshots of the 'multi-layered'[200] and complex legal culture in which the EU ETS is implemented, focusing on the legal interactions between the internal market, the judiciary and environmental law, I have explained why it is impossible to consider any environmental market operating in the EU context neutral, or equally imposable in other jurisdictions. Albeit mere sketches, these snapshots highlight that market discourses in the EU are caught in a spider web of considerations of creating prosperity and competitiveness but also securing integration and environmental protection within the framework of the Treaty competences. Thus, market regulation, which tends to be tied to state measures, is not only concerned with pushing 'back the frontiers of the state'[201] but also with establishing a 'social market economy' in which social and environmental protection is safeguarded. This means that when EU-wide markets are discussed, they exist in a broader legal framework in which a multitude of rationales are followed – not all strictly economic.

Similarly, the snapshots show that debates on environmental law are tightly tied to the internal market; that is, laws in the EU are implemented that can stimulate the internal market and that, moreover, are in legal conformity to it. Any legal reforms, as shown, are equally fixed to the legal structure of the EU, and bound to constitutional principles, such as the subsidiarity principle. Here, the important role of the EU Courts in interpreting EU laws must not be undermined. The Courts have the significant task of interpreting laws, and in doing so they construct markets, as well legitimising their rationale. Ultimately, this chapter demonstrates that it should be impossible to talk about the EU market regime in a neutral fashion, or to overlook the particular market rationale and institutional framework specific to the EU.

---

[200] Description borrowed from D Nelken, 'Disclosing/Invoking Legal Culture: An Introduction' (1995) 4 *Social and Legal Studies* 435, 438. Nelken explains that legal culture is multilayered in the sense that it includes legal norms, legal institutions and their infrastructure, as well as social behaviour and the 'legal consciousness' in creating and applying laws. Similarly Harlow suggests that law and culture can be presented as 'an onion, whose skins can be stripped away to reveal deeper layers'. C Harlow, 'Voices of Difference in a Plural Community' (2002) 50 *American Journal of Comparative Law* 339, 349.
[201] M Egan, *Constructing a European Market* (Oxford University Press, Oxford, 2001) 2.

V. Conclusion

The snapshots of EU legal culture in this chapter are not meant to establish a complete picture of the EU legal order nor of the interactions between market creation, the progressive role of the EU Courts and environmental law therein. What these snapshots do make clear, however, is that the legal role and construction of an environmental regime, such as the EU ETS, can only be determined and appreciated by a close contextual analysis of the terms of the particular legal culture in which the regime is set up. What I will demonstrate in the next two chapters is the utility of the *Economic Efficiency,* the *Private Property Rights,* and the *Command-and-Control* models in law, and how the relevance of the models to discussions about the EU ETS depends on legal culture.

4

Unpacking EU Emissions Trading Discourses (I): The Commission

I. Introduction

In the previous chapter I argued that the EU emissions trading scheme is inevitably an expression of EU legal culture and, as such, demands to be studied in its EU law context. What I now wish to do is to show how this regulatory concept is understood in the EU legal order. The bulk of this examination will be carried out in the two following chapters; here the focus is on demonstrating how emissions trading is identified at the EU level by policy- and lawmakers,[1] and in the next chapter by the judiciary. My analysis in this chapter is based on a series of documents – Communications, a Green Paper, legislation proposals, Directives, as well as press releases, memos and speeches issued mainly by the Commission on the topic of the EU ETS[2] – onto which I map the *Economic Efficiency*, the *Private Property Rights*, and the *Command-and-Control* models when applicable. In light of this exercise, I make two key points.

First, I demonstrate that the *Economic Efficiency*, the *Private Property Rights* and the *Command-and-Control* models operate in these discourses, albeit to different degrees and in different periods.[3] The fact that the models are traceable in the Commission's EU ETS-related narrative, however, proves their applicability in law, and demonstrates that EU emissions trading discourses revolve around a set of questions similar to the general emissions trading debates examined in chapter two – namely, how to allocate regulatory power between the emissions market and the state, and how to define tradable rights in emissions allowances in legal terms. This stands as evidence that the common query in emissions trading discussions in theory, as well as in practice, is a trichotomy of legal questions relating to the role of the state, the market and the legal status of tradable emissions rights.

Second, I demonstrate that over the course of emissions trading debates in the EU, the understanding of emissions trading is far from straightforward. This

[1] Here the Commission.
[2] These documents are fully referenced in section II(B).
[3] The *Economic Efficiency Model* appears most often in these discourses, while the *Command-and-Control Model* emerges primarily in the preliminary discussions on emissions trading. The *Private Property Rights Model*, on the other hand, is relevant chiefly as a consideration voiced by the industry.

regulatory strategy plays various roles and is employed for a bouquet of different reasons: from that of ensuring cost-effective implementation of international law, to creating significant economic opportunities for the Union and its Member States by following a particular regulatory agenda of creating Better Regulation,[4] to centralising regulatory powers and adopting a stronger regulatory framework with the aim of creating 'freer markets' through more rules.[5] In highlighting these regulatory themes – some of them discussed already in the previous chapter – the emphasis is not on the reasons *why* emissions trading in the EU materialised. Indeed, studies of the so-called 'pregnancy period'[6] that eventually resulted in the 'birth' of the EU ETS exist elsewhere.[7] Instead I intend to highlight a different, albeit related, point which is that the various rationales that underpin the EU emissions trading regime are culture-specific,[8] and similarly to the previous chapter, show that as such, this trading regime and any evaluation thereof, is inevitably a reflection of EU legal culture.

In order to map the *Economic Efficiency,* the *Private Property Rights* and the *Command-and-Control* models onto the Commission's EU ETS-related discourses, section II first examines the institutional identity of the Commission and the role that the Commission plays in the EU legal order as the legislative initiator. This legal background complements the discussion on legal culture outlined in the previous chapter and aims to explain how the EU constitutional law framework allows the Commission to play a vital role in the introduction and shaping of emissions trading, and in light of this, explain why it is important to study the Commission's understanding of the EU ETS. In the same section, the legislative history of the EU ETS is briefly summarised with the objective of highlighting the Commission's role therein, as well as orienting the discussion on the key docu-

---

[4] The definition of the Better Regulation agendas, as explained in the previous chapter, is difficult to pin down but it often includes, as its aims, deregulation, simplifying legislation, and reducing administrative burdens so as to facilitate economic growth and create jobs. Commission of the European Communities, 'Communication from the Commission on Better Regulation for Growth and Jobs in the European Union', COM(2005) 97 final.

[5] The 'freer market, more rules' concept is the underpinning idea of market-creation and regulation in the EU. S Vogel, *Freer Markets, More Rules: Regulatory Reform in Advanced Industrial Countries* (Cornell University Press, Ithaca, 1996). This idea is further developed in section III(C)(2).

[6] J Wettestad, 'The Making of the 2003 EU Emissions Trading Directive: An Ultra-Quick Process due to Entrepreneurial Proficiency?' (2005) 5 *Global Environmental Politics* 1, 10.

[7] See ibid, J Lefevere, 'A Climate of Change: An Analysis of Progress in EU and International Climate Change Policy' in J Scott (ed), *Environmental Protection: Environmental Law and Governance* (Oxford University Press, New York, 2009) 171, 183–87, C Damro and P Luaces Méndez, 'Emissions Trading at Kyoto: From EU Resistance to Union Innovation' (2003) 12 *Environmental Politics* 71, M Braun, 'The Evolution of Emissions Trading in the European Union – the Role of Policy Networks, Knowledge and Policy Entrepreneurs' (2009) 34 *Accounting, Organizations and Society* 469, D Ellerman, F Convery and C de Perthuis, *Pricing Carbon: The European Union Emissions Trading Scheme* (Cambridge University Press, Cambridge, 2010).

[8] This is not to say that all possible rationales behind the adoption of the EU ETS are discussed in this chapter. For instance, Schaik and Schunz argue that emissions trading was introduced in the EU legal order, inter alia, so as to fulfil the sustainable development agenda and follow the precautionary principle. See L van Schaik and S Schunz, 'Explaining EU Activism and Impact in Global Climate Politics: Is the Union a Norm- or Interest Driven Actor?' (2012) 50 *Journal of Common Market Studies* 169. The point is rather that whatever reason, it is tied to the EU legal context.

ments that are examined in this chapter and onto which I map the three models. Next, in section III, I explore EU emissions trading discourses, as voiced by the Commission through various press releases, memos, and speeches, as well as in its Communications and a Green Paper concerning emissions trading, and proposals for Directives on emissions trading. By mapping the *Economic Efficiency*, the *Private Property Rights,* and the *Command-and-Control* models onto these documents, I show that variations exist in the Commission's understanding of the purpose and construction of an emissions trading scheme in the EU, and point to how in practice the models' applicability depends on legal culture and various EU-specific regulatory agendas. Subsequently, in section IV, I evaluate these findings, and in the final part, section V, set out the conclusion.

II. The Institutional Identity of the Commission and its Treatment of Emissions Trading as a Regulatory Concept

The role and the legal construction of the EU emissions trading regime is shaped by EU legal culture, particularly by the institutional identity of the Commission in initiating legislation and its ability to influence the form and content of laws in the EU jurisdiction. This section aims to further illustrate this argument from the viewpoint of EU constitutional law, and in light of these considerations, account for the reasons why I examine and apply the *Economic Efficiency*, the *Private Property Rights,* and the *Command-and-Control* models to the Commission's EU ETS- related discourse.

At the outset of this section it is important to stress that the mapping exercise carried out in this chapter is deliberately limited in scope and does not examine any ETS-related narrative of the Council, the Parliament, the Member States, the industry, or, any of the non-governmental organisations (NGOs) – indeed, actors that played a crucial part in the process of adopting emissions trading as part of the EU's *acquis communutaire*.[9] This is because the intention with the mapping exercise is not to examine the EU ETS per se, nor to provide a full illustration of how and why this regulatory regime was established in the EU legal context. Rather the intention is to show that emissions trading is a complex regulatory concept that can be understood and applied in various ways – even within a single jurisdiction and by a particular institution. Targeting this particular objective means that it is sufficient to examine only a selection of EU ETS narratives, which in the case of this chapter is the ETS-related discourse of the Commission.

---

[9] The impact of the various actors are particularly clear in the decision-making process, see J Skjærseth and J Wettestad, *EU Emissions Trading: Initiation, Decision-Making and Implementation* (Ashgate Publishing, Burlington, 2008) ch 5.

A. The Constitutional Role of the Commission

The Commission plays a major role in the EU legal order and is described to operate 'at the very heart of the European Union'.[10] Article 17 TEU provides a list of
various legislative, executive and judicial functions that are entrusted to the
Commission, specifying that the Commission 'shall promote the general interest
of the Union and take appropriate initiatives to that end'.[11] The Commission's
legislative role is to initiate Union legislative acts, which according to Article 17(2)
TEU, is a power that the Commission ultimately monopolises.[12] These proposals
may take a variety of forms but effectively, the Commission can decide therein
whether the Union ought to legislate and, if so, in what legal form and content, as
well as which implementing procedures the proposal should embody.[13] Thus to
examine the Commission's proposal on emissions trading, as is done in this chapter, is to study the key preliminary visions of the EU emissions trading regime and
how it is thought to fit the EU legal order.

   This policy-initiating feature of the Commission is coupled with judicial
powers that enable the Commission to supervise legislation to ensure its proper
implementation across the Union and to bring actions against Member States
that fail to comply with EU law.[14] In this regard the Commission is thought of as
the 'guardian of the Treaties',[15] helping to ensure the effectiveness of EU law. In
the next chapter, the EU ETS cases that are brought by the Commission before the
CJEU are scrutinised. Here it is useful to note that the Commission's judicial
powers indicate that it is relevant to understand the meaning that the Commission
gives the emissions trading regime not only in its legislative proposals but more
generally, as it is the Commission that overlooks whether emissions trading
occurs in accordance with EU law.

   Moreover, the Commission has certain executive powers, including the task of
negotiating on behalf of the EU in international agreements and cooperation with
third countries.[16] In developing and agreeing on the Kyoto Protocol – that led to

---

   [10] S Douglas-Scott, *Constitutional Law of the European Union* (Pearson Education, Harlow, 2002)
53.
   [11] Weiler explains that the key aim of the Commission is, and has been since the Treaty of Rome, to
safeguard and promote further integration in Europe. J Weiler, *The Constitution of Europe: 'Do the New
Clothes Have an Emperor?' and Other Essays on European Integration* (Cambridge University Press,
Cambridge, 1999) 64. On a similar point see Commission of the European Communities, 'Communication
prior to the Laeken European Council, The Future of European Union – European Governance:
Renewing the Community Method', COM(2001) 727 .
   [12] Art 17(2) TEU states that 'Union legislative acts may only be adopted on the basis of a Commission
proposal, except where the Treaties provide otherwise'.
   [13] G Majone, *Dilemmas of European Integration: The Ambiguities and Pitfalls of Integration by Stealth*
(Oxford University Press, Oxford, 2009) 78.
   [14] Art 17(1) TEU states that the Commission 'shall oversee the application of Union law under the
control of the Court of Justice of the European Union'. This procedure is set out in Art 258 TFEU.
   [15] As such, the Commission tends to be seen as the 'motor' of integration for the EU, see P Craig and
G de Burca, *EU Law: Text, Cases and Materials* (5th edn, Oxford University Press, Oxford, 2011) 37.
   [16] The Commission's executive powers also include power of implementation, as well as managing
the budget, Art 17(1) TEU. N Nugent, *The Government and Politics of the European Union* (Oxford

the idea of emissions trading being implemented in the EU – the Commission is said to have played an extraordinarily strong role therein,[17] although it did not formally represent the Union.[18] What this highlights is the Commission's engagement, from the very start, to debates concerned with emissions trading, and it maintained a strong, advocatory role in the enactment and implementation of this trading scheme in the EU – a role that has earned the Commission the title of 'a particularly resourceful "midwife"'[19] that helped deliver the EU ETS. Although this analogy indicates that the Commission did not 'conceive' the EU ETS – as indeed the Directive on emissions trading was adopted by the Council and the Parliament, as explained below – its role in introducing emissions trading to the EU is, nonetheless, significant.[20]

The discussion above highlights two important points. First, it illustrates the Commission's strong commitment to the EU ETS – both as a result of its constitutional identity and due to a broader interest in the EU ETS as a regulatory strategy. Second, it shows the Commission as a 'filter' through which all EU legislative acts must pass, and which, as such, is an important 'internal' component of the EU legal culture. As the Commission thus stands at the centre of affairs with regard to the EU ETS, its narrative on this topic is clearly a useful case study.

To talk about the Commission as a 'single-minded institution'[21] in this sense is, nevertheless, misleading, as this is a fragmented, diverse and pluralistic institution similar to that of the EU as a whole.[22] In fact, preparing the proposal for the EU ETS involved numerous consultation sessions with a range of officials from different Directorate Generals (DG) in the Commission, including that of the Environment, Trade, Internal Market, Enterprise, Transport and Energy, and

University Press, Oxford, 2006) 186–87. Note that the term 'executive' power may be misleading, as the Commission's function in this regard is not entirely state-like but limited to the scope of the Treaty. A Dashwood and D Wyatt, *European Union Law* (5th edn Sweet & Maxwell, London, 2006) 41.

[17] The Commission is reported to have acted as a 16th Member State in this regard. Y Slingenberg, 'The International Climate Policy Developments of the 1990s: The UNFCCC, the Kytoto Protocol, the Marrakech Accords and the EU Ratification Decision' in J Delbeke (ed), *EU Energy Law: The EU Greenhouse Gas Emissions Trading Scheme* (Claeys & Casteels, Leuven, 2006) 15, 23.

[18] The way in which the EU is represented in international environmental negotiations is often through an *ad hoc* and informal negotiation arrangement that speaks from behind the Presidency's nameplate. The role of the Commission in the internal negotiation processes is that it intervenes and is often influential in providing know-how and expertise, see T Delreux, 'The EU as an Actor in Global Environmental Politics' in A Jordan and C Adelle (eds), *Environmental Policy in the EU: Actors, Institutions and Processes* (Routledge, Abingdon, 2013) 287, 294.

[19] Wettestad, 'The Making of the 2003 EU Emissions Trading' (n 6) 2.

[20] Moreover, the Commission is understood to be the 'guardian of the scheme's [EU ETS] integrity and credibility' following its implementation. S Dimas, EU Environment Commissioner, 'Nairobi: Prospects for the Future' (Speech, 30 November 2006) www.eu-un.europa.eu/articles/es/article_6546_es.htm, accessed 14 October 2012.

[21] J Peterson and E Bomberg, *Decision-Making in the European Union* (Macmillan, London, 1999) 39.

[22] Douglas-Scott, *Constitutional Law of the EU* (n 10) 63, E Schön-Quinlivan, 'The European Commission' in A Jordan and C Adelle (eds), *Environmental Policy in the EU: Actors, Institutions and Processes* (Routledge, Abingdon, 2013) 95, 97 and 106–07.

Economic and Financial Affairs,[23] which highlights the complexity both of the EU constitutional regime and emissions trading as a regulatory concept. Yet throughout these deliberations within the Commission, the EU ETS has become, as mentioned in chapter one, the 'Commission's baby',[24] for the support of which the Commission has rallied forcefully. What this chapter aims to do is to examine different visions of the EU ETS that the Commission has promoted, and depict the distinct ways in which the Commission understands emissions trading as a regulatory concept.

B. An Overview of the Legislative Journey of the EU ETS

The legislative history of the EU ETS is short but dynamic. A debate on implementing emissions trading in the EU legal order first took form following the Kyoto Protocol and as the Commission issued two consecutive Communications on this topic.[25] This regulatory idea was significantly developed in the Green Paper on emissions trading that the Commission published in 2000,[26] and further built on in the Commission's Proposal for an emissions trading Directive set out in 2001.[27] Here the Commission argued that the Directive on emissions trading must be based on Article 192 TFEU, meaning that the Council and the Parliament must act in accordance with the ordinary legislative procedure in order to adopt such a legal text. This environmental competence has been amended by the Lisbon Treaty[28] but at the time when the EU ETS was deliberated, Article 192 TFEU provided the Parliament with two readings of the proposal: the first in which the Parliament gives its opinion to the Council, and the second if the Council fails to agree on all points that the Parliament proposes as part of the first-reading amendments.[29] The Parliament's first reading of the EU ETS proposal started in spring 2002, in which the Parliament set forward over 80 suggested amend-

---

[23] Ellerman, Convery and Perthuis, *Pricing Carbon* (n 7) 26–27. More precisely, nine officials are listed as having been particularly useful in advocating for and helping during the adoption and implementation process of the EU ETS, see J Delbeke (ed), *EU Energy Law: The EU Greenhouse Gas Emissions Trading Scheme* (Claeys & Casteels, Leuven, 2006) viii.

[24] J Wettestad, 'European Climate Policy: Toward Centralized Governance?' (2009) 26 *Review of Policy Research* 311, 313.

[25] Commission of the European Communities, 'Communication from the Commission on Climate Change – Towards an EU Post-Kyoto Strategy', COM(1998) 353 and Commission of the European Communities, 'Communication from the Commission on Preparing for Implementation of the Kyoto Protocol', COM(1999) 230.

[26] Commission of the European Communities, 'Green Paper on Greenhouse Gas Emissions Trading Within the European Union', COM(2000) 87 final.

[27] Commission of the European Communities, 'Proposal for a Directive of the European and of the Council establishing a scheme for greenouse gas emission allowance trading within the Community and amending Council Directive 96/61/EC', COM(2001) 581 final.

[28] Art 294 TFEU sets out the post-Lisbon rules on the ordinary legislative procedure, allowing the Parliament three readings.

[29] In case the Council fails to agree to the first-reading amendments, the Parliament has the legislative power to veto, approve or amend the Council's response: Art 251 EC.

ments.[30] Together with the Council, nonetheless, a quick compromise was found and in June 2003, following a second reading, and an 'ultra-quick process' of legislating,[31] a common position was established and the Directive adopted.

However, by 2008, and only three years after the start of emissions trading in the EU, the Commission set forward a proposal, as part of a broader climate and energy package,[32] to revise the Directive.[33] Again, legislative action occurred quickly, and the revised Directive was adopted only six months later during the first Parliamentary reading. These amendments mark a clear shift in the allocation of regulatory power between the Member States and the Commission with regard to managing the emissions trading scheme. Having initially vested wide discretion in the Member States and the private sector to decide, inter alia, the total national level of emissions allowances intended for trading, as well as the monitoring and the verification rules relating to the EU ETS, the revised Directive centralises such decisions by allocating them to the Commission.[34] The revised Directive will be effective from 2013 onwards.[35]

This brief overview is significant for two reasons. First, it roughly lists the chronological legal developments of the EU ETS and second, it puts into context the key documents that are examined in this chapter, which include, more precisely, the two Communications, the Green Paper on emissions trading, the proposal for a Directive on emissions trading, as well as the proposal for a revised Directive on emissions trading, and the two emissions trading Directives. The way these are examined in this chapter is explained next.

III. Mapping Models onto the Commission's EU ETS-Related Discourses

In this section my concern is to study emissions trading as understood by the Commission. This analysis is carried out by analysing the texts listed above, as

---

[30] Skjaerseth and Wettestad, *EU Emissions Trading* (n 9) 43 and ch 5. In short, the Parliament wanted to further widen the coverage of the proposed Directive and to change the allocation methods. The Council, however, pushed for the original version of the proposal to be adopted. Council Directive 2003/87 establishing a scheme for greenhouse gas emission allowance trading within the Community and amending Directive 96/61, [2003] OJ L275/32.

[31] Wettestad, 'The Making of the 2003 EU Emissions Trading' (n 6).

[32] Commission of the European Communities, 'Communication from the Commission on 20 20 by 2020 – Europe's Climate Change Opportunity', COM(2008) 30 final.

[33] Commission of the European Communities, 'Proposal for a Directive amending Directive 2003/87/EC so as to improve and extend the greenhouse gas emission allowance trading system of the Community', COM(2008) 16 final.

[34] As examined in S Bogojević, 'The EU ETS Directive Revised: Yet Another Stepping Stone' (2009) 11 *Environmental Law Review* 279.

[35] Directive 2009/29 of the European Parliament and of the European Council amending Directive 2003/87 so as to improve and extend the greenhouse gas emission allowance trading scheme of the Community, [2009] OJ L140/63.

well as press releases, memos and speeches issued by the Commission concerning these documents and their meaning, and applying the *Economic Efficiency*, the *Private Property Rights* and *Command-and-Control* models thereto when applicable. The purpose of this exercise is to test the applicability of the models in law, and thereby examine the different ways that the allocation of regulatory power between central control (here, the Commission) and the market is understood, as well as the legal status of rights in emissions allowances. What the findings in this chapter show is that over the course of history of the Commission's emissions trading discourses, emissions trading as a regulatory concept is framed differently and applied for a variety of regulatory purposes, including to ensure compliance of international law, create better regulation and create 'more rules' so as to establish a 'freer' carbon market. To each regulatory purpose, different models are seen to emerge and to different extents, which ultimately proves that whether a particular model applies in law is determined by legal culture.

Before I start, it is useful to briefly recap the images of emissions trading projected by the *Economic Efficiency*, the *Private Property Rights* and the *Command-and-Control* models. The *Economic Efficiency Model* sees emissions trading as an economic opportunity and profit centre. In this context, the role of the state is to set out the necessary legal framework to enable these opportunities to arise, including the creation of property rights in emissions allowances, as this is thought to safeguard investments and allow the market to make the most cost-effective decisions concerning the allocation of regulatory responsibility. As the following study shows, this model frequently operates in the Commission's discussions on the EU ETS.

The *Private Property Rights Model* views emissions trading as a pollution control system that allows private property holders to replace governments' control over common resources. Here, the role of the state is restricted to structuring the market by creating tradable private property rights in emission allowances, which the property rights holders are able to allocate on their own terms according to free market forces. Because the Commission sees emissions trading as a legal regime imposed top-down, the *Private Property Rights Model* rarely emerges in the Commission's narrative. However, it is relevant to certain stakeholders' views, which the Commission considers, concerning how emissions trading in the EU ought to be constructed.

In the *Command-and-Control Model*, emissions trading is presented as an administrative regime where regulatory powers are centralised and the market used as a device to ensure cost-effective compliance and implementation of regulatory obligations. This model is present chiefly in the Commission's initial official descriptions of emissions trading in the EU but there are hints of its re-emergence. As is explained below, the carbon crash that occurred in 2006, coupled with the financial market crises, have contributed to a general push toward stronger regulatory oversight of markets, which is reflected in current debates on emissions trading.

Here it is important to also set out a couple of caveats. First, this investigation is not meant to be an exhaustive account of the above-mentioned documents. Rather

I focus on highlighting areas in which the models operate, thus emphasising descriptions of the regulatory power divisions between the market and the states and the legal status of rights in emissions allowances. To a large extent, this is a fairly technical and repetitive exercise but the repetition is a necessary part of being able to highlight the fact that the models exist in the above-mentioned discourses, and as such, in law. Similarly, this chapter does not provide a full portrayal of the legislative developments of the EU ETS. For instance, the adoption of Directive 2008/101,[36] which the EU uses to extend the scope of the EU ETS to include emissions of greenhouse gases from the aviation sector, is omitted.[37] The reason is that this chapter, as well as this book as a whole, is a collection of snapshots of emissions trading discourses – as opposed to a definite account of a particular emissions trading regime. These snapshots illustrate diverse understandings of emissions trading as a regulatory concept, thereby demonstrating the complexity of this regulatory strategy, and highlighting the need to reorient the common approach to thinking, debating and constructing emissions trading schemes.

A. Emissions Trading as an Implementation Mechanism

Emissions trading first emerged in the EU as part of a regulatory narrative concerning the development of regulatory strategies to help the Union and its Member States comply with their commitments under the Kyoto Protocol. In two Communications – 'Climate Change – Towards an EU-Post Kyoto Strategy'[38] and 'Preparing for Implementation of the Kyoto Protocol'[39] – the Commission focused on the practical dimension of the implementation of the Protocol and, in this context, included emissions trading as a compliance mechanism that is able to secure regulatory goals.

These Communications are rarely, if ever, discussed in much detail, or beyond being referred to as the official documents in which the Commission 'first broached the idea of a European trading regime'.[40] Examining the context in

---

[36] Directive 2008/101 of the European Parliament and of the European Council amending Directive 2003/87 so as to include aviation activities in the scheme for greenhouse gas emission allowance trading within the Community, [2009] OJ L8/3.

[37] In short, Directive 2008/101 infers that, subject to certain limitations in Annex I, all flights taking off from or landing at an EU airport are covered by the emissions trading scheme from 2012 onwards. In effect, both ETS-covered flights, and flights that generate emissions outside EU airspace are now required to surrender emission allowances for each tonne of carbon dioxide generated during the relevant flight. This has proven controversial, not the least due to the unilateral nature of this measure, see J Scott and L Rajamani, 'EU Climate Change Unilateralism' (2012) 23 *European Journal of International Law* 469, S Bogojević, 'Legalising Environmental Leadership: A Comment on the CJEU's Ruling in C-366/10 on the Inclusion of Aviation in the EU Emissions Trading Scheme' (2012) 24 *Journal of Environmental Law* 345.

[38] Communication, 'Towards an EU Post-Kyoto Strategy' (n 25) 17.

[39] Communication, 'Preparing for the Implementation of the Protocol' (n 25) 1.

[40] F Convery and L Redmond, 'Market and Price Developments in the European Union Emissions Trading Scheme' (2007) 1 *Review of Environmental Economics and Policy* 88, 89. The Communications

which emissions trading entered regulatory discourses in the EU is nonetheless significant: it shows that emissions trading was primarily narrated in strict compliance terms and seen as a regulatory strategy that the Member States could implement, through public law, to conform to international law obligations. The emphasis on the national governments and the Commission to ensure that emissions trading is implemented highlights that the equally state-centred *Command-and-Control Model* operates in these discourses. This point is illustrated by next analysing the two Communications in turn.

1. *Communication: Climate Change – Towards an EU-Post Kyoto Strategy*

The primary concern of this Communication is the proceedings of a strategy to implement the Protocol and, as such it is hailed as an 'important and necessary step towards fulfilling the reduction commitments undertaken by the European Union in Kyoto'.[41] It is in light of international environmental law that emissions trading was first introduced to the EU legal order as a regulatory mechanism and was thought to grant compliance with international legal commitments. Here emissions trading is examined in a broader framework of flexible mechanisms and explained to function by each party being assigned emissions amounts that they are able to sell, or alternatively, buy extra from other parties, depending on whether they have spare capacity and are willing to sell, or need an additional emissions allowance.[42] This is a straightforward view of how emissions trading works but the Communication flags that any steps to implement international law, and create domestic emissions trading schemes will depend on public law measures.

This public law aspect, and thus also the *Command-and-Control Model*, appears in this Communication by its listing of significant implementation and management roles for the Member States and the Commission in realising an EU emissions trading scheme. For instance, Member States are understood to 'have a major role'[43] in ensuring compliance with the Protocol and implementing emissions trading as a domestic measure. Moreover, the Commission is said to be required to coordinate, in accordance with the principle of subsidiarity, the actions of the Member States, and harmonise the trading schemes to the extent necessary to ensure proper functioning of the internal market.[44] In this regard, the Commission is assigned the task of creating a common framework in which key

---

are similarly described in C Carlarne, *Climate Change Law and Policy: EU and US Approaches* (Oxford University Press, Oxford, 2010) 171.

[41] EUROPA, 'Climate Change – The Commission Presents the First Steps in the Post-Kyoto Strategy to Meet the Commitments of the European Union' (Brussels, 3 June 1998) europa.eu/rapid/pressReleasesAction.do?reference=IP/98/498&format=HTML&aged=1&language=EN&guiLanguage=en, accessed 2 October 2012.

[42] Communication, 'Towards an EU Post-Kyoto Strategy' (n 25) 17.

[43] This is clearly manifested in the fact that the Member States are individually responsible for their targets under the Burden Sharing Agreement. ibid 7, 17–18.

[44] ibid 18.

principles and minimum rules are set out so as to avoid distortion of competition and discrimination.[45] This sets the idea of emissions trading in a broad public law framework, in which emissions trading, similarly to the *Command-and-Control Model*, depend on the multi-level governance of the Union for its existence and function. This is a picture that is state-oriented and clearly distinct from, for instance, the *Private Property Rights Model* that imagines emissions trading as enabling private property holders to manage common resources in lieu of public law systems.

The *Command-and-Control Model* emerges also in the Communication's main criterion of cost-effectiveness, which is listed for the development of a post-Kyoto implementation strategy. Notably, this criterion is not defined in strict economic terms, which would have been aligned with the *Economic Efficiency Model*. Instead it signifies the benefit of reducing pollution, as well as reducing costs of meeting regulatory targets, which in total are deemed 'important for economic and political acceptability of a strategy'.[46] The Commission concludes that only a comprehensive, as opposed to multiple domestic, trading system can grant such cost-effectiveness.[47] The important point to make here is that the understanding of cost-effectiveness of emissions trading strongly resembles that found in the *Command-and-Control Model*, where it similarly infers reduced administrative costs in relation to reducing pollution, and not profit per se, as suggested by the *Economic Efficiency Model*.

What this Communication shows is a *Command-and-Control Model*-related understanding of emissions trading. Here, emissions trading is projected as a regulatory mechanism that promises cost-effective compliance with international law and is heavily reliant on the Member States for implementation and the Commission in ensuring that it accords with the EU legal order. Thus, similarly to the *Command-and-Control Model*, emissions trading is projected as an effective administrative regime.

2. Communication: Preparing for Implementation of the Kyoto Protocol

The second Communication leading up to the implementation of emissions trading in the EU served as an agenda at the 1999 European Council Summit in Cologne, which dealt with regulatory solutions to environmental challenges, including climate change.[48] This document aimed to press Member States to 'go beyond moral commitments'[49] and 'show leadership'[50] by implementing the Protocol. As such, the narrative is predominantly promotional and focuses on the practical dimensions of

---

[45] ibid 18–19.
[46] ibid 6.
[47] ibid 6, 18.
[48] ibid.
[49] EUROPA, 'Preparing for Implementation of the Kyoto Protocol' (Brussels 19 May 1999) europa. eu/rapid/pressReleasesAction.do?reference=IP/99/333&format=HTML&aged=1&language=EN&gui Language=en, accessed 2 October 2012.
[50] Communication, 'Preparing for the Implementation of the Protocol' (n 25) 1.

this implementation. Although emissions trading is not discussed in any depth here, it is part of the debate concerning the implementation procedure of the Protocol,[51] and similarly to the previous Communications, it is understood as a regulatory device that can help achieve the specific regulatory goals cost-effectively.

The *Command-and-Control Model* appears in this Communication in its suggestion that emissions trading in the EU context is a mere regulatory exercise, or 'the best preparation for the Community and its Member States'[52] ahead of the launch of an international emissions trading scheme, which was set to start in 2008. The Commission clarifies that flexible mechanisms, including emissions trading, are 'fundamentally different'[53] from the way the Union and its Member States have organised their environmental policy over the last decades, and as such, gaining experience in this regard is seen as necessary. This new regulatory regime, however, is not envisioned as a substitute for government control, as the *Private Property Rights Model* would have it; rather the Commission is understood to play a vital role in ensuring that any trading scheme complies with the internal market, and in particular with state aid and competition rules, as well as existing EU environmental law policies and other international regimes, such as the World Trade Organization (WTO).[54] This shows that emissions trading is seen to rely on existing public law structures of the EU for its implementation and to function in much similarity to the *Command-and-Control Model*.

Overall the focus of this Communication is on securing the implementation of the Protocol, and in this context, emissions trading plays the secondary role of helping the Union and its Member States with such compliance. Here emissions trading is neither an economic entity, as envisioned in the *Economic Efficiency Model*, nor a substitute for regulatory control, as suggested by the *Private Property Rights Model*. Instead it is portrayed as a compliance mechanism that is tied to a regulatory goal and legal framework, similarly to emissions trading narratives traced in the *Command-and-Control Model*.

3. Theme: Implementation

The above-mentioned Communications clearly orbit a broader theme of implementing the Protocol. This is not surprising if attention is shed on the Commission's broader regulatory objectives at the time. In particular, following the Commission's official 1996 implementation strategy,[55] implementation was of major concern in European environmental law.[56] The Commission argued that achieving goals of

---

[51] ibid 15.
[52] ibid 15.
[53] ibid 14.
[54] ibid 14, 18.
[55] Commission of the European Communities, 'Communication on Implementing Community Environmental Law', COM(96) 500 final.
[56] Implementation is here seen as being at the 'sharp end' of the processes of EU environmental policy, A Jordan, 'The Implementation of EU Environmental Policy: A Policy without a Political Solution?' (1999) 17 *Environment and Planning* 69.

high level of environmental protection 'is only possible if our legal framework is being properly implemented',[57] and stressed that regulatory attention must focus on the application and enforcement procedures, as opposed to creating legal frameworks as an end in itself.[58] In fact, ahead of the international environmental law negotiations at the Rio 'Earth Summit', which later led to the Kyoto Protocol, the Commission highlighted implementation of environmental law and policy as 'an important area for discussion',[59] and pressed to have its own implementation policy 'firmly in place by that time'.[60] Connecting this implementation strategy to the narrative in the above-mentioned Communications helps to explain why emissions trading was framed in a particular way during this period, which highlights that emissions trading was employed as part of a broader EU-specific regulatory agenda.

Another important point to pick up here is that the two Communications offer no other role to emissions trading outside of the implementation framework; it is neither a 'profit-centre', as described in the *Economic Efficiency Model*, nor a replacement for bureaucratic control over rights to use common resources, as explained in the *Private Property Rights Model*. Emissions trading is instead placed in a public law framework in which the Member States and the Commission play vital roles in securing implementation and conformity of emissions trading to existing regulatory regimes – a vision symmetric to the *Command-and-Control Model*.

B. Emissions Trading as an Economic Opportunity: Decentralised Approach

Next the Commission issued a Green Paper and a proposal for an emissions trading Directive that also led to the adoption of the Directive on emissions trading – documents that I now analyse. Over the course of these speedy legislative proceedings, the Commission's discourse on emissions trading changed significantly: having previously adhered to the *Command-and-Control Model*-type of considerations, debating emissions trading in strict compliance terms with regard to international law, it shifted to the *Economic Efficiency Model*-style of deliberation, emphasising economic opportunities that emissions trading is thought to realise. Emissions trading is here understood as putting 'a price tag on the

---

[57] ibid 1.

[58] E Hattan, 'The Implementation of EU Environmental Law' (2003) 15 *Journal of Environmental Law* 273, 286, L Krämer, *EC Environmental Law* (4th edn, Sweet & Maxwell, London, 2000) 281.

[59] Commission, 'Implementing Community Environmental Law' (n 55) 6. The idea that emissions trading is easily implemented was furthered by proponents of emissions trading also at the global stage, see R Baldwin, M Cave and M Lodge, *Understanding Regulation: Theory, Strategy, and Practice* (2nd edn, Oxford University Press, Oxford, 2012) 200.

[60] ibid. A potential implementation deficit was understood to undermine the entire climate change project and the EU's role therein, see A Lenschow, 'Studying EU Environmental Policy' in A Jordan and C Adelle (eds), *Environmental Policy in the EU: Actors, Institutions and Processes* (Routledge, Abingdon, 2013) 49, 66.

environment to make it interesting for companies to reduce pollution',[61] and in this way correct 'mis-pricing by making the value of clean air apparent'.[62] This narrative loudly echoes the *Economic Efficiency Model*, in which emissions trading is similarly described in economic terms as a mechanism that internalises externalities, or in other words, the cost of pollution.

According to the *Economic Efficiency Model*, the role that the state plays in emissions trading regimes is establishing the required legal framework, leaving it to the market to allocate regulatory responsibility the way it sees fit, or according to market forces. Similarly, the Commission portrays emissions trading as part of a broader stream of liberalisation of markets in the EU,[63] where the regulators play a central part in establishing 'necessary structures'[64] for trade but ultimately allows the market to find the best solution and place for emission reductions.[65] Visions of this heavily decentralised and 'results-oriented'[66] – as opposed to rule-based – emissions regime are explored next against the backdrop of the three documents listed.

1. Green Paper on Emissions Trading

The Green Paper launched an EU-wide consultation process concerning the scope, function and structure of emissions trading and gave 'flesh and blood'[67] to the idea of how such a trading scheme ought to work in an EU legal context. In this document the Commission moves away from a *Command-and-Control Model*-type of deliberation, as seen above in the two Communications, and instead the *Economic Efficiency Model* emerges in two particular respects: in the Commission's reliance on the private sector to organise the actual emissions trading, and the portrayal of emissions trading as an economic opportunity.

---

[61] M Wallström, EU Environment Commissioner, 'From Lisbon to Gothenburg: The Business Agenda for Sustainable Development' (Seminar on The European Policy Agenda during the Swedish Presidency, London, 15 March 2001) europa.eu/rapid/pressReleasesAction.do?reference=SPEECH/01/126&format=HTML&aged=1&language=EN&guiLanguage=en, accessed 3 October 2012.

[62] This description is by Vis, who was one of the main authors of the Green Paper, see P Vis, 'Basic Design Options for Emissions Trading' in J Delbeke (ed), *EU Energy Law: The EU Greenhouse Gas Emissions Trading Scheme* (Claeys & Casteels, Leuven, 2006) 39, 46–47. Lefevere, who was part of the team that drafted the proposal for the Directive, describes the EU emissions trading scheme to be concerned with 'getting the prices right'. J Lefevere, 'Greenhouse Gas Emission Allowance Trading in the EU: A Background' (2003) *Yearbook of European Environmental Law* 149, 173.

[63] M Wallström, EU Environment Commissioner, 'Sustainable Energy' (Energieforum, Berlin, 1 February 2001) europa.eu/rapid/pressReleasesAction.do?reference=SPEECH/01/45&format=HTML&aged=1&language=EN&guiLanguage=en, accessed 3 October 2012.

[64] EUROPA, 'Commission Proposes Ratification of Kyoto Protocol and Emissions Trading System' (Brussels, 23 October 2011) europa.eu/rapid/pressReleasesAction.do?reference=IP/01/1465&format=HTML&aged=1&language=EN&guiLanguage=en, accessed 3 October 2012.

[65] S Dimas, EU Environment Commissioner, 'Winning the Fight Against Climate Change: An EU Perspective' (Speech at the University of Cambridge, 13 June 2008) europa.eu/rapid/pressReleasesAction.do?reference=SPEECH/08/333&format=HTML&aged=1&language=EN&guiLanguage=en, accessed 3 October 2012. On a similar note see J Delbeke, 'The Emissions Trading Scheme (ETS): The Cornerstone of the EU's Implementation of the Kyoto Protocol' in J Delbeke (ed), *EU Energy Law: The EU Greenhouse Gas Emissions Trading Scheme* (Claeys & Casteels, Leuven, 2006) 1, 1.

[66] Delbeke, ibid 7.

[67] Skjaerseth and Wettestad, *EU Emissions Trading* (n 30) 39.

The Commission's focus on the private sector is evident in its discussions about the coverage of emissions trading. In the above-mentioned Communications, emissions trading is debated in the context of international law, and as such, is state-focused. Here, however, the Commission's rhetoric changes tune and looks to the private sector. Vis – one of the main authors of the Green Paper[68] – explains that operating emissions trading at the level of individual companies is 'unquestionably the correct level to maximise the economic advantage of emissions trading, as companies know their own costs much better than government officials know the costs for a country as a whole'.[69] The fact that economic factors are emphasised in the discussion of the applicability of emissions trading suggests that the *Economic Efficiency Model* operates here.

The private sector is also thought vital to the process of allocating allowances. The Green Paper devotes considerable time to this issue and considers various possibilities for the allocation of permits, once the cap has been set, in particular comparing free allocation and auctioning. It concludes, however: 'How the permits are allocated does not affect the environmental outcome'.[70] The reason is, the Commission explains, that emissions trading does not reduce emissions, it 'simply provides incentives to find the lowest cost of achieving a given amount of emissions reductions'.[71] It is in fact this mechanism – allowing the market rather than the government to determine the allocation of regulatory obligations via price signalling – that is identified as the strength of emissions trading regimes. The view is that companies can 'better judge the business opportunities of trading, and their potential benefit in engaging in this market'.[72] This description echoes the *Economic Efficiency Model* in two specific ways. First, it praises price as the standard according to which business opportunities, as well as the allocation of regulatory obligations, ought to be measured, and second, it takes emissions trading to adhere to a particular market-mentality in which regulatory power is entrusted to the private sector, not in order to cut emissions but to make a profit. This particular framing of emissions trading as a business opportunity distinguishes this type of discourse from the *Command-and-Control Model,* which furthers emissions trading not for the sake of profit but so as to ensure administrative effectiveness and thus compliance.

However, the fact that the Commission clearly relies on the market to organise emissions trading does not mean, nor does the *Economic Efficiency Model* suggest, that there is no role envisioned for the state in emissions trading regimes. Wallström, the former EU Commissioner for Environment, explains that emissions trading is not 'just about leaving things to market forces, but creating the

[68] J Delbeke (ed), *EU Energy Law: The EU Greenhouse Gas Emissions Trading Scheme* (Claeys & Casteels, Leuven, 2006) xiii.
[69] Vis, 'Basic Design Options for Emissions Trading' (n 62) 40–41.
[70] Green Paper (n 26) 17.
[71] ibid 10.
[72] ibid 8.

necessary structures in which cost-effective incentives can exist'.[73] These 'structures' include, for instance, determining the cap for the total level of emissions that are tradable during a particular period,[74] deciding on rules for emissions allocations, and enforcing penalties – tasks that according to the Green Paper fall within the scope of Member State regulatory discretion.[75] This description of the role of the Member States is obviously different from the *Private Property Rights Model* that imagines deregulation as an act of substituting government control, and the *Command-and-Control Model* that promotes regulatory power to be centralised, as opposed to merely creating 'structures' for trading.

While the Member States are prescribed to set out the relevant 'structures' of emissions trading, the Green Paper is unclear as to what role the Commission ought to play in the emissions trading regime. It lists varying degrees of possible interventions in the emissions market, ranging from mere oversight, so as to ensure conformity between existing EU laws and emissions trading practices, to full harmonisation.[76] The Green Paper explains that the level of intervention ultimately depends on the extent to which common rules are required to safeguard the internal market[77] but that the Commission, in any case, is entrusted with its traditional role under the Treaty of being able to bring the Member States before the court in case of non-compliance.[78] It is relevant to note that the Green Paper refers to different model-types in proposing the different roles for the Commission: it pictures the *Command-and-Control Model* in case of full harmonisation, and the *Economic Efficiency Model* in identifying the Commission's discretion as limited to mere oversight of conformity between EU and national ETS-related laws. Ultimately, the Green Paper suggests two distinct governance structures for emissions trading for the EU legal context.

The *Economic Efficiency Model* appears in the Green Paper also in the way that the Commission promotes emissions trading as an economic opportunity for the private sector. In particular, it predicts all companies involved in emissions trading to incur lower compliance costs, as market-actors will be able to decide whether to increase production and buy additional emissions allowances, or reduce production and sell surplus allowances.[79] On this basis, the Commission sees this trading system as 'an immediate monetary incentive'[80] for the private

---

[73] M Wallström, former EU Environment Commissioner, as quoted in EUROPA, 'Climate Change: Commission Launches European Climate Change Programme and Advocates Twin-Track Approach for Reducing Emissions' (Brussels, 8 March 2000) europa.eu/rapid/pressReleasesAction.do?reference=IP/00/232&format=HTML&aged=1&language=EN&guiLanguage=en, accessed 3 October 2012.

[74] Caps are thus understood to be set according to the 'overall environmental ambitions' of the Member States. Green Paper (n 26) 7–8.

[75] Green Paper (n 26) 24–25. Vis, 'Basic Design Options for Emissions Trading' (n 62) 47.

[76] Green Paper (n 26) 12.

[77] ibid.

[78] ibid 26.

[79] ibid 11.

[80] A Runge-Metzger, 'The Potential Role of the EU ETS for the Development of Long-Term International Climate Policies' in J Delbeke (ed), *EU Energy Law: The EU Greenhouse Gas Emissions Trading Scheme* (Claeys & Casteels, Leuven, 2006) 253, 271.

sector to reduce their emissions, sell surpluses and invest in newer and more energy-efficient installations. This innovation-enhancing picture of emissions trading is significant, in particular because shortly before the EU ETS started operating, it was brought to the Commission's attention that it would cost approximately €600 billion to refurbish and replace old power stations across Europe.[81] Its assertion that emissions trading is 'an opportunity for new technology and for modernising our [Union's] economies',[82] indicates that the Commission sees emissions trading not only as a cheap but also profit-generating solution to an expensive problem. The focus on the economic benefits of emissions trading confirms the existence of the *Economic Efficiency Model* in the Commission's narrative.

Similarly to the above-mentioned Communications, the Green Paper pushes for a quick start of emissions trading and 'before the international emissions trading scheme is launched'.[83] In the Communications, however, the reason for this head start is phrased as 'preparation'[84] for international trading while here the focus is on the economic opportunities that such head start grants. More specifically, gaining 'a leading edge'[85] in using the regulatory mechanism compared to other Parties to the Protocol is deemed crucial not due to any green politics[86] but because, and as Kelemen explains, it grants competitive advantages, including being able to influence and set up rules for an international emissions trading scheme by which competitors must abide.[87] Later, and following the US refusal to ratify the Protocol by mid-2001, becoming a 'forerunner'[88] and taking advantage of this 'window of opportunity'[89] to exert global climate policy leadership became increasingly important in the Commission's rhetoric.[90] What this shows is that emissions trading is presented as an economic opportunity – not only to the private sector but also to the Member States, which overlaps with the economic focus found in the *Economic Efficiency Model*.

[81] ibid 260.

[82] M Wallström, former EU Environment Commissioner, as quoted in EUROPA, 'EU Will Fight to Save Kyoto Agreement' (Brussels, 4 April 2001) europa.eu/rapid/pressReleasesAction.do?reference= MEMO/01/121&format=HTML&aged=1&language=EN&guiLanguage=en, accessed 3 October 2012.

[83] Green Paper (n 26) 10.

[84] See n 52.

[85] Green Paper (n 26) 10.

[86] Kelemen notes that starting in the 1990s – as the awareness of the threat of climate change mounted – domestic political pressure for action to curb green house gases increased in the EU. He argues that the calculus for European policymakers was clear: given that voters would in any case demand domestic action on climate change, it was preferable to promote action at an international level that would force the EU's competitors to undertake costly measures as well. D Kelemen, 'Globalizing EU Environmental Regulation' (2007) 17 *Journal of European Public Policy* 335, 339.

[87] ibid.

[88] Vis, 'Basic Design Options for Emissions Trading' (n 62) 40.

[89] Skjaerseth and Wettestad, *EU Emissions Trading* (n 30) 7.

[90] eg Dimas exclaimed that emissions trading promises the EU to become 'a strong global player'. S Dimas, EU Environment Commissioner, 'Climate Change – International and EU Action' (Speech at the Climate Change Conference, Prague, 31 October 2008) europa.eu/rapid/pressReleasesAction.do?reference =SPEECH/08/570&format=HTML&aged=0&language=EN&guiLanguage=en, accessed 19 September 2012.

The discussion above shows that the Commission positions emissions trading in an economic rationale, analogous to the *Economic Efficiency Model*.[91] Here the Commission projects emissions trading as an economic opportunity that works against the backdrop of a decentralised legal framework, which, in accord with the *Economic Efficiency Model,* is understood to create economic opportunities by allowing the market to find solutions to regulatory dilemmas, including to whom to allocate regulatory responsibility.

2. *Proposal for Directive on Emissions Trading*

The Green Paper was widely well received amongst stakeholders[92] and quickly thereafter the Commission put forward its proposal for a Directive on emissions trading. This document raises numerous issues related to emissions trading, including the environmental value of such a regulatory strategy.[93] Here, however, I focus on the Commission's description of what role the private sector, the Member States and the Commission are seen to play in the emissions trading regime, and the way in which this understanding overlaps with the *Economic Efficiency Model.*

First to note is that this proposal does not stipulate how a market in emissions allowances ought to be organised but instead promotes a deregulatory approach where market forces, as opposed to any central authority, decide on market practices. The Commission explains that[94]

> it [the Commission] is convinced that market structures will arise once the obligations are clear, and the allowances for fulfilling the obligations are established. The Commission wishes the organisation of the market in allowances to be left open to solutions driven by the private sector.

Two points are important to highlight here. First, the fact that it is the private sector, rather than the Member States, or the Commission that is supposed to determine market practice shows that regulatory trust is vested with markets to deliver optimal regulatory solutions.[95] This view is distinct from the *Command-and-Control Model* that is critical toward any suggestion of the ability of markets to work on their own but symmetric to the *Economic Efficiency Model* that understands emissions markets to be able to provide solutions to regulatory dilemmas. Second, the Commission clarifies that it sees emissions allowances as 'obligations' rather

---

[91] This does not mean that the Protocol is no longer relevant to these debates, nor that the assumed implementability of emissions trading is no longer part of the Commission's policy deliberations, see, eg Green Paper (n 26) 4.

[92] M Mehling, 'Emissions Trading and National Allocation in the Member States – An Achilles' Heel of European Climate Policy?' (2005) 5 *Yearbook of European Environmental Law* 113, 124.

[93] Proposal for a Directive on emissions trading (n 27) 4.

[94] ibid 16.

[95] Meadows explains that the reliance on the private sector in this regard is thought to facilitate price discovery, generate greater liquidity, and flexibility, see D Meadows, 'The Emissions Allowance Trading Directive 2003/87/EC Explained' in J Delbeke (ed), *EU Energy Law: The EU Greenhouse Gas Emissions Trading Scheme* (Claeys & Casteels, Leuven, 2006) 63, 86.

than, for instance, private property rights. On this basis, the Commission's vision of emissions trading regimes is distinct from the *Private Property Rights Model* that understands the creation of private property rights as the centre point of trading schemes.

Similarly to the Green Paper, this proposal prescribes a decentralised emissions trading regime in which the Commission plays its traditional role of guarding the Treaty and ensuring that national ETS-measures are in conformity with EU law,[96] whilst the Member States are entrusted the task of determining the structure of the trading scheme and deciding on issues, such as the allocation of allowances and the level of cap.[97] In the view of Runge-Metzger, who was in the Commission's 'boiler room'[98] where the proposal for this Directive was drafted, this particular regulatory structure of the EU ETS is 'pragmatic and practical'.[99] More precisely, he explains that in 'liberal market economies it is logical to hand the responsibility down from governments to private sector players',[100] and in this sense, provide the state only with powers required to establish such a market. What this shows is that key Commission officials envision the emissions market to equate a liberal market, which indicates that the *Economic Efficiency Model* operates in these discourses.

The discussion above shows that the Commission proposes an emissions trading regime that is decentralised: the Member States are vested with decision-making powers to construct the emissions market whilst the Commission is thought to play a supervisory role of ensuring that this construction process adheres to general EU law. It is instead the private sector that is recruited to help drive the trading scheme by, for instance, establishing market practices. In short, the Commission projects emissions trading along the lines of the *Economic Efficiency Model*.

3. Directive on Emissions Trading

The Directive on emissions trading was adopted in 2003, which, as explained in the previous chapter, is a short legal text that establishes a 'basic architecture'[101] for emissions trading in an EU context. Mapping the models onto this legal document shows that the *Economic Efficiency Model* exists therein, and more precisely,

[96] Proposal for a Directive on emissions trading (n 27) 5–6, 11. This means that the Commission needs to ensure that any measure falls in conformity with state aid laws, competition laws, as well as existing environmental laws in the EU jurisdiction.

[97] ibid.

[98] This description is borrowed from F Convery, 'Reflections – The Emerging Literature on Emissions Trading in Europe' (2009) 2 *Review of Environmental Economics and Policy* 121, 123. Convery also counts Jos Delbeke, Mattio Vainio and Peter Zapel as key players in proposing and later implementing the EU ETS.

[99] Runge-Metzger (n 80) 271.

[100] ibid.

[101] J de Cendra de Larragán, 'Too Much Harmonization? An Analysis of the Commission's Proposal to Amend the EU ETS from the Perspective of Legal Principles' in M Faure and M Peeters (eds), *Climate Change and European Emissions Trading: Lessons for Theory and Practice* (Edward Elgar, Cheltenham, 2008) 53, 57.

in the prescription of the allocation of regulatory power between the Member States and the Commission. While the Directive leaves the definition of the legal status of emission allowances open-ended, the Commission seems to understand this right both according to the *Command-and-Control Model;* that is, as a particular regulatory authorisation, and in conformity with the *Economic Efficiency Model* that understands emissions allowances to be part of a cost-efficiency-centred regime. The operation of these two models in the Directive and the Commission's related narrative appears as described next.

The Directive sets out an emissions trading scheme that functions on the pre-condition that all relevant installations must hold a permit in order to be able to engage in industrial activities listed in Annex I.[102] Permit-holders are authorised to emit greenhouse gases from their installations[103] but they must also bear certain obligations, such as monitoring and reporting emissions, as well as surrendering allowances equal to the total emissions of the installation in each calendar year.[104] What is not equally clear from the Directive is the specific legal status of emissions permits, as these are nowhere explicitly defined. As such, the Directive leaves the door to speculations wide open and some scholars, and the industry, have suggested that these ought to be considered as property rights.[105] Vis, however, sees emissions permits as mere obligations:[106]

> It is the idea that emissions trading represents an appropriation of 'property rights' or entitlements that appears to some people as contrary to natural justice. However, such a sentiment makes a number of assumptions that may be wrong. Emissions trading is just a mechanism that allows for greater economic efficiency.

The fact that Vis draws links between emissions permits and economic efficiency suggests that these rights are viewed in accordance with the *Economic Efficiency Model* where the key role of emissions allowances is to secure market-transactions and allow the emissions market to allocate regulatory obligations in the most cost-effective way. Meadows, however, argues that the precise legal nature of this permit is 'a type of tradable administrative authorisation',[107] which highlights an element of the *Command-and-Control Model* in how certain Commission officials think about this issue. On this basis, it may not be altogether clear what type of rights the Directive creates. What, nonetheless, seems obvious from both Vis' and Meadows' description is that these are not defined in accordance with the *Private Property Model* where the right to common resources is thought of in private property right terms and as a symbol of liberty.

---

[102] These include, eg the production and processing of ferrous metals. Directive (n 30) Art 4 and Annex I.

[103] Art 6(1) ibid.

[104] Art 6(1)–(2) ibid.

[105] MJ Mace, 'The Legal Nature of Emission Reductions and EU Allowances: Issues Addressed in an International Workshop' (2005) 2 *Journal of Energy and Environmental Law* 123, 124–26, C Bourbon-Seclet, 'A Tentative Agenda to Improve the "Gold Standard" and Bring Some Contractual Certainty into the System: Part 2' (2008) 23 *Journal of International Banking Law and Regulation* 302, 306.

[106] Vis, 'Basic Design Options for Emissions Trading' (n 62) 41.

[107] Meadows, 'Emissions Allowance Trading Directive Explained' (n 95) 83.

The key provision that determines the power allocation between the Member States and the Commission with regard to constructing the emissions market is codified in Article 9, which is one of the most litigated sections of the Directive.[108] It provides that:

> For each period . . . each Member State shall develop a national plan [NAP] stating the total quantity of allowances that it intends to allocate for that period and how it proposes to allocate them.

This stipulation builds on similar formulations in the Green Paper and the proposal on emissions trading concerning the cap-setting procedure,[109] which plainly entrusts the Member States to determine the total national cap and decide on the initial emissions allowances allocation. According to Vis, the advantage with this system of predetermining national caps and the initial allocations of emissions allowances is that the emissions trading scheme thereafter is 'simpler to administer'[110] and 'the market can develop with greater certainty'.[111] What Vis suggests is that the rationale behind the process of constructing the emissions market is similar to the *Economic Efficiency Model* where market certainty similarly stands as the centrepiece of emissions trading deliberation.

However, this construction process of the emissions market has a public law dimension. The Directive obliges the Member States to follow objective and transparent criteria, listed in Annex III of the Directive, in determining their caps, as well as taking into account the Common Burden Sharing Agreement and public opinions, which, together must be notified to and approved by the Commission.[112] Article 9(3) stipulates the implications of these requirements:

> Within three months of notification of national allocation plans . . . the Commission may reject that plan, or any aspect thereof, on the basis that it is incompatible with the criteria listed in Annex III or with Article 10.

This provision suggests that the Commission holds a strong supervisory role in the process of emissions market creation, with potential veto-rights to national caps. Vis, however, explains that the relationship between the Commission and the Member States in this regard is one of cooperation, and that the Commission's role is 'overseeing the Directive'[113] rather than encroaching on the discretion of

---

[108] Art 9 (n 30) is discussed in detail in ch 5.

[109] Green Paper (n 26) 7–8, Proposal for a Directive on emissions trading (n 27) 5–6.

[110] Vis, 'Basic Design Options for Emissions Trading' (n 62) 41.

[111] Vis explains that ultimately this leads also to greater certainty in the environmental outcome, ibid. Scholars, however, have questioned the extent to which this type of market construction and division of regulatory discretion in fact contributes to market certainty, J de Cendra de Larragán, *Distributional Choices in EU Climate Change Law and Policy: Towards a Principled Approach?* (Kluwer Law International, Alphen aan den Rijn, 2011) 6, C Kemfert and others, 'The Environmental and Economic Effects of European Emissions Trading' in G Michael, R Betz and K Neuhoff (eds), *National Allocation Plans in the EU Emissions Trading Scheme: Lessons and Implications for Phase II* (Earthscan, London, 2007) 441, 443.

[112] Art 9(1) (n 30).

[113] P Vis, 'The First Allocation Round: A Brief History' in J Delbeke (ed), *EU Energy Law: The EU Greenhouse Gas Emissions Trading Scheme* (Claeys & Casteels, Leuven, 2006) 187, 202.

the Member States. This shows that the *Economic Efficiency Model* operates in the Commission's understanding of the scope of central control over the emissions trading scheme. This also suggests that the Commission's view in this regard is distinct both from the *Command-and-Control Model,* in which the central government ment is viewed to play a key role in the construction of markets, and the *Private Property Rights Model* that aims to substitute any bureaucratic control of common resources.

What the short descriptions above highlight is the Commission's understanding of the Directive on two particular issues: the legal status of emissions permits, and the regulatory power allocation between the Commission and the Member States with regard to emissions trading. In these discourses, visions of the *Command-and-Control Model,* as well as the *Economic Efficiency Model* appear in explanations of the legal definition of rights, as encompassed in emission permits. However, in relation to the issue of regulatory power allocation, the Commission aligns with the *Economic Efficiency Model* in promoting limited central control of the emissions market. The fact that two models are applicable in this context seems to follow as a result of the open texture of the Directive.

4. Theme: Better Regulation

During the period in which the Green Paper, the proposal for emissions trading and the Directive were deliberated, the Commission shifted from a compliance-based narrative, found in the two previously mentioned Communications, to economically oriented rhetoric. In particular, the regulatory focus swung from state-focused debates on the implementation of environmental laws, to creating environmental law regimes reliant on the private sector, capable of yielding economic opportunities and helping further the competitiveness of European economies. Emissions trading in this context is presented as a suitable regulatory option, as the Commission indeed understands this trading scheme to create a rich 'carbon economy',[114] and establish new layers of financial activities, such as carbon management.[115] This type of regulatory consideration echoes the *Economic Efficiency Model,* which similarly emphasises profits that emissions trading is thought to promise.

The documents and the discourse highlighted above also demonstrate that the Commission promotes a heavily decentralised legal structure for the emissions trading regime in which the Member States are trusted to set out the necessary framework for emissions trading and the market to establish the relevant trading

---

[114] Slingenberg defines a carbon-economy as a place where scarcity leads to a 'new society conscious of its contribution to climate change', see Y Slingenberg, 'Community Action in the Fight Against Climate Change' in M Onida (ed), *Europe and the Environment: Legal Essays in Honour of Ludwig Krämer* (Europa Law Publishing, Groningen, 2004) 211, 222.

[115] This includes services, such as, accounting, reporting and setting up brokering houses, as well as carbon trade analysts. Runge-Metzger, 'Potential Role of the EU ETS' (n 80) 271–72.

practices. This view is captured by Dimas, the former Commissioner for Environment, who, in reflecting over the Directive, concludes that[116]

> [i]n many instances where the legal framework [the Directive] leaves Member States a choice to either let market forces work or bring in an administrative rule, we have seen administrative rules being chosen. I fear our regulatory minds have re-entered via the back-door in the implementation process of what is a market-based instrument. I do believe we should put more trust in a well-designed market instrument and in more instances give the market the benefit of the doubt.

Dimas' obvious frustration over the implementation of the Directive illustrates two important and correlated points. First, it shows that the hope behind this type of decentralisation is that it will enable markets to operate freely and unfettered by regulation. Second, it demonstrates that market-based instruments, such as the emissions trading scheme, are believed to be able to operate without the interference of Member States, or the Commission. The picture of emissions trading that Dimas thus depicts is one that clearly corresponds to the *Economic Efficiency Model*.

The fact that the Commission sees emissions trading as an opportunity for the EU to improve its competitiveness and stimulate its economy, shows that the Commission is inspired by ecological modernisation.[117] Similarly, the Better Regulation agenda clearly penetrates the Commission's thinking about the functionality of the EU emissions trading regime; for instance, in understanding the EU trading regime as a decentralised governance structure that is able to operate according to market forces. In the previous chapter, I highlighted some of the key leitmotifs underpinning these regulatory trends, including their objective to adopt simple regulation so as to help the industry grow, advance and gain a competitive edge.[118] Indeed, Wiener explicitly refers to the EU ETS as an example of Better Regulation in the EU.[119] The significance of this is twofold. First, it helps to explain why the shift in the Commission narrative changed to focus on economic considerations. Second, and more importantly, it shows that although the *Economic Efficiency Model* and to an extent also the *Command-and-Control Model* appear in the examined documents, their presence can only be understood and explained with reference to the relevant regulatory aims that form part of EU legal culture.

---

[116] S Dimas, EU Environment Commissioner, 'The EU Emissions Trading Scheme – Looking Back and Forward' (Speech at the Green Week Debate on Emissions Trading Scheme, Brussels, 2 June 2005) europa.eu/rapid/pressReleasesAction.do?reference=SPEECH/05/317&format=HTML&aged=1&language=EN&guiLanguage=en, accessed 3 October 2012.
[117] Schaik and Schunz (n 8) 176.
[118] See J Holder and M Lee, *Environmental Protection, Law and Policy* (2nd edn, Cambridge University Press, Cambridge, 2007) 165 and ch 3, section III(C).
[119] J Wiener, 'Better Regulation in Europe' (2006) 59 *Current Legal Problems* 447.

C. Emissions Trading as an Economic Opportunity: Centralised Approach

Only three years after the start of emissions trading in the EU, the Commission proposed to revise the EU ETS regime, leading to a 'major overhaul'[120] of the Directive. Although the Commission judged the first period of emissions trading to have been 'generally positive',[121] in 2006, and following the first publication of verified emissions data from 2005, it surfaced that a surplus of about 44 million emission allowances for 2005 had been issued by national authorities and allowed on the emissions market, causing prices for emissions allowances to plummet.[122] By 2009 the Directive had also been the subject of over 40 proceedings before the EU Courts,[123] which had 'a bearish impact'[124] on the emissions market. Moreover, with the global financial crisis casting a shadow over the use of markets, including carbon markets,[125] the Commission set forward a proposal for the revision of the emissions trading regime in June 2008, with the aim to refine and improve the EU ETS 'in the light of experience gathered'.[126] Having been adopted only six months later, the revised Directive is set to take full effect in 2013.

During the course of the revision proceedings, the Commission retained its focus, seen in the previous period of ETS-discourse, on economic benefits that emissions trading is thought able to help the EU harvest. For instance, the EU ETS is described to be able to secure leadership for the EU in becoming a green economy, boosting 'energy efficiency and security'[127] for the EU. Also, according to Hedegaard, the EU Commissioner for Climate Action, the EU ETS is a key strat-

[120] Connie Hedegaard, EU Commissioner for Climate Action, 'Europe's View on International Climate Policy' (Speech at Harvard Kennedy School, Cambridge, 20 September 2010) europa.eu/rapid/pressReleasesAction.do?reference=SPEECH/10/468, accessed 3 October 2012.

[121] Delbeke, 'The EU ETS' (n 65) 10. Similarly, Vis, 'Basic Design Options for Emissions Trading' (n 62) 212, describes the first allocation period of emissions allowances to have passed 'remarkably well'.

[122] R Betz, K Rogge and J Schleich, 'EU Emissions Trading: An Early Analysis of National Allocation Plans for 2008–12' in M Grubb, R Betz and K Neuhoff (eds), *National Allocation Plans in the EU Emissions Trading Scheme: Lessons and Implications for Phase II* (Earthscan, London, 2007) 361, 366. The Member States are understood to have committed themselves to a 'race-to the bottom', see J Wettestad, P Eikeland and M Nilsson, 'EU Climate and Energy Policy: A Hesitant Supranational Turn?' (2012) 12 *Global Environmental Politics* 67, 76.

[123] Carlarne, *Climate Change Policy* (n 40) 175. The EU ETS case law will be analysed in more detail in the next chapter, here it is important to note that the numerous pending litigation was 'nowhere mentioned' in the Commission's working group on the review of the EU ETS, see J Scott, 'The Multi-Level Governance of Climate Change' in P Craig and G de Burca (eds), *The Evolution of EU Law* (2nd edn, Oxford University Press, Oxford, 2011) 805, 813. However, as the next chapter explains, with the revisions of the EU ETS adopted, the Commission did express hope that this would decrease the number of cases before the EU Courts.

[124] J Maurici, 'Litigation and the EU Emissions Trading Scheme' (2009) 50 *Environmental Law* 7, 24.

[125] L Lohmann, 'Regulatory Challenges for Financial and Carbon Markets' (2009) 2 *Climate and Carbon Law Review* 161.

[126] Proposal for a revised Directive on emissions trading (n 33) 2.

[127] Commission of the European Communities, 'Communication from the Commission on International Climate Policy Post Copenhagen', COM(2010) 86 final, 4.

egy for the EU in 'a global race for green growth and jobs'.[128] Moreover, the fact that one of the key changes in the revised emissions trading regime is a shift from the standard method of allocating allowances free of charge to auctioning has also meant that the Commission sees this regulatory regime as a new source of government revenue able to help control government deficit.[129] These visions are an expression for the *Economic Efficiency Model* in the sense that they emphasise the economic opportunities in emissions trading, or more precisely; creating a so-called 'win-win'[130] regulatory scenario where environmental law helps to stimulate the economy.[131]

The key difference between the Commission's narrative in the documents previously examined and those presently under consideration lies in the understanding of the extent to which the state ought to intervene in emissions market operations. In discussing the framework of the emissions market, the Commission concludes that:[132]

> [T]he market needs to have an appropriate market oversight framework. Such a framework needs to secure fair and efficient trading conditions for all market participants through transparency requirements as well as by preventing and sanctioning market misconduct, in particular insider dealing and market manipulation. Such a framework should also provide safeguards to minimise the risk that the carbon market is used as a vehicle for other illegal activities, such as money laundering or VAT fraud.

This statement highlights two important points. First, it shows the Commission pushing for market control and regulated market practices, which indicates that the Commission has moved away from the view that markets ought to be given 'the benefit of the doubt',[133] as Dimas previously has urged. Yet it also demonstrates that the Commission is only aiming at readjusting the *framework* of emissions market regulation, rather than seeking to entirely harmonise or standardise these market practises, as would have been suggested had the *Command-and-Control Model* been applicable here. Indeed, the Commission explains that the proposal to revise the Directive 'balances the needs for economic efficiency and

---

[128] Hedegaard (n 120).

[129] S describes emissions trading as a new source for revenue, suggesting that it can be useful particularly in financing climate change projects. Stavros Dimas, EU Environment Commissioner, 'Climate Change: Commission Sets out Global Finance Blueprint for Ambitious Action by Developing Nations' (Speech to Press Points, Brussels, 10 September 2009) europa.eu/rapid/pressReleasesAction. do?reference=SPEECH/09/380&format=HTML&aged=1&language=EN&guiLanguage=en, accessed 3 October 2012. Similar analysis is set out in J Werksman and C Voigt, 'Editorial' (2009) 2 *Carbon and Climate Law Review* 133, 133.

[130] Stavros Dimas, EU Environment Commissioner, 'Climate Change in Times of Economic Crises – the Path to a Successful Climate Conference in Copenhagen' (Speech at the Humbold University, Berlin, 6 July 2009) europa.eu/rapid/pressReleasesAction.do?reference=SPEECH/09/332&format= HTML&aged=1&language=EN&guiLanguage=en.

[131] The Stern Review, in particular, is seen to have helped further this view in the EU, see N Stern, *The Economics of Climate Change: The Stern Review* (Cambridge University Press, Cambridge, 2007), as explained in Baldwin, Cave and Lodge (n 59) 194 and Schaik and Schunz (n 8) 176.

[132] Commission of the European Communities, 'Communication Towards an Enhanced Market Oversight Framework for the EU Emissions Trading Scheme', COM(2010) 796 final, 2.

[133] Dimas, 'The EU Emissions Trading Scheme – Looking Back and Forward' (n 116).

fairness between sectors and Member States, and will provide more predictability for industry'.[134] The Commission thus expressed the need to strengthen the emissions market through increased regulatory oversight but in a balanced way and so as to safeguard competition and enhance investments.[135] This view overlaps with the *Economic Efficiency Model,* which similarly prescribes heavier state intervention in emissions markets when transaction costs are high and the market fails to deliver the most cost-effective results.

During the review process, the Commission identifies four main points in the current Directive on emissions trading to discuss and potentially revise: the scope of the Directive, the level of harmonisation, compliance and enforcement mechanisms, and links to third countries.[136] Here I examine only the revised rules relating to the cap-setting procedures, auctioning, and the harmonisation of monitoring and verification rules, as these are thought to alter the balance of power allocation under the current Directive.

1. Directive on Emissions Trading Revised

One of the key changes under the revised Directive is the centralisation of the cap-setting procedure. The revised Directive amends Article 9 in this regard and stipulates that from 2013 onwards a Community-wide quantity of allowances will be issued each year, decreasing by a linear factor of 1.74 per cent.[137] Such a decrease is understood to lead to an overall reduction of emissions at least 20 per cent below 1990 levels by 2020, which is a goal that the Commission targets in its climate change package.[138] As a consequence of this revision, cap-setting powers will be vested with the Commission. This has been called the 'Commission coup',[139] as

---

[134] EUROPA, 'Questions and Answers on the Commission's Proposal to Revise the EU Emissions Trading Scheme' (23 January 2008) europa.eu/rapid/pressReleasesAction.do?reference=MEMO/08/35, accessed 3 October 2012.
[135] Survey as conducted and presented in M Åhman and K Holmgren, 'New Entrant Allocation in the Nordic Energy Sectors: Incentives and Options in the EU ETS' in G Michael, R Betz and K Neuhoff (eds), *National Allocation Plans in the EU Emissions Trading Scheme: Lessons and Implications for Phase II* (Earthscan, London, 2007) 423, 435–36.
[136] Commission of the European Communities, 'Communication on Building a Global Market – Report Pursuant to Article 30 of Directive 2003/87/EC', COM(2006) 676 final, 7.
[137] The level of emissions will compare to the average annual total quantity issued by Member States in their NAPs for the period 2008–12, see revised Directive (n 35) Art 9.
[138] Commission, '20 20 by 2020' (n 32). The EU is also offering to increase its emissions reductions to 30% by 2020 if other major economies in the developed and developing countries commit to undertake global emissions reduction effort, see Commission of the European Communities, Communication, 'Analysis of Options to Move Beyond 20% Greenhouse Gas Emission Reductions and Assessing the Risk of Carbon Leakage', COM(2010) 265 final. Moreover, the EU is offering to increase its emissions reductions to 80–95% by 2050 if other major economies in the developed and developing countries commit to undertake global emissions reduction effort, see Commission of the European Communities, 'Communication from the Commission on a Roadmap from Moving to a Competitive Low Carbon Economy in 2050', COM(2011) 112 final.
[139] J Wettestad, 'Revising EU Emissions Trading: A "Requested Revolution"?' (The European Union and the Fight Against Global Climate Change Lecture Series, 2008) www.fni.no/doc&pdf/jw-081029-ies.pdf, accessed 3 October 2012.

the Commission has monopolised much of the regulatory powers available under the EU emissions trading scheme. This would indeed imply that the *Command-and-Control Model* drives the legal developments with regard to emissions trading. The Commission, however, explains that the reason why these amendments were proposed is the dire impact that the national allocation plans had on the emissions market, proving ineffective both in reaching emissions reduction targets and minimising overall costs of reduction.[140] A central cap, the Commission suggests, provides 'long-term perspective and increased predictability',[141] which is deemed a 'necessity for long-term investments in efficient abatement'.[142] The Commission's attention to the economic impact on the emissions market highlights that it proposes regulatory revision following the rationale of the *Economic Efficiency Model*.

Another far-reaching amendment to the Directive is the change from the current system of so-called 'grandfathering' or, allocating emissions allowances free of charge to auctioning.[143] The Commission proposes auctioning as the basic principle for allocation based on the reason that this allocation system is[144]

> the simplest and generally considered to be the most economically efficient system. This [auctioning] should also eliminate windfall profits and put new entrants and higher than average growing economies on the same competitive footing as existing installations.

This view echoes the *Economic Efficiency Model* in two ways. First, it determines the function of emissions trading based on economic consideration and second, it projects auctioning as the preferred method of emissions allowance allocation, which is in line with the general view of economists.[145] Yet auctioning, as stipulated in the revised Directive, does not allow distribution of permits to be entirely determined by bidding. The Commission is entrusted with the regulation of the timing and the administration of the auctioning process[146] with the aim of ensuring that it is predictable and 'undeniably safe for investments'.[147] Moreover, the Commission is obliged to submit an annual report to the Parliament and the Council on the functioning of the European carbon market, including the process

---

[140] Proposal for a revised Directive (n 33) 2.

[141] ibid 7.

[142] ibid.

[143] Revised Directive (n 35) Art 10 provides that from '2013 onwards, Member States shall auction all allowances which are not allocated free of charge'.

[144] Proposal for a revised Directive (n 33) 14.

[145] Literature on this topic is abundant, see, eg D Ellerman, B Buchner and C Carraro (eds), *Allocation in the European Emissions Trading Scheme: Rights, Rents and Fairness* (Cambridge University Press Cambridge, 2007), C Holderness, 'The Assignment of Rights, Entry Effects, and the Allocation of Resources' in R Epstein (ed), *Economics of Property Law* (Edward Elgar, Cheltenham, 2007), S Weishaar, 'CO2 Emission Allowance Allocation Mechanisms, Allocative Efficiency and the Environment: A Static and Dynamic Perspective' (2007) 24 *European Journal of Law and Economics* 29.

[146] Revised Directive (n 35) Art 10(4). Commission Regulation 1031/2010 of 12 November 2010 on the timing, administration and other aspects of auctioning of greenhouse gas emission allowances pursuant to Directive 2003/87/EC of the European Parliament and of the Council establishing a scheme for greenhouse gas emission allowances trading within the Community, [2010] OJ L 302/1.

[147] Revised Directive (n 35) Art 10(4).

of auctioning.[148] Additionally, the Directive restricts the Member States from using auctioning revenues entirely according to their will; the Directive proposes 50 per cent of the revenue to be invested in nine different climate-related projects,[149] and requires 10 per cent of the total quantity of allowances that are auctioned in the EU as a whole to be distributed amongst certain Member States for the 'purpose of solidarity'.[150] The actual legal implications of these stipulations, and the extent to which the Commission may in fact interfere with auctioning at Member State level are still uncertain.[151] At the very least, what the above shows is that the revised Directive sets out a market-based allocation system with a firm regulatory oversight. This could suggest that the *Command-and-Control Model*-type of considerations operate here but as these provisions were proposed by the Commission so as to stimulate growth, it appears it is the *Economic Efficiency Model* that dominates these deliberations.

It is important to note, however, that the application of auctioning under the Directive is restricted in scope. More precisely, auctioning emission allowances applies only to the power sector; sectors considered carbon sensitive, such as the heating industry, will receive free permits until 2027 according to harmonised EU-wide rules.[152] The Commission sees this restriction as necessary on the basis that it protects certain energy-intensive actors in the EU that are subject to international competition, and that would be put at an 'economic disadvantage' in relation to industries that are not subject to comparable regulation.[153] With the aim of avoiding the over-allocation of free permits to these sectors, the Commission is vested with the regulatory discretion to set benchmarks for free emissions permits.[154] Similarly to the *Command-and-Control Model*, the Commission thus recognises the need to artificially construct competition in the emissions market so as to safeguard the EU industries against its competitors.

Under the revised Directive, the Commission further harmonises the EU emissions trading regime by codifying monitoring and reporting rules,[155] as well as

---

[148] ibid Art 10(5).

[149] Note that the extent of this requirement is uncertain, as Member States are encouraged rather than obliged to invest in these projects, which include instance financing the development of renewable energies and research and development of energy efficiency, see ibid Art 10 (3)(a)–(i).

[150] ibid Art 10(2)(a).

[151] The Commission has, nonetheless, proposed to amend so as to clarify the provisions of the Directive on the timing of auctions of emissions and Commission Regulation 1031/2010, see Commission of the European Communities, 'Proposal for a Decision of the European Parliament and of the Council amending Directive 2003/87/EC clarifying provisions on the timing of auctions of greenhouse gas allowances', COM(2012) 416 final. Commission Regulation amending Regulation (EU) No 1031/2010 in particular to determine the volumes of greenhouse gas emission allowances to be auctioned in 2013–20 (provisional version).

[152] ibid Art 10a.

[153] Proposal for a revised Directive (n 32) 16.

[154] Commission Decision 2011/278/EU of 27 April 2011 determining transitional Union-wide rules for harmonised free allocation of emission allowances pursuant to Article 10a of Directive 2003/87/EC of the European Parliament and of the Council, [2011] L130/1.

[155] Commission Regulation (EU) 601/2012 of 21 June 2012 on the monitoring and reporting of greenhouse gas emissions pursuant to Directive 2003/87/EC of the European Parliament and of the Council, [2012] OJ L181/30.

verification rules.[156] The purpose of this regulatory centralisation, the Commission explains, is to help create an even playing field between market actors across the emissions market. This is thought to contribute to predicable market practices that can 'directly affect investment decisions'.[157] The Commission acknowledges that regulations and detailed rules in this regard may lead to higher administrative costs but it concludes that this outcome is 'justified, as administrative costs in the longer term would be much lower'.[158] This projects the *Economic Efficiency Model*-type of rationale where temporary high costs validate long-term economic solutions.

The discussion above offers a brief overview of the Commission's narrative concerning the revised Directive and its official explanation to some of the key changes stipulated therein. The key implication of the revised emissions trading regime is the centralisation of regulatory powers, which give the Commission a stronger role in managing and overlooking the function of the emissions market. The way in which the Commission interprets this change is similar to the *Economic Efficiency Model* that equally allows for a stronger central managerial role in cases where this helps improve market security and activity.

2. *Theme: Freer Markets, More Rules*

The revised Directive has significantly changed the emissions trading regime: the process of cap-setting is centralised, monitoring and verification methods are standardised, and emissions allowances are, as a general rule, distributed by auction. Considering that these activities are carried out either by the Commission, or under its supervision, the revised emissions trading scheme clearly centralises regulatory powers in the Commission's favour. What the discussion above shows is that the Commission sees these legislative changes as necessary steps in safeguarding the emissions market and inducing confidence in emissions trading – especially following the initial crash in carbon prices. This understanding of heavier regulation for the sake of stabilising markets suggests that the *Economic Efficiency Model*, which similarly appreciates state intervention when the market demands it, operates here.

Thus the key difference between the Commission's narratives here and during the previous period of ETS-debates is the focus on safeguarding economic benefits, which the emissions market is thought to deliver, through a strong regulatory framework. This idea of creating more rules so as to further market activity and integration is a regulatory theme deeply embedded in the EU legal culture. As

---

[156] Commission Regulation (EU) 600/2012 of 21 June 2012 on the verification of greenhouse gas emission reports and tonne-kilometre and the accreditation of verifiers pursuant to Directive 2003/87/EC of the European Parliament and of the Council, [2012] OJ L181/1.

[157] Council of the European Communities, 'Review of the European Union Emissions Trading Scheme' (Council Conclusions, Brussels, 4 July 2007) register.consilium.europa.eu/pdf/en/07/st11/st11429.en07.pdf, accessed 4 October 2012.

[158] Proposal for a revised Directive (n 33) 6.

demonstrated in the previous chapter, the EU is 'regulatory in nature',[159] and the development of the internal market builds upon a strong and expanding regulatory structure. Indeed, Vogel uses the phrase; 'freer markets, more rules' to explain how in the EU legal order, competition and cross-border trade is enhanced via rules and centralised governance.[160] This shows that the way in which the Commission understands the legal developments of emissions trading in the EU is a reflection not only of the *Economic Efficiency Model* but also more broadly of EU legal culture.

IV. Reflections

The analysis above only provides glimpses of how the Commission's understanding of the EU emissions trading scheme and the legal features of this regime have developed over the course of the 10-year period that the above study covers. What these glimpses, nonetheless, show are the different turns that the Commission's ETS-related discourse has taken. In the initial debates, the Commission promotes emissions trading as a promising implementation strategy that can guarantee compliance with international environmental law. At this point, implementation was, as highlighted, one of the Commission's core regulatory concerns. In the two periods of emissions trading deliberation that followed – the first concerning the initial Directive, and the second the revised Directive – the Commission's emphasis shifts from implementation to economic opportunities that emissions trading is thought to realise. Although the focus turns to economic considerations in both, each period sees the Commission present a different picture of how the emissions trading scheme ought to be constructed and managed. In particular, the extent to which the private sector is entrusted with setting out and controlling the actual trading practices differs. In relation to the initial Directive, the Commission shows a deep confidence in the private sector, which ultimately indicates that the Commission sees the EU ETS as a regime where market forces are allowed to allocate, for instance, regulatory responsibility. This vision relates to certain aspects of the Better Regulation agenda, in particular the way in which it depicts the reduction of administrative regulation and deregulation more generally as a way of helping create economic opportunities for EU economies. Discussions of the revised Directive, however, show that the Commission's perception of the extent to which the private sector can remain unregulated in the emissions trading regime has changed. This is clear in how the Commission presses for a stronger market oversight through centralisation of regulatory power, and in the increased number of ETS-related rules and regulations. Establishing more rules in order to stabilise the emissions market and create stability for the relevant market-actors could be seen as forming part of a

---

[159] Ch 3, section III(C).
[160] Vogel (n 5).

general regulatory trend following recent financial turbulences.[161] Even so, it is symptomatic also of a deeper regulatory philosophy of market-creation and regulation in the EU, that is, the idea of enhancing market activity through wide-reaching market-rules. These 'turns' in the Commission's ETS-related narrative may not appear particularly dramatic but they highlight two important points.

First, they demonstrate that the Commission's understanding of emissions trading as a regulatory concept is in flux. This finding may not appear surprising considering that the EU ETS is generally seen to be *in vivo* an 'experiment,'[162] which is stipulated to change[163] and, which is thought of as a 'learning-by-doing' experience.[164] What the analysis above indicates, however, is a slightly different point, which is that the Commission's understanding of the EU ETS is undeniably linked to different regulatory agendas relevant to EU legal culture, and as these change, so does the use and focus of the EU emissions trading regime. Effectively, this shows that emissions trading, as a regulatory concept, derives its meaning from the particular regulatory lens through which law- and policymakers observe it and, as such, the legal culture in which it operates.

Second, the various narratives on this topic establish that different models from chapter two operate here at different times. Notably the *Economic Efficiency Model* surfaces most often over the course of these debates, which may be explained by the fact that the team that drafted the Green Paper, and the remaining official document relevant for the creation of the EU ETS, are mainly economists.[165] The *Command-and-Control Model* appears also but chiefly in state-based discussions, as exemplified by the Communications where the focus is on the implementation and compliance with international environmental law. The *Private Property Rights Model*, on the other hand, seems to be absent from the Commission's ETS-based rhetoric. The obvious reason for this is that the Commission is itself a bureaucratic component and part of a multi-governance regulatory structure that the *Private Property Rights Model* would seek to abolish. The fact that EU law has not developed a sense of 'property'[166] may be another reason for the neglect of the

---

[161] See J Stiglitz, *Freefall: Free Markets and the Sinking of the Global Economy* (Allen Lane London, 2010).

[162] D MacKenzie, *Material Markets: How Economic Agents are Constructed* (Oxford University Press, Oxford, 2009) 166.

[163] Art 30 of the Directive (n 30) stipulates that the scope of the emissions trading regime can be broadened to include additional sectors, and as of 2008, Member States can individually include other greenhouse gases above carbon dioxide in the scheme.

[164] Green Paper (n 26) 10.

[165] Jos Delbeke, head of unit, and Arthur Runge-Metzger, Mattio Vainio, Peter Zapfel and Peter Vis were central to the implementation of the EU ETS and are all economists. Olivia Hartridge is a political scientist and Damien Medows, Yvon Slingberg and Jürgen Lefevere are lawyers. As listed in Ellerman, Convery and de Perthuis, *Pricing Carbon* (n 7) 26.

[166] Art 345 TFEU states that the Treaties 'shall in no way prejudice the rules in Member States governing the system of property ownership'. Manea explains that the fact that the definition and treatment of property are not centralised at the EU level means that the definition and treatment of emissions allowances cannot be easily harmonised across the Union, see S Manea, 'Defining Emissions Entitlements in the Constitution of the EU Emissions Trading System' (2012) 1 *Transnational Environmental Law* 303, 310.

Private Property Rights Model in the EU. This indeed fits the argument of this book that emissions trading schemes are undoubtedly reflections of legal cultures in which they exist.

This is not to say, however, that *Private Property Rights Model*-type of considerations are generally non-existent in the EU ETS-context and not considered by the Commission. For instance, during a stakeholder meeting with the industry and NGOs, the Commission suggested that public authorities ought to be able to intervene in the emissions market so as to 'smooth the peaks and troughs of price fluctuations'.[167] The stakeholders, however, responded by expressing 'mistrust . . . towards the intervention of public authorities in private markets',[168] and in the final proposal for a Directive on emissions, this suggestion is no longer included. These hints of the *Private Property Rights Model* in the stakeholder's view of emissions trading serves to show that although the Commission does not voice this particular model in its own rhetoric, the *Private Property Rights Model* is, nonetheless, part of its deliberation.

There are, however, a number of important limitations to the way in which the models are applied in the analysis above. To start with, and as explained in chapter two, these models are imperfect: they are my own and they reflect the way in which I see emissions trading schemes to be perceived in selected emissions trading scholarship. Mapping these fixed models onto dynamic discourses, such as the Commission's ETS-related debates, is challenging, as it means attempting to categorise the odd rhythms of EU regulatory practice. As a result, the exercise carried out in this chapter is not very smooth, especially as, at times, the models overlap. I am also aware of the fact that the reader may see the models as operating differently in the above-listed discourse. The point, however, is not to argue that a particular model represents the precise way in which the Commission understands emissions trading. My aim is rather to show that different models – albeit to different degrees and at times only as mere hints – operate here, which stands as evidence for two points.

First, it demonstrates that emissions trading discourse in the EU is complex and that even in the narrative of one particular institution, traces of different visions of how emissions trading regimes ought to be constructed and applied, exist. Second, it highlights that the common query in emissions trading scholarship, and more precisely the trichotomy of legal questions relating to the role of the state, the market and the legal status of tradable emissions rights identified in chapter two, is relevant also in practice. However, the fact that the *Private Property Rights Model* was found to be applicable to the Commission's ETS-related narrative to a lesser extent than the other two models helps to show that the question of rights per se is not as important in this context as the question of the allocation of

---

[167] Commission of the European Communities, 'Chairmain's Summery Record of Stakeholer Consultation Meeting with Industry and Environmental NGOs' (Brussels, 17 September 2001) ec.europa.eu/clima/documentation/ets/docs/record_of_stakeholder_consultation_meeting_en.pdf, accessed 4 October 2012.
[168] ibid.

regulatory power between public authorities – both at EU and national level – and the private sector. In this way, the models also help highlight the difference in emphasis concerning these core questions, as seen by the Commission and the emissions trading scholarship more generally.

V. Conclusion

As explained at the outset of this chapter, my aim in mapping the *Economic Efficiency*, the *Private Property Rights*, and the *Command-and-Control* models onto the Commission's ETS-related discourse has not been to provide an exhaustive account of the EU ETS, nor to explain the full legal developments of this trading scheme. Rather my objective is to show evidence of the applicability of the models in law. The significance of this is to demonstrate that emissions trading discourses in the EU are complex and dynamic and deal with a similar set of questions as emissions trading scholars do – although to a lesser extent questions of rights. However, the fact that rights, in the Commission's view, are not as central to the debate on emissions trading, as is the allocation of regulatory power, proves a second crucial point, which is that the applicability of the models is intrinsically tied to legal culture. This also helps to reinforce the key argument in the previous chapter; namely, the EU emissions trading regime can only be properly understood in the context of the EU legal milieu.

5

Unpacking EU Emissions Trading Discourses (II): EU Courts

I. Introduction

This chapter constitutes the second part of my case study of how emissions trading as a regulatory concept is conceived in the EU legal context. Here I build on the analysis developed in the previous chapter and move from the study of policy- and lawmakers' ETS-related discourse to examining the EU ETS case law, focusing on how judges reason and give meaning to emissions trading, as well as how the CJEU responds to the idea of an EU market in emissions allowances as projected by the applicants. I map the *Economic Efficiency,* the *Private Property Rights,* and the *Command-and-Control* models onto these ETS-related judicial discourses when applicable, and as in the previous chapter, my aim therewith is to provide an example of how emissions trading, even in a single jurisdiction, admits of different understandings. In this way, I intend to make visible some of the legal complexities involved in conceptualising emissions trading, and in particular, I wish to make two points in this chapter.

First, I show that the main legal problem that the EU Courts address in the EU ETS case law is rooted in the question of to whom the regulatory power required to construct and manage the EU emissions trading regime is to be allocated. Mapping the *Economic Efficiency,* the *Private Property Rights,* and the *Command-and-Control* models onto these judicial discourses and demonstrating that these – albeit to different degrees – are applicable, helps to illustrate that distinct understandings of emissions trading as a regulatory concept exist in the courtroom. This study thus shows the usefulness of the models in fleshing out the discrepancies and giving an insight into the EU ETS case law, as well as contributing with an explanation as to why the EU ETS regime has been, and continues to be fiercely litigated.

Second, I demonstrate that the CJEU, when delivering its ETS-related judgments, plays a pivotal role in constructing the EU emissions market. More precisely, the EU ETS case law sees the EU Courts decide on the legitimate degree of regulatory discretion vested at the national and the EU level to determine emissions allowance caps, which means that they determine at what level of governance legislation is justifiable. EU ETS litigation is also significant because the Court's understanding of the trading regime is proven to have a direct impact on market prices for emissions allowances.[1] This illustrates that the EU emissions market and the EU Court's interpretations thereof demand to be analysed within the same analytical framework, which further validates the argument set out in chapter three; namely, that in the EU legal context and at the EU level, markets, the judiciary, and environmental law exist in a close symbiosis and, as such, must be analysed as parts of a broader jigsaw rather than as distinct entities.

The structure of this chapter is as follows. In section II, I introduce the reader to EU ETS jurisprudence first against a general backdrop of climate change litigation and thereafter by explaining how this set corpus of case law is inherently EU-specific. I make this latter point by matching the type of actions that comprise the EU ETS case law with the CJEU's particular areas of jurisdiction and its specific constitutional role in interpreting, applying and articulating EU law. This exercise serves to highlight the importance of legal culture, as well as explain why it is important to study the CJEU's understanding of emissions trading as a regulatory concept. Next, in section III, I analyse a selection of EU ETS cases by mapping the *Economic Efficiency,* the *Private Property Rights,* and the *Command-and-Control* models onto the judicial proceedings when applicable. The aim with this methodology is the same as in the previous chapter; that is, to demonstrate that the models emerge in law, which is further used to highlight that various conceptualisations of emissions trading as a regulatory concept operate in the EU legal order. Subsequently, I evaluate my findings in section IV, and in section V, I discuss the possible implications that the revised Directive[2] on emissions trading may have on the type of actions brought before the EU Courts in the future. Lastly, in section VI, the findings in this chapter are summarised.

Before starting I need to set out a couple of caveats. First, this chapter is not intended as a normative study in which a particular argument, or view analysed as part of the EU ETS legal proceedings is preferred, nor do I suggest how diverging judicial discourses relating to the EU ETS can or ought to be reconciled. The purpose here is merely to show that different understandings of emissions trading exist and to highlight these through the application of the *Economic Efficiency,* the *Private Property Rights,* and the *Command-and-Control* models to the relevant case law. It is through the applicability of the models that I seek to attest the core of my book, which is to unpack legal dilemmas embedded in emissions trading as a regulatory concept, and more precisely, to show that emissions regulatory regimes are complex and can be envisioned and applied in multiple ways and for different regulatory reasons.

Second, this chapter is an examination of how the EU Courts understand and interpret the EU emissions trading regime but it is neither a general, nor a comprehensive study of how the EU Courts work or, interpret cases in a more general

---

[1] See section III(A)(1).

[2] Directive 2009/29 of the European Parliament and of the European Council amending the Directive 2003/87 so as to improve and extend the greenhouse gas emission allowance trading scheme of the Community, [2009] OJ L140/63 (revised Directive).

EU context. The fact that this chapter relies on EU constitutional law to explain why a certain kind of legal questions occur in EU ETS judicial proceedings serves, nonetheless, to show that this emissions trading scheme can only be properly understood in the legal environment in which it operates.

II. EU ETS Jurisprudence and the EU Courts

The number of EU ETS cases has swiftly mushroomed since the EU emissions trading scheme started operating in 2005. Only in the first four years following its enactment, the Directive was challenged in more than 40 cases.[3] The EU ETS jurisprudence can be classified as part of a broader group of climate change litigation,[4] which is a legal genre that in recent years has experienced an increasing upward trend in legal proceedings more generally.[5] Much climate change litigation in other jurisdictions focuses on using existing legal venues through, for instance, torts, judicial review, and human rights to establish new legal claims centred round the impact of climate change,[6] and thereby to try to mitigate, prevent or adapt to climate change.[7] As such, scholarship in this area tends to cast the spotlight on questions, such as, to what extent civil liability and the judiciary can be used to take measures to reduce the effects of climate change,[8] and investigate

---

[3] As Singh Ghaleigh explains, these 40 cases dwarf 25 and 17 respective legal actions brought under Council Regulation 2037/2000 of 16 September 2009 on substances that deplete the ozone layer, [2009] OJ L286/1, and Council Directive 96/62 of 27 September 1996 on ambient air quality assessment and management, [1996] OJ L296/55 – two other key EU regulations on pollution control. N Singh Ghaleigh, 'Emissions Trading Before the European Court of Justice: Market Making in Luxembourg' in D Freestone and C Streck (eds), *Legal Aspects of Carbon Trading: Kyoto, Copenhagen and Beyond* (Oxford University Press, Oxford, 2009) 367, 374.

[4] C Hilson, 'Climate Change Litigation: A Social Movement Perspective' (Legal and Criminological Consequences of Climate Change, 2010) www.reading.ac.uk/web/FILES/law/Climate_Change_Litigation_13_July_SSRN_2010.pdf, accessed 6 June 2011. Defining 'climate change litigation' is contentious. Markell and Ruhl argue that this type of litigation refers to cases in which the party, or tribunal decisions 'directly or expressly raise an issue of fact or law regarding the substance or policy of climate change causes and impacts'. From this viewpoint, the EU ETS case law qualifies as climate change litigation on the basis that the Directive is the key EU environmental law to deal with challenges of climate change. D Markell and JB Ruhl, 'An Empirical Survey of Climate Change Litigation in the United States' (2010) 40 *Environmental Law Reporter* 10644, 10647.

[5] Osofsky sees an 'explosion of climate change litigation' see H Osofsky, 'Climate Change Litigation as Pluralist Legal Dialogue?' (2007) 26 *Stanford Environmental Law Journal* 181, 184.

[6] Such as, eg 'carbon torts'. Markell and Ruhl, 'Litigation in the United States' (n 4) 10646.

[7] Singh Ghaleigh, 'Emissions Trading before the European Court of Justice' (n 3) 385–86.

[8] There is a vast amount of literature on this topic, see M Faure and M Peeters (eds), *Climate Change Liability* (Edward Elgar, Cheltenham, 2011), R Lazarus, 'Super Wicked Problems and Climate Change: Restraining the Present to Liberate the Future' (2009) 94 *Cornell Law Review* 1153, N Singh Ghaleigh, '"Six Honest Serving-Men": Climate Change Litigation as Legal Mobilization and the Utility of Typologies' (2010) 1 *Climate Law* 31, J Peel, 'Issues in Climate Change Litigation' (2011) 1 *Climate and Carbon Law Review* 15, L Heinzerling, 'Climate Change in the Supreme Court' (2008) 38 *Environmental Law* 1, K Engel, 'Courts and Climate Policy: Now and in the Future' in B Rabe (ed), *Greenhouse Governance: Adressing Climate Change in America* (Brookings Institute Press, Washinton DC, 2010), H Osofsky, 'Adjudicating Climate Change across Scales' in B William and O Hari (eds), *Adjudicating*

to what degree the courts are or, can be employed as a venue for political resistance – particularly when the legislator proves inapt for legal action.[9] In this context, the courts are said to have become a 'critical forum in which the future of GHG-emission [greenhouse gas] regulation and responsibility are debated',[10] which, in turn raises important questions regarding the role that the judiciary plays or ought to play in public governance.[11] To date, climate change litigation has received considerable legal attention in the US,[12] where the typical example of such legal action is driven by NGOs, who act as plaintiffs and most commonly before the federal and state courts.[13]

Following this description, however, EU ETS jurisprudence stands in contrast to typical climate change litigation. Rather than pressing for new climate change related claims through established legal venues, or using the courtroom with a broader political motive, EU ETS litigation predominately raises questions that stand at the heart of the EU legal order; and more precisely, it demands that the regulatory competences between the Commission and the Member States are drawn.[14] It is thus in light of the constitutional structure of the EU, and the role of the EU Courts in addressing competence-based dilemmas that the essence of EU ETS case laws can be made sense of. This section considers the specific constitutional role and jurisdictional scope of the EU Courts, and against this background explains the type of ETS-based proceedings that reach the courtroom at the EU level. These considerations, it is important to highlight, are not aimed at providing an exhaustive account of the constitutional features and functions of the EU Courts, nor adding to the rich debate on EU constitutional law. Rather the objective is to show that EU ETS litigation inherently involves questions of EU law, which are further shaped by the extent to which applicants are allowed to challenge these laws before the EU Courts. Similarly to the two previous chapters, this section emphasises the importance of legal culture in unpacking complexities of emissions trading regimes.

Climate Change: State, National and International Approaches (Cambridge University Press, Cambridge, 2009) 373.

[9] According to Ewing and Kysar, the judiciary is capable of helping combat climate change through a system of 'prods and pleas'. This refers to the capacity of different authorities to push each other to action; that is, in the case of climate change litigation, judges are understood to perform their roles with a view toward catalysing activity somewhere else in the system. This means that the role of the court is ultimately to activate a series of actors including governments, businesses and non-governmental groups to take measures to make international agreements both effective and possible. B Ewing and D Kysar, 'Prods and Pleas: Limited Government in an Era of Unlimited Harm' (2011) 121 *Yale Law Journal* 350.

[10] H Osofsky, 'The Continuing Importance of Climate Change Litigation' (2010) 1 *Climate Law* 3, 4.

[11] D Markell and JB Ruhl, 'An Empirical Assesment of Climate Change in the Courts: A New Jurisprudence or Business as Usual?' (2012) 64 *Florida Law Review* 15.

[12] For an overview of the relevant literature see Hilson, 'Climate Change Litigation' (n 4).

[13] Markell and Ruhl, 'Litigation in the United States' (n 4) 10649.

[14] This is not to say that the EU judicial branch never can be mobilised to secure rights for particular social groups, see H Schepel and E Blankenburg, 'Mobilizing the European Court of Justice' in G de Burca and J Weiler (eds), *The European Court of Justice* (Oxford University Press, New York, 2001) 9–42.

A. The Constitutional Role of the EU Courts

The CJEU, consisting of the General Court and the Court of Justice, plays a seminal constitutional part in the EU legal order. Article 19 TEU, which sets out the basic rules governing the EU Courts, stipulates that the CJEU 'shall ensure that in the interpretation and application of the Treaties law is observed'. Since regulatory competences are attributed to the Union as listed in the Treaty,[15] this interpretative role is essential in observing and effectively deciding who – between the Union and its Member States – gets to do what in the EU legal order. As such, the CJEU is undoubtedly the key institution in the EU's constitutional architecture.[16]

Relying on Article 19 TEU, the CJEU has over the years progressively developed a wide constitutional base both for its own rulings and for EU law more broadly. For instance, the EU Courts have given effect to measures that were not directly mentioned as an EU competence in the Treaty – environmental protection, as described in chapter three[17] is an example thereof – asserted supremacy and direct effect of EU law over national jurisdictions,[18] and developed a normative framework that governs the relationship between the institutions and the Member States.[19] The manner in which the EU Courts have been able to progress in this way has a great deal to do with the ambiguity of the Treaty provisions. As described by Lord Denning, the Treaty 'lacks precision [and] uses words and phrases without defining what they mean',[20] which has meant that in utilising Article 19 TEU, the CJEU has, by 'observing' EU law, de facto articulated its purpose and meaning. As a result of this type of gap-filling role, the CJEU has engaged with 'constitution-making',[21] and in the process, cemented its own role as the Union institution with the highest authority to make these types of structure decisions.

There observations are well known in the academic community but what is of relevance to note in this chapter are the broad interpretative powers entrusted to the CJEU in exercising its jurisdictions. Namely, it is within the framework of these that the EU ETS cases appear and are given their legal meaning. Three

---

[15] Art 5(1) TEU.

[16] T Tridimas, *The General Principles of EU Law* (2nd edn, Oxford University Press, Oxford, 2006) 18, E Scotford, *The Role of Environmental Principles in the Decisions of the European Union Courts and New South Wales Land and Environment Court* (DPhil thesis, University of Oxford, 2010) ch 4.

[17] Ch 3, section III(B).

[18] Literature on this point is vast, see, eg J Weiler, 'A Quiet Revolution: The European Court of Justice and its Interlocutors' (1994) 26 *Comparative Political Studies* 510, K Alter, 'The European Court's Political Power' (1996) 19 *West European Politics* 458, G Garrett, 'The Politics of Legal Integration in the European Union' (1995) 49 *International Organization* 171.

[19] J Weiler, *The Constitution of Europe: 'Do the New Clothes Have an Emperor?' and Other Essays on European Integration* (Cambridge University Press, Cambridge, 1999) 189.

[20] *Bulmer v Bollinger* [1974] 2 WLR 202, as cited in S Douglas-Scott, *Constitutional Law of the European Union* (Pearson Education, Harlow, 2002) 208.

[21] Weiler, 'The Constitution of Europe' (n 19).

jurisdictions in particular – as stipulated in Articles 263, 276 and 258 TFEU – are important to highlight in this regard.[22]

B. EU ETS Case Law and the Jurisdictions of the EU Courts

The CJEU enjoys a wide array of jurisdictions and three that are of particular relevance here. First, the CJEU has the power, according to Article 263 TFEU, to order Union acts to be annulled. Article 263(2) TFEU stipulates that these actions can be brought against any of the institutions, listing various grounds for review, including lack of competence, essential procedural infringement and misuse of power. To date, most EU ETS actions have appeared within the scope of Article 263 TFEU; the most frequent cause being the use of the Commission's regulatory powers under the Directive to review Member States' emissions allowance caps – the so-called national allocation plans (NAP).[23] Two distinct groups have used Article 263 TFEU in this regard: the Member States and the industries covered by the Directive. Since Article 263(2) TFEU provides the Member States with the status of 'privileged applicants' – meaning that they do not have to show any special interest in the case to gain standing – cases initiated by the national governments have all been admitted to the EU Courts. Private operators, on the other hand, are according to the Treaty 'non-privileged applicants' and, as such, must comply with the notoriously restrictive conditions under Article 263(4) TFEU to gain standing.[24] As a result, all actions relying on Article 263(4) TFEU have to date been found inadmissible.[25] This point is crucial as it shows that EU ETS jurisprudence is distinct from the more general prototype of climate change litigation that, as described earlier, is driven by NGOs. Moreover, the fact that the EU Courts are constitutionally restricted in hearing cases from private operators means that EU ETS litigation is almost exclusively driven by the Member States and the Commission, which, indeed is one of the key features of this particular series of ETS-based climate change jurisprudence.

The second CJEU jurisdiction is codified in Article 267 TFEU and allows the Court of Justice to interpret the Treaties and EU law, as well as the validity of acts of institutions upon a national court or tribunal making a preliminary reference. This process of interpretation is recognised as the 'jewel in the crown'[26] of EU constitutional law, as it is through these processes that the Court has progressed to secure authoritative interpretations of EU law, establishing, for instance, direct

---

[22] The CJEU's other jurisdictions are discussed in P Craig, *EU Administrative Law* (2nd edn, Oxford University Press, Oxford 2012) ch 10.

[23] Section III(A).

[24] As set out in Case 25/62 *Plaumann & Co v Commission* [1963] ECR 95. The Court has been equally restrictive in allowing standing to ensure that environmental standards are met, see L Krämer, 'Environmental Justice in the European Court of Justice' in J Ebbesson and P Okowa (eds), *Environmental Law and Justice in Context* (Cambridge University Press, Cambridge, 2009) 195, 199 and 209. This is further discussed in section III(A)(2).

[25] See n 76.

[26] Craig, *EU Administrative Law* (n 22) 263.

effect of EU law.[27] Moreover, this type of interpretation is crucial to the EU legal order as it helps secure uniformity in applying EU law throughout 27 different national jurisdictions, without the Court of Justice ruling on all cases itself.[28] One important feature of Article 267 TFEU-type of cases is that the Court of Justice does not rule on the validity of the conflicting views before the court but it nonetheless offers an authoritative view of what it believes EU law to mean. The Court is thus often seen laying down fundamental principles of the European Union legal system through the judicial dialogue of preliminary reference procedures.[29] To date, a number of preliminary references have been issued in relation to the EU ETS[30] but only two have been ruled on: one from the French administrative court concerning the question whether the Directive is compatible with the principle of equal treatment,[31] and one from the United Kingdom regarding the validity of Directive 2008/101 in the light of a series of international law provisions and principles of international customary law.[32] Similarly to the previous category of EU ETS case law, Article 267 TFEU-type of actions have sought to challenge the regulatory competences of the EU to legislate both in light of EU law and international law.

The CJEU enjoys a third jurisdiction over enforcement cases between the Commission and the Member States as stipulated in Article 258 TFEU. Typically these cases are brought by the Commission against Member States, or between two Member States for failure to fulfil Treaty obligations.[33] With regard to the EU ETS, the Commission has brought two such cases: against Italy[34] and Finland[35] for their failure to implement the Directive according to the set time limit. In both instances the EU Courts made the relevant declarations owing to the incomplete transposition of the Directive.

The above descriptions are significant for two reasons. First, they categorise EU ETS cases to date and show that these are moulded according to particular judicial frameworks specific to the EU, and more precisely, the CJEU's jurisdictions. The fact that the most common EU ETS case is an action challenging the Commission's

---

[27] See Case 26/62 *Van Gend en Loos v Nederlandse Administratie der Belastingen* [1963] ECR 1, as well as F Mancini and D Keeling, 'From CILFIT to ERT: The Constitutional Challenge facing the European Court' (1991) 11 *Yearbook of European Law* 1, J Cohen, 'The European Preliminary Reference and US Supreme Court Review of State Court Judgments: A Study in Comparative Judicial Federalism' (1996) 44 *American Journal of Comparative Law* 421, ibid.

[28] K Lenaerts and K Gutman, '"Federal Common Law" in the European Union: A Comparative Perspective from the United States' (2006) 54 *American Journal of Comparative Law* 1, 15–16.

[29] T Tridimas, 'Knocking on Heaven's Door: Fragmentation, Efficiency and Defiance in the Preliminary Reference Procedure' (2003) 40 *CML Review* 9.

[30] eg C-203/12 *Billerud Karlsborg Aktiebolag v Naturvårdsverket* [2012] OJ C184/7, C-566/11 *Iberdrola v Spanish State* [2011] OJ C39/8.

[31] Case C-127/07 *Société Arcelor Atlantique et Lorraine and Others v Premier Ministre, Ministre de l'Écologie et du Développement Durable and Ministre de l'Économie, des Finances et de l'Industrie* [2008] ECR I-9895 .

[32] Case C-366/10 *Air Transport Association of America, American Airlines, Inc, Continental Airlines, Inc, United Airlines, Inc v Secretary of State for Energy and Climate Change* [2011] OJ C260/9.

[33] Art 259 TFEU.

[34] Case C-122/05 *Commission v Italy* [2006] ECR I-65.

[35] Case C-107/05 *Commission v Finland* [2006] ECR I-10.

powers under the Directive, or EU's regulatory powers more broadly, similarly highlights that the issue of competence stands at the heart of EU ETS juris-prudence. This adds to the argument that this particular series of climate change litigation is a reflection of the EU's competence-focused legal culture.

Second, they show that the EU Courts have a wide platform in interpreting the EU ETS or, in other words, defining the EU's regulatory boundaries and deter-mining the legitimate level and allocation of regulatory powers – a question that the models in chapter two show is central to emissions trading discourses. Considering that the CJEU has by tradition 'added flesh to the barish bones of the treaty',[36] and in this way delivered the final interpretation of what the purpose and aim of EU law is, it is clear that the EU Court's understanding of the Directive is crucial – not the least because the text of the Directive is, as described in chapter three, 'lite' and open-textured.[37] Applying the *Economic Efficiency,* the *Private Property Rights,* and the *Command-and-Control* models to these judicial dis-courses next shows that this textual openness allows for various interpretations of the meaning and significance of the EU emissions trading regime.

III. Mapping Models onto EU ETS-Related Judicial Discourses

In this section my concern is to study the EU ETS case law, and in particular the way in which the EU Courts, the Commission and some of the applicants concep-tualise emissions trading as a regulatory concept therein. This analysis is carried out by studying the two groups of EU ETS case law as listed above: actions for annulment and preliminary references, as indeed these are the only two categories of EU ETS jurisprudence that have resulted in litigation. I examine this selection of cases by mapping the *Economic Efficiency,* the *Private Property Rights,* and the *Command-and-Control* models onto the relevant judicial proceedings when applicable. Thus I employ the same methodology as in the previous chapter. The various meanings, distinctions and overlaps relating to the use of the *Economic Efficiency,* the *Private Property Rights,* and the *Command-and-Control* models are set out in chapters two and four; still it is useful to briefly recap on the type of regime that each model envisions in furthering emissions trading as a regulatory mechanism, as well as point out the extent to which the models emerge in the case law analysed next.

According to the *Economic Efficiency Model,* the purpose of emissions trading is to create a profit-centre in selling and buying emissions allowances. The narrative

---

[36] Douglas-Scott, *Constitutional Law of the EU* (n 20) 213.
[37] See ch 3, section II(A). The question as to what extent the EU Courts ought to be considered the 'oracle' in cases of vague laws, see J Scott and S Sturm, 'Courts as Catalysts: Re-Thinking the Judicial Role in New Governance' (2006) 13 *Colombia Journal of European Law* 565.

of this model is market-centred, projecting market forces as optimal in allocating regulatory responsibilities. As the market is left to work 'on its own', the role of the state is envisioned to be minimal, unless regulatory intervention is required to stabilise the carbon market. Similarly as illustrated in the previous chapter,[38] the Commission aligns with the *Economic Efficiency Model*-type of considerations also in EU ETS jurisprudence, and to a certain extent, so does the Court of Justice.

The *Private Property Rights Model* sees emissions trading as a regime that replaces bureaucratic control over common resources. This type of trading system is envisioned to function through the creation of private property rights; private property holders are left to trade these on their own terms, which, in effect, is seen to amount to private, as opposed to state-controlled, management of the access to and use of the commons. This model, however, is not voiced in the ETS-related judiciary discourses examined in this chapter.

The *Command-and-Control Model* views emissions trading as an administrative law regime that uses the market as a mere device to comply with a certain regulatory goal. This model thus thinks of emissions trading as a state-based regime in which the role of the state is left unchallenged albeit allowing, to a certain degree, decentralisation of regulatory implementation procedures. This conceptualisation appears most often in the judgments of the General Court but also in some of the Court of Justice's rhetoric, as well as in certain judicial proceedings brought by private operators covered by the Directive.

Before I start, a couple of important limitations to the following case study need to be set out. First, the *Economic Efficiency,* the *Private Property Rights,* and the *Command-and-Control* models are applied in this study so as to help better *understand* reality. That is not to say that these models are, or can be, perfectly mapped onto the EU ETS judicial proceedings, and as such, this exercise is not always very smooth. Obviously, the reason is that the reality is far too complex to be captured in a model – or even in three. What the models, nonetheless, help to illustrate is that distinct understandings of emissions trading, as a regulatory concept, exist in EU ETS-related judicial discourses, and thereby show that emissions trading cannot be conceptualised in uniform nor in straightforward terms.

Moreover, this chapter does not provide an exhaustive account of the EU ETS case law but rather focuses on two types of EU ETS-related actions: Articles 263 TFEU (analysing actions brought by the Member States[39] and challenges by private operators[40] separately) and 267 TFEU. In examining these types of cases, I do not offer a full review of the judicial deliberation therein but focus on points raised where any of the *Economic Efficiency,* the *Private Property Rights,* and the *Command-and-Control* models appear. As such, and similarly to the mapping exercise carried out in the previous chapter, I provide quick snapshots of the actual texts analysed, which, additionally, are to a large extent technical and repetitive. The reason for the snapshots is not to analyse EU ETS jurisprudence per se

---

[38] Ch 4, sections III(B)–(C).
[39] According to Art 263(2) TFEU.
[40] According to Art 263(4) TFEU.

but rather to trace the applicability of the models in law, and thereby be able to demonstrate that the EU Courts, the Commission and the applicants perceive emissions trading, as a regulatory concept, in distinct ways. The technicality and the repetition is thus part of this exercise.

As a practical note it should be mentioned that certain judgments examined hereafter were decided prior to the Lisbon Treaty. However, in analysing these, references will primarily be to the EU Courts by their current name. Moreover, and as noted in the previous chapters, the EU ETS Directive has been revised. However, since to date all case law on this topic is concerned with the initial EU ETS legal framework, this original legal text is the central point for discussion in this chapter.

A. EU ETS Case Law: Actions for Annulment

The bulk of EU ETS jurisprudence relies on Article 263 TFEU, contesting the allocation of regulatory powers under the Directive between, on the one hand, the Commission in reviewing the NAPs, and the Member States in implementing the Directive, on the other hand. Here, it is useful to briefly highlight the main rules – encapsulated in Articles 9, 10 and 11 of the Directive – for determining a NAP, as these constitute the areas of dispute between parties in the relevant case law. Article 9 stipulated that Member States:

[S]hall develop a national plan [NAP] stating the total quantity of allowances that it intends to allocate for that period and how it proposes to allocate them.

This sets out the general obligation on the part of the national authorities to which the Directive sets out a number of further qualifications. First, the Member States must notify their NAP to the Commission and the other Member States, under a specific time schedule,[41] and second, the Member States must follow 'objective and transparent criteria' in determining its NAP, taking into account criteria listed in Annex III,[42] as well as comments from the public.[43] It is on these criteria that the Commission may 'reject that plan, or any aspect thereof',[44] which is a key regulatory discretion entrusted to the Commission under the Directive that is limited by two conditions. First, the Commission may reject a NAP only within three months of its notification, and second, it must give reasons for such a decision.[45] Ultimately, the final decision on the NAP is entrusted to the Member States but these still need to fulfil certain conditions, such as providing information

---

[41] Council Directive 2003/87 establishing a scheme for greenhouse gas emission allowance trading within the Community and amending Directive 96/61, [2003] OJ L275/32, Art 9(1).

[42] These include, inter alia, taking into account targets committed to under the Kyoto Protocol, other environmental laws and state aid provisions, as well as various stipulations on providing information. M Mehling, 'Emissions Trading and National Allocation in the Member States – An Achilles' Heel of European Climate Policy?' (2005) 5 *Yearbook of European Environmental Law* 113, 144–51.

[43] Directive (n 40) Art 9(3).

[44] ibid.

[45] ibid.

regarding the final quantity of emissions allowances they intend to allocate, and the allocation method they aim to use.[46]

These provisions are seemingly very technical but in application they give rise to important competence questions – as clearly illustrated by EU ETS jurisprudence. More precisely, the typical action for annulment in EU ETS cases concerns the Commission's decision to reject a particular NAP, leaving the Court to interpret whether the Commission's reasoning for doing so is in line with Article 9(3) of the Directive. Mapping the *Economic Efficiency,* the *Private Property Rights* and the *Command-and-Control* models onto these judicial proceedings shows that the General Court and the Commission have distinct views on this subject. As a rule, the Commission relies on the *Economic Efficiency Model*-type of arguments in pleading for a strong regulatory overview of establishing NAPs. The Commission's view of its role under the Directive is to provide the necessary regulatory structures that will ensure stability in the emissions market. The Commission therefore looks at the *impact* that a particular NAP would have on the emissions market in deciding to what extent its regulatory intervention in reviewing the NAP stretches. This position is similar to the *Economic Efficiency Model* in the way that the Commission measures its regulatory powers against how well the market is able to operate without such regulatory intervention.

The General Court, on the other hand, takes a *Command-and-Control Model*-inspired approach in delivering its judgments concerning the EU ETS. More specifically, the General Court frames emissions trading as an administrative tool and articulates a clear rejection of examining the *effects* on the emissions market in weighing the Commission's competences. The Court's focus is instead on creating a trading system that ensures legal certainty for Member States. This state-focus reinforces the argument that the General Court aligns with the *Command-and-Control Model* in depicting emissions trading.

1. Challenges brought by the Member States

In examining EU ETS actions brought by the Member States challenging the Commission's regulatory powers under the Directive, I focus on two cases in particular: *Estonia v Commission*[47] and *Poland v Commission,*[48] and in brief their respective appeals: *Commission v Estonia*[49] and *Commission v Poland.*[50] These concern the so-called Phase II of emissions trading, which required the NAPs to be coordinated with the Kyoto Protocol commitments. Moreover, it follows the carbon crash in 2006, which saw prices in emissions allowances plummet due to the over-allocation of emissions allowances.[51] Mapping the models onto judicial proceedings from this trading period shows that the Commission consistently

---

[46] In this regard, Member States must conclude their final NAP in accordance with Art 11(1) ibid.
[47] Case T-263/07 *Estonia v Commission* [2009] ECR II-3463.
[48] Case T-183/07 *Poland v Commission* [2009] ECR II-3395.
[49] Case C-505/09 *Commission v Estonia*, 29 March 2012, not yet reported.
[50] Case C-504/09 *Commission v Poland*, 29 March 2012, not yet reported.
[51] Ch 4, section III(C).

applies the *Economic Efficiency Model* in its reasoning, and explicitly refers to the collapse of carbon prices as a confirmation of the need to look to market impacts in allocating regulatory power. However, the General Court is affirmative in its use of *Command-and-Control Model*-type of considerations, depicting emissions trading as a mere administrative tool that is fitted around competences set out for the Member States and the EU institutions to regulate in this regard.

The General Court heard the two actions from Poland and Estonia on two consecutive days and factually these cases are identical. The Commission had rejected the NAPs from the two Member States on the basis that their assessment data of emission quantities, on which emissions allowances were determined, did not match the Commission's own set of data. Poland and Estonia's core claim is that the Commission overstepped its regulatory powers in this regard; rather than simply reviewing the NAPs, the Commission replaced these with its own emissions measurements and thereby de facto determined emissions ceilings for Member States.[52]

In the Polish case, the Commission's key argument is an expression of the *Economic Efficiency Model*. It argues that a correct assessment of NAPs:[53]

> [M]ust enable a situation to be avoided in which surpluses of allowances build up, thereby risking a 'collapse in the market' as happened during the trading period from 2005 to 2007.

This shows that the Commission focuses on the *impacts* of the NAPs on the emissions market and the viability of the ETS regime to control the total level of emissions allowances in determining its regulatory competence to review emissions quantitative data under Article 9(3) of the Directive. In fact, the Commission clearly articulates this, claiming that its reviewing powers are not limited to assessing the quality of data but taking into account 'the reaction which the market is likely to have in relation to the quality of those data'.[54] On this basis, the Commission explains that it had to reject the NAP in question, as it would have added an immediate surplus of emissions allowances to the emissions market, which would have 'an effect on the price of those allowances'.[55] Thus, in the Commission's view, should a market crash loom due to the way in which the Member States have drawn their NAPs, it would be empowered to reject such NAPs. This close correlation between regulatory power and market impact shows that the Commission furthers a vision of emissions trading related to the *Economic Efficiency Model*.

The General Court, however, delivers a different view of the Commission's role in the emissions trading regime. The General Court summarises that the Commission's power to review the NAPs is severely limited and does not include taking into account the effects of the NAPs on the emissions market. More

---

[52] *Estonia v Commission* (n 47) paras 36–40, *Poland v Commission* (n 48) paras 48–59.
[53] *Poland v Commission* (n 48) para 64.
[54] ibid para 67.
[55] ibid.

precisely, it explains that even if a NAP would add an excess of emissions allowances and thereby contribute to a possible collapse of the emissions market, this[56]

> cannot justify maintaining the contested decision in force in a community governed by the rule of law such as the Community, since that act was adopted in breach of the distribution of powers between the Member States and the Commission, as defined in the Directive.

The reference to the rule of law here is significant because it highlights the importance of legal culture in appreciating the General Court's understanding of what the core concern in this case is. To elucidate this point, it is useful to briefly contrast two possible visions – although others exist – of the meaning of the rule of law, and to show how this applies to the EU legal order. For instance, according to Hayek, the principle of the rule of law is crucial to restrict arbitrary government actions and safeguard individual freedom.[57] To Hayek, this law is not about legality, as indeed he states 'This rule has little to do with the question of whether all actions of government are legal in the juridical sense'.[58] Rather he uses the term to imply limits to the scope of legislation and coercive powers of the state to interfere with the individual; that is, allowing the state to act only in cases defined in advanced by the law.[59] Hayek's version of the rule of law is thus an idea that resembles beliefs held by the *Private Property Rights Model* regarding the ability of law to safeguard the individual against state coercion. In the context of the EU legal order, however, the rule of law has a different focus – one that parallels the *Command-and-Control Model*. It is codified in Article 2 TEU[60] and is applied to secure violations of EU law through court access, aiming to see to that the corpus of EU law is respected. This process is understood to create 'autonomous influence of law and legal rulings extend[ing] to the political process itself'.[61] Ultimately, the rule of law at the EU level allows the EU to effectively influence Member State behaviour, compelling Member State compliance via available court venues,[62] whilst basing this particular coexistence of national legal orders and the EU jurisdiction on constitutional law.[63] What this discussion aims to show – without engaging with the meaning of the principle of the rule of law per se – is that there are multiple ways, each inherently culture-specific, to understand how power structures in an emissions trading scheme are determined at the mention of the

---

[56] ibid para 129.

[57] Hayek draws the distinction between a permanent framework in which all actions are known beforehand and within which the 'productive activity is guided by individual decisions', on the one hand, and the 'direction of economic activity by a central authority', on the other hand, which, Hayek explains, is the general distinction between the rule of law and arbitrary government. FA Hayek, *The Road to Serfdom* (Routledge and Kegan Paul, London and Henley, 1976) 44, 54.

[58] ibid 61.

[59] ibid 62.

[60] Art 2 TEU states that thus the Union is 'this founded on . . . the rule of law'.

[61] K Alter, *Establishing the Supremacy of European Law: Making of an International Rule of Law in Europe* (Oxford University Press, Oxford, 2001) 3.

[62] ibid.

[63] J Shaw, *Law of the European Union* (3rd edn, Palgrave, London, 2000) 191.

rule of law. Here, the General Court's reference to this rule in the context of competences signals that its focus in analysing emissions trading is on ensuring that
the power balance between the Member States and the institutions is secured, and
that regulatory compliance on state level is achieved. From this perspective, the
reference to the rule of law is significant in showing the EU-specific meaning that
the General Court gives ETS litigation. Moreover, the focus on the state, as
opposed to on the individual or the market, suggests that the *Command-and-Control
Model* – in contrast to the *Private Property Rights,* or the *Economic Efficiency* models –
operates in the General Court's deliberation.

Similarly to the Polish case, in *Estonia v Commission* the Commission pleads for
a teleological interpretation of the Directive, arguing that its reviewing powers
encompass the discretion to reject the NAPs on the basis that the Member States
have fixed emissions allowance ceilings that are unable to entail an increase in the
price of carbon.[64] In particular, the Commission emphasises the importance of
effective price signalling in emissions trading, concluding that if its powers to
review the NAPs are limited to only assessing the quality of the data therein, as
opposed to evaluating the impact of these on the market, oversupply of allowances will follow, which the Commission takes to 'completely undermin[e] the
effects of the Directive as a tool to reduce emissions'.[65] What this line of argument
highlights, as argued previously, is that the Commission relies on the *Economic
Efficiency Model*-type of considerations in describing its regulatory role in correlation to the needs of the market.

In this judgment, the General Court states that the Directive is of primary
importance in the EU's fight against global warming, which, the Court defines as
'one of the greatest social, economic and environmental threats which the world
currently faces'.[66] However, with regard to the question whether the Commission's
reviewing powers extend to assessing impacts on the emissions market, the
General Court concludes:[67]

> [I]n a community governed by the rule of law, administrative measures must be adopted
> in compliance with the competences attributed to various administrative bodies.

This statement reflects the *Command-and-Control Model* in two specific ways. First,
it shows that the General Court identifies emissions trading as a mere 'administrative measure', which is analogous to the *Command-and-Control Model* – and not
as a profit-centre, or a substitute for a state-controlled governance regime, which
are the views of emissions trading in the *Economic Efficiency* and the *Private Property
Rights* models respectively. Second, it demonstrates that the General Court emphasises the rule of law in interpreting regulatory power under the Directive, which,
in the EU context, as explained above, is a *Command-and-Control Model*-inspired
view on how to construct an emissions trading regime. Again, this is different

---

[64] *Estonia v Commission* (n 47) 42.
[65] ibid.
[66] ibid para 49.
[67] ibid para 50.

from the *Economic Efficiency* and the *Private Property Rights* models where regulatory power is either allocated to central government so that the necessary structures for a stable and profitable market can be established or, alternatively, to property holders with the aim of empowering these, through private property rights, to overturn bureaucratic control of common resources.

The Commission appealed both above-mentioned judgments to the Court of Justice on the basis that the General Court, inter alia, erred in law in its interpretation of the scope and the objective of Article 9(3).[68] This helps to highlight, as does the application of the models to these judiciary proceedings, that the way in which the Commission views the allocation of regulatory power in emissions trading, and ultimately emissions trading as a regulatory concept, is distinct from the vision that the General Court holds. The Court of Justice, nonetheless, dismissed the appeals in two very similar judgments. The core of the CJEU's reasoning relates to the importance of assuring that the allocation of regulatory power under the Directive is in line with the intentions of the legislator – even if this leads to higher emissions levels.[69] It states:

> In the present case, even supposing that the approach favoured by the Commission could improve the functioning of the European Union scheme for greenhouse gas emissions trading and thus make it possible to achieve more efficiently the objective of reducing greenhouse gas emissions substantially, that fact could not alter the allocation of powers between the Member States and the Commission as provided for in Articles 9 and 11 of Directive 2003/87.

This statement elucidates that the CJEU, similarly to the General Court, identifies the allocation of regulatory competence as the chief concern in EU ETS litigation. It also shows that the Court acknowledges the impact that the EU emissions trading regime may have on combating climate change but the CJEU does not weigh this in its interpretation of the Commission's competences. This approach overlaps with the Opinion of Advocate General Trstenjak, in which she argues that the 'Consideration of the smooth operation of the trading system does not justify conferring on the Commission additional *extra legem* powers'.[70] What this shows is that the Court of Justice, similarly to the General Court, frames ETS litigation as a competence question concerning the limits of the regulatory power between the Member States and the EU institutions, and in this way adheres to the *Command-and-Control Model* that is equally state-focused.

In effect, these appeals go to the heart of EU constitutional law in the sense that they deal with the principle of subsidiarity.[71] In an area of shared competence,

[68] *Commission v Estonia* (n 49), *Commission v Poland* (n 50).

[69] *Commission v Estonia*, para 80 and *Commission v Poland*, para 78.

[70] Opinion of AG Trstenjak delivered on 17 November, Case C-504/09 *Commission v Poland*, 29 March 2012, not yet reported, para 84, Opinion of AG Trstenjak delivered on 17 November, Case C-505/09 *Commission v Estonia*, 29 March 2012, not yet reported, para 79.

[71] A Biondi, 'Subsidiarity in the Courtroom' in A Biondi, P Eeckhout and S Ripley (eds), *EU Law After Lisbon* (Oxford University Press, Oxford, 2012) 211, 223–24, X Groussot and S Bogojević, 'Subsidiarity as a Procedural Safeguard of Federalism' in L Azoulai (ed), *The European Union as a Federal Order of Competences* (Oxford University Press, Oxford, forthcoming). Indeed, Lenaerts refers

such as the environment, the Member States are allowed to legislate in so far as that regulatory activity has not been harmonised.[72] What the CJEU thus seeks to establish is whether the Union legislator has fully harmonised the rules concerning the construction and operation of the EU ETS according to Article 5 TEU or, whether the Member States still enjoy a wide discretion in this regard.[73] The Court states that according to the wording of the Directive, the intention of the European Union policymakers is to empower the Commission only to verify the conformity of the NAPs with the criteria set out in the Directive,[74] meaning that the Commission's review power is limited to review of legality.[75] In stating this, the CJEU makes clear that it is up to the legislator to decide how the emissions trading regime should operate, refraining from delivering prescriptive judgments on whether this particular trading scheme ought to be made stricter so as to ensure a stable EU carbon market (as envisioned by the *Economic Efficiency Model*), or protect the rights of the emissions allowance-holders (as projected by the *Private Property Rights Model*). Rather, the CJEU projects the EU emissions regime in light of the EU's constitutional principles and confirms the General Court's state-focused deliberation – analogous to the *Command-and-Control Model*.

These snapshots of the ETS judgments show at least two things. First, they demonstrate that distinct narratives exist in the courtroom, each portraying emissions trading as a regulatory concept differently. The Commission aligns with the *Economic Efficiency Model*, focusing on the function of the market and based on this outlook, arguing that power allocation must be assigned according to the need to stabilise the operation of the emissions market. The EU Courts, however, centre their judicial deliberation on competences, and the need to provide legal certainty for Member States to comply with the assigned rules under the Directive – an idea similar to the *Command-and-Control Model*. As such, the EU Courts define emissions trading to be a mere administrative system that is cut to fit power divisions between the Member States and the institutions in light of EU constitutional law – irrespective of possible adverse emissions market impacts.

2. Challenges brought by Private Operators

The second group of litigants that bring actions for annulment are private operators covered by the Directive. As noted earlier, the Member States enjoy the status of 'privileged applicants' and as such have direct access to the EU Courts. Individual operators, however, must fulfil the restrictive criteria under Article 263(4) TFEU in

to emissions trading as a prime example of an environmental law fulfilling the subsidiarty principle. K Lenaerts, 'The Principle of Subsidiarity and the Environment in the European Union: Keeping the Balance of Federalism' (1993) 17 *Fordham International Law Journal* 846.

[72] Art 5 TEU. This point is highlighted by the General Court in both *Estonia v Commission* (n 47) para 52 and *Poland v Commission* (n 48) para 52.
[73] *Commission v Estonia* (n 49) para 81, *Commission v Poland* (n 50) para 79, Opinion of AG Trstenjak in *Commission v Poland* (n 70) para 62.
[74] *Commission v Poland* (n 50) para 47.
[75] *Commission v Estonia* (n 49) para 48.

order to get standing, which they have failed to do in all instances with regard to challenging the Commission's regulatory competences under the Directive.[76] In this regard, what is important to highlight is the type of reasoning that leads the General Court – in concurrence with the Commission – to reject actions for annulment from private operators, and how this links to the *Command-and-Control Model*. Here this is illustrated in short by examining one of the first actions of annulment brought by private litigants: *EnBW Energie Baden Württemberg v Commission*.[77]

In this case, EnBW brought an action challenging the Commission's decision to approve a German NAP that contained so-called 'transfer rules'.[78] These rules allow operators, who have decommissioned old plans with new installations, to enjoy the same number of emissions allowances that they would have been granted, had they continued to operate their old plant. The purpose of this provision, Germany explained, is to reward investments in clean energy. The applicant, on the other hand, argued that this constituted state aid, as it allowed its key competitor to benefit from an excess of emission allowances and thus enjoy a competitive advantage on the emissions allowance market.[79]

This judgment is centred on the question of whether EnBW was allowed standing to challenge the contested decision. Here the General Court investigated whether annulment of the contested decision was 'capable of having legal consequences'[80] that could have bestowed an advantage on EnBW. In deciding this particular point, the Court looked at whether individual operators incurred any rights from the Commission's decision on the NAP. The Court concluded – and in doing so delivered the punch line in this case – that the Commission's role of review under the Directive is not concerned with the creation of rights but to provide 'legal certainty for the Member States'.[81] In other words, the Commission's approval of the NAPs is viewed as necessary only for the Member States to know how to allocate their emissions allowances nationally.[82] On this basis, the General Court found the contested decision unable to bestow an advantage on EnWB and subsequently announced the application inadmissible.[83]

---

[76] This list includes Case T-489/04 *US Steel Kosice v Commission* [2007] ECR II-127, Case C-503/07 *Saint-Gobain Glass Deutschland v Commission* [2008] ECR I-2217, Case T-193/07 *Gorazdze Cement v Commission* [2008] OJ C301/36, Case T-197/07 *Grupa Ozarow v Commission* [2008] OJ C301/37, Case T-198/07 *Cementownia 'Warta' v Commission* [2008] OJ C301/38, Case T-241/07 *Buzzi Unicem v Commission* [2009] OJ C6/30 .

[77] Case T-387/04 *EnBW Energie Baden-Württemberg AG v Commission* [2007] ECR II-1195 (*EnBW*),

[78] More precisely, the Commission had issued a decision rejecting the German NAP but only to the extent that it provided for ex-post adjustments to the allocation of emission allowances, and so, the transfer rules were approved, ibid paras 40–47.

[79] ibid paras 31–36.

[80] ibid para 96.

[81] ibid para 117. Similarly, in Art 263(2) TFEU actions, the General Court clarifies that the Commission's review power under Art 9(3) of the Directive aims to 'provide legal certainty for the Member States and, in particular to permit them to be sure, within a short time, how they may allocate emission allowances and manage the allowance trading scheme on the basis of their NAP during the allocation period in question'. See Case T-369/07 *Latvia v Commission* [2011] OJ C139/29, para 54.

[82] *EnBW* (n 77) para 96.

[83] ibid para 123.

The significance of the Court's conclusion is twofold. First, it demonstrates that its focus is on legal certainty for the *Member States,* as opposed to *market* stability (which is the focus of the Commission's judicial narrative) in interpreting governance structures in the EU emissions trading regime. This state-centered perspective shows that the *Command-and-Control Model* is applicable to the Court's deliberation, which, considering that the Commission furthers the *Economic Efficiency Model*-based arguments, illustrates that significantly different understandings of what constitutes the core legal dilemma in emissions trading exist in the courtroom. Moreover, it highlights that the General Court's understanding of rights in the EU emissions trading context is similar to the *Command-and-Control Model* in the sense that it is state-focused and hints to the importance of regulatory compliance at the state-level. Its view on emissions allowances is thus not positioned so as to empower emissions allowance holders to substitute state-control of common resources – as is the case in the *Private Property Rights Model* – nor to induce investments and thus confidence in the emissions market, which is the position of the *Economic Efficiency Model.*

Investigating standing more generally, it is clear that its purpose is to regulate the level at which intervention in the regulatory processes is allowed.[84] Moreover, looking at standing in the EU context, and in light of an early study by Stein and Vining, it is clear that the EU Courts' focus and conceptualisation of the standing provisions, including the requirement to show 'direct concern' for non-privileged applicants, ultimately manifests a deeper interest in maintaining the delicate balance between the Member States' and the Commission's regulatory powers at the EU level.[85] What this means is that private applicants are left to seek judicial protection via national jurisdictional venues,[86] and according to the preliminary reference procedure,[87] as opposed to being allowed to challenge political proceedings directly at the international level. Arguably this judicial approach sits uncomfortably with the idea of 'an ever closer Union'[88] but it fits well with the *Command-and-Control Model* and the General Court's reasoning in EU ETS cases

---

[84] Sunstein explains the development of laws on standing in the US, their different impacts at different periods and engages in a more general debate on standing as a regulatory concept, see C Sunstein, 'Standing and the Privatization of Public Law' (1988) 88 *Colombia Law Review* 1432, 1461.

[85] E Stein and J Vining, 'Citizen Access to Judicial Review of Administrative Action in a Transnational and Federal Context' (1976) 70 *American Journal of International Law* 219, 233. Similarly, Krämer explains that Art 263(4) TFEU was originally intended to be narrow simply because EU legislation was initially adopted by the Council of Ministers, where the Governments of the Member States were represented, see L Krämer, 'Seal Killing, the Inuit and EU Law' (2012) 21 *Review of European Community and International Environmental Law* 291.

[86] The CJEU has developed the doctrine of 'direct effect' that permits individuals to rely on EU law before national courts. C Harlow, 'European Administrative Law and the Global Challenge' (Robert Schuman Centre For Advanced Studies, Working Paper No 98/23, 1998) www.eui.eu/DepartmentsAndCentres/RobertSchumanCentre/Publications/WorkingPapers/9823.aspx, accessed 12 October 2012.

[87] 294/83 *Les Verts v European Parliament* [1986] ECR 1339.

[88] Art 1 TEU.

– here as exemplified by *EnBW Energie Baden Württemberg v Commission* – as well as with more recent environmental protection cases.[89]

It is worth nothing that following the Treaty of Lisbon, the provisions on standing are amended so that 'individual concern' does not have to be proven for regulatory acts that are of 'direct concern' to the applicant and that do not entail implementing measures.[90] This revised provision was tested in *Arcelor v Parliament and Council*,[91] where the Court found that the Directive cannot 'in any event, be regarded as being a regulatory act which does not entail implementing measures within the terms of the fourth paragraph of Article 263 TFEU'.[92] What this means is that individual operators can never directly challenge the Directive, or the Commission's powers therein,[93] which reinforces the analysis above and the argument that the *Command-and-Control Model* operates in the Court's interpretation of ETS cases concerning Article 236(4) TFEU.

This brief overview of legal actions brought by private operators covered by the Directive shows that the General Court's narrative is state-focused. Moreover, by interpreting private actions as inadmissible, it is clear that the Court permits the Member States, as opposed to individuals, or market actors to challenge the regulatory processes of the EU emissions trading regime. This highlights the important factor of legal culture in understanding ETS-based climate change litigation in the EU, and the Court's vision of emissions trading as a regulatory concept.

B. EU ETS Case Law: Preliminary Reference

To date, two EU ETS-related preliminary references have been decided by the CJEU – *Arcelor*[94] and *Air Transport Association of America*[95] – both testing the limits of the EU's regulatory power in constructing and managing the EU emissions regime. Here only the first judgment will be examined,[96] providing an example of where the Court's narrative is in line with arguments and rhetoric common to the *Economic Efficiency Model,* whilst the applicant from the national court – a steel manufacturer covered by the Directive – depicts the EU emissions trading regime in accordance with the *Command-and-Control Model.* The importance of this finding is that it shows that variations may exist in how the General Court and

---

[89] B Müller, 'Access to the Courts of the Member States for NGOs in Environmental Matters under European Union Law' (2011) 23 *Journal of Environmental Law* 505.

[90] Art 263(4) TFEU. See also H Vedder, 'Treaty of Lisbon and European Environmental Law and Policy' (2010) 22 *Journal of Environmental Law* 285, 297.

[91] Case T-16/04 *Arcelor v Parliament and Council* [2010] ECR II-00211.

[92] ibid para 123.

[93] Similarly in *Latvia v Commission* (n 81) para 33, the General Court states that for the right to bring an action for annulment, the Treaty draws 'a clear distinction' between the right of Union institutions and Member States, on the one hand, and legal persons and individuals, on the other hand.

[94] See n 31.

[95] See n 32.

[96] I have analysed the case *Air Transport Association of America* elsewhere, see S Bogojević, 'Legalising Environmental Leadership: A Comment on the CJEU's Ruling in C-366/10 on the Inclusion of Aviation in the EU Emissions Trading Scheme' (2012) 24 *Journal of Environmental Law* 345.

the Court of Justice conceptualise the EU emissions trading regime, which adds to the complexity of emissions trading debates, as well as highlights their cultural specificity.

The French Conseil d'État employed the preliminary reference procedure to enquire whether the Directive was valid in light of the principle of equal treatment, in so far as it was applicable to installations in the steel sector but not to other sectors, such as the aluminium and the plastic industries.[97] It is useful to note that the applicant in the main proceedings was the world's largest volume producer of steel, a so-called 'carbon fat cat'[98] that profited hugely from the sale of excess emissions allowances in 2006.[99] The applicant, nonetheless, challenged the validity of the Directive through the national courts, claiming that since the Directive failed to cover the chemical and plastic sectors – that is, the applicant's main competitors – it thus breached several constitutional principles, including the right to property, the freedom of establishment, and the principle of equal treatment.[100] What is remarkable about this plea was that despite the economic benefits that the applicant enjoyed from the Directive, its view of emissions trading did not relate to the *Economic Efficiency Model* where emissions trading schemes are thought of as a profit-centre; but rather, the applicant focused on the administrative obligations imposed by the Directive – such as applying for emissions allowance permits and having to surrender these – and from this viewpoint portrayed the EU emissions trading regime as a set of regulatory burdens restricting and discriminating against its economic activities.[101] Although the applicant's argument was that these regulatory impositions were illegal, the fact that emissions trading as a regulatory concept is framed as an administrative state-controlled regime shows that *Command-and-Control Model*-based descriptions operated in the applicant's emissions trading discourse.

Considering whether the Directive breaches the principle of equal treatment, the Court of Justice, however, imagines emissions trading similarly to the *Economic Efficiency Model*. To start with, the Court's narrative reflects economic considerations: it deliberates on the 'supply and demand for allowances'[102] and takes into consideration the costs of compliance 'of individual undertakings'.[103] The latter point stands in sharp contrast to the previous EU ETS case law where the General Court focuses on the compliance of the Member States, which signals that the Court of Justice and the General Court view emissions trading differently. Moreover, in considering whether the Directive is compatible with the principle of equal treatment, the Court of Justice, similarly to the *Economic Efficiency Model*

---

[97] *Société Arcelor Atlantique* (n 31) para 22.

[98] R Elsworth and others, *Carbon Fat Cats 2011: The Companies Profiting from the EU Emissions Trading Scheme* (Sandbag, London, 2011) 1.

[99] Case C-127/07 *Arcelor Atlantique and Lorraine and Others v Commission* [2008] OJ C44/8, Opinion of AG Maduro, para 57.

[100] *Société Arcelor Atlantique* (n 31) para 20.

[101] ibid.

[102] ibid para 33.

[103] ibid.

and the Commission in the previously analysed cases, looks at the *impact* that a wider scope of sectors covered by the Directive would have on the carbon market. It concludes that a broader coverage[104]

> would have made the management of the allowance trading scheme more difficult and increased the administrative burden, so that the possibility that the functioning of the scheme would have been disturbed at the time of its implementation as a result of that inclusion cannot be excluded.

This emphasis on the *function* of the emissions market is analogous to the *Economic Efficiency Model*, and again different from the General Court's commitment to the *Command-and-Control Model*-type of considerations, in focusing exclusively on the regulatory competences between the Member States and the institutions in deciding the governance structures of the EU emissions trading regime. Additionally, the Court of Justice stresses that the emissions trading scheme is 'novel and complex'[105] and in risk of being burdened by too many participants early on. On this basis, the Court finds that the EU legislator's 'step-by-step' approach, treating the chemical and the plastic sectors differently from the steel industry pursuant to Article 30 of the Directive, is justified.[106] This pragmatic and impact-focused approach to debating governing structures of the EU emissions trading scheme shows that the Court of Justice bases its deliberations on *Economic Efficiency Model*-type of visions of emissions trading as a regulatory regime.

In summary, what is clear from the study of the EU ETS-related preliminary reference is that the Court of Justice is pragmatic and looks to the impact and function of the emissions trading scheme in interpreting the legitimate scope of the carbon market. As such, the Court of Justice provides a results-oriented vision of emissions trading, similarly to the *Economic Efficiency Model*.

IV. Reflections

The analysis above provides snapshots of the meaning given to emissions trading in EU ETS jurisprudence. What these snapshots show is that distinct conceptualisations of emissions trading take form in the EU case law, ultimately contributing to a complex and conflicting emissions trading discourse. Mapping the models onto these judicial debates helps to highlight discrepancies therein and illustrate distinct outlooks on emissions trading and the governance structure that this trading system is thought to create as understood by the EU Courts, the Commission and the listed private operators.

---

[104] ibid para 65.
[105] ibid para 61.
[106] AG Maduro describes the emissions trading scheme along the same lines to the Court of Justice, Opinion AG Maduro (n 99) para 44.

More precisely, this chapter shows that the Commission centres its narrative on the market and looks to the need of ensuring market stability in deciding the extent of its regulatory powers under the Directive. This view correlates with the *Economic Efficiency Model* in the sense that it is impact-based, and in this regard, pragmatic as to what role the state ultimately plays in the carbon market. The Commission's portrayal of emissions trading in these judicial discourses fits well with its law- and policy-based narrative examined in the previous chapter. There, the Commission similarly applies the *Economic Efficiency Model* first, so as to support a decentralised regulatory structure for emissions trading, and then to advocate for a centralised regime[107] – in both instances looking at the needs of the carbon market in deciding on the emissions trading governance structures.

Interpreting the scope of the emissions market, the Court of Justice is equally impact-focused – at least in ruling on the described preliminary reference procedure. For instance, it justifies the limited scope of the Directive, and thus unequal treatment, on the basis of the effects a broad coverage of the industrial sector would have on the workability of the emissions trading regime. The fact that the *Economic Efficiency Model* thus operates in the Court of Justice's deliberation is particularly interesting considering that the General Court shows alignment in its ETS-specific judgments with the *Command-and-Control Model*. Indeed, the General Court stresses the significance of legal security for the *Member States* (as opposed to the market, or the rights holders as proposed by the *Economic Efficiency* or the *Private Property Rights* models respectively), rejects the Commission's market-focused line of reasoning, and provides a strict reading of competence divisions in interpreting the regulatory regime for emissions trading. The General Court clearly 'speaks the language of constitutional law',[108] which is illustrated also by its references to the subsidiary principle. Moreover, mapping the *Command-and-Control Model* onto Article 263(4) TFEU cases demonstrates that from the perspective of the General Court, emissions trading is a state-focused administrative regime, which, as such, is primarily for the Member States to challenge. As exemplified in *Société Arcelor Atlantique*, some applicants share the view of the General Court and project emissions trading as a state-controlled regulatory regime. What these mixes of narratives suggest is that different expressions and understandings of emissions trading, as a regulatory concept and governance structure, exist in the courtroom. This is a crucial finding, especially considering the CJEU's constitutional role in articulating the purpose of EU law.

The fact that the two Courts are seen to approach environmental regimes differently is not novel. In analysing the EU Courts and the EU case law, Krämer concludes that the General Court views 'the environment as one factor in society among many, rather than a general interest which cannot be placed at the same

---

[107] Ch 4, section III(B) and (C).

[108] J Scott, 'The Multi-Level Governance of Climate Change' in P Craig and G de Burca (eds), *The Evolution of EU Law* (2nd edn, Oxford University Press, Oxford, 2011) 805, 811.

level as vested interests',[109] while he finds that the Court of Justice is 'more innovative and creative'.[110] The reason for this relates back to chapter three and the importance of legal culture. In this context, it is significant to flag that the General Court and the Court of Justice occupy different jurisdictions. The General Court covers mainly cases that are brought by private persons, or companies against an EU institution. The Court of Justice, on the other hand, deals in essence with actions that are brought by the Commission against a Member State, preliminary references issued by national courts, and appeals against judgments of the General Court.[111] These different types of legal venues impact on how the Court responds to the various actions; that is, the General Court is constrained by the conditions set out in Article 263 TFEU (which are far narrower in scope in comparison to the interpretative breadth entrusted to the Court of Justice under Article 267 TFEU) in delivering its verdicts. As such, the Court of Justice tends to deliver 'meta-teleological or broad, system-level purposive interpretation'[112] aimed primarily at enhancing integration.[113] Another important, and related point is that due to the different type of actions that the two Courts deal with, they have developed overlapping yet slightly different expertise.[114] For instance, much competition law develops through challenges by private parties, and the General Court is the central judicial institution in this particular field of EU law.[115] What this suggests is that the General Court's heavy diet of competition law makes it more focused on economic analysis,[116] thus it understands the Commission's *Economic Efficiency Model*-inspired claims differently from the Court of Justice. Investigating the impact that the structure and constitutional roles vested with these two judicial institutions have on the outcome of the EU case law offers an intriguing new line of enquiry.[117] The point to make here, however, is that the judicial construction of emissions trading regimes clearly is culture-specific.

---

[109] L Krämer, 'The European Court of Justice' in A Jordan and C Adelle (eds), *Environmental Policy in the EU: Actors, Institutions and Processes* (Routledge, Abingdon, 2013) 113, 128, L Krämer, 'On the Court of First Instance and the Protection of the Environment' in G Bándi (ed), *The Impact of ECJ Jurisprudence on Environmental Law* (Szent István Társulat, Budapest, 2009) 95.

[110] Krämer, 'The European Court' (n 109) 127.

[111] ibid.

[112] G Conway, 'Introduction and Overview – Interpretation and the European Court of Justice' in G Conway (ed), *The Limits of Legal Reasoning and the European Court of Justice* (Cambridge University Press, Cambridge, 2012) 1, 3.

[113] The Court has often used 'effectiveness' to expand on EU criminal law competences, see E Herlin-Karnell, *The Constitutional Dimension of European Criminal Law* (Hart Publishing, Oxford, 2012).

[114] Expertise here is understood in simple terms, meaning skills and knowledge that is specific to a particular group. E Fisher, 'The Rise of Transnational Environmental Law and the Expertise of Environmental Lawyers' (2012) 1 *Transnational Environmental Law* 43, 48.

[115] D Chalmers, G Davies and G Monti, *European Union Law* (2nd edn, Cambridge University Press, Cambridge, 2010) 147.

[116] I am thankful to Stephen Weatherill for this comment.

[117] Such an enquiry could also include an examination of how the predominately male composition of the EU Court impacts its reasoning, J Shaw, 'Gender and the Court of Justice' in G de Búrca and J Weiler (eds), *The European Court of Justice* (Oxford University Press, Oxford, 2001) 87.

The relevance of legal culture in appreciating the judiciary's view of emissions trading regimes is equally obvious in two further instances. First, examining the main legal dilemma in EU ETS jurisprudence shows that these are ultimately questions concerning EU constitutional law. Indeed, the snapshots above demonstrate that the EU ETS case law is chiefly concerned with the allocation of regulatory power to construct and manage the emissions trading regime. To date, the General Court has consistently interpreted the Directive as establishing an extensively decentralised regulatory regime where the Member States, rather than the Commission, enjoy regulatory discretion in setting up and supervising the operation of the carbon market – irrespective of the impact that this governance structure may have on the emissions trading system. The EU ETS judgments are thus framed as competence questions, and decided accordingly. In other words, they orbit questions of EU law.

Second, legal culture offers an explanation as to why the topic of the legal status and significance of *rights* in emissions allowances – which, as shown in chapter two, form an important part of emissions trading scholarship[118] – is not a central question before the EU judiciary. First, however, it should be noted that in *United Kingdom v Commission*, the General Court briefly refers to the possibility of emissions allowances being '"property" having commercial value',[119] and in *EnBW Energie Baden Württemberg v Commission*, the Commission suggests that emissions allowances are equivalent to 'an intangible asset the value of which was determined by the market'.[120] Over and above these basic observations, the relevant judicial discourse adds nothing further to this debate. What is more, in *EnBW Energie Baden Württemberg v Commission*, the General Court found that due to the *lack of rights* stemming from the Commission's approval of NAPs, private installation covered by the Directive could not enjoy standing.[121] The fact that EU law has not developed a sense of 'property',[122] however, is a plausible explanation as to why the CJEU stops at considering the legal nature of emissions allowances. It also explains why the

[118] As described in ch 2, the bulk of emissions trading literature discusses at great length the importance of vesting emissions allowances with a legal status that will ensure stability in the carbon market – often assumed to be property rights. The reason why this tends to be considered a crucial point is because emissions trading, as a regulatory idea, emerged in economic literature, in which the creation of property rights in emissions allowances is thought a prerequisite for an emissions market, see H Demsetz, 'Toward a Theory of Property Rights' (1967) 57 *American Economic Review* 347, G Libecap, 'Property Rights Allocation of Common Pool Rescources' in C Ménard and M Ghertman (eds), *Regulation, Deregulation, Reregulation: Institutional Perspectives* (Edward Elgar, Cheltenham, 2009) 27, R Stavins, 'Transaction Costs and Tradeable Permits' (1995) 29 *Journal of Environmental Economics and Management* 133, R Sandor, 'Creating New Markets: The Chicago Climate Exchange' in I Kaul and P Conceicao (eds), *The New Public Finance: Responding to Global Challenges* (Oxford University Press, Oxford, 2006) 390, D Cole, 'Clearing the Air: Four Propositions About Property Rights and Environmental Protection' (1999) 10 *Duke Environmental Law and Policy Forum* 103, J Stavang, 'Property in Emissions? Analysis of the Norwegian GHG ETS with References also to the UK and the EU' (2005) 17 *Environmental Law and Management* 209, S Manea, 'Defining Emissions Entitlements in the Constitution of the EU Emissions Trading System' (2012) 1 *Transnational Environmental Law* 303.
[119] Case T-178/05 *United Kingdom v Commission* [2005] ECR II-4807, para 161.
[120] *EnBW Energie Baden Württemberg v Commission* (n 77) para 22.
[121] ibid section III(A)(2).
[122] Ch 4, section IV, Manea (n 118) 310.

Private Property Right Model, which positions the creation of private property rights at the centre of emissions trading discussions, fails to emerge in EU ETS-based judicial discourses. Again, this shows the significance of legal culture in emissions trading scholarship.

Unpacking ETS-specific judicial discourses through the application of the *Economic Efficiency,* the *Private Property Rights,* and the *Command-and-Control* models is, as explained in the previous chapters, limited in numerous ways. First, the models are subjective and reflect how I view and thus bundle various emissions trading discussions as part of distinct narratives. Second, the fact that the case law examined in this chapter provides only snapshots of the key arguments surfacing in EU ETS jurisprudence is another limitation. Third, the finding that the EU ETS cases are interpreted through a competence-focused lens may seem an all too obvious conclusion, especially considering the constitutional role of the CJEU.[123] The emphasis of my argument, however, lies elsewhere. My claim in this chapter is that emissions trading is a complex regulatory concept, which – as illustrated through an analysis of a series of glimpses of EU ETS jurisprudence – is given distinct meanings in the judicial discourses that, moreover, can only be properly understood against the backdrop of the legal environment in which the trading scheme operates.

V. Looking Ahead

The case law analysis above shows that the sheer volume of EU ETS jurisprudence orbits the question of how to allocate regulatory power between the Commission and the Member States in determining the NAPs, which involves an interpretation of Article 9 of the Directive. Cap-setting procedures are generally thought of as the 'hornets' nest',[124] as they involve taking into consideration a series of recommendations and rules and stakeholders' viewpoints while respecting specific emissions targets. In this case, Article 9 is described as the 'Achilles' heel' of EU climate policy[125] because it is by far the most litigated provision in the EU ETS regime. Its vulnerability to litigation has proven to have a real impact on the emissions market, as manifested in the fall in prices for emissions allowances following judgments in *Poland v Commission*[126] and *Estonia v Commission*.[127] More precisely, following the General Court's verdict to annul the contested decisions in the two

---

[123] F Jacobs, 'Is the Court of Justice of the European Communities a Constitutional Court?' in D Curtin and D O'Keeffe (eds), *Constitutional Adjudication in European Community and National Law – Essays for the Hon Mr Justice T-F O'Higgins* (Butterworth, Dublin, 1992) 25, 32.

[124] C Stone, *The Gnat is Older than Man – Environment and Human Agenda* (Princeton University Press, Princeton, 1993) 1 as cited in ibid 113.

[125] Mehling (n 42) 128.

[126] See n 48.

[127] See n 47.

above-discussed cases, market prices for emissions allowances fell by 2.3 per cent.[128] As a result, Dimas, the former EU Environment Commissioner, urged Member States to act swiftly and prepare new NAPs so as to 'minimise the regulatory uncertainty created by the court ruling'.[129] The significance of this is that it demonstrates that Court rulings have a real impact on the operation of the emissions market,[130] and thus that carbon markets cannot be thoroughly examined outside the sphere of law.

NAP-related EU ETS cases may, however, be judged to have a short impact considering that under the revised Directive, and from 2013 onwards, the Commission will centrally decide on caps.[131] On this note, and as a response to the judgment in *Poland v Commission* and *Estonia v Commission*, Dimas explained:[132]

> The Commission is fully committed to ensuring the integrity, predictability and stability of the system [the EU emissions trading scheme]. Fundamental changes were agreed last December to the cap-setting process from 2013, guaranteeing a healthy development of the European carbon market.

What Dimas seems to suggest is that a centrally set cap will be able to avoid market volatility, and ultimately litigation. This idea of reducing the number of court cases by centralising the process of determining the cap is widely shared among scholars and it is based on a deeper belief that the process of constructing emissions markets is separable from the operation of emissions markets. In chapter one, I highlighted the landmark piece on emissions trading by Ackerman and Stewart, in which they identify four administrative tasks in setting up an emissions trading scheme, ranking cap-setting on the top of the list, before concluding that 'that's that'.[133] This type of description is significant for a number of reasons. First, it portrays the construction of emissions trading schemes, and the cap-setting process as a mere technicality before the actual trading starts, thus creating a clear divide between the operation and the function of emissions trading, which equally creates a state/market distinction. Moreover, it envisions a minimal role for the state or, as described by Stewart in a more recent publication, the state is seen to play a 'simplified

---

[128] J van Zeben, 'Case Note: Respective Powers of the European Member State and Commission Regarding Emissions Trading and Allowance Allocation' (2010) 12 *Environmental Law Review* 216, 223.

[129] As cited in EUROPA, 'Emissions Trading: Commission Takes New Decisions on Estonia and Polish National Allocation Plans for 2008–12' (Brussels, 11 December 2009) europa.eu/rapid/press ReleasesAction.do?reference=IP/09/1907&format=HTML&aged=1&language=EN&guiLanguage=en, accessed 9 October 2012.

[130] G Dari-Mattiacci and J van Zeben, 'Legal and Market Uncertainty in Market-Based Instruments: The Case of the EU ETS' (2011) 19 *New York University Environmental Law Journal*.

[131] Revised Directive (n 2) Art 9 provides that 'The Community-wide quantity of allowances issued each year starting in 2013 shall decrease in a linear manner beginning from the mid-point of period 2008 to 2012'.

[132] EUROPA, 'Emission Trading System: Statement by Commissioner Stavros Dimas on the Court Rulings related to the Commission Decisions on the Estonian and Polish National Allocation Plans for 2008–12' (Brussels, 24 September 2009) europa.eu/rapid/pressReleasesAction.do?reference=IP/09/1355 &format=HTML&aged=1&language=EN&guiLanguage=en, accessed 11 October 2012.

[133] B Ackerman and R Stewart, 'Reforming Environmental Law' (1985) 37 *Stanford Law Review* 1333, 1347.

role'.[134] This is indeed the key reason why emissions trading is often predicted to reduce litigation.[135] It should be noted that these observations are made in a US-based legal context[136] but as illustrated by Dimas' statement above, key EU officials seem to hold similar assumptions. These predictions, nonetheless, sit uncomfortably with the fact that the steel industry together with, and under the umbrella of, the European Confederation of Iron and Steel Industries (EUROFER), has already earmarked the Commission's decisions on benchmarking for litigation.[137] Benchmarking, as explained in the previous chapter, forms part of the centralised cap-setting procedure, allowing the Commission to determine the level at which certain carbon heavy industry will receive free emissions allowance permits.[138] The key reason behind this legal action is the belief that the Commission has overstepped its competences in deciding on the benchmark levels.[139] With the snapshots set out in this chapter of EU ETS litigation in mind – and especially the wide applicability of the *Command-and-Control Model* to the General Court's discourse – it seems obvious that a centralised cap is an unlikely panacea to the high volume of EU ETS case law. Competence testing is essentially the core of EU law, and as such an inherent part of EU ETS legal culture.

VI. Conclusion

The analysis in this chapter – an examination of how emissions trading as a regulatory concept is understood by the EU Courts, the Commission and applicants in EU ETS case law – provides the second step in unpacking emissions trading discourses using the EU ETS as a case study. As a preliminary step to this case study,

---

[134] R Stewart, 'Instrument Choice' in D Bodansky, J Brunnée and E Hey (eds), *The Handbook of International Environmental Law* (Oxford University Press, Oxford, 2007) 145, 156.

[135] Ackerman and Stewart, 'Reforming Environmental Law' (n 133), R Stewart, 'Economic Incentives for Environmental Protection: Opportunities and Obstacles' in R Revesz, P Sands and R Stewart (eds), *Environmental Law, the Economy and Sustainable Development: The United States, the European Union and the International Community* (Cambridge University Press, Cambridge, 2000) 171, 202, D Ellerman, 'Are Cap-and-Trade Programs More Environmentally Effective than Conventional Regulation?' in J Freeman and C Kolstad (eds), *Moving to Markets in Environmental Regulation: Lessons From Twenty Years of Experience* (Oxford University Press, Oxford, 2007) 48–63. These cap/trade, or construction/trading distinctions are clearly described in D Driesen, 'Capping Carbon' (2010) 1 *Environmental Law* 1.

[136] G Pring, 'A Decade of Emissions Trading in the USA: Experience and Observations for the EU' in M Peeters and K Deketelaere (eds), *EU Climate Change Policy: The Challenge of New Regulatory Initiatives* (Edward Elgar, Cheltenham, 2006) 188, 195.

[137] ENDS, 'EU Steel Industry to sue over ETS Benchmarks' (Brussels, 4 April 2011) www.endseurope.com/25989/eu-steel-industry-to-sue-over-ets-benchmarks, accessed 10 October 2012.

[138] Revised Directive (n 2) Art 10a.

[139] SteelOrbis, 'EUROFER to Challenge EC Decision on Benchmarks for Steel' (4 April 2011) www.steelorbis.com/steel-news/latest-news/eurofer-to-challenge-ec-decision-on-benchmarks-for-steel-591841.htm, accessed 10 June 2011. The contested Decision is Commission Decision 2011/278/EU of 27 April 2011 determining transitional Union-wide rules for harmonised free allocation of emission allowances pursuant to Article 10a of Directive 2003/87/EC of the European Parliament and of the Council, [2011] L130/1.

I stressed the importance of legal culture in analysing the EU ETS in chapter three. Against this legal background, in chapter four, I illustrated how the Commission's narrative on emissions trading has developed to respond to different regulatory objectives, and how the regulatory focus, governance structure and thus also the conceptualisation of the EU emissions trading regime has changed over time. In this chapter I have pointed to a variety of understandings of the EU emissions trading regime by examining ETS-related judicial discourses, and focusing on the meaning given to this regulatory strategy by the EU Courts. These different nuances in conceptualising emissions trading as a regulatory concept – either within the EU legal context, or elsewhere – are rarely identified in environmental law scholarship, and in the next chapter I examine why this is the case.

6

The 'Honeymoon' in
Environmental Law Scholarship

I. Introduction

To this point, my focus in this book has been upon how emissions trading is conceptualised as a regulatory concept by scholars, policy- and lawmakers, and in the
courtroom. Moreover, I have highlighted the importance of legal culture in
understanding the various shapes that these conceptualisations take. What this
study has shown, albeit principally through snapshots, is at least two things. First,
it has illustrated the breadth of different environmental and non-environmental
problems that emissions trading is thought to respond to, including creating
competitive economies, substituting bureaucratic control of common resources,
and complying with international environmental law.[1] Second, it has demonstrated that the key dilemma underpinning emissions trading discourse, and what
in fact distinguishes the different visions of emissions trading apart, is the view of
the role that the state, the market and rights in emissions allowances play or ought
to play in emissions trading regimes. This kaleidoscopic picture of emissions
trading stands in contrast to what I described in chapter one to be a generically
uniform prism through which emissions trading scholarship tends to view
and engage with this subject.[2] Having identified the problem with how emissions
trading schemes are perceived in law at the start of this book and thereafter, in
chapters two to five, provided case studies, focusing on the EU ETS, which have
exposed the legal complexities involved in emissions trading, I now intend to
explore why environmental law scholarship has failed to investigate, or at least
recognise, such complexities. In particular, I wish to make two points in this
chapter.

The starting point for this chapter is that emissions trading has enjoyed a long
'honeymoon'[3] in environmental law scholarship. The honeymoon consists of
promoting and preferring emissions trading above other regulatory strategies

---

[1] Chs 2 and 4.
[2] Ch 1, sections I–II.
[3] Description borrowed from L Heinzerling, 'The Environment' in M Tushnet and P Cane (eds), *The Oxford Handbook of Legal Studies* (Oxford University Press, Oxford, 2003) 701, 712. I have used the honeymoon analogy in an earlier publication, see S Bogojević, 'Ending the Honeymoon: Deconstructing
Emissions Trading Discourses' (2009) 21 *Journal of Environmental Law* 443.

without, however, engaging with legal complexities embedded in conceptualising, scrutinising, applying and/or managing emissions trading schemes. In examining this phenomenon, I try to identify ways in which environmental law scholarship manages to oversimplify emissions trading, treating it as a mere tool – which indeed is a manifestation of the honeymoon.

The second point relates to the explanation of *why* environmental law scholarship enjoys this honeymoon, which is an enquiry that stands at the heart of this chapter. Here I give details of the framework and the nature of emissions trading debates in environmental law scholarship. More precisely, I show that strong tendencies exist to dichotomise emissions trading discussions according to 'market versus state' distinctions, as well as to focus on the global context and transferability of laws in debating this regulatory option. These frameworks, coupled with the interdisciplinary, promotional and pragmatic features of the emissions trading literature are contributory factors to the marginalisation of the relevance of law and the importance of legal specificities to emissions trading, which, accumulatively create a perception of emissions trading as a straightforward regulatory mechanism, imposable across environmental settings and public law contexts. An investigation into these frameworks and the nature of emissions trading discussions exposes the assumptions that underpin this oversimplified picture of emissions trading as a regulatory concept and thus helps to explain why the honeymoon persists in environmental law scholarship.

The significance of drawing a map of how emissions trading is approached in environmental law scholarship is twofold. First, it marks the start of a debate on how to create a coherent and rigid framework of analysis for emissions trading in law, which includes thinking critically of the way in which scholars debate and view emissions trading as a regulatory concept within the umbrella of environmental law. The motive is to better appreciate current methodologies so as to be better equipped in fleshing out legal aspects of emissions trading schemes.[4] This exercise is thus distinct both from critiquing the use of market mechanisms in environmental law, and suggesting that environmental law scholars must adopt my methodology employed in this book to their respective studies of emissions trading regimes.

Second, it forms part of a maturing process that environmental law scholarship as an intellectual enterprise is currently undergoing.[5] Understanding the type of challenges that environmental law scholars face in committing to a certain scholarly field and mapping environmental law methodologies are examples of important steps toward helping environmental scholarship mature and think more critically about itself as a subject.[6] By examining *how* environmental law scholarship projects

---

[4] In other words, to develop an environmental law expertise in relation to emissions trading. On the point about expertise, see E Fisher, 'The Rise of Transnational Environmental Law and the Expertise of Environmental Lawyers' (2012) 1 *Transnational Environmental Law* 43.

[5] E Fisher and others, 'Maturity and Methodology: Starting a Debate about Environmental Law Scholarship' (2009) 21 *Journal of Environmental Law* 213.

[6] ibid 243–49. See also E Scotford, *Environmental Principles and the Evolution of Environmental Law* (Hart Publishing, Oxford, 2013).

emissions trading as a simple regulatory tool and *why* it commits to this view, this chapter contributes to this maturing process. Considering that the honeymoon is attributed to a lack of scholarly reflection of complexities behind emissions trading, this exercise is particularly pressing.

This chapter is structured as follows. In section II, I briefly clarify the notion of a 'honeymoon' in environmental law, or more precisely, how Heinzerling uses, as well as the way in which I employ the term in this chapter. Subsequently, in section III, I identify the reasons why the honeymoon exists. Here I list the interdisciplinary (or, more precisely, the relationship between economics and environmental law), pragmatic and promotional function of environmental law scholarship, as well as environmental law scholarship's tendency to create, or enhance market/state dichotomies, and the global outlook through which emissions trading schemes tend to be defined in environmental law literature, as contributory factors to the honeymoon.

A common theme in this list of reasons is immaturity of methodology, which is clearly projected in the way that environmental law scholarship addresses the use of emissions markets in environmental law as straightforward, without establishing a robust scholarly process through which to critically assess legal aspects relating to such trading. In section IV, I evaluate these findings and in reflecting on how environmental law scholarship can mature, I draw parallels between the approach to emissions trading in environmental law scholarship and common public/private distinctions in legal scholarship. In particular, I show that the way, in which environmental law scholarship perceives law as marginal, or technical in the context of carbon markets, is analogous to tendencies in legal scholarship to distinguish between the state and the market. This exercise is brief but it shows that in order to create a more robust and mature methodology of analysis for emissions trading in law, environmental law scholars need to think critically about how they engage with the application of markets in environmental law, and thus revaluate its approach to the relationship between the market and the (multi-level) state with regard to emissions trading. In section V, I set out and summarise the conclusions of this chapter.

Four points should be made clear before starting. First, my intention in this chapter is not to point fingers at current environmental law scholarship from a methodological pedestal and argue that methodologies applied in this book are more 'mature' or 'better' than existing ones. The reasons that I list as the source of the honeymoon are ultimately methodological challenges that I faced in conducting research for this book, which overlap with methodological challenges that environmental law scholars are confronted with in studying this topic. As such, this chapter seeks to reflect on, rather than to prescribe environmental law methodologies.

Second, this chapter does not assess the extent to which the framework of analysis for emissions trading applied in the previous chapters – that is, the use of the *Economic Efficiency*, the *Private Property Rights*, and the *Command-and-Control* models to demonstrate and flesh out legal complexities embedded in emissions trading discourses – manages to respond to the methodological challenges posed by the honeymoon. Rather it acts as a springboard to this discussion, which is set out in the next and final chapter of this book.

Third, the focus in this chapter is on literature from earlier chapters; that is predominately environmental law scholarship concerning the EU ETS, stemming from academic communities in the UK/EU. However, I rely heavily on US literature because much of emissions trading scholarship stems from the US, and indeed also the concept of the honeymoon.

II. Defining the 'Honeymoon' in Environmental Law Scholarship

According to Heinzerling, all market-based mechanisms,[7] including pollution trading schemes, are enjoying a 'long honeymoon'[8] in legal scholarship. Written as part of a commentary on environmental law scholarship, Heinzerling uses the notion of a honeymoon to critique the manner in which legal scholars have engaged, or rather failed to engage 'carefully and critically',[9] in debates on market mechanisms. In this context, she makes two related points. First, she focuses her criticism on the way in which environmental law scholarship has spiralled into 'irrational exuberance'[10] to conclude that market mechanisms are not only the solution to *some* environmental problems but that they in fact are the *only* solution.[11] Second, she tracks this academic exuberance to the US, the sulphur dioxide programme and the Emergency Planning and Community Rights-to-Know-Act – two market mechanisms that are widely considered successful due to their achievement in reducing chemical use and release at a far lower cost than traditional regulation.[12] Heinzerling explains that based on these two regulatory experiences, scholars encourage the application of market mechanisms to other environmental settings without, however, taking contextual differences into consideration.[13] The key argument that Heinzerling thus furthers in observing environmental law scholarship is not an outright rejection of the use of market mechanisms but rather a criticism and warning to environmental lawyers in promoting this particular regulatory strategy to be applied 'everywhere at once'.[14]

---

[7] Market mechanisms include effluent taxes, emissions trading schemes or, any environmental requirement that enlists the market in the service of environmental protection. J Nash, 'Too Much Market? Conflict between Tradable Pollution Allowances and the "Polluter Pays" Principle' (2000) 24 *Harvard Environmental Law Review* 465, 482.
[8] Heinzerling, 'Environment' (n 3) 712.
[9] ibid 713.
[10] ibid.
[11] ibid.
[12] ibid 712–13.
[13] ibid 713.
[14] ibid.

In this chapter I align myself closely with Heinzerling's critique of environmental law scholarship. In fact, I position the 'honeymoon' analogy at the heart of the problem that this chapter addresses but I also build on Heinzerling's above-listed arguments in three distinct ways. To start with, I focus my study on the honeymoon and the reasons why it persists with references to emissions trading schemes, and in particular the EU ETS, as opposed to market-based mechanisms more broadly. Second, the significance of the honeymoon period in the context of this chapter is not only scholars' 'irrational exuberance' over the application of market-mechanisms in environmental law but also, and more importantly, a systematic approach in environmental law scholarship to overlook legal complexities and specificities embedded in conceptualising, establishing and operating this regulatory strategy. Third, I trace the source of the honeymoon not only to isolated cases of successful regulatory experiences with market mechanisms but more broadly to the existing frameworks of analysis for emissions trading schemes in law. In particular, I demonstrate that there is a tendency to compartmentalise emissions trading debates into 'market versus state' camps and, as such, to dichotomise without thoroughly recognising the overlaps and intersections between the two. This particular framework, the focus on global characteristics and use of emissions trading, as well as the interdisciplinary, pragmatic and promotional nature of emissions trading debates in environmental law scholarship contribute to the honeymoon in two ways: they oversimplify and/or overlook legal questions and legal particularities of emissions trading, and subsequently also undermine the role that environmental law scholarship plays or ought to play in analysing this regulatory strategy.

In sum, the 'honeymoon' in this chapter refers to an oversimplification of emissions trading from a legal perspective. Next I show how the honeymoon manifests itself in environmental law scholarship and explore the reasons why it persists.

III. Why the Honeymoon in Environmental Law Scholarship Exists

Exposing reasons why emissions trading schemes enjoy a honeymoon in environmental law scholarship, or in other words why these regulatory strategies are treated as simple regulatory tools, is a difficult and controversial task for at least three reasons. First, it is difficult to engage in such a scrutiny without offending other scholars or appearing arrogant, or indeed both.[15] Second, this exercise requires analysing a very long and still ongoing debate. Discussions on emissions trading started with Coase's[16] analysis of the social cost of externalities or, pollution

---

[15] D Rhode, 'Legal Scholarship' (2002) 115 *Harvard Law Review* 1327, 1327.
[16] R Coase, 'The Problem of Social Cost' (1960) 3 *Journal of Law and Economics* 1. The influence of this article on environmental law scholarship is further explained in section III(A).

and have over the years expanded to regulatory debates in a range of different legal settings and academic communities. Obviously, and as stated at the outset of this chapter, my intention is not to cover the full 50 years of this debate but that raises the question regarding the validity of my assessment. Third, despite the seemingly long debate on this topic, emissions trading scholarship is in comparison to other more established legal areas still a very young subject, or indeed 'not yet mature'.[17] According to Bodansky, it is only with time and experience that a new legal field develops a robust scholarship that asks more challenging questions.[18] From this viewpoint, my explanations for the honeymoon may appear simply premature.

Against the backdrop of these points and before starting, it is important to clarify the purpose of understanding why the honeymoon exists. To start with, I do not claim that all legal scholarship on this topic assumes that trading schemes are simple and uniform from a legal perspective.[19] In fact, in defining the honeymoon, Heinzerling recognises that there is 'a handful of scholars . . . who have taken the time to look carefully, and critically'[20] at legal complexities of emissions trading and thus have not committed their scholarship to the honeymoon. Moreover, I acknowledge that my list of reasons as to why the honeymoon exists is non-exhaustive, yet it contains a common theme of methodological challenges that environmental law scholars grapple with working in this area. Understanding these challenges, and how they result in a failure to execute robust legal analysis of emissions trading in law, will better equip scholars from a methodological viewpoint to create revised frameworks of analysis and thereby pave the way for thorough legal scrutiny on this topic and an end to the honeymoon. To do so, is not a question of waiting for environmental law scholarship to mature, as such maturity can only be reached by dissecting methodologies and thinking critically about methods used to understand environmental laws.[21] In this regard, I identify five aspects of the current state of environmental law scholarship that has prolonged the honeymoon: its relationship with economics (interdisciplinary element), its pragmatic and promotional nature, its tendency to create and be insistent on strong dichotomies (market/state), as well as its fascination with the global context and examining laws through a global outlook. It is to this analysis that I now turn.

---

[17] F Convery, 'Reflections – The Emerging Literature on Emissions Trading in Europe' (2009) 2 *Review of Environmental Economics and Policy* 121, 123. This belief is engrained more generally in environmental law scholarship. Fisher and others, 'Maturity and Methodology' (n 5) 218, explain how this environmental law scholarship is often thought of as the 'Peter Pan of legal scholarship – "the discipline that never grew up"'.

[18] D Bodansky, *The Art and Craft of International Environmental Law* (Harvard University Press, Cambridge, Massachusetts, 2010) 35. Note that Bodansky refers to international environmental law.

[19] Indeed, in ch 1, section III(C) I acknowledge that there are scholars who take a more sophisticated view of emissions trading and who do not merely consider that emissions trading is a tool, imposable everywhere.

[20] Heinzerling, 'Environment' (n 3) 713.

[21] Fisher and others, 'Maturity and Methodology' (n 5) 213.

A. Interdisciplinarity of Environmental Law Scholarship

The first[22] reason why the honeymoon exists is related to the interdisciplinary nature of environmental law scholarship.[23] Its subject-matter is by itself inter-disciplinary[24] and there is a 'methodological expectation'[25] that this scholarship be interdisciplinary. In the case of emissions trading debates, which are dominated by economists, such methodological expectations demand that environmental law scholarship challenges and engages with claims from non-legal disciplines. However, due to its failure to do so, environmental law scholarship has created an image of emissions trading where the relevance of legal scholarship and law, com-pared to economics, is marginal. Two interrelated explanations underlie this approach, each contributing to the honeymoon.

The first reason why environmental law scholarship fails to engage with interdis-ciplinary debates on emissions trading is that there is no established methodology for such activity. Emissions trading scholarship is hugely influenced by economics, not the least because emissions trading, as a regulatory idea, derives from this dis-cipline.[26] As explained in chapters one and two, emissions trading is based on a theory concerning the optimal solution to the allocation of social cost for pollu-tion. Coase, an economist, articulated this theory by claiming that pollution is an externality for which a bargaining system ought to be created, allowing the right to pollute to be traded to the highest bidder.[27] This idea was quickly developed by at least four other economists; Crocker,[28] Montgomery[29] Demsetz[30] and Dales,[31] who investigated a similar theory's applicability also to other commons, including water

---

[22] This numerical ordering does not reflect the importance of the reasons listed.

[23] Heinzerling described environmental law as 'pervasively interdisciplinary'. Heinzerling 'Environment' (n 3) 702.

[24] eg any legal regulation and legal activity that falls within the field of environmental law is sup-ported and legitimised by, eg the work of biologists, chemists, economists, engineers, geneticists and physicists, and, additionally, each is underpinned by cultural assumptions, and circumstantial factors. J Holder and M Lee, *Environmental Protection, Law and Policy* (2nd edn, Cambridge University Press, Cambridge, 2007) xii. Emissions trading is a typical 'shared paradigm' where a variety of intellectual disciplines are involved in considering the shape that the emissions market ought to take, including considerations as wide apart as metrology, international and domestic politics, and industry lobbying. D MacKenzie, F Muniesa and L Siu, 'Introduction' in D MacKenzie, F Muniesa and L Siu (eds), *Do Economists Make Markets? On the Performativity of Economics* (Princeton University Press, Princeton, 2007) 1, 15–16.

[25] Fisher and others, 'Maturity and Methodology' (n 5) 232.

[26] ibid 703.

[27] Coase, 'The Problem of Social Cost' (n 16) 3.

[28] T Crocker, 'The Structuring of Atmospheric Pollution Control System' in H Wolozin (ed), *The Economics of Air Pollution* (WW Norton & Co, New York City, 1966) 61.

[29] W Montgomery, 'Markets in Licenses and Efficient Pollution Control Programs' (1972) 5 *Journal of Economic Theory* 395.

[30] H Demsetz, 'The Cost of Transacting' (1968) 82 *Quarterly Journal of Economics* 33, H Demsetz, 'Toward a Theory of Property Rights' (1967) 57 *American Economic Review* 347.

[31] J Dales, 'Land, Water, and Ownership' (1968) 1 *Canadian Journal of Economics* 791, J Dales, *Pollution, Property and Prices: An Essay in Policy-Making and Economics* (University of Toronto Press, Toronto, 1970).

and land. Collectively, these studies are the 'academic and experimental platform'[32] that made emissions trading in practice possible. What this means is that if environmental law scholars want to 'carefully and critically' scrutinise emissions trading, they need to understand a wide array of topics that the theory covers, including Coase's theorem, economic ideas about creating a bargaining system and property rights, as well as regulatory theory and its application.[33] Such an exercise is obviously methodologically challenging but in failing to engage with these interdisciplinary debates, or even only acknowledging the difficulties therewith, theoretical claims regarding emissions trading remain untested from a legal perspective.[34] This is remarkable considering that theory-based emissions trading literature tends not to discuss emissions trading schemes per se but rather examines more generally various theories about the optimal solution to the allocation of resources in various commons.[35] This makes it easy to assume that differences between how theory and the law define emissions trading exist. However, as environmental law scholarship fails to recognise the possibility of such differences and challenge non-legal claims, the role of law in interdisciplinary debates is left to seem marginal, and thereby the honeymoon is prolonged.

The second reason why environmental law scholarship has failed to engage more critically with non-legal contributions on emissions trading is self-doubt, or the common belief held by legal and non-legal scholars alike, that in order to engage with emissions trading, legal scholars need to be equipped with special skills, and most obviously understand economics.[36] Markets are generally understood to be the domain of economists,[37] and equally market mechanisms, including emissions trading, is strongly assumed to be based on economic calculations that are best understood from an economic viewpoint.[38] This view is clearly reflected in the composition of policy- and lawmaking institutions; for instance, the majority of officials drafting the EU ETS were economists,[39] and it is widely held that the extent to which emissions trading schemes are applied in various jurisdictions and environmental settings depends on whether economists are involved in the decision-making process. Stavins verbalises this correlation by stating that 'Traditional regulatory programs require regulators with a technical or legal-based skill-set. Market-based

[32] D Ellerman, F Convery and C de Perthuis, *Pricing Carbon: The European Union Emissions Trading Scheme* (Cambridge University Press, Cambridge, 2010) 9.
[33] Fisher and others, 'Maturity and Methodology' (n 5) 238.
[34] See how this argument is set out against environmental law scholarship more broadly, ibid.
[35] G Brown, 'Renewable Natural Resource Management and Use Without Markets' (2000) 38 *Journal of Economic Literature* 875.
[36] Fisher and others, 'Maturity and Methodology' (n 5) 226.
[37] See N Fligstein, *The Architecture of Markets: An Economic Sociology of Twenty-First-Century Capitalist Societies* (Princeton University Press, Princeton, 2001).
[38] M Lee, *EU Environmental Law: Challenges, Change and Decision-Making* (Hart Publishing, Oxford, 2005) 185.
[39] With regard to the creation of the EU ETS, Jos Delbeke, Head-of-unit, and Arthur Runge-Metzger, Mattio Vainio, Peter Zapfel and Peter Vis were central to the implementation of the EU ETS and are all economists. Others include Olivia Hartride (political scientist) and Damien Medows, Yvon Slingberg and Jürgen Lefevere (lawyers). Ellerman, Convery and Perthuis, *Pricing Carbon* (n 32) 26.

instruments require an economics orientation'.[40] On a similar basis, it is explained that the EU officials, who were in favour of emissions trading when emissions trading was initiated in the EU legal order, were 'disposed to market approaches'[41] and thus able to understand 'the importance of market signals as animators of environmentally responsible behaviour'.[42] Equally, in the US, the fact that the Environmental Defence Fund (EDF) is one of the great proponents of implementing emissions trading in the US legal context, is explained with reference to its composition: 'EDF has always had a good number of economists on its staff'.[43] Such views allow the honeymoon to persist, as they are left uncontested by environmental law scholars and insinuate that the importance of law, in comparison with economics, is marginal in the context of emissions trading.

Following these methodological challenges, the way in which the honeymoon manifests itself in environmental law scholarship concerns the *focus*, as opposed to the quality, of emissions trading debates. More precisely, the fact that economics is dominant in these discussions determines the type of questions that are discussed and considered pressing. This further defines how emissions trading as a regulatory strategy is perceived. Freeman and Kolstad help to elucidate this point:[44]

> [E]conomists, for example, focus on the potential of regulation to generate cost savings, whereas legal scholars tend to focus more on procedural regularity and fairness in instrument design, as well as how tool selection might affect the balance of power among the different institutions of government, such as the courts and the executive branch. Economists worry about front-end design issues that affect efficiency, including the point of regulation, the system of allocating entitlements, and the cost of implementation. Lawyers translate these choices into statutes and regulations but traditionally spend most of their energy on the back-end struggles over liability and compliance that frequently lead to legal challenges.

The point of this statement is clear: lawyers and economists view regulation differently and thus emphasise different aspects of law as important. This may seem an obvious point to make, yet it is an important one to highlight in the context of interdisciplinary emissions trading debates, as it explains why economics-related features of emissions trading, dealing with topics such as design issues or efficiency, inevitably are in focus. Two brief examples show that this indeed is the case.

---

[40] R Stavins and B Whitehead, 'Market-Based Environmental Politics' in J Dryzek and D Schlosberg (eds), *Debating the Earth: The Environmental Politics Reader* (Oxford University Press, Oxford, 2005) 229, 232.

[41] Here, reference is made to Catherine Day, who served in the Cabinet of Peter Sutherland's Directorate General for Competition. Ellerman, Convery and Perthuis, *Pricing Carbon* (n 32) 27.

[42] Here reference is made to Wallström, the former EU Commissioner for Environment, ibid.

[43] C Schroeder, 'Public Choice and Environmental Policy' in D Farber and A O'Connell (eds), *Research Handbook on Public Choice and Public Law* (Edward Elgar, Cheltenham, 2010) 450, 476.

[44] J Freeman and C Kolstad, 'Prescriptive Environmental Regulations versus Market-Based Incentives' in J Freeman and C Kolstad (eds), *Moving to Markets in Environmental Regulation: Lessons After Twenty Years of Experience* (Oxford University Press, Oxford, 2006) 3, 6–7.

First, the previous chapter demonstrated that one of the most pressing legal questions relating to emissions trading in practice – at least in the EU legal context – is the process of determining caps. In emissions trading literature, however, this subject has attracted only a modest scholarly debate. Driesen explains that this is due to economists focusing on *trading*-specific questions, as opposed to policy matters, which cap-setting is understood to represent.[45] In section D, I will highlight how such cap-*and*-trading distinctions create market and state dichotomies in emissions trading scholarship. Here, the focus on primarily trading matters is highlighted as a symptom of the influence of economics on the type of questions that are thought of as important in relation to emissions trading.

Second, a major recent study of 'excellent' and 'most valuable literature' on emissions trading,[46] concludes that nine topics have been most significant in this regard – eight of which have economic focus.[47] Interestingly, this survey establishes that 'the [emissions trading] literature is poor because there has been little understanding of how institutional rules have been the dominant force in shaping the outcome in the market'.[48] Ultimately, what this proves is that economics has had a real impact on the type of questions that are considered 'valuable' to investigate with regard to emissions trading but also that there is a gap and a strong need for legal scholarship in this area, in particular in analysing the intersections between emissions markets and policy and law, as opposed to setting these apart.

In sum, what the discussion above shows is that the interdisciplinary nature of emissions trading debates involve methodological challenges that make emissions trading a difficult subject for environmental law scholars to claim. Yet failing to engage in these interdisciplinary debates leaves the impression that law is irrelevant. It is in this prevailing, non-legal focus of emissions trading as a regulatory mechanism that the honeymoon manifests itself.

B. Pragmatic Approach in Environmental Law Scholarship

The second reason why the honeymoon exists is that the bulk of environmental law scholarship adopts a pragmatic approach to analysing emissions trading. This

---

[45] D Driesen, 'Capping Carbon' (2010) 1 *Environmental Law* 1, 9–10. Also L Heinzerling, 'Selling Pollution, Forcing Democracy' (1995) 14 *Stanford Environmental Law Journal* 300, 302–03. Note that both Driesen and Heinzerling refer to Dales, *Pollution Property, and Price* (n 31) as an example of scholarship that has contributed to the creation of this particular cap-*and*-trade distinction. Note that, similarly, the Commission has marked a difference between the procedure of determining the cap – which, under the Directive is a task entrusted to the Member States to set according to their 'overall environmental ambitions' – in the context of emissions trading. Commission of the European Communities, 'Green Paper on Greenhouse Gas Emissions Trading Within the European Union', COM(2000) 87 final, 7–8.

[46] Convery, 'Emerging Literature on Emissions Trading' (n 17) 122–23. This study included a survey of 52 research practitioners in the emissions trading field.

[47] These include: emissions reductions, allocation, competitiveness, distributional issues, new entrants, markets, finance, and trading. ibid 123. These questions are of economic focus if Freeman's and Kolstad's (n 44) distinction between focal points in economics and law is followed.

[48] ibid 133.

kind of scholarship serves primarily to describe and prescribe legal developments in this area and so deals mainly with questions of how emissions trading schemes operate, or ought to be reformed.[49] Utility-based literature of this kind is valuable in its own right; however, by focusing on functional issues, environmental law scholarship presents itself, as well as the legal aspects of emissions trading, as merely instrumental. As a result, law is viewed as a simple 'toolbox' and emissions trading a mere tool[50] – therein the honeymoon. Indeed, law is often, and in particular among non-lawyers, thought to have chiefly an instrumental function, or a so-called 'technical-serviant role'[51] to translate policies into 'operational language'.[52] This view is especially strong in environmental law, which, according to Coyle and Morrow, is essentially thought of as a series of statutory limitations on the exercise of private entitlements to protect the environment, valuable only instrumentally, 'rather than as an end in itself'.[53] Two things account for this honeymoon, and more specifically the pragmatic approach to emissions trading in environmental law scholarship.

First, much environmental law scholarship is descriptive because it had to grow up with environmental law itself.[54] Heinzerling explains, from a US perspective, how prior to the first environmental statutes, environmental law scholarship did not exist, which means that the key occupation of environmental law scholars has been to comment on issues of statutory content and design.[55] This has had two further implications, both contributing to the honeymoon. First, it has meant that environmental law scholarship is intimately tied to the practice and operation of

---

[49] In the context of the EU ETS, much environmental law scholarship, including my own, is concerned with reforms of this trading scheme, see, eg J van Zeben, '(De)Centralized Law-Making in the Revised EU ETS' (2009) 3 *Carbon and Climate Law Review* 340, M Peeters and S Weishaar, 'Exploring Uncertainties in the EU ETS: "Learning by Doing" Continues Beyond 2012' (2009) 1 *Carbon and Climate Law Review* 88, J Sim, 'EU ETS Allocation: Evaluation of Present System and Options Beyond 2012' (2006) 30 *Zeitschrift für Energiewirtschaft* 285, P Vis, 'Basic Design Options for Emissions Trading' in J Delbeke (ed), *EU Energy Law: The EU Greenhouse Gas Emissions Trading Scheme* (Claeys & Casteels, Leuven, 2006) 39, S Bogojević, 'The EU ETS Directive Revised: Yet Another Stepping Stone' (2009) 11 *Environmental Law Review* 279, G Schwarze, 'Including Aviation into the European Union Emissions Trading Scheme' (2007) 16 *European Environmental Law Review* 10.

[50] Assuming that environmental law is simply about functional matters (ie law being a type of 'toolbox' and thus focusing on mere 'instrumentality' as the law) is a typical misconception in present legal scholarship. E Fisher, 'Unpacking the Toolbox: Or Why the Public/Private Divide is Important in EC Environmental Law' in M Freedland and J-B Auby (eds), *The Public Law/Private Law Divide: Une Entente Assez Cordiale? la Distinction du Droit Public et du Droit Privé: Regards Français et Britanniques* (Hart Publishing, Oxford, 2006) 215, 217.

[51] J Weiler, 'Community, Member States and European Integration: Is the Law Relevant?' (2008) 21 *Journal of Common Market Studies* 39, 39. Weiler refers to Union law in this context. On this point, see also M Maduro, *We the Court: The European Court of Justice and the European Economic Constitution – A Critical Reading of Article 30 of the EC Treaty* (Hart Publishing, Oxford, 2002) 13–14.

[52] Weiler, 'Community, Member States and European Integration' (n 51).

[53] S Coyle and K Morrow, *Philosophical Foundations of Environmental Law: Property, Rights and Nature* (Hart Publishing, Oxford, 2004) 2–3.

[54] Heinzerling, 'Environment' (n 3) 701. Similar discussion in E Fisher, B Lange and E Scotford, *Environmental Law: Text, Cases and Materials* (Oxford University Press, Oxford, 2013) ch 1.

[55] Heinzerling, 'Environment' (n 3) 701.

law.[56] More precisely, environmental law scholarship is commonly expected by legislators, as well as by the industry and non-governmental organisations (NGOs) to explain how a certain law works or ought to function, so as to be able to plan how to proceed with legal reforms and investments respectively.[57] In the case of emissions trading, the industry's interest in the future and operation of these trading regimes is clearly reflected in the type of emissions trading scholarship that is published on this topic.[58] Ultimately, what this means with regard to the honeymoon is that it is perpetuated by the traditions of environmental law scholarship and expectations imposed on environmental law scholars to produce technical and practice-oriented reports on law.

Second, and interrelated with the previous point, environmental law scholarship adopts a pragmatic approach to studying emissions trading as a response to the high speed and scope of legal developments.[59] Climate change law and policy, in particular, are one of the fastest, 'if not the fastest'[60] moving legal areas in the EU and at international level. The case of the EU ETS, as explained in chapter four, is a prime example of such a fast-progressing area of law: the Directive[61] was implemented within only two years of its initiation and revised within six months of the proposal for revision.[62] The high pace and high number of laws, policy proposals, international negotiations and meetings about emissions trading add to the honeymoon by creating a methodological challenge for environmental lawyers working in this field attempting in obtaining an overview of the relevant policy and legal developments, at the same time, as managing to produce in-depth and thorough analyses that are not merely descriptive, or fragmented. This challenge is layered with an ever increasing and high-pressured demand from within the scholarship itself to produce emissions trading-related analysis, as clearly

---

[56] Fisher and others, *Environmental Law* (n 54) ch 1. Along the same lines but much more forceful, Schlag describes legal scholarship as 'case law journalism'. Discussing the state of legal scholarship more broadly and in the US context, Schlag argues that it offers little more than comments on recent court rulings. P Schlag, 'Spam Jurisprudence, Air Law, and the Rank Anxiety of Nothing Happening (A Report on the State of the Art)' (2009) 97 *Georgetown Law Journal* 803, 821–23.

[57] Heinzerling, 'Environment' (n 3) 703.

[58] See, eg S Deatherage, *Carbon Trading Law and Practice* (Oxford University Press, Oxford, 2011), A Brohé, N Eyre and N Howarth, *Carbon Markets: An International Business Guide* (Earthscan, London, 2009), R Antes, B Hansjürgen and P Letmathe, *Emissions Trading and Business* (Physica-Verlag HD, Heidelberg, 2010), R Bayon, A Hawn and K Hamilton, *Voluntary Carbon Markets An International Business Guide to What They Are and How They Work* (2nd edn, Earthscan, London, 2009).

[59] Similar note set out in Fisher and others, 'Maturity and Methodology' (n 5) 229, relating to environmental law scholarship more broadly. Also Macrory notes on the complexities of environmental law scholarship as a result of its fast-developing legislative and policy base, R Macrory, '"Maturity and Methodology": A Personal Reflection' (2009) 21 *Journal of Environmental Law* 251, 252–53.

[60] J Lefevere, 'A Climate of Change: An Analysis of Progress in EU and International Climate Change Policy' in J Scott (ed), *Environmental Protection: European Law and Governance* (Oxford University Press, New York, 2009) 171, 171.

[61] Council Directive 2003/87 establishing a scheme for greenhouse gas emission allowance trading within the Community and amending Directive 96/61, [2003] OJ L275/32.

[62] Commission Communication, '20 20 by 2020 – Europe's Climate Change Opportunity', COM(2008) 30 final, Directive 2009/29 of the European Parliament and of the European Council amending the Directive 2003/87 so as to improve and extend the greenhouse gas emission allowance trading scheme of the Community, [2009] OJ L140/63.

reflected in the growing number of journals specialising in climate and carbon law.[63] This state of affairs has induced environmental law scholars to commit their scholarship to chiefly commenting on legal designs and options for emissions trading and thereby maintaining the honeymoon in environmental law scholarship.

Ultimately what the discussion above shows is that the honeymoon exists in part due to the practice-oriented nature of environmental law scholarship and in part due to the high-paced nature of legal developments relating to emissions trading regimes. These reasons are clearly interlinked, and their effect on the legal scholarship on emissions trading has been to portray legal aspects relating to emissions trading regimes as mere technicalities.

C. Promotional Environmental Law Scholarship

A third reason for the honeymoon, and the persistence of the image that emissions trading is straightforward, relates to the promotional nature of emissions trading debates in environmental law scholarship. This 'promotional' aspect is manifested in that much emissions trading discussion in environmental law scholarship focuses on endorsing, rather than critically assessing emissions trading regimes, and as such overlooks and/or oversimplifies the legal complexities involved. The basis for such scholarship is related to the previous point regarding the close nexus between environmental law scholarship and the practice of law. Indeed most scholarship that is promotional in this context is aimed primarily at policy- and lawmakers and the industry, rallying support for the use of this regulatory strategy in environmental law.[64] The honeymoon manifests itself in two ways in this regard.

First, promotional environmental law scholarship on emissions trading overlooks legal and contextual complexities involved with emissions trading, and calls for trading regimes to be applied to all environmental settings – without attending to legal specificities of such suggestions.[65] Chapter one provided a long list of examples of how emissions trading schemes and their use in environmental law is addressed with forceful zest.[66] This list includes portraying emissions trading as a system able to create 'win-win' solutions[67] that involves no losers, and which in

---

[63] In only three years, at least three different journals specialising on climate law have been established: *Climate Law* (2010), *International Journal of Climate Change Strategies and Management* (2009), and *Carbon and Climate Law Review* (2008). This, in addition to bourgeoning literature on climate law being published in traditional environmental law journals.

[64] See, eg D Schoenbrod, R Stewart and K Wyman, *Breaking the Logjam: Environmental Protection that Will Work* (Yale University Press, New Haven, 2010), B Ackerman and R Stewart, 'Reforming Environmental Law' (1985) 37 *Stanford Law Review* 1333, and n 58.

[65] Heinzerling, 'Environment' (n 3) 713. As explained, Heinzerling refers to market mechanisms more broadly.

[66] Section II.

[67] G Boyle, 'Greenhouse Gas Emissions Trading and Duties of the State: A Preliminary Review of Alberta's Specified Gas Emitters Regulation' (2008) 2 *Climate and Carbon Law Review* 160.

times of climate change, we have 'no choice but to implement',[68] or even, which ought to be employed at all times, 'unless one can show they are somehow deficient'.[69] This kind of scholarship is useful in crystallising possible advantages with emissions trading but as Heinzerling explains, it prolongs the honeymoon in the sense that it advances an image of emissions trading being applicable 'everywhere at once'[70] – without mentioning the legal probability or complexities of such a view.

Second, and following from the former point, emissions trading schemes tend to be furthered as simple regulatory strategies, which is also the reason why they are believed to be imposable in different regulatory contexts. This is apparent in two ways. First, emissions trading is commonly referred to as a 'simple solution',[71] applicable to complex environmental problems, such as climate change. The key belief underpinning this view is that emissions trading schemes are understood to grant great flexibility, in particular being extendable to new sectors, market actors, and gases with allegedly greater ease than direct regulation.[72] Second, emissions trading is presented as straightforward both in its construction and operation. As explained in chapter one, in a landmark piece on emissions trading, Ackerman and Stewart identify four bureaucratic tasks in the setting up and managing of emissions trading schemes before concluding that 'that's that'.[73] This kind of oversimplification is not a rarity present only in this particular article but is a general approach to describing the construction process of emissions trading.[74] Similarly, this description is part of a broader argument that suggests that emissions trading is easier to establish than direct regulation[75] and that a generic step-by-step design model exists for creating emissions trading schemes.[76] What these descriptions create is a sentiment that emissions trading is 'intuitively simple',[77]

---

[68] This assumption is described in R Baldwin, 'Regulation Lite: The Rise of Emissions Trading' (2008) 2 *Regulation and Governance* 193, 194.

[69] As explained in Freeman and Kolstad, 'Prescriptive Environmental Regulation versus Market-Based Incentives' (n 44) 5.

[70] Heinzerling, 'Environment' (n 3) 713. As previously explained, Heinzerling refers to market mechanisms more broadly.

[71] B Hansjürgen, 'Concluding Observations' in B Hansjürgen (ed), *Emissions Trading for Climate Policy: US and European Perspectives* (Cambridge University Press, Cambridge, 2005) 222, 223. Hansjürgen refers to the EU ETS in this regard.

[72] ibid. For a fuller list of the reasons that are used to promote emissions trading, see R Baldwin, M Cave and M Lodge, *Understanding Regulation: Theory, Strategy, and Practice* (2nd edn, Oxford University Press, Oxford, 2012) 198–200.

[73] Ackerman and Stewart, 'Reforming Environmental Law' (n 64) 1347. These include setting the cap, establishing an auction system for emissions allowances, a title registry, and a penalty system.

[74] Indeed the term 'cap-and-trade' serves to indicate that emissions trading schemes based on this system are easy to set up. Driesen, 'Capping Carbon' (n 45).

[75] ibid 11.

[76] ibid, T Tietenberg, *Emissions Trading: Principles and Practice* (2nd edn, Resources for the Future, Washington DC, 2006) 17, D Mavrakis and P Konidari, 'Classification of Emissions Trading Scheme Design Characteristics' (2003) 13 *European Environment* 48, 52. This point is described in ch 1, section II.

[77] J Skjærseth and J Wettestad, *EU Emissions Trading: Initiation, Decision-Making and Implementation* (Ashgate Publishing, Burlington, 2008) 154.

which is a depiction employed in order to push for endorsement of this regulatory strategy. This shows that projecting emissions trading as a straightforward regulatory process is the underlying motive of promotion-focused environmental law scholarship. On this ground, the honeymoon persists.

As explained earlier, Heinzerling specifically criticises the extent to which environmental law scholarship has 'spiralled into irrational exuberance'[78] to further market-based mechanisms to all environmental law problems. The discussion above shows that in the context of emissions trading, such exuberance can be traced to the aim of seeking to mobilise support for the use of this regulatory strategy, which is also why emissions trading is projected as easy and straightforward. Promotional environmental law scholarship thus perpetuates the honeymoon.

D. Framing Dichotomies: Market versus State

The fourth reason why the honeymoon exists in environmental law scholarship is the tendency to entrench and commit to dichotomous framing[79] of emissions trading debates according to market/state distinctions. This dichotomy is expressed in the framing of market mechanisms, here as exemplified by emissions trading, as a regulatory strategy that is distinct from direct regulation on the basis that the latter is state-controlled while the former operates via market mechanisms.[80] Two camps lead such debates:[81] one that emphasises various capabilities of markets[82] to manage pollution *better* than state-based regulation because it operates via market mechanisms, and another that focuses on market failures and inequalities produced by economies to argue for central management of pollution control systems. Both camps are underpinned by a particular vision and ideology concerning what the market and the state do, or ought to do. On the one side, the market is charged with theories regarding *government* failure, or the so-called loss of faith in the state, which the market is understood to remedy by establishing a more effective and transparent management system. On the other side, the government is seen as a necessary actor

---

[78] Heinzerling, 'Environment' (n 3) 713.
[79] The significance of 'framing' is discussed in ch 2, section II. Here it simply refers to a particular categorisation of a specific topic, which ultimately affects the way in which the subject in question is studied and understood. S Jasanoff, 'Heaven and Earth' in S Jasanoff and M Martello (eds), *Earthly Politics: Local and Global in Environmental Governance* (MIT Press, Cambridge, Mass, 2004) 31. See also L Heinzerling, 'Climate Change in the Supreme Court' (2008) 38 *Environmental Law* 1, 7–8, J Mashaw, *Greed, Chaos, and Governance: Using Public Choice to Improve Public Law* (Yale University Press, New Haven, 1997) 1.
[80] This presumption is fleshed out in N Graham, 'The Mythology of Environmental Markets' in D Grinlinton (ed), *Property Rights and Sustainability* (Martinus Nijhoff Publishers, Leiden, 2011) 149, 160.
[81] J Holder and M Lee, *Environmental Protection, Law and Policy* (2nd edn, Cambridge University Press, Cambrdige, 2007) xii.
[82] Discussions on markets 'swim in a sea of discourse'. H White, 'Modeling Discourse in and around Markets' (2000) 27 *Poetics* 117, 118. Here, however, I focus on environmental markets, and more precisely emissions markets in environmental law scholarship.

to fix *market* failures.[83] Ultimately, each camp upholds ideal and oversimplified[84] versions of the 'state' or the 'market' to the effect that any discussion about emissions markets and market reforms fall either with the market, at the one end of the spectrum, or with direct regulation; that is, the state-entrenched view, at the other – thus creating state/market distinctions in environmental law scholarship.[85] In both instances, the opportunity to recognise the symbiotic and legally complex relationship between markets and the state is overlooked, and thus the honeymoon in environmental law scholarship is prolonged. This dichotomy, and the honeymoon, is visible in the following five examples of how emissions markets and the state are described in environmental law scholarship.

In the first camp, emissions markets tend to be regarded as politically neutral regulatory systems.[86] The idea is that emissions markets are democratic institutions, which allow market actors to secure agreements on their own terms[87] and according to what the majority sees fit.[88] Along these lines, Sunstein presents emissions markets as being 'democracy reinforcing'.[89] This view is based on the idea that emissions trading systems demand attention to be fixed at pollution levels and by focusing on the overall environmental quality – as opposed to specific technologies – they inspire the public's participation in deliberating environmental goals.[90] These descriptions are contrasted with state-controlled regulatory regimes where decisions regarding 'how', 'where' and 'who' should reduce emissions are fettered by political choice and vested interests.[91] In fact, the underlying argument is that the creation of emissions markets will 'help to reclaim community control over decisions about our government from distant and bureaucratic and selfish factions'.[92] This is a clear example of state/market distinctions in environmental law scholarship where emissions markets are understood to deliver regulatory choices independently from the state.

---

[83] Stern, for instance, argues that climate change is the biggest market failure to date, N Stern, *The Economics of Climate Change: The Stern Review* (Cambridge University Press, Cambridge, 2007) 1.

[84] According to Ackerman and Heinzerling, depictions of markets tend to be simple enough to 'fit on bumper stickers'. F Ackerman and L Heinzerling, *Priceless: On Knowing the Price of Everything and the Value of Nothing* (New York Press, New York City, 2004) 25.

[85] For a similar point in relation to market/state distinctions in administrative law, see A Aman Jr, 'Administrative Law for a New Century' in M Taggart (ed), *The Province of Administrative Law* (Hart Publishing, Oxford, 1997) 90, 110.

[86] On a related note, Satz argues that environmental markets tend to be considered as being 'the same everywhere' and in that sense uniform. D Satz, *Why Some Things Should Not Be For Sale* (Oxford University Press, Oxford, 2010) 92.

[87] B Ackerman and R Stewart, 'Reforming Environmental Law: The Democratic Case for Market Incentives' (1988) 13 *Colombia Journal of Environmental Law* 171.

[88] D Pearce and E Barbier, *Blueprint for Sustainable Development* (Earthscan, London, 2000) 2. Note that Pearce and Barbier discuss environmental markets more broadly.

[89] C Sunstein, 'Panel II: Public Versus Private Environment Regulation' (1994) 21 *Ecological Law Quarterly* 455, 459.

[90] As described and cited in Heinzerling, 'Selling Pollution' (n 45) 302.

[91] In particular, emissions trading is understood to circumvent any 'coercive' central planning, J Wiener, 'Global Environmental Regulation: Instrument Choice in the Legal Context' (1999) 108 *Yale Law Journal* 677, 775.

[92] As described and cited in Heinzerling, 'Selling Pollution' (n 45) 302.

Second, environmental markets are commonly portrayed as superior[93] to other regulatory options in implementing environmental policies. For example, markets are described as being in a 'much better position'[94] to decide where most pollution reduction is achieved with each investment under the presumption that 'the market always knows best'.[95] The singularity of the market in achieving regulatory goals cost-effectively is often contrasted with direct regulation, such as end-of-pipe pollution control methods, which are thought of as costly and burdensome due to their micro-management by central government.[96] In effect, this kind of description frames emissions markets as different from state-managed regulation on the basis of efficiency[97] but in doing so it also suggests that markets operate in a legal vacuum, or separately from the state.

Third, the first camp depicts emissions markets as autonomous entities, that is, distinct from the state, by employing stigmatised rhetoric to describe regulation.[98] For example, emissions trading systems tend to be referred to as *economic instruments*, and markets prefixed as 'free', whilst direct regulation is labelled as *command*-and-*control*.[99] These distinct categorisations not only portray traditional regulation in a derogatory fashion, suggesting that public authority dictates environmental control,[100] but also insinuate that emissions markets are *economic* regulatory options – working outside the control of the state.[101] Although environmental law scholars have acknowledged the apparent bias of these labels,[102] the fact is that

[93] ibid.

[94] R de Witt Wijnen, 'Emissions Trading under Article 17 of the Kyoto Protocol' in D Freestone and C Streck (eds), *Legal Aspects of Implementing the Kyoto Protocol Mechanisms: Making Kyoto Work* (Oxford University Press, Oxford, 2005) 403, 403.

[95] This attitude is described in F Ackerman and L Heinzerling, *Priceless: On Knowing the Price of Everything and the Value of Nothing* (New York Press, New York City, 2004) 25. The Commission has, at times, expressed similar views with regard to the EU ETS, see ch 4 and Commission of the European Communities, 'Green Paper on Greenhouse Gas Emissions Trading Within the European Union', COM(2000) 87 final.

[96] R Stewart, 'Economic Incentives for Environmental Protection: Opportunities and Obstacles' in R Revesz, P Sands and R Stewart (eds), *Environmental Law, the Economy and Sustainable Development: The United States, the European Union and the International Community* (Cambridge University Press, Cambridge, 2000) 171, 182, J Wiener and B Richman, 'Mechanism Choice' in D Farber and A O'Connell (eds), *Research Handbook on Public Choice and Public Law* (Edward Elgar, Cheltenham, 2010) 363, 370, Freeman and Kolstad, 'Prescriptive Environmental Regulation versus Market-Based Incentives' (n 44) 4.

[97] Button describes that there is a strong tendency with the use of emissions trading schemes to 'leave it up to the market' to organise market practices. J Button, 'Carbon: Commodity or Currency? The Case for an International Carbon Market Based on the Currency Model' (2008) 32 *Harvard Environmental Law Review* 571, 582. Similarly, and according to popular jargon, government are urged to leave the markets to 'do their work' P Krugman, 'The Green Economy', *New York Times*, New York, 5 April 2010.

[98] Traditional and alternative regulation as defined in J Dryzek, *The Politics of the Earth: Environmental Discourses* (2nd edn, Oxford University Press, Oxford, 2005) 135.

[99] M Jacobs, *The Green Economy: Environment, Sustainable Development, and the Politics of the Future* (Pluto Press, London, 1991) 151.

[100] M Lee, *EU Environmental Law: Challenges, Change and Decision-Making* (Hart Publishing, Oxford, 2005) 183.

[101] Jacobs, *The Green Economy* (n 99).

[102] R Macrory, 'Regulating in a Risky Environment' (2001) 54 *Current Legal Problems* 619, Lee, *EU Environmental Law* (n 100) 184.

such bias is symptomatic of a deeper mistrust in the state to manage the environment,[103] which underpins the state/market dichotomy in environmental law scholarship and adds to the honeymoon.

In the second camp, the scholarly focus shifts to market failures and the alleged inabilities of the market to further environmental protection. Here, environmental law scholarship seeks to challenge the 'naïve belief'[104] in the 'magic of markets'[105] and to emphasise 'the flaws of the markets'[106] that are thought to have been forgotten. One such flaw is described as the inequitable nature of carbon markets. In this context, emissions trading regimes are defined as simple bargaining systems over pollution, in which the 'rich may get away with what the poor cannot afford to commit'.[107] Similarly, references to 'hot-spots' – that is, high local concentrations of pollution – are used to claim that the application of markets in environmental law ultimately leads to uneven levels of distribution of pollution, affecting poor areas the most.[108] Along the same line, markets in environmental law are defined as unethical. The argument is that in order for markets to function, nature has to be price-tagged or, in other words, transferred into a 'commodity'.[109] Since nature is seen as 'priceless',[110] markets are rejected as unsuitable for environmental protection purposes. This type of rhetoric describes environmental markets equally derogatory as the previous camp, which refers to direct regulation as 'command-and-control'. In effect, each camp highlights its preference as to how society more broadly should

---

[103] Lee, *EU Environmental Law* (n 100) 184. As an example see Ackerman and Stewart, 'Reforming Environmental Law' (n 64).

[104] Ackerman and Heinzerling, *Priceless* (n 95) 24.

[105] N Deakin and K Walsh, 'The Enabling State: The Role of Markets and Contracts' (1996) 74 *Public Administration* 33, 35.

[106] Ackerman and Heinzerling, *Priceless* (n 95) 24.

[107] As cited in Emission, Trading Policy Statement, 'General Principles for the Creation, Banking and the Use of Emission Reduction Credits EPA' 51 *Federal Regulation* 381. From a discourse perspective, Goodin explains how polluting tends to be alluded to as 'sins', see R Goodin, 'Selling Environmental Indulgences' (1994) 47 *Kyklos* 573. Particularly in international environmental law, developed countries raise concerns regarding inequalities between developed and developing countries in negotiations on and solutions to climate change, see, eg L Rajamani, 'The Increasing Current and Relevance of Rights-Based Perspectives in the International Negotiations on Climate Change' (2010) 22 *Journal of Environmental Law* 391, 395.

[108] E Rehbinder, 'Market-Based Incentives for Environmental Protection' in R Revesz, P Sands and R Stewart (eds), *Environmental Law, the Economy and the Sustainable Development* (Cambridge University Press, Cambridge, 2000) 245, 245. This is thought to occur due to uneven market powers – a key concern in international environmental law and the relationship between developed and developing. For this discussion – in the context of CDM see J Parikh and K Parikh, 'The Kyoto Protocol: An Indian Perspective' (2004) 5 *International Review for Environmental Strategies* 127, 139, H van Asselt and J Gupta, 'Stretching Too Far? Developing Countries and the Role of Flexible Mechanisms Beyond Kyoto' (2009) 28 *Stanford Environmental Law Journal* 311, 355.

[109] According to Nash, this description of emissions markets leading to 'commodification' of common resources is a common technique to tarnish the use of environmental markets in the public eye. J Nash, 'Framing Effect and Regulatory Choice' (2006) 82 *Notre Dame Law Review* 313, 315. Similarly, *The Guardian* notes that the narratives in debating emissions trading are clearly biased, for instance, stating that under emissions trading pollution can be 'redeemed' alludes to methods of the Catholic Church in the 16th century saving sinners from eternal damnation upon the exchange of money. S Manea, 'The Carbon Market – Gone in a Puff of Smoke?', *The Guardian*, London, 24 January 2011. Also Stern makes a similar point *The Stern Review* (n 83) 193.

[110] Ackerman and Heinzerling, *Priceless* (n 95).

be managed: according to market forces in the case of the former and via public authorities, 'specially trained to secure environment protection'[111] in the case of the latter. The honeymoon persists in these debates not because each camp has a particular preference in regulatory mechanism but because both camps fail to recognise the co-production and interrelationship between markets and the state in environmental law.

Ultimately, the above discussion is a very rough overview of the type of arguments that dichotomise emissions market debates in environmental law scholarship. As an important caveat, I do not argue that all environmental law scholarship is polarised in the manner described above,[112] nor do I claim that environmental law scholars are blind to the obvious role that the state plays in creating a legal framework for emissions markets.[113] Yet the idea of market and state as polar opposites is not only a 'constitutive feature of late modernity'[114] but also deeply engrained in environmental law methodologies. The effect of such a distinction is to construct an image of markets as distinct from the state or, more dramatically, from law. What this means is that important overlaps between, for instance, judicial discourse and market construction are overlooked, just as the complex and dynamic relationship between markets and the state in the context of emissions trading are oversimplified. On this basis, the honeymoon in environmental law scholarship is maintained.

E. Global Outlook on Emissions Trading in Environmental Law Scholarship

The fifth reason why the honeymoon exists in environmental law scholarship is the global outlook through which emissions trading tends to be discussed.[115] The effect of such a global approach is the projection of emissions trading as a uniform regulatory instrument, imposable in public law from jurisdiction to jurisdiction without much consideration of cultural particularities. Emissions trading debates that commit to this type of framing date mainly after the Kyoto Protocol,[116] as this international treaty first set out the legal framework for a global emissions trading scheme. Although the Protocol does not demand uniformity in Parties' compliance,

---

[111]   ibid.

[112]   Lazarus, for instance, argues that any reference to markets as opposed to the state are unhelpful for a fruitful environmental law debate. R Lazarus, 'Panel II: Public Versus Private Environment Regulation' (1994) 21 *Ecological Law Quarterly* 438.

[113]   Stewart, 'Economic Incentives' (n 96) 174, Wiener, 'Global Environmental Regulation' (n 91) 783, Lee, *EU Environmental Law* (n 100) 186.

[114]   E Fisher, 'Expertise and the WTO SPS Agreement' (ESIL-ASIL Research Forum, Helsinki, 2–3 October 2009) (the conference paper on file with the author).

[115]   S Bogojević, 'Global Gazing: Viewing Markets Through the Lens of Emissions Trading Discourses' in B Jessup and K Rubenstein (eds), *Environmental Discourses in Public and International Law* (Cambridge University Press, Cambridge, 2012) 331.

[116]   Kyoto Protocol to the United Nations Framework Convention on Climate Change, opened for signature 11 December 1997, 37 ILM 22 (entered into force 16 February 2005).

or in creating national emissions trading schemes,[117] Fogel argues that it, nonetheless, pictures environmental problems and their solutions through a so-called 'global gaze'.[118] This means that the environment, as well as policy and law are simplified and generalised so as to enable international law to 'rule by afar'.[119] This inherent global approach of international treaties has in certain regards filtered through to how environmental law scholarship understands emissions trading schemes that respond to the Protocol. In the case of the EU ETS, this is manifested in the way that this trading regime is reduced to a simple design structure that can be applied elsewhere. This view is projected in the following three ways.

First, a common description of the EU ETS emphasises a global profile because it is thought that the EU ETS will eventually become a global carbon market.[120] As highlighted in chapters three and four,[121] the EU emissions trading regime is envisaged to become the 'world prototype'[122] and a 'blueprint'[123] for future international emissions trading, as well as the 'nucleus of a much larger global carbon market',[124] and the 'global standard-setter'[125] with regard to carbon trading. One of the most dominant reasons for this global approach is the idea that the EU ETS is able to secure economic benefits for the EU by being a model for other carbon markets.[126] This is rhetoric typical of policy- and lawmakers at the EU level, however, academics[127] and the judiciary[128] mimic it. The effect of these narratives is to

---

[117] See ch 3, section II(A)(1).

[118] C Fogel, 'The Local, the Global, and the Kyoto Protocol' in S Jasanoff and M Martello (eds), *Earthly Politics: Local and Global in Environmental Governance* (MIT Press, Cambridge, Massachusetts, 2004) 103, 121.

[119] ibid.

[120] Citing Gordon Brown delivering a key note speech in 2007 on the UNFFFC, as quoted in S-J Clifton, *A Dangerous Obsession: The Evidence against Carbon Trading and for Real Solutions to Avoid a Climate Crunch* (Friends of the Earth, London, 2009) 17.

[121] Ch 3 explains how this type of rhetoric contributes to the idea that emissions trading is 'on the move', and ch 4 shows how the Commission has, at times, emphasised the 'global' features of emissions trading as a way of presenting this regulatory regime as an economic opportunity for the EU.

[122] A Engels, 'Market Creation and Transnational Rule-Making: The case of CO2 Emissions Trading' in M-L Djelic and K Sahlin-Andersson (eds), *Transnational Governance: Institutional Dynamics of Regulation* (Cambridge University Press, Cambridge, 2006) 329, 343.

[123] Y Slingenberg, 'The International Climate Policy Developments of the 1990s: The UNFCCC, the Kytoto Protocol, the Marrakech Accords and the EU Ratification Decision' in J Delbeke (ed), *EU Energy Law: The EU Greenhouse Gas Emissions Trading Scheme* (Claeys & Casteels, Leuven, 2006) 15, 35.

[124] EUROPA, 'Climate Change: Commission welcomes final adoption of Europe's climate and energy package' (12 December 2008) europa.eu/rapid/press-release_IP-08-1998_en.htm, accessed 17 October 2012.

[125] Commission of the European Communities, 'Communication: A Single Market for 21st Century Europe', COM(2007) 724 final.

[126] Ch 4, section III(B) and (C).

[127] See, eg J Wettestad, 'The Making of the 2003 EU Emissions Trading Directive: An Ultra-Quick Process due to Entrepreneurial Proficiency?' (2005) 5 *Global Environmental Politics* 1, 17, A Runge Metzger, 'The Potential Role of the EU ETS for the Development of Long-Term International Climate Policies' in J Delbeke (ed), *EU Energy Law: The EU Greenhouse Gas Emissions Trading Scheme* (Claeys & Casteels, Leuven, 2006) 253.

[128] The CJEU is seen to acknowledge EU climate change leadership in EU ETS recent case law, S Bogojević, 'Legalising Environmental Leadership: A Comment on the CJEU's Ruling in C-366/10 on the Inclusion of Aviation in the EU Emissions Trading Scheme' (2012) 24 *Journal of Environmental Law* 345.

frame a particular perception of the EU ETS as a regulatory mould, which, depending on its success, can impact the structure of emissions trading schemes elsewhere – regardless of legal culture.

Second, and related to the above, the possibility of 'linking' the EU ETS to other emissions trading schemes assigned to the international climate change regime plays a crucial part in why the global features of this emissions trading regime are emphasised. In short, linking means that each emissions allowance under the EU ETS may be identified, or linked to an assigned amount under the Protocol, and its successor, and as such allow cross-market trade to take place.[129] Since the idea is that the EU ETS 'should only be the beginning'[130] of an international emissions trading regime, linking provides the means to expand the trading system globally. What is important to highlight following these opportunities is that, as a result, the EU ETS is seen as 'an open architecture'[131] to which other trading schemes can easily connect. This has, however, meant that the actual legal particularities of the EU ETS regime are overlooked, as linking via contracts and agreements is possible.[132] Arguably, this type of linking is introduced so as to avoid having to agree on one international emissions trading model[133] but what it does is imply that emissions trading schemes can form a global emissions trading scheme – centred around the EU ETS – without much attention to legal culture. In this way, the honeymoon is maintained and prolonged.

Third, the global approach to emissions trading is linked to a broader regulatory idea of the possibility to 'cross-hybridize'[134] this regulatory strategy. As explained by Heinzerling, the successful story of emissions trading with sulphur dioxide in the US has inspired scholars to urge policy- and lawmakers to apply and replicate emissions trading schemes elsewhere with the assumption that they will work equally well.[135] Notably, Heinzerling only discusses the cross-application of emissions trad-

[129] M Mehling, 'Linking Emissions Trading Schemes' in D Freestone and C Streck (eds), *Legal Aspects of Carbon Trading: Kyoto, Copenhagen, and Beyond* (Oxford University Press, Oxford, 2009) 108, N Anger, 'Emissions Trading Beyond Europe: Linking Schemes in a Post-Kyoto World' (2008) 30 *Energy Economics* 2028.

[130] D Meadows, 'The Emissions Allowance Trading Directive 2003/87/EC Explained' in J Delbeke (ed), *EU Energy Law: The EU Greenhouse Gas Emissions Trading Scheme* (Claeys & Casteels, Leuven, 2006) 63, 100.

[131] R Dornau, 'The Emissions Trading Scheme of the European Union' in D Freestone and C Streck (eds), *Legal Aspects of Implementing the Kyoto Protocol Mechanisms: Making Kyoto Work* (Oxford University Press, Oxford, 2005) 417, 430. Similar description in Hansjürgen, 'Concluding Observations' (n 71) 223.

[132] Nash makes this point in discussing linking in international environmental law more generally stating that such a system enables national emissions markets to take the form and shape that national government can decide between themselves. Nash, 'Too much Market?' (n 7) 534. See also J Wiener, 'Global Environmental Regulation: Instrument Choice in the Legal Context' (1999) 108 *Yale Law Journal* 677.

[133] Nash ibid and Wiener ibid.

[134] Term borrowed from J Wiener, 'Convergence, Divergence, and Complexity in the US and European Risk Regulation' in N Vig and M Faure (eds), *Green Giants? Environmental Policies of the United States and the European Union* (MIT Press, Cambridge, 2004) 73.

[135] Heinzerling, 'Environment' (n 3) 713. See also M Hanemann, 'Cap-and-Trade: A Sufficient or Necessary Condition for Emission Reduction?' (2010) 26 *Oxford Review of Economic Policy* 225, 227.

ing to different environmental settings, however, the US regulatory example is often cited as 'an inspiration'[136] for the EU ETS legal construction. In fact, certain 'design' features of the US trading scheme were replicated in the EU ETS[137] with the belief that their success in the US would be equally applicable in the EU. Hansjürgen elucidates this by claiming that:[138]

> With regard to the chosen design options for the European emissions trading market, important lessons from the US experience have been adopted. There is little reason to think that these design options would not work with regard to the ETS.

This highlights the idea that emissions trading designs – irrespective of legal context – are transferable across public law settings. Equally, and as described above, the EU ETS is promoted as the future design structure upon which other emissions trading schemes will be based.[139] Lack of attention to legal specificities in furthering such regulatory goals and thus assuming that emissions trading schemes are generic regulatory mechanisms, however, help to further the honeymoon.

The crucial point to pick up here is not that the EU ETS – deriving from international environmental law, inspired by the US pollution control history, and aiming to become the future centre for global carbon markets – constitutes a problem per se. The difficulty, and the contribution to the honeymoon, lies in the fact that this global view on emissions trading is underpinned by the belief that emissions trading schemes can be replicated across jurisdictions generically. Emphasising its potentially global application, without acknowledging the huge impact that legal culture has on emissions trading regimes, frames emissions trading an easily applicable tool that will seek to achieve the sought-for regulatory results at all times and in all public law settings. Hence, the honeymoon exists in environmental law scholarship.

IV. Reflections: Long Honeymoon, Sweet Ending?

What we see from the exposé above are two things. First, it shows that emissions trading schemes are experiencing a long honeymoon in environmental law scholarship. This honeymoon expresses itself in various ways: the prevailing economics-centred literature, technical and descriptive reports of emissions trading laws and their developments, promotional depictions of emissions trading as straightforward regulatory strategy, dichotomous accounts of emissions markets

---

[136] J Delbeke, 'Putting the Emerging Global Carbon Market on Solid Footing' (Speech For the Opening of ICAP Global Cabron Market Forum, 19–20 May 2008) www.icapcarbonaction.com/index.php?option=com_content&view=article&id=18&Itemid=17&lang=ja, accessed 11 September 2012.

[137] Ellerman, Convery, Perthuis, *Pricing Carbon* (n 32) 3, J Skjærseth and J Wettestad, *EU Emissions Trading: Initiation, Decision-Making and Implementation* (Ashgate Publishing, Burlington, 2008) 154, Convery, 'Emerging Literature on Emissions Trading in Europe' (n 5) 127.

[138] Hansjürgen, 'Concluding Observations' (n 71) 223.

[139] See section III(E).

and the state, and the global, as opposed to culture-specific, outlook on emissions trading regimes. What these manifestations have in common is that they over-simplify and/or overlook legal aspects of emissions trading. Thereby they under-mine the role of environmental law in understanding emissions trading. This is a pretty dire picture of the state of environmental law scholarship but as I have stated throughout this chapter, the purpose of this exercise has not been to blacklist the environmental law community that contributes to the honeymoon but rather to understand *why* environmental law scholars are induced to do so.

This takes me to the second point, which concerns the cause for the honey-moon's existence. The exercise above points to five reasons: the specific nature of emissions trading debates; that is, its interdisciplinary, pragmatic and promotional character, as well as the framing of emissions trading schemes according to market/state distinctions, and the fascination of environmental law scholarship with the global context and the transferability of laws. These reasons are interre-lated in two ways. First, they are underpinned by various methodological chal-lenges, including the challenge to engage in complex interdisciplinary debates, deal with high-paced legal developments and the pressures from the practice, industry, as well as the scholarship itself to respond quickly to legal changes relevant to emis-sions trading. The key reason why these challenges are difficult to overcome is that this area of legal scholarship is still immature, meaning that robust methodologies through which to face these issues have yet to be established.[140] Second, they high-light a common theme of how environmental law scholarship approaches the use of markets in environmental law. The fact that emissions trading schemes concern the creation of an emissions *market* entrenches the market/state dichotomy, as well as the scholarship's lack of confidence to engage more forcefully in interdisciplin-ary debates. Also in the pragmatic and the promotional debates on emissions trad-ing, the fact that emissions trading is a *market* is used to further it as simple, and in the case of the global framing of emissions trading, global. What this means, and what the exercise of mapping methodologies applied to analysing emissions trad-ing in environmental law scholarship demonstrates, is that the first step toward ending the honeymoon is to think more critically about the way in which markets in environmental law are approached.

Here it is useful to briefly look at legal studies more generally, and the common trend therein to understand and portray markets as operating independently from regulation, or the state. Arguably the entire history of legal thought, since the turn of the century, is the history of the decline of a particular set of distinc-tions.[141] These distinctions, taken together, constitute a particular way in which scholars think about the social world, and it may be regarded as an ideological

---

[140] Fisher and others, 'Maturity and Methodology' (n 5).

[141] Literature on this topic is vast, see, eg C Sampford, 'Law, Institutions and the Public/Private Divide' (1991) 20 *Federal Law Review* 185, M Freedland and J-B Auby (eds), *The Public Law/Private Law Divide: Une Entente Assez Cordiale? la Distinction du Droit Public et du Droit Privé: Regards Français et Britanniques* (Hart Publishing, Oxford, 2006) 1, J Freeman, 'Private Role in Public Governance' (2000) 75 *New York University Law Review* 543, D Kennedy, 'The Stages of the Decline of the Public/Private Distinction' (1982) 130 *University of Pennsylvania* 1349.

classification, and one that is commonly associated with liberal political theory.[142] Equally, environmental law rests upon such a distinction: that of the public and the private. More precisely, environmental law is seen as relying, on the one hand, on certain presuppositions about the relationship between the private realm of individual rights, and, on the other hand, on the public realm of collective interest and choice.[143] In effect, environmental law is often perceived as a series of attempts to resolve clashes between public and private interests as they arise.[144] Although the public/private dichotomy is widely contested, it remains employed, connoting familiar distinctions.[145] The most common caricature of the public/private division is manifested in the private sphere being portrayed as a spontaneous order built on cooperation, consent and contract, compared with the coerced order of the public sphere, the state, created by legal regulation.[146] The idea of law, which runs from this distinction, suggests that within the private sphere, affairs between individuals are managed via one-to-one agreements, even in the absence of law, while, on the other hand, in the public law sphere, relationships between the state and individual citizens are uniformly managed by the state. The public/private distinction is subsequently relying on a different set of distinctions concerning the administration of the public and the private,[147] which affects not only the perception of the two spheres but also the kind of legal rules that are applied thereto. Following this distinction, the market is clearly part of the private ambit, mainly because market actions by market participants are understood as being 'irreducibly individualistic' or rather, a negation of 'collective action'.[148] The argument is that individual acts, albeit interconnected in the market, are not a matter of common decision-making, and therefore they are private.[149] The essence of the public/private distinction is thus the conviction that it is possible to conceive of social and economic life apart from government and law. In fact, herein lies the power of the words 'public' and 'private'.[150]

What this short overview of public/private distinctions shows is that by adhering to similar divisions, whatever falls within the private sphere, such as the market, will be understood as not law at all and therefore irrelevant for lawyers to scrutinise.

---

[142] These include state/society, public/private, individual/group, right/power, property/sovereignty, legislature/judiciary, objective/subjective, freedom/coercion, science/politics dichotomies. For the latter distinction see E Fisher, *Risk, Regulation and Administrative Constitutionalism* (Hart Publishing, Oxford, 2010). See also P Cane, 'Public Law and Private Law: A Study of the Analysis and Use of a Legal Concept' in J Eekelaar and J Bell (eds), *Oxford Essays in Jurisprudence* (Clarendon Press, Oxford, 1987) 57.

[143] Coyle and Morrow, *Philosophical Foundation of Environmental Law* (n 53) 160.

[144] ibid 184.

[145] J Freeman, 'Private Role in Public Governance' (2000) 75 *New York University Law Review* 543, 551.

[146] Sampford, 'Law, Institutions' (n 141) 187–88.

[147] J Allison, *A Continental Distinction in the Common Law: A Historical and Comparative Perspective on English Law* (Clarendon Press, Oxford, 1996).

[148] A Preda, *Framing Finance: The Boundaries of Markets and Modern Capitalism* (Chicago University Press, Chicago, 2009) 7.

[149] ibid 103–04.

[150] Sampford, 'Law, Institutions' (n 141) 187–88.

Arguably this would be the most extreme case of the public/private, or state/market distinctions, yet unwrapping the five reasons underpinning the honeymoon shows that there are hints of this type of assumption, in particular comparing the extent to which law in relation to economics is perceived as significant in interdisciplinary debates on emissions trading. What this shows is that the need for environmental law scholarship to mature and to think critically about its approach toward the use of markets in environmental law is pressing.

V. Conclusion

My aim in this chapter has been to map current methodologies of analysis for emissions trading schemes in law so as to expose what underpins the oversimplified views of emissions trading regimes in law. What this investigation has shown is that a common theme of immaturity of methodologies in environmental law scholarship, and in particular, a lack of 'critical and careful' method with which to study the application of markets in environmental law, has resulted in emissions trading schemes being perceived as straightforward tools. While identifying this state of affairs, I have not assessed whether the methodology developed in this book – that is, the use of the *Economic Efficiency,* the *Private Property Rights,* and the *Command-and-Control* models to unpack emissions trading discourses and highlight legal dilemmas and discrepancies underpinning the understanding of emissions trading as a regulatory concept – manages to respond to the challenges underlying the honeymoon. It is to this consideration, and the general conclusions of this book, that I now turn.

7

Conclusions

I. Beyond Uniformity of Emissions Trading Schemes

This book set the ambitious goal of re-configuring the way in which scholars discuss and portray emissions trading schemes as a regulatory concept. Over the course of the previous six chapters I have made three points in particular. First, emissions trading schemes are complex regulatory strategies that respond to a wide range of environmental and non-environmental goals, including creating profit-centres, establishing a governance regime aimed at substituting state control of common resources, and ensuring regulatory compliance. Second, the particular purpose entrusted to emissions trading has, as a corollary, a distinct governance structure according to which an emissions trading regime may be constructed and managed. These governance structures differ in the legal status upon which emissions rights are created and in the vision of the role that the state plays, or ought to play, in the construction and management of the emissions market. Third, these features of governance structures are culture-specific, which is a significant reminder of the importance of law in understanding not only how emissions trading schemes function but also what meaning is given to them as regulatory strategies.

Ultimately this book has provided a revised prism through which to view emissions trading as a regulatory strategy. Through snapshots of emissions trading discourses as voiced by scholars, as well as law- and policymakers and the judiciary in the EU legal context, I have painted a pluralistic view of emissions trading and brought to light legal complexities involved in conceptualising and applying emissions trading in law. The importance of this exercise has been to discard any suggestion that emissions trading is a simple and generic regulatory mechanism and to set out a framework for analysis, in which emissions trading schemes are critically assessed from a legal perspective.

Much of this book has been concerned with pointing to legal complexities relating to emissions trading, without providing any solutions to resolve these. This is because this book aims to guide the reader to legal questions, dilemmas and themes that should be thought about when emissions trading is discussed, as opposed to dictating to the reader what exactly to think on this subject.[1] In this final chapter it is convenient to summarise my findings, which I will set out in a

---

[1] This approach is inspired by E Fisher, B Lange and E Scotford, *Environmental Law: Text, Cases and Materials* (Oxford University Press, Oxford, 2013).

two-limbed conclusion. In the first limb, I focus on the book's reconfiguration of the common understanding of emissions trading schemes as a regulatory concept and, in the second limb, I highlight the methodological significance of this project, which I sum up and explain against the backdrop of the honeymoon in environmental law. It is to this exercise that I now turn.

II. Summary of Analysis

This book started with a broad and bold explanation of the need to revise the dominant prism through which emissions trading schemes, as a legal device, tend to be viewed and described. My description of this prism is that it sees emissions trading as a simple tool, imposable across jurisdictions, and, on this basis, I argued that its revision was a necessity. Throughout this book I have returned to this point; highlighting areas of complexity in conceptualising, as well as applying, emissions trading schemes, I have underlined the demand for a robust legal approach to the study of this regulatory strategy, as well as showed that the strategy is neither straightforward nor uniform.

The starting point of my analysis was the deconstruction of emissions trading literature, resulting in the elaboration of the *Economic Efficiency*, the *Private Property Rights*, and the *Command-and-Control* models. Categorising emissions trading debates according to the models has been indispensable to this project, not least because the mere fact that different models exist – each model encapsulating distinct understandings of the purpose and function of emissions trading – demonstrates that emissions trading schemes are complex regulatory strategies. In particular, the models have shown how emissions trading is understood as a regulatory concept in environmental law and environmental law scholarship, and more importantly, highlighted the co-produced nature of markets, states and law in these debates.

First, the models show that emissions trading schemes respond to a variety of regulatory goals, including creating economic opportunities (the *Economic Efficiency Model*), establishing a private property-based governance regime of common resources (the *Private Property Rights Model*), and ensuring regulatory compliance (the *Command-and-Control Model*). What this means is that emissions trading is a rich regulatory concept that is far more nuanced than the common presumption that emissions trading corrects a market failure,[2] or more generally, regulates a commons. This also proves that any suggestion that emissions trading schemes are simple or generic regulatory strategies is misplaced.

---

[2] See, eg F Convery and L Redmond, 'Market and Price Developments in the European Union Emissions Trading Scheme' (2007) 1 *Review of Environmental Economics and Policy* 88, R Stewart, 'Models for Environmental Regulation: Central Planning Versus Market-Based Approaches' (1992) 19 *Boston College Environmental Affairs Law Review* 547, Commission of the European Communities, 'Green Paper on Market-Based Instruments for Environment and Related Policy Purposes', COM(2007) 140 final.

Second, the models highlight that, underlying the distinct regulatory objectives imposed on emissions trading schemes, some form of governance authority that restrains the use of commons resources is imagined. According to the *Economic Efficiency Model* the regulatory authority lies within the market, as it is according to market forces that emissions allowances are allocated; in the *Private Property Rights Model* private property holders are invested with regulatory authority in deciding, on their own terms, whether to sell, keep, squander or safeguard their property rights in emissions allowances; and in the *Command-and-Control Model* the regulatory power is entrusted to the central government. What this shows is that emissions trading discourses address legal dilemmas of 'how' and 'to whom' to allocate regulatory power, that is, power to construct and organise emissions trading schemes. Considering that each model imagines a different regulatory authority governing emissions trading, it follows that each model refers to a distinct governance structure, differing as to the legal status of emissions allowances and the roles that the market and the state play or ought to play in emissions trading. The importance of this exercise is to show that emissions trading schemes are able to establish a range of different governance structures and, as such, to demonstrate that emissions trading regimes are neither uncomplicated nor uniform. Moreover, it proves that we must think carefully about the role of the state, markets and rights in discussing the use of markets as control systems in environmental law.

Third, through their applicability in law, the models help to flesh out discrepancies in the conceptualisation of emissions trading in a particular legal context and illustrate that the meaning given to emissions trading derives from legal culture. The EU ETS was taken as a case study. Applying the models to the ETS-related discourses of law- and policymakers, and the judiciary at the EU level, reveals distinct visions of the role emissions trading schemes operate in the EU legal setting. This is apparent in chapter four, which highlights the Commission's dynamic view of emissions trading, shifting from a *Command-and-Control Model*-inspired projection of regulation as a mere compliance system to the *Economic Efficiency Model*-based view of emissions trading as an economic opportunity. Similarly, chapter five shows that the General Court frames legal questions concerning the EU ETS as competence questions (a *Command-and-Control Model*-type of consideration), whilst the Court of Justice (at least in the preliminary reference procedure) and the Commission, acting chiefly as the defendant, focus on economic impact in conceptualising and defining the structures of the emissions trading regime (an *Economic Efficiency Model*-based view).

It is interesting, albeit not surprising, that the *Private Property Rights Model* is not applicable to EU ETS-related discourses to the same extent, or at all, as the *Economic Efficiency* or the *Command-and-Control* models. Here it is useful to consider the findings in chapter three. They explain how the EU jurisdiction builds on integration through a multi-level governance system, in which markets, judicial market-interpretation and market-construction, and law are intertwined – a regulatory reality distinct from the aims of the *Private Property Rights Model*, which seeks to substitute for central governance of common resources emissions markets. In other words, the obvious reason as to why the *Private Property Rights Model* fails to emerge in the EU-specific case study is because the EU is itself a bureaucratic component, and part of a multi-governance regulatory structure that the *Private Property Rights Model* would seek to abolish. An interrelated reason is that much legal scholarship and legal thought at the EU level is tied to integration and furthers the creation of the internal market through legislation and policy-oriented scholarship.[3] As such, ideas related to public choice, which underpin the *Private Property Rights Model,* are equally absent, or at least less frequent, in the EU legal community. Moreover, the fact that EU law has not developed a sense of 'property',[4] as briefly discussed in chapters four and five, is another explanation for the lack of the *Private Property Rights Model* in the EU. What this shows is that the applicability of the models in law is dependent on legal culture, which also demonstrates that conceptualisations and constructions of emissions trading schemes are culture-specific.

This point is further clarified in chapter four, which illustrates a strong correlation between dominant regulatory agendas in the EU and the regulatory goals imposed on the EU ETS by law- and policymakers at the EU level. For instance, the Commission promoted emissions trading as a promising implementation strategy that could guarantee compliance by the EU with international law at the time when implementation was its key regulatory agenda. Also, chapter five shows the significance of legal culture in relation to the type of litigants and legal questions that are admitted to the courtroom, as well as how judges discuss and interpret the emissions trading regime according to an EU constitutional law perspective. This constitutional law focus helps to explain why ETS-specific challenges from private parties are dismissed and why the core legal questions deliberated before the Court concern the balance of competences between the Commission and the Member States. Ultimately, what this mapping exercise highlights is the utility of the models. In particular, it demonstrates the complexity involved in understanding emissions trading as a regulatory concept – even in a single jurisdiction – and shows that emissions trading schemes are not an instrumental set of rules, or an empty design structure that is imposable across jurisdictions but, rather, an image of legal culture in itself.[5]

[3] R van Gestel and H-W Micklitz, 'Revitalizing Doctrinal Legal Research in Europe: What About Methodology?' in U Neergaard, R Nielsen and L Roseberry (eds), *European Legal Method – Paradoxes and Revitalisation* (DJOP Publishing, Copenhagen, 2011) 25, 41–44. Ch 3, section III(C).
[4] Art 345 TFEU states that the Treaties 'shall in no way prejudice the rules in Member States governing the system of property ownership'. Ch 4, section IV and ch 5, section IV.
[5] The importance of legal culture to this study is greatly influenced by E Fisher, *Risk Regulation and Administrative Constitutionalism* (Hart Publishing, Oxford, 2010).

III. The End of the Honeymoon?

What the above discussion has done is to recapitulate the core findings of this book relating to the *Economic Efficiency,* the *Private Property Rights* and the *Command-and-Control* models, and the way in which these models help to reveal the kaleidoscopic understandings of emissions trading that exist in environmental law scholarship and in the EU legal context. My analysis, however, has not been limited to explaining *how* emissions trading is conceptualised but explained, further, *why* emissions trading schemes are generally thought to be simple and uniform regulatory tools. This is the real issue in this book: the belief commonly held in emissions trading discourses that emissions trading schemes are straightforward and that these can be applied across jurisdictions and environmental settings with equal success. Chapter six pointed to the immaturity of methodologies in environmental law scholarship as a key reason why such oversimplification of environmental law persists. Developing a robust methodology in this field is difficult: emissions trading debates are frequently economics-centred, technical, descriptive and promotional; they generally adopt a dichotomous framing of emissions markets in relation to states, and emphasise global, as opposed to culture-specific, aspects of emissions trading. The combined effect of this is to create a perception of emissions trading schemes as easy, economy-based tools to which law is only marginally relevant – a vision that persists because environmental law scholarship fails to challenge it. In Heinzerling's terms, this is the honeymoon that emissions trading currently enjoys in environmental law scholarship.[6] The significance of the models is that they challenge this honeymoon, and they do so in at least two ways.

First, the models show that the understandings of the role of markets, the state, and rights in common resources are co-produced. What this means is that the way in which the market is thought of in an emissions trading context links to ideas of the role of the state, as well as conceptions of rights in emissions allowances. The models illustrate that considerable variation is available in the types of relationship that the state, the market, and property holders in emissions allowances may enter: the *Economic Efficiency Model* sees the market operating 'freely' but relies on the possibility of the state intervening when market stability demands it; the *Private Property Rights Model* thinks of private property holders as the centrepiece of emissions trading and the market as a forum in which they can agree on their own terms to whom and how to allocate rights in emissions allowances – the central authority is only thought of as relevant in granting private property rights; and in the *Command-and-Control Model* the state is understood to play the central role in regulating pollution, using emissions markets as a device and creating licences and permits in emissions allowances, rather than private property

---

[6] L Heinzerling, 'The Environment' in M Tushnet and P Cane (eds), *The Oxford Handbook of Legal Studies* (Oxford University Press, Oxford, 2003) 701, 712.

rights. Under each model, the roles of the state, the market and rights in emissions allowances are differently defined but the understanding of each is intrinsically linked to the understanding of the other two.

The importance of this finding is that it refutes the tendency, which chapter six explains exists in environmental law scholarship, to polarise discussions on emissions markets according to state/market distinctions. Such distinctions suggest that regulatory power rests either in the market or the state, that limiting the power of the market thus means extending the power of the state, or that a particular institutional problem is shifted or even solved by making a regulatory power transfer. What this kind of market/state distinction ultimately does is construct an image of emissions markets as distinct from the state, or even from the law and, from this perspective, it prolongs the honeymoon in environmental law scholarship. Chapter six explained how this view of emissions trading is also the result of the dominance of economics in interdisciplinary emissions trading debates, which marginalise the significance of legal analysis of emissions markets. However, as this book shows, the application of emissions markets in environmental law does not correspond to the 'retreat' of the state, or to the marginal relevance of law to understanding emissions trading as a regulatory strategy but, rather, it encourages environmental law scholarship to examine further the overlaps between market, states, and rights and how these exist symbiotically in emissions trading regimes.

Second, the models show that underlying emissions trading discourses lies a story of governance. As explained above, emissions trading debates revolve around the dilemma of how and to whom to allocate regulatory power,[7] which, in the case of the EU ETS, are questions concerning the allocation of regulatory power between the Commission and the Member States to manage and construct the trading regime. This regulatory power-sharing, as chapter five shows, has given rise to fierce litigation relating to the interpretations of competences in regulating the environment at the EU level.[8] Governance, in this context, is thus not a mere organisation of regulatory powers, but an imperative reflection of legal culture and the rationale of a particular legal system. What this demonstrates is that emissions markets cannot exist in any pre-political state or legal vacuum, in a form readily imposable across jurisdictions, as suggested from the viewpoint of the honeymoon in environmental law scholarship. Rather, emissions markets are crucially part of, and reliant on, law. This point further highlights a key problem

---

[7] Indeed, exploring the affect on the balance of power among different government institutions is arguably a typical preoccupation of lawyers, see M Loughlin, *Public Law and Political Theory* (Clarendon Press, Oxford, 1992), similar finding in J Freeman and C Kolstad, 'Prescriptive Environmental Regulations versus Market-Based Incentives' in J Freeman and C Kolstad (eds), *Moving to Markets in Environmental Regulation: Lessons After Twenty Years of Experience* (Oxford University Press, Oxford, 2006) 3, 6.

[8] EU ETS litigation also raises questions regarding the extent of the EU's competences to adopt laws that have legal implications beyond the EU jurisdiction, see S Bogojević, 'Legalising Environmental Leadership: A Comment on the CJEU's Ruling in C-366/10 on the Inclusion of Aviation in the EU Emissions Trading Scheme' (2012) 24 *Journal of Environmental Law* 345.

in considering emissions trading from a legal viewpoint: there is a need to show that the use of emissions trading has not meant that the 'province of law',[9] or more precisely, environmental law scholarship, has shrunk but, instead, that there is a real need for it to develop a clearer picture of the different types of governance structures that emissions trading regimes are able to create, and what their implications are, or could be.

Throughout this book I have repeatedly stated the limits of the use of the *Economic Efficiency*, the *Private Property Rights* and the *Command-and-Control* models, in particular because they reflect my idiosyncratic perception of how the relevant literature and debates describe emissions trading, and how they fit into discourses in law. Also, I have recognised that there is a great deal of literature that takes a more sophisticated view of emissions trading, that does not merely consider that emissions trading is a tool imposable everywhere, or that emissions markets exist outside of law. The models should not be taken too literally; their aim is to highlight complexities in emissions trading and to show how markets, states and rights in emissions trading are interlinked. As such, the models set out a revised framework of analysis for emissions trading schemes in law. This methodological tool may not be flawless or suitable for all purposes but, importantly, it ends the honeymoon in environmental law scholarship by refuting any suggestion that emissions trading is a simple form of regulation, and by pointing to governance issues as a starting point for legal investigations on this topic.

IV. Looking Ahead

As I have stated from the outset, this study is only the first step in a much broader project on the use of markets as a control mechanism in environmental law. Continuing to dig deeper into this topic, and as the next step, I identify four interlinked strands of enquiry.

A possible first step in this project is to broaden the examination of emissions allowance trading through the application of the *Economic Efficiency*, the *Private Property Rights* and the *Command-and-Control* models to include markets applied to other type of commons, such as: fisheries,[10] biodiversity[11] and water.[12] The

---

[9] Phrase borrowed from M Taggart (ed), *The Province of Administrative Law* (Hart Publishing, Oxford, 1997).

[10] There is a vast amount of literature on this topic. In the EU context, the Commission has recently proposed to reform the common fisheries policy by creating a market in fisheries quotas, see Commission of the European Communities, 'Proposal for a Regulation on the Common Fisheries Policy', COM(2011) 425 final.

[11] See, eg M Drechsler and F Hartig, 'Conserving Biodiversity with Tradable Permits under Changing Conservation Costs and Habitat Restoration Time Lags' (2011) 70 *Ecological Economics* 533.

[12] Literature on water rights is extensive and covers different jurisdictions, see, eg L Godden, 'Governing Common Resources: Environmental Markets and Property in Water' in A McHarg and others (eds), *Property and the Law in Energy and Natural Resources* (Oxford University Press, Oxford, 2010).

significance of such an investigation is to test the models' applicability not only to a particular legal culture but also to different environmental contexts within a specific legal context.[13] Such an exercise would act as a springboard to fleshing out potential divergences between environmental markets and their functions in distinct environmental contexts, possibly leading to the creation of different models – to the three used in this book – through which to illustrate this.

Continuing along the line of market investigation, chapter three leaves a fertile ground for further examination of the interconnections between the judiciary, the market and environmental law more broadly, and not only in the context of the EU emissions trading regime. This step leads to two overlapping paths of investigation. One is to examine EU environmental law, or more precisely, the way in which the market integration rationale, specific to the EU, shapes and challenges this area of law. Such an examination does not follow a market versus environmental dichotomy but rather aims to investigate how market-, trade- and environmental objectives compete, evolve and are ultimately co-produced in the EU legal order. An interrelated path of examination focuses, more particularly, on the CJEU, and the way in which, through its interpretative role, it constructs environmental governance regimes both within and outside the EU jurisdiction.[14] The legal implications of this particular authority are to be considered against the EU's internal and external environmental law competences,[15] and how the judiciary interprets these so as to expand on the EU's regulatory- and its own judicial powers.

The second possible next step is to investigate further the role of the 'state' in the use of environmental markets. The *Economic Efficiency*, the *Private Property Rights* and the *Command-and-Control* models demonstrate that scholars, as well as the judiciary and the law- and policymaker at the EU level, view this role differently in the context of emissions trading regimes. My focus here has been narrow, using a simplistic picture of the multilevel regime structure relevant to the EU, where the 'central' and the 'local' state powers refer to the Commission and the Member States respectively. There is thus a need to map a far more nuanced administrative framework for the use of markets in EU environmental law, and illustrate the complex regulatory state mechanisms that stand behind it. An intriguing line of enquiry in this context is to investigate the different type of expertise[16] that each relevant institution holds, and how a particular package of skills and knowledge, as well as the composition and the constitutional role of the various institutions impact the construction and understanding of environmental

[13] Indeed, according to Heinzerling (n 6) the honeymoon lies in the fact that markets are understood to operate similarly in all environmental settings.
[14] See n 8. A Stone Sweet, 'Judicialization and the Construction of Governance' (1999) 32 *Comparative Political Studies* 147, 161. The role of the judicial practice in protecting the environment is similarly investigated in the context of international environmental law, see F Francioni, 'Realism, Utopia and the Future of International Environmental Law' (Law 2012/11, EUI Working Papers, 2012).
[15] G Marín Durán and E Morgera, *Environmental Integration in the EU's External Relations: Beyond Multilateral Dimensions* (Hart Publishing, Oxford, 2012).
[16] Defined as particular skills and knowledge, see E Fisher, 'The Rise of Transnational Environmental Law and the Expertise of Environmental Lawyers' (2012) 1 *Transnational Environmental Law* 43.

markets. Chapters four and five illustrate the importance of legal culture in the EU institution's conceptualisation of the EU emissions trading schemes, and so, the objective is to develop this argument further.

The third strand of enquiry concerns the creation of rights in environmental markets. As the *Economic Efficiency*, the *Private Property Rights* and the *Command-and-Control* models demonstrate, 'rights' in emissions trading encompass a wide range of understandings, ranging from rights as mere permits to private property rights. Moreover, what is defined as 'property rights', or what is thought of as 'property', is contextual and culture-specific and not always similarly defined across various regulatory frameworks.[17] There is therefore a need to further explore how 'property' rights are thought of and constructed in different jurisdictions and environmental settings, not only so as to better understand the legal implications of the creation of markets to control the use of common resources, but also so as to clarify and develop the complex relationship between environmental law and property law.[18]

The final and the most important step, which, moreover, underlies all previous strands of enquiry, is to consider how environmental markets, various state-actors relevant to the setting up and operating such a scheme, as well as rights created in this market, interrelate and how this co-production impacts the structure of a particular environmental market regime. The need to examine this trichometry is one of the key messages in this book. Chapter two hints of the fact that there is a need to position and analyse these issues in a broader regulatory framework,[19] and thereby examine, inter alia, the type of actors (both private and public) involved, to whom regulatory power is allocated, how this power is transferred, and the subsequent legal implications. Such an enquiry is significant as it answers both how different common resources are controlled, as well as which factors influence the particular control system.

These four lines of enquiry are neither conclusive nor exhaustive. They are, nonetheless, important starting points toward better understanding the use of markets to regulate the environment, as well as real intellectual challenges for the author.

---

[17] K Gray, 'Property in a Queue' in G Alexander and E Penalver (eds), *Property and Community* (Oxford University Press, Oxford, 2009) 169, 192, R Barnes, *Property Rights and Natural Resources* (Hart Publishing, Oxford, 2009) 9.

[18] For an example of such scholarship, see E Scotford and R Walsh, 'Property Rights in English Environmental Law – Contingent Rights in Shifting Legal Context' (Symposium on the Interface of Public and Private Law Concepts of Property, King's College London, 14 June 2012) (paper on file with the author).

[19] eg also with regard to parking, R Epstein, 'The Allocation of the Commons: Parking on Public Roads' (2002) 31 *Journal of Legal Studies* 515.

V. Conclusion

To sum up this book, it is useful to draw an analogy between its findings and the story of the Wizard of Oz.[20] This may seem unlikely but the Wizard and emissions trading are comparable in the sense that each enjoys a special status in its respective domain: the Wizard is understood to possess the most forceful and potent magic in Oz, whilst emissions trading enjoys a high profile in environmental law: it is considered superior to other direct regulation options[21] and, in the EU legal context, is thought of as the 'flagship measure',[22] one of the 'cornerstones',[23] and the 'jewel in the crown'[24] of the EU's climate change policy. In other words, both the Wizard and emissions trading are regarded as pre-eminent and powerful amongst their peers. When confronted by Dorothy and her friends, the Wizard, however, confesses that he is not a great Wizard but instead 'just a common man'.[25] Over the course of the past six chapters, I have similarly demonstrated that emissions trading is not the type of regulatory strategy it is often assumed to be – that is, simple and generic. Rather, emissions trading schemes are complex governance regimes, applied for a range of regulatory objectives, which mirror the legal cultures in which they operate – in this sense, they are 'just' very complicated environmental regulation.

The relevance of the analogy is that the Wizard is not what Dorothy and her friends expected him to be – the greatest Wizard of all, but that, nonetheless, the Wizard proves helpful in leading Dorothy and her company to what they initially demanded of him. Here, I have similarly emphasised that emissions trading schemes are unable to provide the level of simplicity and uniformity that is often demanded or expected of them as a regulatory strategy – but I have also argued that this does not mean that emissions trading schemes ought to be disregarded. The value of this book, like the value of the story of the Wizard of Oz, is as an opportunity to understand why emissions trading schemes are perceived as straightforward regulatory strategies, and to establish a methodology through which such reasons may be challenged – just as Dorothy and her friends

---

[20] This analogy was first set out in S Bogojević, 'Global Gazing: Viewing Markets Through the Lens of Emissions Trading Discourses' in B Jessup and K Rubenstein (eds), *Environmental Discourses in Public and International Law* (Cambridge University Press, Cambridge, 2012) 331.

[21] L Heinzerling, 'Selling Pollution, Forcing Democracy' (1995) 14 *Stanford Environmental Law Journal* 300, 302.

[22] Stavros Dimas, EU Environment Commissioner, 'Improving Environmental Quality through Carbon Trading' (Speech at the Carbon Expo Conference, Köln, 2 May 2007) europa.eu/rapid/press-ReleasesAction.do?reference=SPEECH/07/265, accessed 19 September 2012.

[23] Case C-127/07 *Arcelor Atlantique and Lorraine and Others v Commission* [2008] OJ C44/8, Opinion of AG Maduro, para 2.

[24] Stavros Dimas, EU Environment Commissioner, 'Climate Change – International and EU Action' (Speech at the Climate Change Conference, Prague, 31 October 2008) europa.eu/rapid/pressReleases-Action.do?reference=SPEECH/08/570&format=HTML&aged=0&language=EN&guiLanguage=en, accessed 19 September 2012.

[25] L Baum, *The Wizard of Oz* (Templar Publishing, Surrey, 2007) 104.

were challenged in the course of following the 'yellow brick road'. Ultimately, this book has shown that there is a need critically and carefully to assess emissions trading schemes in law, and has provided an analytical framework for doing so.

BIBLIOGRAPHY

F Ackerman and L Heinzerling, *Priceless: On Knowing the Price of Everything and the Value of Nothing* (New York Press, New York City, 2004).

B Ackerman and R Stewart, 'Reforming Environmental Law: The Democratic Case for Market Incentives' (1988) 13 *Colombia Journal of Environmental Law* 171.

—— —— 'Reforming Environmental Law' (1985) 37 *Stanford Law Review* 1333.

M Åhman and K Holmgren, 'New Entrant Allocation in the Nordic Energy Sectors: Incentives and Options in the EU ETS' in G Michael, R Betz and K Neuhoff (eds), *National Allocation Plans in the EU Emissions Trading Scheme: Lessons and Implications for Phase II* (Earthscan, London, 2007).

A Alchian, *Pricing Society* (The Institute of Economic Affairs, Leicester, 1967).

J Aldy and R Stavins, 'Climate Policy Architecture for the Post-Kyoto World' (2008) 50 *Environment* 7.

—— ——, 'Introduction: International Policy Architecture for Global Climate Change' in A Joseph and S Robert (eds), *Architectures for Agreement: Addressing Global Climate Change in the Post-Kyoto World* (Cambridge University Press, Cambridge, 2007).

J Allison, *A Continental Distinction in the Common Law: A Historical and Comparative Perspective on English Law* (Clarendon Press, Oxford, 1996).

K Alter (ed), *The European Court's Political Power: Selected Essays* (Oxford University Press, Oxford, 2009).

—— *Establishing the Supremacy of European Law: Making of an International Rule of Law in Europe* (Oxford University Press, Oxford, 2001).

A Aman Jr, 'Administrative Law for a New Century' in M Taggart (ed), *The Province of Administrative Law* (Hart Publishing, Oxford, 1997).

M Andersen and I Massa, 'Ecological Modernization: Origin, Dilemmas and Future Directions' (2000) 2 *Environmental and Planning Law Journal* 337.

T Anderson and D Leal, 'Rethinking the Way We Think' in J Dryzek and D Schlosberg (eds), *Debating the Earth: The Environmental Politics Reader* (Oxford University Press, Oxford, 2005).

—— —— *Free Market Environmentalism* (Westview Press, Oxford, 1993).

—— —— 'Free Market Versus Political Environmentalism' (1992) 15 *Harvard Journal of Law and Public Policy* 297.

N Anger, 'Emissions Trading Beyond Europe: Linking Schemes in a Post-Kyoto World' (2008) 30 *Energy Economics* 2028.

R Antes, B Hansjürgen and P Letmathe, *Emissions Trading and Business* (Physica-Verlag HD, Heidelberg, 2010).

K Anttonen, M Mehling and K Upston-Hooper, 'Breathing Life into the Carbon Market Legal Frameworks of Emissions Trading in Europe' (2007) 16 *European Environmental Law Review* 96.

K Armstrong, 'Governance and the Single Market' in P Craig and G de Burca (eds), *The Evolution of EU law* (Oxford University Press, Oxford, 1999).

K Arrow, *Social Choice and Individual Values* (Yale University Press, New Haven, 1963).

J Austin, 'A Plea For Excuses' (1956) 57 *Aristotelian Society* 57.

R Baldwin, 'Better Regulation: The Search and the Struggle' in R Baldwin, M Cave and M Lodge (eds), *The Oxford Handbook of Regulation* (Oxford University Press, Oxford, 2010).

—— 'Regulation Lite: The Rise of Emissions Trading' (2008) 2 *Regulation and Governance* 193.

—— 'Is Better Regulation Smarter Regulation?' (2005) *Public Law* 485.

——, M Cave and M Lodge, 'Regulation – The Field and the Developing Agenda' in R Baldwin, M Cave and M Lodge (eds), *The Oxford Handbook of Regulation* (Oxford University Press, Oxford, 2010).

—— —— ——, *Understanding Regulation: Theory, Strategy, and Practice* (2nd edn, Oxford University Press, Oxford 2012).

C Barnard, *The Substantive Law of the EU: The Four Freedoms* (3rd edn, Oxford University Press, Oxford, 2010).

R Barnes, *Property Rights and Natural Resources* (Hart Publishing, Oxford, 2009).

L Baum, *The Wizard of Oz* (Templar Publishing, Surrey, 2007).

W Baumol and W Oates, *The Theory of Environmental Policy* (2nd edn, Cambridge University Press, Cambridge, 1988).

R Bayon, A Hawn and K Hamilton, *Voluntary Carbon Markets An International Business Guide to What They Are and How They Work* (2nd edn, Earthscan, London, 2009).

S Bell and D McGillivray, *Environmental Law* (7th edn, Oxford University Press, Oxford, 2008).

M Betsill, 'Global Climate Change Policy: Making Progress or Spinning the Wheels?' in R Axelrod, D Downie and N Vig (eds), *The Global Environment: Institutions, Law, and Policy* (CQ Press, Washington DC, 2005).

R Betz, K Rogge and J Schleich, 'EU Emissions Trading: An Early Analysis of National Allocation Plans for 2008–12' in M Grubb, R Betz and K Neuhoff (eds), *National Allocation Plans in the EU Emissions Trading Scheme: Lessons and Implications for Phase II* (Earthscan, London, 2007).

A Biondi, 'Subsidiarity in the Courtroom' in A Biondi, P Eeckhout and S Ripley (eds), *EU Law After Lisbon* (Oxford University Press, Oxford, 2012).

P Birnie, A Boyle and C Redgwell, *International Law and the Environment* (3rd edn, Oxford University Press, Oxford, 2009).

W Block, 'Environmental Problems, Private Property Rights Solutions' in W Block (ed), *Economics and the Environment: A Reconciliation* (The Frasier Institute, Vancouver, 1990).

D Bodansky, 'A Tale of Two Architectures: The Once and Future UN Climate Change Regime' (2011) 43 *Arizona State Law Journal* 697.

—— *The Art and Craft of International Environmental Law* (Harvard University Press, Cambridge, Massachusetts, 2010).

——, J Brunnée and E Hey, 'International Environmental Law: Mapping the Field' in D Bodansky, J Brunnée and E Hey (eds), *The Oxford Handbook of International Environmental Law* (Oxford University Press, Oxford, 2007).

N Boeger, 'Minimum Harmonisation, Free Movement and Proportionality' in P Syrpis (ed), *The Judiciary, the Legislature and the EU Internal Market* (Cambridge University Press, Cambridge, 2012).

S Bogojević, 'Global Gazing: Viewing Markets Through the Lens of Emissions Trading Discourses' in B Jessup and K Rubenstein (eds), *Environmental Discourses in Public and International Law* (Cambridge University Press, Cambridge, 2012).

—— 'Legalising Environmental Leadership: A Comment on the CJEU's Ruling in C-366/10 on the Inclusion of Aviation in the EU Emissions Trading Scheme' (2012) 24 *Journal of Environmental Law* 345.

—— 'Ending the Honeymoon: Deconstructing Emissions Trading Discourses' (2009) 21 *Journal of Environmental Law* 443.

—— 'The EU ETS Directive Revised: Yet Another Stepping Stone' (2009) 11 *Environmental Law Review* 279.

M Bond and D Farrier, 'Transferable Water Allocations-Property Rights or Shimmering Mirage' (1996) 13 *Environmental and Planning Law Journal* 213.

C Bourbon-Seclet, 'A Tentative Agenda to Improve the "Gold Standard" and Bring Some Contractual Certainty into the System: Part 2' (2008) 23 *Journal of International Banking Law and Regulation* 302.

—— 'Legal Aspects of Climate Change in Europe: Is the European Emission Trading Scheme Greater than the Sum of the Parts? Part 1' (2008) 23 *Journal of International Banking Law and Regulation* 252.

G Boyle, 'Greenhouse Gas Emissions Trading and Duties of the State: A Preliminary Review of Alberta's Specified Gas Emitters Regulation' (2008) 2 *Climate and Carbon Law Review* 160.

M Braun, 'The Evolution of Emissions Trading in the European Union – the Role of Policy Networks, Knowledge and Policy Entrepreneurs' (2009) 34 *Accounting, Organizations and Society* 469.

A Brohé, N Eyre and N Howarth, *Carbon Markets: An International Business Guide* (Earthscan, London, 2009).

J Broome, *Counting the Cost of Global Warming* (White Horse Press, Isle of Harris, 1992).

G Brown, 'Renewable Natural Resource Management and Use Without Markets' (2000) 38 *Journal of Economic Literature* 875.

E Brubaker, *Property Rights in the Defence of Nature* (Earthscan, London, 1958).

A Bryman, *Social Research Methods* (3rd edn, Oxford University Press, Oxford, 2008).

J Buchanan and G Tullock, *The Calculus of Consent: Logical Foundations of Constitutional Democracy* (University of Michigan Press, Ann Arbor, 1965).

T Burns, 'Better Lawmaking? An Evaluation of Lawmaking in the European Community' in P Craig and C Harlow (eds), *Lawmaking in the European Union* (Kluwer Law International, London 1998).

J Button, 'Carbon: Commodity or Currency? The Case for an International Carbon Market Based on the Currency Model' (2008) 32 *Harvard Environmental Law Review* 571.

M Callon, 'An Essay on Framing and Overflowing: Economic Externalities Revisited by Sociology' in M Callon (ed), *The Laws of the Markets* (Blackwell Publishers, Oxford, 1998).

P Cane, 'Public Law and Private Law: A Study of the Analysis and Use of a Legal Concept' in J Eekelaar and J Bell (eds), *Oxford Essays in Jurisprudence* (Clarendon Press, Oxford, 1987).

C Carlarne, *Climate Change Law and Policy: EU and US Approaches* (Oxford University Press, Oxford, 2010).

—— and D Farber, 'Law Beyond Borders: Transnational Responses to Global Environmental Issues' (2012) 1 *Transnational Environmental Law* 13.

D Chalmers, 'Inhabitants in the Field of EC Environmental Law' in P Craig and G de Burca (eds), *The Evolution of EU Law* (1st edn, Oxford University Press, Oxford, 1999).

D Chalmers, G Davies and G Monti, *European Union Law* (2nd edn, Cambridge University Press, Cambridge, 2010).

D Chalmers, *et al*, *European Union Law: Text and Materials* (Cambridge University Press, Cambridge, 2006).

M Chan, 'Lessons Learned from the Financial Crisis: Designing Carbon Markets for Environmental Effectiveness and Financial Stability' (2009) 2 *Climate and Carbon Law Review* 152.

G Chichilnisky and G Heal, 'Markets for Tradable Carbon Dioxide Emission Quotas: Principles and Practice' in G Chichilnisky and G Heal (eds), *Environmental Markets: Equity and Efficiency* (Colombia University Press, New York, 2001).

—— ——, 'Introduction' in G Chichilnisky and G Heal (eds), *Environmental Markets: Equity and Efficiency* (Colombia University Press, New York City, 2000).

R Cichowski, 'Integrating the Environment: The European Court and the Construction of Supranational Policy' (1998) 5 *Journal of European Public Policy* 387.

C Cinnamon, 'Climate Change Policies an Ocean Apart: United States and European Union Climate Change Policies Compared' (2006) 14 *Penn State Environmental Law Review* 435.

R Coase, 'The Problem of Social Cost' (1960) 3 *Journal of Law and Economics* 1.

J Cohen, 'The European Preliminary Reference and US Supreme Court Review of State Court Judgments: A Study in Comparative Judicial Federalism' (1996) 44 *American Journal of Comparative Law* 421.

D Cole, 'Clearing the Air: Four Propositions About Property Rights and Environmental Protection' (1999) 10 *Duke Environmental Law and Policy Forum* 103.

Commission of the European Communities, 'Communication from the Commission on a Roadmap from Moving to a Competitive Low Carbon Economy in 2050', COM(2011) 112 final.

—— 'Communication from the Commission on 20 20 by 2020 – Europe's Climate Change Opportunity', COM(2008) 30 final.

—— 'Commission Proposal for a Council Directive Introducing a Tax on Carbon Dioxide Emissions and Energy', COM(92) 226 final.

—— 'Commission White Paper on European Governance', COM(2001) 428.

Commission of the European Communities, 'Communication from the Commission on Better Regulation for Growth and Jobs in the European Union', COM(2005) 97 final.

—— 'Communication from the Commission on Climate Change – Towards an EU Post-Kyoto Strategy', COM(1998) 353.

—— 'Communication from the Commission on Preparing for Implementation of the Kyoto Protocol', COM(1999) 230.

—— 'Communication from the Commission on Smart Regulation in the European Union', COM(2010) 543 final.

—— 'Communication from the Commission on Building a Global Market – Report Pursuant to Article 30 of Directive 2003/87/EC', COM(2006) 676 final.

—— 'Communication from the Commission on Implementing Community Environmental Law', COM(96) 500 final.

—— 'Communication from the Commission on International Climate Policy Post Copenhagen', COM(2010) 86 final, 4.

Commission of the European Communities, 'Communication prior to the Laeken European Council, The Future of European Union – European Governance: Renewing the Community Method', COM(2001) 727.

—— 'Communication from the Commission on Towards an Enhanced Market Oversight Framework for the EU Emissions Trading Scheme', COM(2010) 796 final.

—— 'Communication from the Commission on a Single Market for 21st Century Europe', COM(2007) 724 final.

—— 'Green Paper on Greenhouse Gas Emissions Trading Within the European Union', COM(2000) 87 final.

—— 'Green Paper on Market-Based Instruments for Environment and Related Policy Purposes', COM(2007) 140 final.

—— 'Proposal for a Decision of the European Parliament and of the Council amending Directive 2003/87/EC clarifying provisions on the timing of auctions of greenhouse gas allowances', COM(2012) 416 final.

—— 'Proposal for a Directive amending Directive 2003/87/EC so as to improve and extend the greenhouse gas emission allowance trading system of the Community', COM(2008) 16 final.

—— 'Proposal for a Directive of the European and of the Council establishing a scheme for greenhouse gas emission allowance trading within the Community and amending Council Directive 96/61/EC', COM(2001) 581 final.

—— 'Proposal for a Regulation on the Common Fisheries Policy', COM(2011) 425 final.

Commission of the European Communities, 'White Paper on Completing the Internal Market', COM(85) 310 final.

Commission of the European Communities, Communication, 'Analysis of Options to Move Beyond 20% Greenhouse Gas Emission Reductions and Assessing the Risk of Carbon Leakage', COM(2010) 265 final.

—— Notice from the Commission on the Definition of the Relevant Market for the Purposes of Community Competition Law, [1997] OJ C372/5.

—— Proposal for a Regulation on the Common Fisheries Policy, COM(2011) 425 final.

—— 'Commission Working Paper on Better Regulation and the Thematic Strategies for the Environment', COM(2005) 446 final.

F Convery, 'Reflections – The Emerging Literature on Emissions Trading in Europe' (2009) 2 *Review of Environmental Economics and Policy* 121.

—— and L Redmond, 'Market and Price Developments in the European Union Emissions Trading Scheme' (2007) 1 *Review of Environmental Economics and Policy* 88.

G Conway, 'Introduction and Overview – Interpretation and the European Court of Justice' in G Conway (ed), *The Limits of Legal Reasoning and the European Court of Justice* (Cambridge University Press, Cambridge, 2012).

J Costonis, 'The Chicago Plan: Incentive Zoning and the Preservation of Urban Landmarks' (1972) 85 *Harvard Law Review* 574.

R Cotterrell, 'Is there a Logic of Legal Transplants?' in D Nelken and J Feest (eds), *Adapting Legal Cultures* (Hart Publishing, Oxford, 2001).

—— 'The Concept of Legal Culture' in D Nelken (ed), *Comparing Legal Cultures* (Darthmouth Publishing, Aldershot, 1997).

S Coyle and K Morrow, *Philosophical Foundations of Environmental Law: Property, Rights and Nature* (Hart Publishing, Oxford, 2004).

P Craig, *EU Administrative Law* (2nd edn, Oxford University Press, Oxford 2012).

—— 'The Evolution of the Single Market: Unpacking the Premises' in C Barnard and J Scott (eds), *The Law of the Single European Market* (Hart Publishing, Oxford, 2002).

—— and G de Burca (eds), *The Evolution of EU Law* (2nd edn, Oxford University Press, Oxford 2011).

—— —— *EU Law: Text, Cases and Materials* (5th edn, Oxford University Press, Oxford, 2011).

P Craig and G de Burca, *EU Law: Text, Cases and Materials* (4th edn, Oxford University Press, Oxford, 2008).

R Craufurd Smith, 'The Evolution of Cultural Policy in the European Union' in P Craig and G de Burca (eds), *The Evolution of EU Law* (Oxford University Press, Oxford, 2011).

T Crocker, 'The Structuring of Atmospheric Pollution Control System' in H Wolozin (ed), *The Economics of Air Pollution* (WW Norton & Co, New York City, 1966).

H Dagan and M Heller, 'The Liberal Commons' (2001) 110 *Yale Law Journal* 549.

J Dales, *Pollution, Property and Prices: An Essay in Policy-Making and Economics* (University of Toronto Press, Toronto, 1970).

—— 'Land, Water, and Ownership' (1968) 1 *Canadian Journal of Economics* 791.

C Damro and P Luaces Méndez, 'Emissions Trading at Kyoto: From EU Resistance to Union Innovation' (2003) 12 *Environmental Politics* 71.

G Dari-Mattiacci and J van Zeben, 'Legal and Market Uncertainty in Market-Based Instruments: The Case of the EU ETS' (2011) 19 *New York University Environmental Law Journal*.

É Darier (ed), *Discourses of the Environment* (Blackwell Publishers, Oxford, 1999).

A Dashwood and D Wyatt, *European Union Law* (5th edn Sweet & Maxwell, London, 2006).

G Davies, 'Subsidiarity: The Wrong Idea, in the Wrong Place, at the Wrong Time' (2006) 43 *CML Rev* 63.

G de Burca and J Scott, 'Introduction' in G de Burca and J Scott (eds), *Law and New Governance in the EU and the US* (Hart Publishing, Oxford, 2006).

J de Cendra de Larragán, *Distributional Choices in EU Climate Change Law and Policy: Towards a Principled Approach?* (Kluwer Law International, Alphen aan den Rijn, 2011).

—— 'Too Much Harmonization? An Analysis of the Commission's Proposal to Amend the EU ETS from the Perspective of Legal Principles' in M Faure and M Peeters (eds), *Climate Change and European Emissions Trading: Lessons for Theory and Practice* (Edward Elgar, Cheltenham, 2008).

R de Witt Wijnen, 'Emissions Trading under Article 17 of the Kyoto Protocol' in D Freestone and C Streck (eds), *Legal Aspects of Implementing the Kyoto Protocol Mechanisms: Making Kyoto Work* (Oxford University Press, Oxford, 2005).

B de Witte, 'Non-market Values in Internal Market Legislation' in N Shuibhne (ed), *Regulating the Internal Market* (Edward Elgar Publishing, Cheltenham, 2006).

N Deakin and K Walsh, 'The Enabling State: The Role of Markets and Contracts' (1996) 74 *Public Administration* 33.

S Deatherage, *Carbon Trading Law and Practice* (Oxford University Press, Oxford, 2011).

K Deketelaere and M Peeters, 'Key Challenges of EU Climate Change Policy: Competence, Measures and Compliance' in M Peeters and K Deketelaere (eds), *EU Climate Change Policy: The Challenge of New Regulatory Initiatives* (Edward Elgar, Cheltenham, 2006).

J Delbeke, 'The Emissions Trading Scheme (ETS): The Cornerstone of the EU's Implementation of the Kyoto Protocol' in J Delbeke (ed), *EU Energy Law: The EU Greenhouse Gas Emissions Trading Scheme* (Claeys & Casteels, Leuven, 2006).

—— (ed), *EU Energy Law: The EU Greenhouse Gas Emissions Trading Scheme* (Claeys & Casteels, Leuven, 2006).

T Delreux, 'The EU as an Actor in Global Environmental Politics' in A Jordan and C Adelle (eds), *Environmental Policy in the EU: Actors, Institutions and Processes* (Routledge, Abingdon, 2013).

H Demsetz, 'The Cost of Transacting' (1968) 82 *Quarterly Journal of Economics* 33.

—— 'Toward a Theory of Property Rights' (1967) 57 *American Economic Review* 347.

J Derrida, *Writing and Differences* (Chicago University Press, Chicago, 1978).
—— *Of Grammatology* (Johns Hopkins University Press, Baltimore, 1974).
D Dinan, *Ever Closer Union: An Introduction to European Integration* (3rd edn, Palgrave Macmillan, Hampshire, 2005).
E Donald, 'Environmental Markets and Beyond: Three Modest Proposals for the Future of Environmental Law' (2001) 29 *Capital University Law* 245.
R Dornau, 'The Emissions Trading Scheme of the European Union' in D Freestone and C Streck (eds), *Legal Aspects of Implementing the Kyoto Protocol Mechanisms: Making Kyoto Work* (Oxford University Press, Oxford, 2005).
S Douglas-Scott, *Constitutional Law of the European Union* (Pearson Education, Harlow, 2002).
A Downs, *An Economic Theory of Democracy* (Harper, New York, 1957).
M Drechsler and F Hartig, 'Conserving Biodiversity with Tradable Permits under Changing Conservation Costs and Habitat Restoration Time Lags' (2011) 70 *Ecological Economics* 533.
D Driesen, 'Capping Carbon' (2010) 1 *Environmental Law* 1.
—— 'Economic Instruments for Sustainable Development' in B Richardson and S Wood (eds), *Environmental Law for Sustainability* (Hart Publishing, Oxford, 2006) 277.
—— 'What's Property Got To Do With It?: A Review Essay of "Pollution and Property: Comparing Ownership Institutions for Environmental Protection" by Daniel Cole' (2003) 30 *Ecology Law Quarterly* 1003.
—— 'Is Emissions Trading an Economic Incentive Program?: Replacing the Command and Control/Economic Incentive Dichotomy' (1998) 55 *Washington and Lee Law Review* 289.
J Dryzek, 'Paradigms and Discourses' in D Bodansky, J Brunnée and E Hey (eds), *The Oxford Handbook of International Environmental Law* (Oxford University Press, Oxford, 2007).
—— *The Politics of the Earth: Environmental Discourses* (2nd edn, Oxford University Press, Oxford, 2005).
D Dudek, R Stewart and J Wiener, 'Environmental Policy for Eastern Europe: Technology-Based Versus Market-Based Approaches' (1992) 17 *Colombia Journal of Environmental Law* 1.
J Dunoff, 'Levels of Environmental Governance' in D Bodansky, J Brunnée and E Hey (eds), *The Oxford Handbook of International Environmental Law* (Oxford University Press, Oxford, 2007).
M Egan, *Constructing a European Market* (Oxford University Press, Oxford, 2001).
C Egenhofer and others, *The EU Emissions Trading Scheme: Taking Stock and Looking Forward* (Mistra, Brussels, 2006).
D Ellerman, 'Are Cap-and-Trade Programs More Environmentally Effective than Conventional Regulation?' in J Freeman and C Kolstad (eds), *Moving to Markets in Environmental Regulation: Lessons From Twenty Years of Experience* (Oxford University Press, Oxford, 2007).
——, F Convery and C de Perthuis, *Pricing Carbon: The European Union Emissions Trading Scheme* (Cambridge University Press, Cambridge, 2010).
—— and P Joskow, *The European Union's Emissions Trading System in Perspective* (Pew Center on Global Climate Change, Arlington VA, 2008).
—— B Buchner and C Carraro (eds), *Allocation in the European Emissions Trading Scheme: Rights, Rents and Fairness* (Cambridge University Press Cambridge, 2007).

D Ellerman and others, *Markets for Clean Air: The US Acid Rain Program* (Cambridge University Press, New York City, 2000).

R Elsworth and others, *Carbon Fat Cats 2011: The Companies Profiting from the EU Emissions Trading Scheme* (Sandbag, London, 2011).

K Engel, 'Courts and Climate Policy: Now and in the Future' in B Rabe (ed), *Greenhouse Governance: Adressing Climate Change in America* (Brookings Institute Press, Washinton DC, 2010).

A Engels, 'Market Creation and Transnational Rule-Making: The case of CO2 Emissions Trading' in M-L Djelic and K Sahlin-Andersson (eds), *Transnational Governance: Institutional Dynamics of Regulation* (Cambridge University Press, Cambridge, 2006).

R Epstein, 'Carbon Dioxide: Our Newest Pollutant' (2010) 43 *Suffolk University Law Review* 797.

—— 'The Allocation of the Commons: Parking on Public Roads' (2002) 31 *Journal of Legal Studies* 515.

T Etty and others, 'Transnational Dimensions of Climate Governance' (2012) 1 *Transnational Environmental Law* 235.

B Ewing and D Kysar, 'Prods and Pleas: Limited Government in an Era of Unlimited Harm' (2011) 121 *Yale Law Journal* 350.

D Farber and A O'Connell, 'A Brief Trajectory of Public Choice and Public Law' in D Farber and A O'Connell (eds), *Research Handbook on Public Choice and Public Law* (Edward Elgar, Cheltenham, 2010).

S Farrall, T Ahmed and D French (eds), *Criminological and Legal Consequences of Climate Change* (Hart Publishing, Oxford, 2012).

M Faure and M Peeters (eds), *Climate Change and European Emissions Trading: Lessons for Theory and Practice* (Edward Elgar, Cheltenham, 2008).

M Faure and M Peeters (eds), *Climate Change Liability* (Edward Elgar, Cheltenham, 2011).

E Fisher, 'The Rise of Transnational Environmental Law and the Expertise of Environmental Lawyers' (2012) 1 *Transnational Environmental Law* 43.

—— *Risk Regulation and Administrative Constitutionalism* (Hart Publishing, Oxford, 2010).

—— 'Unpacking the Toolbox: Or Why the Public/Private Divide is Important in EC Environmental Law' in M Freedland and J-B Auby (eds), *The Public Law/Private Law Divide: Une Entente Assez Cordiale? la Distinction du Droit Public et du Droit Privé: Regards Français et Britanniques* (Hart Publishing, Oxford, 2006).

——, B Lange and E Scotford, *Environmental Law: Text, Cases and Materials* (Oxford University Press, Oxford, 2013).

—— and others, 'Maturity and Methodology: Starting a Debate about Environmental Law Scholarship' (2009) 21 *Journal of Environmental Law* 213.

N Fligstein, *The Architecture of Markets: An Economic Sociology of Twenty-First-Century Capitalist Societies* (Princeton University Press, Princeton, 2001).

C Fogel, 'The Local, the Global, and the Kyoto Protocol' in S Jasanoff and M Martello (eds), *Earthly Politics: Local and Global in Environmental Governance* (MIT Press, Cambridge, Mass, 2004).

M Foucault, *The Order of Things: An Archeology of the Human Science* (Routledge, London, 2002).

—— *Discipline and Punish: The Birth of the Prison* (Penguin Books, Harmondsworth, 1991).

—— *The History of Sexuality* (Penguin Books, Harmondsworth, 1981).

F Francioni, 'Realism, Utopia and the Future of International Environmental Law' (Law 2012/11, EUI Working Papers, 2012).

M Freeden, *Ideology: A Very Short Introduction* (Oxford University Press, New York, 2003).

M Freedland and J-B Auby (eds), *The Public Law/Private Law Divide: Une Entente Assez Cordiale? la Distinction du Droit Public et du Droit Privé: Regards Français et Britanniques* (Hart Publishing, Oxford, 2006).

J Freeman, 'Private Role in Public Governance' (2000) 75 *New York University Law Review* 543.

J Freeman and C Kolstad, 'Prescriptive Environmental Regulations versus Market-Based Incentives' in J Freeman and C Kolstad (eds), *Moving to Markets in Environmental Regulation: Lessons After Twenty Years of Experience* (Oxford University Press, Oxford, 2006).

D Freestone, 'The UN Framework Convention of Climate Change, the Kyoto Protocol, and the Kyoto Mechanisms' in D Freestone and C Streck (eds), *Legal Aspects of Implementing the Kyoto Protocol Mechanisms* (Oxford University Press, Oxford, 2005).

L Friedman, 'Some Comments on Cotterrell and Legal Transplants' in D Nelken and J Feest (eds), *Adapting Legal Cultures* (Hart Publishing, Oxford, 2001).

—— 'The Concept of Legal Culture: A Reply' in D Nelken (ed), *Comparing Legal Cultures* (Dartmouth Publishing, Aldershot, 1997).

G Garrett, 'The Politics of Legal Integration in the European Union' (1995) 49 *International Organization* 171.

M Ghertman, 'The Puzzle of Regulation, Deregulation and Reregulation' in C Ménard and M Ghertman (eds), *Regulation, Deregulation, Reregulation: Institutional Perspectives* (Edward Elgar, Cheltenham, 2009).

J Gibson and G Caldeira, 'The Legal Cultures of Europe' (1996) 30 *Law and Society Review* 55.

R Gill, 'Discourse Analysis' in M Bauer and G Gaskell (eds), *Qualititative Research with Text, Image and Sound: A Practical Handbook* (Sage, London, 2000).

L Godden, 'Governing Common Resources: Environmental Markets and Property in Water' in A McHarg and others (eds), *Property and the Law in Energy and Natural Resources* (Oxford University Press, Oxford, 2010).

R Goodin, 'Selling Environmental Indulgences' (1994) 47 *Kyklos* 573.

L Gormley, 'The Internal Market: History and Evolution' in N Shuibhne (ed), *Regulating the Internal Market* (Edward Elgar Publishing, Cheltenham, 2006).

N Graham, 'The Mythology of Environmental Markets' in D Grinlinton (ed), *Property Rights and Sustainability* (Martinus Nijhoff Publishers, Leiden, 2011).

K Gray, 'Property in a Queue' in G Alexander and E Penalver (eds), *Property and Community* (Oxford University Press, Oxford, 2009).

X Groussot and S Bogojević, 'Subsidiarity as a Procedural Safeguard of Federalism' in L Azoulai (ed), *The European Union as a Federal Order of Competences* (Oxford University Press, Oxford, forthcoming).

N Gunningham and D Sinclair, 'Regulatory Pluralism: Designing Policy Mixes for Environmental Protection' (1999) 21 *Law and Policy* 49.

——, P Grabosky and D Sinclair, *Smart Regulation: Designing Environmental Policy* (Clarendon Press, Oxford, 1998).

A Haagsma, 'The European Community's Environmental Policy: A Case-Study in Federalism' (1989) 12 *Fordham International Law Journal* 311.

R Hahn and G Hester, 'Marketable Permits: Lessons for Theory and Practice' (1989) 16 *Ecological Law Quarterly* 361.

R Hahn and G Hester, 'Where Did All the Markets Go? An Analysis of EPA's Emissions Trading Program' (1989) 6 *Yale Journal on Regulation* 109.

M Hajer, 'Coalitions, Practices, and Meaning in Environmental Politics: From Acid Rain to BSE' in D Howarth and J Torfing (eds), *Discourse Theory in European Politics: Identity, Policy and Governance* (Palgrave Macmillan, Hampshire, 2005).

—— *The Politics of Environmental Discourse: Ecological Modernization and the Policy Process* (Clarendon Press, Oxford, 1995).

—— 'Discourse Coalition and the Institutionalisation of Practice: The Case of Acid Rain in Britain' in F Fischer and J Forester (eds), *The Argumentative Turn in Policy and Planning* (UCL Press, London, 1993).

M Hanemann, 'Cap-and-Trade: A Sufficient or Necessary Condition for Emission Reduction?' (2010) 26 *Oxford Review of Economic Policy* 225.

B Hansjürgen, 'Concluding Observations' in B Hansjürgen (ed), *Emissions Trading for Climate Policy: US and European Perspectives* (Cambridge University Press, Cambridge, 2005).

G Hardin, 'The Tragedy of the Unmanaged Commons: Population and the Disguise of Providence' in R Andelson (ed), *Commons Without Tragedy* (Shepheard-Walwyn Publishers, London, 1991).

—— 'The Tragedy of the Commons' (1968) 162 *Science* 1243.

A Harding, 'Comparative Law and Legal Transplantation in South East Asia' in D Nelken and J Feest (eds), *Adapting Legal Cultures* (Hart Publishing, Oxford, 2001).

C Harlow, 'Voices of Difference in a Plural Community' (2002) 50 *American Journal of Comparative Law* 339.

B Harrison, C Smith and B Davies, *Introductory Economics* (Macmillan Press, London, 1992).

E Hattan, 'The Implementation of EU Environmental Law' (2003) 15 *Journal of Environmental Law* 273.

F A Hayek, *The Road to Serfdom* (Routledge and Kegan Paul, London and Henley, 1976).

R Haythornthwaite, 'Better Regulation in Europe' in S Weatherill (ed), *Better Regulation* (Hart Publishing, Oxford, 2007).

G Heal, 'Markets and Sustainability' in R Revesz, P Sands and R Stewart (eds), *Environmental Law, the Economy and Sustainable Development: The United States, the European Union and the International Community* (Cambridge University Press, Cambridge, 2000).

L Heinzerling, 'Climate Change in the Supreme Court' (2008) 38 *Environmental Law* 1.

—— 'The Environment' in M Tushnet and P Cane (eds), *The Oxford Handbook of Legal Studies* (Oxford University Press, Oxford, 2003).

—— 'Selling Pollution, Forcing Democracy' (1995) 14 *Stanford Environmental Law Journal* 300.

M Heller, *The Gridlock Economy: How Too Much Ownership Wrecks Markets, Stops Innovation, and Costs Lives* (Basic Books, New York City, 2008).

D Helm and D Pearce, 'Economic Policy Towards the Environment: An Overview' in D Helm (ed), *Economic Policy Toward the Environment* (Blackwell Publishers, Oxford, 1991) 1.

E Herlin-Karnell, *The Constitutional Dimension of European Criminal Law* (Hart Publishing, Oxford, 2012).

C Hilson, *Regulating Pollution. A UK and EC Perspective* (Hart Publishing, Oxford, 2000).

J Holder and M Lee, *Environmental Protection, Law and Policy* (2nd edn, Cambridge University Press, Cambridge, 2007).

C Holderness, 'The Assignment of Rights, Entry Effects, and the Allocation of Resources' in R Epstein (ed), *Economics of Property Law* (Edward Elgar, Cheltenham, 2007).

D Howarth and J Torfing (eds), *Discourse Theory in European Politics: Identity, Policy and Governance* (Palgrave Macmillan, Hampshire, 2005).

F Jacobs, 'Is the Court of Justice of the European Communities a Constitutional Court?' in D Curtin and D O'Keeffe (eds), *Constitutional Adjudication in European Community and National Law – Essays for the Hon Mr Justice T-F O'Higgins* (Butterworth, Dublin, 1992).

M Jacobs, *The Green Economy: Environment, Sustainable Development, and the Politics of the Future* (Pluto Press, London, 1991).

J Jans and H Vedder, *European Environmental Law – After Lisbon* (4th edn, Europa Law Publishing, Groningen, 2011).

——, H Sevenster and J Janssen, 'Environmental Spill-Overs Into General Community Law' (2008) 31 *Fordham International Law Journal* 1360.

S Jasanoff, 'Heaven and Earth' in S Jasanoff and M Martello (eds), *Earthly Politics: Local and Global in Environmental Governance* (MIT Press, Cambridge, Mass, 2004).

—— 'The Idiom of Co-Production' in S Jasanoff (ed), *States of Knowledge: The Co-Production of Science and Social Order* (Routledge, London, 2004).

B Jessup and K Rubenstein (eds), *Using Environmental Discourses to Traverse Public and International Environmental Laws* (Cambridge University Press, Cambridge, 2012).

C Joerges, 'What is Left of the European Economic Constitution? A Melancholic Euology' (2005) 30 *EL Rev* 461.

C Joerges, 'The Europeanization of Private Law as a Rationalization Process and as a Contest of Disciplines – an Analysis of the Directive on Unfair Terms in Consumer Contracts' (1995) 3 *European Environmental Law Review* 175.

J Johnston, 'Problems of Equity and Efficiency in the Design of International Greenhouse Gas Cap-and-Trade Schemes' (2009) 33 *Harvard Environmental Law Review* 405.

A Jordan, 'The Implementation of EU Environmental Policy: A Policy without a Political Solution?' (1999) 17 *Environment and Planning* 69.

D Kelemen, 'Globalizing EU Environmental Regulation' (2007) 17 *Journal of European Public Policy* 335.

C Kemfert and others, 'The Environmental and Economic Effects of European Emissions Trading' in G Michael, R Betz and K Neuhoff (eds), *National Allocation Plans in the EU Emissions Trading Scheme: Lessons and Implications for Phase II* (Earthscan, London, 2007).

R Kemp, 'Why Not In My Backyard? A Radical Interpretation of Public Opposition to the Deep Disposal of Radioactive Waste in the United Kingdom' (1990) 22 *Environment and Planning* 1239.

D Kennedy, 'The Stages of the Decline of the Public/Private Distinction' (1982) 130 *University of Pennsylvania* 1349.

C Knill and D Liefferink, 'The Establishment of EU Environmental Policy' in A Jordan and C Adelle (eds), *Environmental Policy in the EU: Actors, Institutions and Processes* (Routledge, Abingdon, 2013).

L Krämer, 'The European Court of Justice' in A Jordan and C Adelle (eds), *Environmental Policy in the EU: Actors, Institutions and Processes* (Routledge, Abingdon, 2013).

—— 'Seal Killing, the Inuit and EU Law' (2012) 21 *Review of European Community and International Environmental Law* 291.

—— 'Environmental Justice in the European Court of Justice' in J Ebbesson and P Okowa (eds), *Environmental Law and Justice in Context* (Cambridge University Press, Cambridge, 2009).

L Krämer, 'On the Court of First Instance and the Protection of the Environment' in G Bándi (ed), *The Impact of ECJ Jurisprudence on Environmental Law* (Szent István Társulat, Budapest, 2009).

—— 'Some Reflections on the EU Mix of Instruments on Climate Change' in M Peeters and K Deketelaere (eds), *EU Climate Change Policy: The Challenge of New Regulatory Initiatives* (Edward Elgar, Cheltenham, 2006).

—— *Casebook on EU Environmental Law* (Hart Publishing, Oxford, 2002).

—— *EC Environmental Law* (4th edn, Sweet & Maxwell, London, 2000).

R Lazarus, 'Super Wicked Problems and Climate Change: Restraining the Present to Liberate the Future' (2009) 94 *Cornell Law Review* 1153.

—— *The Making of Environmental Law* (Chicago University Press, Chicago, 2004).

—— 'Panel II: Public Versus Private Environment Regulation' (1994) 21 *Ecological Law Quarterly* 438.

M Lee, *EU Environmental Law: Challenges, Change and Decision-Making* (Hart Publishing, Oxford, 2005).

J Lefevere, 'A Climate of Change: An Analysis of Progress in EU and International Climate Change Policy' in J Scott (ed), *Environmental Protection: European Law and Governance* (Oxford University Press, New York, 2009).

—— 'Greenhouse Gas Emission Allowance Trading in the EU: A Background' (2003) *Yearbook of European Environmental Law* 149.

P Legrand, 'What "Legal Transplants"?' in D Nelken and J Feest (eds), *Adapting Legal Cultures* (Hart Publishing, Oxford, 2001).

—— 'Against a European Civil Code' (1997) 60 *MLR* 44.

K Lenaerts, 'The Principle of Subsidiarity and the Environment in the European Union: Keeping the Balance of Federalism' (1993) 17 *Fordham International Law Journal* 846.

—— and K Gutman, '"Federal Common Law" in the European Union: A Comparative Perspective from the United States' (2006) 54 *American Journal of Comparative Law* 1.

A Lenschow, 'Studying EU Environmental Policy' in A Jordan and C Adelle (eds), *Environmental Policy in the EU: Actors, Institutions and Processes* (Routledge, Abingdon, 2013).

D Levi-Faur, 'The Global Diffusion of Regulatory Capitalism' (2005) 598 *ANNALS of the American Academy of Political and Social Science* 12.

G Libecap, 'Property Rights Allocation of Common Pool Rescources' in C Ménard and M Ghertman (eds), *Regulation, Deregulation, Reregulation: Institutional Perspectives* (Edward Elgar, Cheltenham, 2009).

L Lohmann, 'Regulatory Challenges for Financial and Carbon Markets' (2009) 2 *Climate and Carbon Law Review* 161.

—— 'Carbon Trading: A Critical Conversation on Climate Change, Privatisation and Power' (2006) 48 *Development Dialogue* 4.

M Loughlin, *Public Law and Political Theory* (Clarendon Press, Oxford, 1992).

C Lyons, 'Perspectives on Convergence Within European Integration' in P Beaumont, C Lyons and N Walker (eds), *Convergence and Divergence in European Public Law* (Hart Publishing, Oxford, 2001).

MJ Mace, 'The Legal Nature of Emission Reductions and EU Allowances: Issues Addressed in an International Workshop' (2005) 2 *Journal of Energy and Environmental Law* 123.

D MacKenzie, *Material Markets: How Economic Agents are Constructed* (Oxford University Press, Oxford, 2009).

——, F Muniesa and L Siu, 'Introduction' in D MacKenzie, F Muniesa and L Siu (eds), *Do Economists Make Markets? On the Performativity of Economics* (Princeton University Press, Princeton, 2007).

R Macrory, *Regulation, Enforcement and Governance in Environmental Law* (Hart Publishing, Oxford, 2010).

—— '"Maturity and Methodology": A Personal Reflection' (2009) 21 *Journal of Environmental Law* 251.

—— 'Regulating in a Risky Environment' (2001) 54 *Current Legal Problems* 619.

M Maduro, *We the Court: The European Court of Justice and the European Economic Constitution – A Critical Reading of Article 30 of the EC Treaty* (Hart Publishing, Oxford, 2002).

—— and L Azoulai (eds), *The Past and Future of EU Law: The Classics of EU Law Revisited on the 50th Anniversary of the Rome Treaty* (Hart Publishing, Oxford, 2010).

G Majone, *Dilemmas of European Integration: The Ambiguities and Pitfalls of Integration by Stealth* (Oxford University Press, Oxford, 2009).

—— 'The European Commission as Regulator' in G Majone (ed), *Regulating Europe* (Routledge, Abingdon, 1996).

—— 'The Rise of Statutory Regulation in Europe' in G Majone (ed), *Regulating Europe* (Routledge, Abingdon, 1996).

—— 'Introduction' in G Majone (ed), *Deregulation or Re-Regulation? Regulatory Reform in Europe and the United States* (Pinter Publishers, London, 1990).

R Malloy, *Law in a Market Context: An Introduction to Market Concepts in Legal Reasoning* (Cambridge University Press, Cambridge, 2004).

F Mancini and D Keeling, 'From CILFIT to ERT: The Constitutional Challenge facing the European Court' (1991) 11 *Yearbook of European Law* 1.

S Manea, 'Defining Emissions Entitlements in the Constitution of the EU Emissions Trading System' (2012) 1 *Transnational Environmental Law* 303.

G Marín Durán and E Morgera, *Environmental Integration in the EU's External Relations: Beyond Multilateral Dimensions* (Hart Publishing, Oxford, 2012).

D Markell and JB Ruhl, 'An Empirical Assesment of Climate Change in the Courts: A New Jurisprudence or Business as Usual?' (2012) 64 *Florida Law Review* 15.

—— —— 'An Empirical Survey of Climate Change Litigation in the United States' (2010) 40 *Environmental Law Reporter* 10644.

R Martella, 'Market-based Regulation under the Clean Air Act' (2010) 4 *Carbon and Climate Law Review* 139.

J Mashaw, 'Public Law and Public Choice: Critique and Rapprochment' in D Farber and A O'Connell (eds), *Research Handbook on Public Choice and Public Law* (Edward Elgar, Cheltenham, 2010).

——, *Greed, Chaos, and Governance: Using Public Choice to Improve Public Law* (Yale University Press, New Haven, 1997).

I Massa and M Andersen, 'Special Issue Introduction: Ecological Modernization' (2000) 2 *Journal of Environmental Policy and Planning* 265.

J Maurici, 'Litigation and the EU Emissions Trading Scheme' (2009) 50 *Environmental Law* 7.

D Mavrakis and P Konidari, 'Classification of Emissions Trading Scheme Design Characteristics' (2003) 13 *European Environment* 48.

J McAdam (ed), *Climate Change and Displacement* (Hart Publishing, Oxford, 2012).

D Meadows, 'The Emissions Allowance Trading Directive 2003/87/EC Explained' in J Delbeke (ed), *EU Energy Law: The EU Greenhouse Gas Emissions Trading Scheme* (Claeys & Casteels, Leuven, 2006).

M Mehling, 'Linking Emissions Trading Schemes' in D Freestone and C Streck (eds), *Legal Aspects of Carbon Trading: Kyoto, Copenhagen, and Beyond* (Oxford University Press, Oxford, 2009).

—— 'Emissions Trading and National Allocation in the Member States – An Achilles' Heel of European Climate Policy?' (2005) 5 *Yearbook of European Environmental Law* 113.

E Meijer and J Werksman, 'Keeping it Clean – Safeguarding the Environmental Integrity of the Clean Development Mechanism' in D Freestone and C Streck (eds), *Legal Aspects of Carbon Trading: Kyoto, Copenhagen, and Beyond* (Oxford University Press, Oxford, 2005).

G Michael, 'Seeking Fair Weather: Ethics and the International Debate on Climate Change' (1995) 71 *International Affairs* 463.

J Mill, *On Liberty; and Other Essays* (Oxford University Press, Oxford, 1991).

J Mintz, 'Economic Reform of Environmental Protection: A Brief Commentary on a Recent Debate' (1991) 15 *Harvard Environmental Law Review* 149.

W Montgomery, 'Markets in Licenses and Efficient Pollution Control Programs' (1972) 5 *Journal of Economic Theory* 395.

B Morgan and K Yeung, *An Introduction to Law and Regulation: Texts and Materials* (Cambridge University Press, Cambridge, 2007).

B Müller, 'Access to the Courts of the Member States for NGOs in Environmental Matters under European Union Law' (2011) 23 *Journal of Environmental Law* 505.

A Myrick Freeman III, 'Economics' in D Jamieson (ed), *A Companion to Environmental Philosophy* (Blackwell Publishing, Oxford, 2001).

S Napolitano and others, 'The US Acid Rain Program: Key Insights from the Design, Operation, and Assessment of a Cap-and-Trade Program' (2007) 20 *The Electricity Journal* 47.

J Nash and R Revesz, 'Markets and Geography: Designing Marketable Permit Schemes to Control Local and Regional Pollutants' (2001) 28 *Ecological Law Quarterly* 569.

J Nash, 'Framing Effect and Regulatory Choice' (2006) 82 *Notre Dame Law Review* 313.

—— 'Too Much Market? Conflict between Tradable Pollution Allowances and the "Polluter Pays" Principle' (2000) 24 *Harvard Environmental Law Review* 465.

D Nelken, 'Comparatists and Transferability' in D Nelken (ed), *Beyond Law in Context: Developing a Sociological Understanding of Law* (Ashgate, Surrey, 2009).

—— 'Using the Concept of Legal Culture' (2004) 29 *Australian Journal of Legal Philosophy* 1.

—— 'Towards a Sociology of Legal Adaption' in D Nelken and J Feest (eds), *Adapting Legal Cultures* (Hart Publishing, Oxford, 2001).

—— 'Disclosing/Invoking Legal Culture: An Introduction' (1995) 4 *Social and Legal Studies* 435.

D Nonini, 'The Global Idea of "the Commons"' in D Nonini (ed), *The Global Idea of 'the Commons'* (Berghahn Books, New York, 2007).

N Nugent, *The Government and Politics of the European Union* (Oxford University Press, Oxford, 2006).

J O'Hara, *A New American Tea Party: The Counterrevolution Against Bailouts, Handouts, Reckless Spending and More Taxes* (John Wiley & Sons, Hoboken, New Jersey, 2010).

A Ogus, *Regulation: Legal Form and Economic Theory* (Clarendon Press, Oxford, 1994).

E Olivi, 'The EU Better Regulation Agenda' in S Weatherill (ed), *Better Regulation* (Hart Publishing, Oxford, 2007).

C Olsen Lundh, 'Koldioxidhandeln Inom EU ETS – Stärkt och Expanderad?' (2008) 2 *Europarättslig Tidskrift* 350.

E Orts, 'Reflexive Environmental Law' (1995) 89 *Northwestern University Law Review* 1227.

H Osofsky, 'The Continuing Importance of Climate Change Litigation' (2010) 1 *Climate Law* 3.

—— 'Adjudicating Climate Change across Scales' in B William and O Hari (eds), *Adjudicating Climate Change: State, National and International Approaches* (Cambridge University Press, Cambridge, 2009).

—— 'Climate Change Litigation as Pluralist Legal Dialogue?' (2007) 26 *Stanford Environmental Law Journal* 181.

E Ostrom, *Governing the Commons: The Evolution of Institutions for Collective Action* (Cambridge University Press, Cambridge, 1990).

J Parikh and K Parikh, 'The Kyoto Protocol: An Indian Perspective' (2004) 5 *International Review for Environmental Strategies* 127.

M Paterson, 'International Justice and Global Warming' in B Holden (ed), *The Ethical Dimensions of Global Change* (Macmillan, London, 1996).

J Peel, 'Issues in Climate Change Litigation' (2011) 1 *Climate and Carbon Law Review* 15.

——, L Godden and R Keenan, 'Climate Change Law in an Era of Multi-Level Governance' (2012) 1 *Transnational Environmental Law* 245.

M Peeters, 'Enforcement of the EU Greenhouse Gas Emissions Trading Scheme' in M Peeters and K Deketelaere (eds), *EU Climate Change Policy: The Challenge of New Regulatory Initiatives* (Edward Elgar, Cheltenham, 2006).

—— 'Emissions Trading as a New Dimension to European Environmental Law: The Political Agreement of the European Council on Greenhouse Gas Allowance Trading' (2003) 12 *European Environmental Law Review* 82.

—— 'Towards a European System of Tradable Pollution Permits?' (1993) 2 *Tilburg Foreign Law Review* 117.

—— and S Weishaar, 'Exploring Uncertainties in the EU ETS: "Learning by Doing" Continues Beyond 2012' (2009) 1 *Carbon and Climate Law Review* 88.

J Peterson and E Bomberg, *Decision-Making in the European Union* (Macmillan, London, 1999).

A Pigou, *Wealth and Welfare* (Macmillan, London, 1912).

R Posner, 'Nobel Laureate: Ronald Coase and Methodology' (1993) 7 *Journal of Economic Perspectives* 195.

S Prechal, *Directives in EC Law* (Oxford University Press, Oxford, 2005).

A Preda, *Framing Finance: The Boundaries of Markets and Modern Capitalism* (Chicago University Press, Chicago, 2009).

G Pring, 'A Decade of Emissions Trading in the USA: Experience and Observations for the EU' in M Peeters and K Deketelaere (eds), *EU Climate Change Policy: The Challenge of New Regulatory Initiatives* (Edward Elgar, Cheltenham, 2006).

N Questiaux, 'Implementing EC Law in France: The Role of the French Conseil d'Etat' in P Craig and C Harlow (eds), *Lawmaking in the European Union* (Kluwer International London, 1998).

C Radaelli, 'Whither Better Regulation for the Lisbon Agenda?' (2007) 14 *Journal of European Public Policy* 190.

L Rajamani, 'The Increasing Current and Relevance of Rights-Based Perspectives in the International Negotiations on Climate Change' (2010) 22 *Journal of Environmental Law* 391.

L Raymond, 'The Emerging Revolution in Emissions Trading Policy' in B Rabe (ed), *Greenhouse Governance: Addressing Climate Change in America* (The Brookings Institute, Washington DC, 2010).

E Rehbinder, 'Market-Based Incentives for Environmental Protection' in R Revesz, P Sands and R Stewart (eds), *Environmental Law, the Economy and the Sustainable Development* (Cambridge University Press, Cambridge, 2000).

R Repetto, *America's Climate Problem: The Way Forward* (Earthscan, London, 2011).

—— *NYU Casebook: Environmental Law and Policy* (Foundation Press, New York City, 2008).

—— 'Federalism and Environmental Regulation: An Overview' in R Revesz, P Sands and R Stewart (eds), *Environmental Law, the Economy and Sustainable Development: The United States, the European Union and the International Community* (Cambridge University Press, Cambridge, 2000).

D Rhode, 'Legal Scholarship' (2002) 115 *Harvard Law Review* 1327.

A Rieser, 'Prescription for the Commons: Environmental Scholarship and the Fishing Quotas Debate' (1999) 23 *Harvard Environmental Law Review* 395.

B Rittberger and J Richardson, 'Old Wine in New Bottles? The Commission and the Use of Environmental Policy Instruments' (2003) 81 *Public Administration* 575.

M Rodi, 'Legal Aspects of the European Emissions Trading Scheme' in B Hansjürgen (ed), *Emissions Trading for Climate Policy: US and European Perspectives* (Cambridge University Press, Cambridge, 2005).

C Rose, 'Expanding the Choice for the Global Commons: Comparing Newfangled Tradable Allowance Schemes to Old-Fashioned Common Property Regimes' (1999) 10 *Duke Environmental Law and Policy Forum* 45.

N Rose, *Powers of Freedom: Reframing Political Thought* (Cambridge University Press, Cambridge, 1999).

J-J Rousseau, *The Social Contract and Discourses* (Dent, London, 1913).

JB Ruhl, 'Thinking of Environmental Law as a Complex Adaptive System: How to Clean Up the Environment by Making a Mess of Environmental Law' (1997) 34 *Houston Law Review* 933.

A Runge Metzger, 'The Potential Role of the EU ETS for the Development of Long-Term International Climate Policies' in J Delbeke (ed), *EU Energy Law: The EU Greenhouse Gas Emissions Trading Scheme* (Claeys & Casteels, Leuven, 2006).

C Sampford, 'Law, Institutions and the Public/Private Divide' (1991) 20 *Federal Law Review* 185.

P Samuelson and W Nordhaus, *Economics* (McGraw-Hills Book Co, London, 2005).

R Sandor, 'Creating New Markets: The Chicago Climate Exchange' in I Kaul and P Conceicao (eds), *The New Public Finance: Responding to Global Challenges* (Oxford University Press, Oxford, 2006).

P Sands, 'European Community Environmental Law: The Evolution of a Regional Regime of International Environmental Protection' (1991) 100 *Yale Law Journal* 2511.

D Satz, *Why Some Things Should Not Be For Sale* (Oxford University Press, Oxford, 2010).

H Schepel and E Blankenburg, 'Mobilizing the European Court of Justice' in G de Burca and J Weiler (eds), *The European Court of Justice* (Oxford University Press, New York, 2001).

P Schlag, 'Spam Jurisprudence, Air Law, and the Rank Anxiety of Nothing Happening (A Report on the State of the Art)' (2009) 97 *Georgetown Law Journal* 803.

D Schoenbrod, R Stewart and K Wyman, *Breaking the Logjam: Environmental Protection that Will Work* (Yale University Press, New Haven, 2010).

C Schroeder, 'Public Choice and Environmental Policy' in D Farber and A O'Connell (eds), *Research Handbook on Public Choice and Public Law* (Edward Elgar, Cheltenham, 2010).

R Schütze, *European Constitutional Law* (Cambridge University Press, Cambridge, 2012).

—— *From Dual to Cooperative Federalism: The Changing Structure of European Law* (Oxford University Press, Oxford, 2009).

G Schwarze, 'Including Aviation into the European Union Emissions Trading Scheme' (2007) 16 *European Environmental Law Review* 10.

E Schön-Quinlivan, 'The European Commission' in A Jordan and C Adelle (eds), *Environmental Policy in the EU: Actors, Institutions and Processes* (Routledge, Abingdon, 2013).

E Scotford, *Environmental Principles and the Evolution of Environmental Law* (Hart Publishing, Oxford, 2013).

—— *The Role of Environmental Principles in the Decisions of the European Union Courts and New South Wales Land and Environment Court* (DPhil thesis, University of Oxford, 2010).

A Scott, 'Foreword' in E Brubaker (ed), *Property Rights in the Defence of Nature* (Earthscan, London, 1995).

J Scott, 'The Multi-Level Governance of Climate Change' in P Craig and G de Burca (eds), *The Evolution of EU Law* (2nd edn, Oxford University Press, Oxford 2011).

—— 'From Brussels with Love: The Transatlantic Travels of European Law and the Chemistry of Regulatory Attraction' (2009) 57 *American Journal of Comparative Law* 897.

—— *Environmental Law* (Longman, London, 1998).

—— and L Rajamani, 'EU Climate Change Unilateralism' (2012) 23 *European Journal of International Law* 469.

—— and S Sturm, 'Courts as Catalysts: Re-Thinking the Judicial Role in New Governance' (2006) 13 *Colombia Journal of European Law* 565.

J Shaw, 'Gender and the Court of Justice' in G de Búrca and J Weiler (eds), *The European Court of Justice* (Oxford University Press, Oxford, 2001).

—— *Law of the European Union* (3rd edn, Palgrave, London, 2000).

—— and R Stroup, 'Global Warming and Ozone Depletion' in W Block (ed), *Economics and the Environment: A Reconciliation* (The Frasier Institute, Vancouver, 1990).

J Sim, 'EU ETS Allocation: Evaluation of Present System and Options Beyond 2012' (2006) 30 *Zeitschrift für Energiewirtschaft* 285.

A Sinden, 'The Tragedy of the Commons and the Myth of a Private Property Solution' (2007) 78 *University of Colorado Law Review* 533.

N Singh Ghaleigh, '"Six Honest Serving-Men": Climate Change Litigation as Legal Mobilization and the Utility of Typologies' (2010) 1 *Climate Law* 31.

—— 'Emissions Trading Before the European Court of Justice: Market Making in Luxembourg' in D Freestone and C Streck (eds), *Legal Aspects of Carbon Trading: Kyoto, Copenhagen and Beyond* (Oxford University Press, Oxford, 2009).

J Skjærseth and J Wettestad, *EU Emissions Trading: Initiation, Decision-Making and Implementation* (Ashgate Publishing, Burlington, 2008).

Y Slingenberg, 'The International Climate Policy Developments of the 1990s: The UNFCCC, the Kytoto Protocol, the Marrakech Accords and the EU Ratification Decision' in J Delbeke (ed), *EU Energy Law: The EU Greenhouse Gas Emissions Trading Scheme* (Claeys & Casteels, Leuven, 2006).

—— 'Community Action in the Fight Against Climate Change' in M Onida (ed), *Europe and the Environment: Legal Essays in Honour of Ludwig Krämer* (Europa Law Publishing, Groningen, 2004).

S Sorrell and J Skea, 'Introduction' in S Sorrell and J Skea (eds), *Pollution For Sale: Emissions Trading and Joint Implementation* (Edward Elgar Publishing, Cheltenham, 1999).

J Stavang, 'Property in Emissions? Analysis of the Norwegian GHG ETS with References also to the UK and the EU' (2005) 17 *Environmental Law and Management* 209.

R Stavins, 'Market-Based Environmental Policies: What Can We Learn from US Experience (and Related Research)?' in J Freeman and C Kolstad (eds), *Moving to Markets in Environmental Regulation: Lessons from Twenty Years of Experience* (Oxford University Press, Oxford, 2007).

—— 'Policy Instruments for Climate Change: How Can National Governments Address a Global Problem?' (1997) *University of Chicago Legal Forum* 293.

—— 'Transaction Costs and Tradeable Permits' (1995) 29 *Journal of Environmental Economics and Management* 133.

—— and B Whitehead, 'Market-Based Environmental Politics' in J Dryzek and D Schlosberg (eds), *Debating the Earth: The Environmental Politics Reader* (Oxford University Press, Oxford, 2005).

E Stein and J Vining, 'Citizen Access to Judicial Review of Administrative Action in a Transnational and Federal Context' (1976) 70 *American Journal of International Law* 219.

N Stern, *The Economics of Climate Change: The Stern Review* (Cambridge University Press, Cambridge, 2007).

R Stewart, 'Instrument Choice' in D Bodansky, J Brunnée and E Hey (eds), *The Handbook of International Environmental Law* (Oxford University Press, Oxford, 2007).

—— 'A New Generation of Environmental Regulation?' (2001) 29 *Capital University Law Review* 21.

—— 'Economic Incentives for Environmental Protection: Opportunities and Obstacles' in R Revesz, P Sands and R Stewart (eds), *Environmental Law, the Economy and Sustainable Development: The United States, the European Union and the International Community* (Cambridge University Press, Cambridge, 2000).

—— 'Introduction' in R Revesz, P Sands and R Stewart (eds), *Environmental Law, the Economy and Sustainable Development: The United States, the European Union and the International Community* (Cambridge University Press, Cambridge, 2000).

—— 'Models for Environmental Regulation: Central Planning Versus Market-Based Approaches' (1992) 19 *Boston College Environmental Affairs Law Review* 547.

—— 'Regulation, Innovation, and Administrative Law: A Conceptual Framework' (1981) 69 *California Law Review* 1256.

—— and J Wiener, 'The Comprehensive Approach to Global Climate Policy: Issues of Design and Practicality' (1992) 9 *Arizona Journal of International and Comparative Law* 83.

J Stiglitz, 'Government Failure vs Market Failure: Principles of Regulation' in E Balleisen and D Moss (eds), *Government and Markets: Toward a New Theory of Regulation* (Cambridge University Press, Cambridge, 2010).

—— *Freefall: Free Markets and the Sinking of the Global Economy* (Allen Lane London, 2010).

A Stone Sweet, 'The European Court of Justice' in P Craig and G de Burca (eds), *The Evolution of EU Law* (Oxford University Press, Oxford, 2011).

—— *The Judicial Construction of Europe* (Oxford University Press, Oxford, 2004).

—— 'Judicialization and the Construction of Governance' (1999) 32 *Comparative Political Studies* 147.

C Stone, *The Gnat is Older than Man – Environment and Human Agenda* (Princeton University Press, Princeton, 1993).

C Streck, 'Joint Implementation: History, Requirements, and Challenges' in D Freestone and C Streck (eds), *Legal Aspects of Carbon Trading: Kyoto, Copenhagen, and Beyond* (Oxford University Press, Oxford, 2005).

R Stroup and S Goodman, 'Property Rights, Environmental Resources, and the Future' (1992) 15 *Harvard Journal of Law and Public Policy* 427.

H Sue, 'Climate' in D Jamieson (ed), *A Companion to Environmental Philosophy* (Blackwell Publishing, Oxford, 2001).

W Sunderlin, *Ideology, Social Theory, and the Environment* (Rowman and Littlefield Publishers, Lanham, 2003).

C Sunstein, 'Panel II: Public Versus Private Environment Regulation' (1994) 21 *Ecological Law Quarterly* 455.

—— 'Standing and the Privatization of Public Law' (1988) 88 *Colombia Law Review* 1432.

E Szyszczak, 'State Intervention and the Internal Market' in T Tridimas and P Nebbia (eds), *European Union Law for the Twenty-First Century: Rethinking the New Legal Order* (Hart Publishing, Oxford, 2004).

M Taggart (ed), *The Province of Administrative Law* (Hart Publishing, Oxford, 1997).

G Teubner, 'Legal Irritants: Good Faith in British Law or How Unifying Law Ends Up in New Divergences' (1998) 61 *MLR* 11.

B Thompson, 'Markets for Nature' (2000) 25 *William and Mary Environmental Law and Policy* 261.

T Tietenberg, *Emissions Trading: Principles and Practice* (2nd edn, Resources for the Future, Washington DC, 2006).

—— 'The Tradable Permits Approach to Protecting the Commons: What Have We Learned?' in E Ostrom and others (eds), *The Drama of the Commons* (National Resource Council, Washington DC, 2003).

—— *Emissions Trading, An Exercise in Reforming Pollution Policy* (Resources for the Future, Johns Hopkins University Press, Washington DC, 1985).

J Torfing, 'Discourse Theory: Achievements, Arguments, and Challenges' in D Howarth and J Torfing (eds), *Discourse Theory in European Politics: Identity, Policy and Governance* (Palgrave Macmillan, Hampshire, 2005).

T Tridimas, *The General Principles of EU Law* (2nd edn, Oxford University Press, Oxford, 2006).

—— 'Knocking on Heaven's Door: Fragmentation, Efficiency and Defiance in the Preliminary Reference Procedure' (2003) 40 *CML Review* 9.

J Usher, 'The Gradual Widening of European Community Policy on the Basis of Articles 100 and 235 of the EEC Treaty' in J Schwarze and H Schermers (eds), *Structure and Dimension of European Community Policy* (Nomos, Baden Baden, 1988).

H van Asselt, 'Emissions Trading: The Enthustiatic Adoption of an "Alien" Instrument?' in A Jordan and others (eds), *Climate Change Policy in the European Union* (Cambridge University Press, Cambridge, 2010).

—— and J Gupta, 'Stretching Too Far? Developing Countries and the Role of Flexible Mechanisms Beyond Kyoto' (2009) 28 *Stanford Environmental Law Journal* 311.

R van Gestel and H-W Micklitz, 'Revitalizing Doctrinal Legal Research in Europe: What About Methodology?' in U Neergaard, R Nielsen and L Roseberry (eds), *European Legal Method – Paradoxes and Revitalisation* (DJOP Publishing, Copenhagen, 2011).

M van Hoecke and M Warrington, 'Legal Cultures, Legal Paradigms and Legal Doctrine: Towards a New Model for Comparative Law' (1998) 47 *ICLQ* 495.

L van Schaik and S Schunz, 'Explaining EU Activism and Impact in Global Climate Politics: Is the Union a Norm- or Interest Driven Actor?' (2012) 50 *Journal of Common Market Studies* 169.

J van Zeben, 'Case Note: Respective Powers of the European Member State and Commission Regarding Emissions Trading and Allowance Allocation' (2010) 12 *Environmental Law Review* 216.

—— '(De)Centralized Law-Making in the Revised EU ETS' (2009) 3 *Carbon and Climate Law Review* 340.

H Vedder, 'Treaty of Lisbon and European Environmental Law and Policy' (2010) 22 *Journal of Environmental Law* 285.

P Vis, 'Basic Design Options for Emissions Trading' in J Delbeke (ed), *EU Energy Law: The EU Greenhouse Gas Emissions Trading Scheme* (Claeys & Casteels, Leuven, 2006).

—— 'The First Allocation Round: A Brief History' in J Delbeke (ed), *EU Energy Law: The EU Greenhouse Gas Emissions Trading Scheme* (Claeys & Casteels, Leuven, 2006).

D Vogel, 'Environmental Policy in the European Community' in S Kamieniecki (ed), *Environmental Politics in the International Arena: Movements, Parties, Organizations, and Policy* (State University of New York Press, Albany, 1993).

S Vogel, 'Why Freer Markets Need More Rules' in M Landy, M Levin and M Shapiro (eds), *Creating Competitive Markets: The Politics of Regulatory Reform* (Brookings Institution Press, Washington DC, 2007).

—— *Freer Markets, More Rules: Regulatory Reform in Advanced Industrial Countries* (Cornell University Press, Ithaca, 1996).

I von Homeyer, 'The Evolution of EU Environmental Governance' in J Scott (ed), *Environmental Protection: European Law and Governance* (Oxford University Press, New York City, 2009).

M von Unger, D Conway and J Hoogzaad, *Carbon Offsetting in Europe Post 2012: Kyoto Protocol, EU ETS, and Effort Sharing* (Climate Focus, Frankfurt am Main, 2012).

A Warleigh, 'Purposeful Opportunists? EU Institutions and the Struggle over European Citizenship' in R Bellamy and A Warleigh (eds), *Citizenship and Governance in the EU* (London, Continuum, 2001).

H Waxman, 'An Overview of the Clean Air Act Amendments of 1990' (1991) 21 *Environmental Law* 1721.

S Weatherill, 'The Challenge of Better Regulation' in S Weatherill (ed), *Better Regulation* (Hart Publishing, Oxford, 2007).

—— *Cases and Materials on EU Law* (8th edn, Oxford University Press, Oxford, 2007).

—— and P Beaumont, *EU Law* (3rd edn, Penguin Publishing, London, 1999).

J Webber, 'Culture, Legal Culture, and Legal Reasoning: A Comment on Nelken' (2004) 29 *Australian Journal of Legal Philosophy* 27.

J Weiler, 'Community, Member States and European Integration: Is the Law Relevant?' (2008) 21 *Journal of Common Market Studies* 39.

—— *The Constitution of Europe: 'Do the New Clothes Have an Emperor?' and Other Essays on European Integration* (Cambridge University Press, Cambridge, 1999).

—— 'A Quiet Revolution: The European Court of Justice and its Interlocutors' (1994) 26 *Comparative Political Studies* 510.

J Weiler, 'The Transformation of Europe' (1991) 100 *Yale Law Journal* 2403.

S Weishaar, 'CO2 Emission Allowance Allocation Mechanisms, Allocative Efficiency and the Environment: A Static and Dynamic Perspective' (2007) 24 *European Journal of Law and Economics* 29.

J Werksman and C Voigt, 'Editorial' (2009) 2 *Carbon and Climate Law Review* 133.

M Wetherell, 'Themes in Discourse Research: The Case of Diana' in M Wetherell, S Taylor and S Yates (eds), *Discourse Theory and Practice: A Reader* (Sage, London, 2001).

J Wettestad, 'European Climate Policy: Toward Centralized Governance?' (2009) 26 *Review of Policy Research* 311.

—— 'The Making of the 2003 EU Emissions Trading Directive: An Ultra-Quick Process due to Entrepreneurial Proficiency?' (2005) 5 *Global Environmental Politics* 1.

——, P Eikeland and M Nilsson, 'EU Climate and Energy Policy: A Hesitant Supranational Turn?' (2012) 12 *Global Environmental Politics* 67.

R Whish and D Bailey, *Competition Law* (Oxford University Press, Oxford, 2012).

G White, *Climate Change and Migration: Security and Borders in a Warming World* (Oxford University Press, Oxford, 2011).

H White, 'Modeling Discourse in and around Markets' (2000) 27 *Poetics* 117.

F Wieacker, 'Foundations of European Legal Culture' (1990) 38 *American Journal of Comparative Law* 1.

J Wiener, 'Better Regulation in Europe' (2006) 59 *Current Legal Problems* 447.

—— 'Convergence, Divergence, and Complexity in the US and European Risk Regulation' in N Vig and M Faure (eds), *Green Giants? Environmental Policies of the United States and the European Union* (MIT Press, Cambridge, 2004).

—— 'Something Borrowed for Something Blue: Legal Transplants and the Evolution of Global Environmental Law' (2001) 27 *Ecological Law Quarterly* 1295.

—— 'Global Environmental Regulation: Instrument Choice in the Legal Context' (1999) 108 *Yale Law Journal* 677.

—— and B Richman, 'Mechanism Choice' in D Farber and A O'Connell (eds), *Research Handbook on Public Choice and Public Law* (Edward Elgar, Cheltenham, 2010).

L Wittgenstein, *Philosophical Investigations* (4th edn, Wiley-Blackwell, West Sussex, 2009).

K Wyman, 'The Property Rights Challenge in Marine Fisheries' (2008) 50 *Arizona Law Review* 511.

—— 'Why Regulators Turn to Tradeable Permits: A Canadian Case Study' (2002) 52 *University of Toronto Law Journal* 419.

G Xu, 'The Role of Property Law in Economic Growth' in M Faure and J Smits (eds), *Does Law Matter? On Law and Economic Growth* (Intersentia, Cambridge, 2011).

B Yandle and A Morriss, 'The Technologies of Property Rights: Choice Among Alternative Solutions to Tragedies of the Commons' (2001) 28 *Ecology Law Quarterly* 123.

L Zedner, 'Comparative Research in Criminal Justice' in L Noaks ,M Maguire and M Levi (eds), *Contemporary Issues in Criminology* (University of Wales Press, Cardiff, 1995).

INDEX